ANNUAL EDITIONS

Sociology

Thirty-Fourth Edition

05/06

EDITOR

Kurt Finsterbusch

University of Maryland, College Park

Kurt Finsterbusch received a bachelor's degree in history from Princeton University in 1957 and a bachelor of divinity degree from Grace Theological Seminary in 1960. His Ph.D. in sociology, from Columbia University, was conferred in 1969. Dr. Finsterbusch is the author of several books, including *Understanding Social Impacts* (Sage Publications, 1980), *Social Research for Policy Decisions* (Wadsworth Publishing, 1980, with Annabelle Bender Motz), and *Organizational Change as a Development Strategy* (Lynne Rienner Publishers, 1987, with Jerald Hage). He is currently teaching at the University of Maryland, College Park, and, in addition to serving as editor for *Annual Editions: Sociology*, he is also editor of *Annual Editions: Social Problems,* and McGraw-Hill/Dushkin's *Taking Sides: Clashing Views on Controversial Social Issues.*

McGraw-Hill/Dushkin

2460 Kerper Blvd., Dubuque, IA 52001

Visit us on the Internet
http://www.dushkin.com

Credits

1. **Culture**
   Unit photo—© by PhotoDisc, Inc.
2. **Socialization and Social Control**
   Unit photo—© by PhotoDisc, Inc.
3. **Groups and Roles in Transition**
   Unit photo—© Getty Images/Jacobs Stock Photography.
4. **Stratification and Social Inequalities**
   Unit photo—© Getty Images/ Ryan McVay.
5. **Social Institutions: Issues, Crises, and Changes**
   Unit photo—© CORBIS/Royalty Free.
6. **Social Change and the Future**
   Unit photo—© Getty Images/ PhotoLink/D. Normark.

Copyright

Cataloging in Publication Data
Main entry under title: Annual Editions: Sociology. 2005/2006.
1. Sociology—Periodicals. I. Finsterbush, Kurt, comp. II. Title: Sociology.
ISBN 0–07–310836–7   658'.05   ISSN 0277–9315

© 2006 by McGraw-Hill/Dushkin, Dubuque, IA 52001, A Division of The McGraw-Hill Companies.

Thirty-fourth Edition

Cover image © Photos.com
Printed in the United States of America   1234567890QPDQPD987654   Printed on Recycled Paper

Editors/Advisory Board

Members of the Advisory Board are instrumental in the final selection of articles for each edition of ANNUAL EDITIONS. Their review of articles for content, level, currentness, and appropriateness provides critical direction to the editor and staff. We think that you will find their careful consideration well reflected in this volume.

Preface

In publishing ANNUAL EDITIONS we recognize the enormous role played by the magazines, newspapers, and journals of the public press in providing current, first-rate educational information in a broad spectrum of interest areas. Many of these articles are appropriate for students, researchers, and professionals seeking accurate, current material to help bridge the gap between principles and theories and the real world. These articles, however, become more useful for study when those of lasting value are carefully collected, organized, indexed, and reproduced in a low-cost format, which provides easy and permanent access when the material is needed. That is the role played by ANNUAL EDITIONS.

The new millennium has arrived with difficult new issues such as how to deal with new levels of terrorism, while many of the old issues remain unresolved. There is much uncertainty. Almost all institutions are under stress. The political system is held in low regard because it seems to accomplish so little, to cost so much, and to focus on special interests more than the public good. The economy is in a recession in the short term and in the long term it suffers from foreign competition, trade deficits, economic uncertainties, and a worrisome concentration of economic power in the hands of relatively few multinational corporations. Complaints about the education system continue, because grades K–12 do not teach basic skills well and college costs are too high. Health care is too expensive, many Americans lack health care coverage, and some diseases are becoming resistant to our medicines. The entertainment industry is booming, but many people worry about its impact on values and behavior. News media standards seem to be set by the tabloids. Furthermore, the dynamics of technology, globalization, and identity groups are creating crises, changes, and challenges. Crime rates have declined somewhat, but they are still at high levels. The public is demanding more police, more jails, and tougher sentences, but less government spending. Government social policies seem to create almost as many problems as they solve. Laborers, women, blacks, and many other groups complain of injustices and victimization. The use of toxic chemicals has been blamed for increases in cancer, sterility, and other diseases. Marriage and the family have been transformed, in part by the women's movement and in part by the stress that current conditions create for women who try to combine family and careers. Schools, television, and corporations are commonly vilified. Many claim that morality has declined to shameful levels. Add to all this the problems of population growth, ozone depletion, and global warming, and it is easy to be pessimistic. Nevertheless, crises and problems also create opportunities.

The present generation may determine the course of history for the next 200 years. Great changes are taking place, and new solutions are being sought where old answers no longer work. The issues that the current generation faces are complex and must be interpreted within a sophisticated framework. The sociological perspective provides such a framework. It expects people to act in terms of their positions in the social structure, the political, economic, and social forces operating on them, and the norms that govern the situation.

Annual Editions: Sociology 05/06 should help you to develop the sociological perspective that will enable you to determine how the issues of the day relate to the way that society is structured. The articles provide not only information but also models of interpretation and analysis that will guide you as you form your own views. In addition, both the *topic guide* and the *World Wide Web* pages can be used to further explore the book's topics.

This thirty-fourth edition of *Annual Editions: Sociology* emphasizes social change, institutional crises, and prospects for the future. It provides intellectual preparation for acting for the betterment of humanity in times of crucial change. The sociological perspective is needed more than ever as humankind tries to find a way to peace, prosperity, health, and well-being that can be maintained for generations in an improving environment. The numerous obstacles that lie in the path of these important goals require sophisticated responses. The goals of this edition are to communicate to students the excitement and importance of the study of the social world and to provoke interest in and enthusiasm for the study of sociology.

Annual Editions: Sociology depends upon reader response in order to develop and change. You are encouraged to return the postage-paid *article rating form* at the back of the book with your opinions about existing articles, recommendations of articles you think have sociological merit for subsequent editions, and advice on how the anthology can be made more useful as a teaching and learning tool.

Kurt Finsterbusch
Editor

Dedicated to Meredith Ramsay for all that we share.

Contents

UNIT 1
Culture

The concepts in bold italics are developed in the article. For further expansion, please refer to the Topic Guide and the Index.

UNIT 2
Socialization and Social Control

UNIT 3
Groups and Roles in Transition

The concepts in bold italics are developed in the article. For further expansion, please refer to the Topic Guide and the Index.

UNIT 4
Stratification and Social Inequalities

The concepts in bold italics are developed in the article. For further expansion, please refer to the Topic Guide and the Index.

The concepts in bold italics are developed in the article. For further expansion, please refer to the Topic Guide and the Index.

UNIT 5
Social Institutions: Issues, Crises, and Changes

The concepts in bold italics are developed in the article. For further expansion, please refer to the Topic Guide and the Index.

UNIT 6
Social Change and The Future

The concepts in bold italics are developed in the article. For further expansion, please refer to the Topic Guide and the Index.

The concepts in bold italics are developed in the article. For further expansion, please refer to the Topic Guide and the Index.

Topic Guide

This topic guide suggests how the selections in this book relate to the subjects covered in your course. You may want to use the topics listed on these pages to search the Web more easily.

On the following pages a number of Web sites have been gathered specifically for this book. They are arranged to reflect the units of this *Annual Edition.* You can link to these sites by going to the DUSHKIN ONLINE support site at *http://www.dushkin.com/online/.*

ALL THE ARTICLES THAT RELATE TO EACH TOPIC ARE LISTED BELOW THE BOLD-FACED TERM.

Violence

Wealth

Welfare

Women

Work and unemployment

World Wide Web Sites

The following World Wide Web sites have been carefully researched and selected to support the articles found in this reader. The easiest way to access these selected sites is to go to our DUSHKIN ONLINE support site at *http://www.dushkin.com/online/*.

AE: Sociology 05/06

The following sites were available at the time of publication. Visit our Web site—we update DUSHKIN ONLINE regularly to reflect any changes.

General Sources

Library of Congress
http://www.loc.gov

Examine this extensive Web site to learn about resource tools, library services/resources, exhibitions, and databases in many different subfields of sociology.

Social Science Information Gateway (SOSIG)
http://sosig.esrc.bris.ac.uk

SOSIG is an online catalog of Internet resources relevant to social science education and research. Resources are selected by librarians or subject specialists.

Sociological Tour Through Cyberspace
http://www.trinity.edu/~mkearl/index.html

Prepared by Michael Kearl at Trinity University, this extensive site provides essays, commentaries, data analyses, and links on death and dying, family, the sociology of time, social gerontology, social psychology, and more.

UNIT 1: Culture

New American Studies Web
http://www.georgetown.edu/crossroads/asw/

This eclectic site provides links to a wealth of resources on the Web related to American studies: gender studies, environment, race, and more. It is of great help when doing research in demography, genealogy, and population studies.

Anthropology Resources Page
http://www.usd.edu/anth/

Many cultural topics can be accessed at this site from the University of South Dakota. Click on the links to find information about differences and similarities in values and lifestyles among the world's peoples.

Human Rights and Humanitarian Assistance
http://www.etown.edu/vl/humrts.html

Through this part of the World Wide Web Virtual Library, you can conduct research into a number of human-rights topics in order to gain a greater understanding of issues affecting indigenous peoples in the modern era. The site also provides links to many other subjects related to sociology.

UNIT 2: Socialization and Social Control

Center for Leadership Studies
http://www.situational.com

The Center for Leadership Studies (CLS) is organized for the research and development of the full range of leadership in individuals, teams, organizations, and communities.

Crime Times
http://www.crime-times.org

This interesting site lists research reviews and other information regarding causes of criminal, violent, and psychopathic behavior. It is provided by the Wacker Foundation, publishers of *Crime Times*.

Ethics Updates/Lawrence Hinman
http://ethics.acusd.edu

This site provides both simple concept definition and complex analysis of ethics, original treatises, and sophisticated search-engine capability. Subject matter covers the gamut, from ethical theory to applied ethical venues. There are many opportunities for user input.

National Institute on Drug Abuse (NIDA)
http://165.112.78.61/

Use this site index of the National Institute on Drug Abuse for access to NIDA publications and communications, information on drugs of abuse, and links to other related Web sites.

UNIT 3: Groups and Roles in Transition

The Gallup Organization
http://www.gallup.com

Links to an extensive archive of public opinion poll results and special reports on a huge variety of topics related to American society are available on this Gallup Organization home page.

Marriage and Family Therapy
http://www.aamft.org/index_nm.asp

This site has links to numerous marriage and family therapy topics. Online directories, books and articles are also available.

The North-South Institute
http://www.nsi-ins.ca/ensi/index.html

Searching this site of the North-South Institute—which works to strengthen international development cooperation and enhance gender and social equity—will help you find information on a variety of issues related to social transitions.

PsychNet/American Psychological Association
http://www.apa.org/topics/homepage.html

By exploring this site, you will be able to find links to an abundance of articles and other resources related to interpersonal relationships throughout the life span.

SocioSite: Feminism and Woman Issues
http://www.pscw.uva.nl/sociosite/TOPICS/Women.html

Open this enormous sociology site of the University of Amsterdam's Sociological Institute to gain insights into a number of issues that affect both men and women. It provides biographies of women through history, an international network for women in the workplace, links to gay studies, affirmative action, family and children's issues, and much more. Return to the site's home page for many other sociological links.

UNIT 4: Stratification and Social Inequalities

Americans With Disabilities Act Document Center

http://www.jan.wvu.edu/links/adalinks.htm

This Web site contains copies of the Americans With Disabilities Act of 1990 (ADA) and ADA regulations. This Web site also provides you with links to other Internet sources of information concerning disability issues.

American Scientist

http://www.amsci.org/amsci/amsci.html

Investigating this Web site of the *American Scientist* will help students of sociology to access a variety of articles and to explore issues and concepts related to race and gender.

Give Five

http://www.independentsector.org/give5/givefive.html

The Give Five Web site is a project of Independent Sector, a national coalition of foundations, voluntary organizations, and corporate giving programs working to encourage giving, volunteering, not-for-profit initiatives, and citizen action.

Joint Center for Poverty Research

http://www.jcpr.org

Finding research information related to poverty is possible at this site. It provides working papers, answers to FAQs, and facts about who is poor in America. Welfare reform is also addressed.

NAACP Online: National Association for the Advancement of Colored People

http://www.naacp.org

The principal objective of the NAACP is to ensure the political, educational, social, and economic equality of minority group citizens in the United States.

UNIT 5: Social Institutions: Issues, Crises, and Changes

Center for the Study of Group Processes

http://www.uiowa.edu/~grpproc/

The mission of the Center for the Study of Group Processes includes promoting basic research in the field of group processes and enhancing the professional development of faculty and students in the field of group processes.

International Labour Organization (ILO)

http://www.ilo.org

ILO's home page leads to links that describe the goals of the organization and summarizes international labor standards and human rights. Its official UN Web site locator can point to many other useful resources.

IRIS Center

http://www.iris.umd.edu

The project on Institutional Reform and the Informal Sector (IRIS) aims to understand transitional and developing economies. Examine this site to learn about research into government institutions and policies that helps to promote successful economic change in the global age.

National Center for Policy Analysis

http://www.ncpa.org

Through this site, you can reach links that provide discussions of an array of topics that are of major interest in the study of American politics and government from a sociological perspective, including regulatory policy, affirmative action, and income.

National Institutes of Health (NIH)

http://www.nih.gov

Consult this site for links to extensive health information and scientific resources of interest to sociologists from the NIH, one of eight health agencies of the Public Health Service.

UNIT 6: Social Change and The Future

Human Rights and Humanitarian Assistance

http://www.etown.edu/vl/humrts.html

Through this part of the World Wide Web Virtual Library, you can conduct research into a number of human-rights concerns around the world. The site also provides links to many other subjects related to important social issues.

The Hunger Project

http://www.thp.org

Browse through this nonprofit organization's site to explore how it tries to achieve its goal: the end to global hunger through leadership at all levels of society. The Hunger Project contends that the persistence of hunger is at the heart of the major security issues threatening our planet.

Terrorism Research Center

http://www.terrorism.com/index.shtml

The Terrorism Research Center features definitions and original research on terrorism, counterterrorism documents, a comprehensive list of Web links, and monthly profiles of terrorist and counterterrorist groups.

United Nations Environment Program (UNEP)

http://www.unep.ch

Consult this home page of UNEP for links to environmental topics of critical concern to sociologists. The site will direct you to useful databases and global resource information.

William Davidson Institute

http://www.wdi.bus.umich.edu

The William Davidson Institute at the University of Michigan Business School is dedicated to the understanding and promotion of economic transition. Consult this site for discussion of topics related to the changing global economy and the effects of globalization in general.

We highly recommend that you review our Web site for expanded information and our other product lines. We are continually updating and adding links to our Web site in order to offer you the most usable and useful information that will support and expand the value of your Annual Editions. You can reach us at: *http://www.dushkin.com/annualeditions/*.

UNIT 1
Culture

Unit Selections

1. **The Kindness of Strangers**, Robert V. Levine
2. **The Mountain People**, Colin M. Turnbull
3. **The Atrophy of Social Life**, D. Stanley Eitzen
4. **Self-Reliance: Those Rugged Individuals**, Joannie Fischer
5. **What's So Great About America?**, Dinesh D'Souza

Key Points to Consider

- What do you think are the core values in American society?

- What are the strengths and weaknesses of cultures that emphasize either cooperation or individualism?

- What is the relationship between culture and identity?

- What might a visitor from a primitive tribe describe as shocking and barbaric about American society?

- What are you most proud about American culture and why?

 **Links: www.dushkin.com/online/**
These sites are annotated in the World Wide Web pages.

New American Studies Web
http://www.georgetown.edu/crossroads/asw/

Anthropology Resources Page
http://www.usd.edu/anth/

Human Rights and Humanitarian Assistance
http://www.etown.edu/vl/humrts.html

The ordinary, everyday objects of living and the daily routines of life provide a structure to social life that is regularly punctuated by festivals, celebrations, and other special events (both happy and sad). These routine and special times are the stuff of culture, for culture is the sum total of all the elements of one's social inheritance. Culture includes language, tools, values, habits, science, religion, literature, and art.

It is easy to take one's own culture for granted, so it is useful to pause and reflect on the shared beliefs and practices that form the foundations for our social life. Students share beliefs and practices and thus have a student culture. Obviously the faculty has one also. Students, faculty, and administrators share a university culture. At the national level, Americans share an American culture. These cultures change over time and especially between generations. As a result, there is much variety among cultures across time and across nations, tribes, and groups. It is fascinating to study these differences and to compare the dominant values and signature patterns of different groups.

The two articles in the first subsection deal with some of the variety among cultures. In the first the author studies the differences between various places in the prevalence of helping behavior and then tries to explain these differences. The second article, by Colin Turnbull, reports how the Ik tribe suffered the loss of its tribal lands and was forced to live in a harsh environment. This environmental change caused a terrifying change in its culture. When a society's technology is very primitive, its environment has a profound impact on its social structure and culture. We would expect, therefore, that such a momentous change in the tribe's environment would require some interesting adaptations. The change that occurred, however, was shocking. Literally all aspects of life changed for the tribe's members in a disturbingly sinister way. Moreover, the experience of this tribe leads Turnbull to question some of the individualistic tendencies of America.

In the next subsection, three authors focus on American culture. Stanley Eitzen raises concerns about the increasing isolation of individuals in America. Since social interaction "is the basic building block of intimate relationships, small groups, formal organizations, communities, and societies … [he] believes we should be concerned by some disturbing trends in our society that hinder or even eliminate social interaction and that indicate a growing isolation as individuals become increasingly separated from their neighbors, their co-workers, and even their family members." Among the factors that contribute to this isolation are changing residences, changing jobs, divorce, new technologies, less visiting with neighbors, both parents working, TV viewing patterns, consumerism, and time pressures. In the next article Joannie Fischer looks at American culture from a historical perspective. Americans have a culture that idealizes rugged individualism and self-reliance and Fischer explains the religious and intellectual foundations for this culture. The final article of this section argues that America has much to be proud about. Its author, Dinesh D'Souza, is an immigrant himself so he can see America both as an outsider and as an insider. He is able to identify many wonderful aspects of America that amaze and attract foreigners. He emphasizes the whole population's sense of equality and freedom of choice, in addition to the wealth that even the poor have here, when compared to the poor in other countries.

The Kindness of Strangers

People's willingness to help someone during a chance encounter on a city street varies considerably around the world

Robert V. Levine

I'll never forget a lesson that I learned as a boy growing up in New York City. One day, when I was perhaps six years old, I was walking with my father on a crowded midtown street. All of a sudden, the normal flow of pedestrian traffic backed up as people tried to avoid a large object on the sidewalk. To my astonishment, the object turned out to be a human being, a man lying unconscious against a building. Not one of the passing herd seemed to notice that the obstacle was a man. Certainly no one made eye contact. As we shuffled by, my father—the model of a loving, caring gentleman—pointed to a bottle in a paper bag and told me that the poor soul on the sidewalk "just needed to sleep it off." When the drunken man began to ramble senselessly, my father warned me not to go near, saying "You never know how he'll react." I soon came to see that day's lesson as a primer for urban adaptation.

Yet many years later I had a very different experience while visiting a market in Rangoon. I had spent the previous 12 months traveling in poor Asian cities, but even by those standards this was a scene of misery. In addition to being dreadfully poor, the residents had to contend with the sweltering climate, ridiculously dense crowds and a stiff wind blowing dust everywhere. Suddenly a man carrying a huge bag of peanuts called out in pain and fell to the ground. I then witnessed an astonishing piece of choreography. Appearing to have rehearsed their motions many times, a half dozen sellers ran from their stalls to help, leaving unattended what may have been the totality of their possessions. One put a blanket under the man's head; another opened his shirt; a third questioned him carefully about the pain; a fourth fetched water; a fifth kept onlookers from crowding around too closely; a sixth ran for help. Within minutes, a doctor arrived, and two other locals joined in to assist. The performance could have passed for a final exam at paramedic school.

The Good, the Bad and the Ugly

Rousseau wrote that "cities are the sink of the human race." But as my experiences in New York and Rangoon make clear, not all cities are the same. Places, like individuals, have their own personalities. Which environments most foster altruism? In which cities is a person in need likely to receive help? I have spent most of the past 15 years systematically exploring these questions.

My students and I have traveled across the United States and much of the world to observe where passersby are most likely to aid a stranger. In each of the cities we surveyed, we conducted five different field experiments. Our studies focused on simple acts of assistance, as opposed to Oskar Schindler-like heroism: Is an inadvertently dropped pen retrieved by a passing pedestrian? Does a man with an injured leg receive assistance picking up a fallen magazine? Will a blind person be helped across a busy intersection? Will someone try to make change for a quarter (or its foreign equivalent) when asked? Do people take the time to mail a stamped and addressed letter that has apparently been lost?

Our first studies were done in the early 1990s, when my students and I visited 36 cities of various sizes in different regions of the United States. The results did nothing to dispel my childhood impressions of New York. In an assessment that combined the results of these five experiments, New York came out dead last—36th out of 36. When we included a sixth measure of kindness toward strangers (per capita contribution to United Way), New York only moved up to 35th on the list. Overall, we found that people in small and medium-sized cities in the Southeast were the most helpful and that residents of large Northeastern and West Coast cities were the least.

One of the advantages of testing so many places is that we could see how other social, economic and environmen-

An illustration from a Victorian-era children's Bible depicts the famous story Jesus is said to tell in Luke 10:25–37: A man is attacked by thieves and left injured by the roadside; the only one to come to his aid is a passing Samaritan, a member of a group despised by Jews of that era. This parable about the willingness of one stranger to help another is especially relevant in modern times, because so many people live in cities and are surrounded daily by people they do not know. How likely is one to encounter a "good Samaritan" today? The author and his students probed that question and found that the answer varies considerably from place to place.

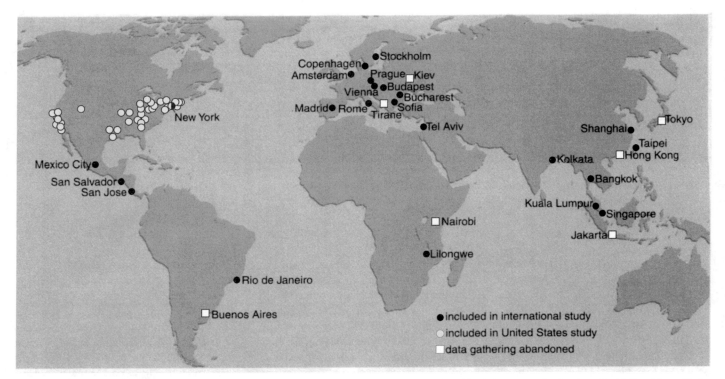

Figure 1. Tests of helpfulness span the globe. The author's 1994 study of helping was limited to 36 U.S. cities *(light gray, yellow),* but his more recent work includes 23 cities *(black, red),* 22 of them located in other countries. In a few places, attempts to gather information about helpfulness of strangers had to be abandoned *(square, blue).*

tal indicators correlated with our experimental results. Far and away the best predictor, we found, was population density. This parameter was more closely tied to the helpfulness of a city than were the crime rate, the pace of life, the prevailing economic conditions or environmental stressors—say, noise or air pollution. We could readily make a case that, overall, people in more crowded cities were much less likely to take the time to help. New York was Exhibit A.

This finding is, of course, easy enough to understand. Crowding brings out the worst in us. Urban critics have demonstrated that squeezing too many people into too small a space leads, paradoxically enough, to alienation, anonymity and social isolation. Ultimately, people feel less responsible for their behavior toward others—especially strangers. Previous research had shown that city dwellers are more likely to do one another harm. Our study indicated that they are also less likely to do one another good and that this apathy increases with the degree of crowding.

But do all big cities exhibit this pattern? It was no surprise to find that densely packed cities like New York do not measure up to the communitarian standards of their smaller and calmer counterparts in the Southeast and Midwest. But as my experience in Rangoon showed, one comes across pockets of village cohesiveness in the most urban places. How do big-city dwellers from various countries compare? In particular, how does New York measure up to other large cities worldwide?

To answer these questions, for six summers Ara Norenzayan and more than 20 other adventurous students from my university worked with me to carry out five separate experiments in large cities around the world. In all, we ran nearly 300 trials of helpfulness that involved feigning blindness, dropped more than 400 pens, approached some 500 people while pretending to have a hurt leg or to be in need of change, and strategically lost almost 800 letters. To relate our findings to the situation in the United States, we used results for the same five

experiments carried out in New York during our earlier study.

Problems in Translation

Psychologists who mount elaborate field studies are keenly aware that observing what doesn't work in experiments is sometimes as instructive as observing what does. True to this rule, our first noteworthy finding was that ways of measuring helping do not always translate cleanly across cultures. Two experiments in particular—those that involved asking for change and losing letters—simply do not have the same functional meaning in many countries that they have in the United States.

The lost-letter test was the most troublesome. This experiment entails leaving stamped, addressed envelopes in a visible location on the street and then recording the percentage of these letters that get delivered. One problem we encountered was that people literally ran away from the letters in some cities. In Tel Aviv, in particular, where unclaimed packages have all too often turned out to contain bombs, people actively avoided our suspicious-

Three measures of helpfulness were found to translate reasonably well between cultures. For one test, the experimenter would drop a pen, apparently by accident and seemingly without noticing, at a moment when a stranger approaching the sidewalk would see it fall. If this person pointed out the dropped pen to the experimenter, a positive result was entered in the tally, which gauged the helpfulness of 424 people in all. In a second set of tests, the experimenter donned a leg brace and walked with a limp. when a passerby approached within 20 feet, the experimenter would drop several magazines on the sidewalk, seemingly by accident, and then struggle to pick them up. If the passing stranger helped gather up the magazines or even offered to help, the trial was scored positively. A total of 493 people were tested in this way. For a third test, the experimenter would feign blindness and approach the curb at a busy intersection just as the traffic light facing him turned green. He would then wait on the sidewalk for a passerby to offer aid. If one did so while the light was still green, the experiment would be scored positively; if not, it would be scored negatively. The author and his students completed a total of 281 trials of this nature.

looking envelopes. In El Salvador, our experimenter was informed about a popular scam in which shysters were intentionally dropping letters: When a good Samaritan picked one up, a con man appeared, announcing that he had lost the letter and that it contained cash (it didn't), then demanding the money back with enough insistence to intimidate the mild-mannered. Not surprisingly, very few letters were touched in El Salvador.

In many developing countries, we found that local mailboxes are either unattended or nonexistent. As a result, mailing a letter in these places requires walking to a central post office, rather than simply going to the letter box on the nearest corner. In Tirane, Albania (where we eventually gave up our attempts to gather data), we were warned not to bother with this experiment, because even if a letter were posted, it probably wouldn't arrive at its destination. (Of course, postal unreliability is also a factor in some more affluent nations.) And most problematic of all, in several countries we found that letters and postal communication are irrelevant to many residents' lives. In retrospect, we should have known better and been less ethnocentric when we designed the experiment. After all, what can one expect in India, for example, where the illiteracy rate is 52 percent?

The asking-for-change experiment also encountered a variety of problems in translation. In this study, the experimenter would ask someone walking in the opposite direction for change for a quarter (in the United States) or the equivalent in other currencies. Between monetary inflation and the widespread use of prepaid telephone cards, however, we learned that the need for particular coins has disappeared in many parts of the world. In Tel Aviv, for example, no one seemed to understand why a person might require small change. In Calcutta (a city that has now officially changed its name to Kolkata), our experimenter had difficulty finding anyone who had small-value bills and coins—reflecting a general shortage all over India at that time. In Buenos Aires, capital of the struggling Argentine economy, we wondered how to score the response of a person who replied that he was so broke that he couldn't even make change. In a few cities, people were afraid to exchange any money with strangers. In Kiev (another city for which we eventually gave up collecting data), where thieves run rampant, visitors are warned never to open a purse or wallet on the street.

In the end, we limited our cross-national comparisons to the tests in which the experimenter pretended to be blind, to have an injured leg or to accidentally drop a pen. Even these situations, we found, occasionally suffered in translation. In the hurt-leg trials, for example, we learned that a mere leg brace was sometimes insufficient to warrant sympathy. Take Jakarta, where experimenter Widyaka Nusapati reported that people don't usually bother to help someone with a minor leg injury. Perhaps if the limb were missing, Nusapati observed, the test might be valid there.

We found that in some cities, such as Tokyo and in parts of the United States, traffic light controls give off distinctive sounds so that the visually impaired will know when it is safe to walk, making it less likely that people would consider a blind person crossing an intersection as someone in need of aid. And, in a curious twist, the experimenter in Tokyo felt so compelled by the surrounding norms of civility that he found it nearly impossible to fake blindness or a hurt leg to attract well-meaning helpers. As a result, Tokyo could not be included in our final ranking.

Despite these difficulties, we ran the three tests successfully in 23 different countries—the largest cross-national comparison of helping ever conducted. What we found suggests a world of difference in the willingness of urbanites to reach out to strangers. In the blind-person experiment, for example, subjects in five cities—Rio de Janeiro, San Jose (Costa Rica, not California), Lilongwe, Madrid and Prague—helped the pedestrian across the street on every occasion, whereas in Kuala Lumpur and Bangkok help was offered less than half the time. If you have a hurt leg in downtown San Jose, Kolkata or Shanghai, our results show that you are more than three times more likely to receive help picking up a fallen magazine than if you are struggling on the streets of New York or Sofia. And if you drop your pen behind you in New York, you have less than one-third the chance that you do in Rio of ever seeing it again.

The two highest-ranking cities are in Latin America: Rio and San Jose. Overall, we found that people in Portuguese- and Spanish-speaking cities tended to be among the most helpful: The other three such cities on our list, Madrid, San Salvador and Mexico City, each scored well above average. Considering that some of these places suffer from long-term political instability, high crime rates and a potpourri of other social, economic and environmental ills, these positive results are noteworthy.

Social psychologist Aroldo Rodrigues, who is currently a colleague of mine at California State University, Fresno, spent

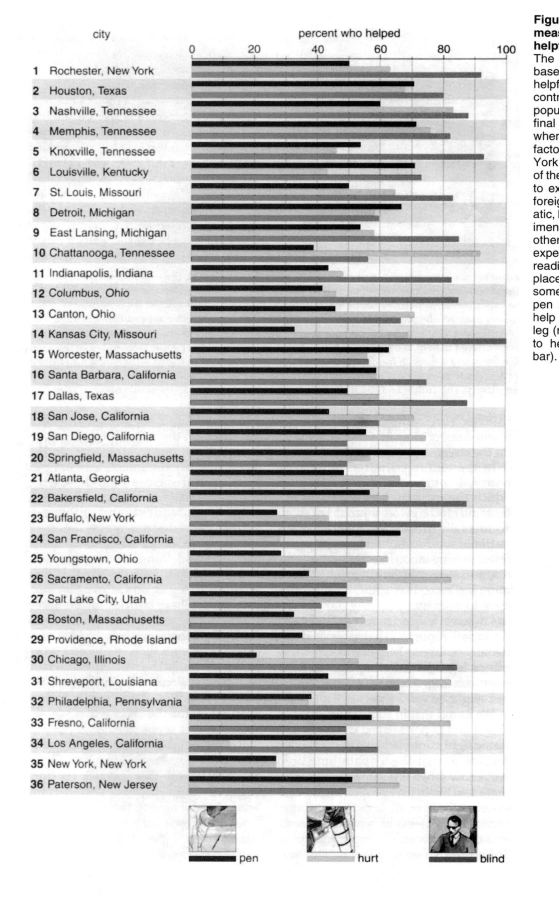

Figure 2. Author's 1994 study measured the general level of helpfulness in 36 U.S. cities. The published ranking was based on five experiments of helpfulness and on per-capita contribution to United Way, a popular charity campaign. (The final ranking differs somewhat when giving to United Way is not factored in. In that case, New York moves to the very bottom of the list.) The author's attempts to extend the same analysis to foreign cities proved problematic, because some of the experiments did not translate well to other cultures. Only three of the experimental yardsticks proved readily applicable in most places: willingness to help someone who had dropped a pen (upper bar), willingness to help someone with an injured leg (middle bar) and willingness to help a blind person (lower bar).

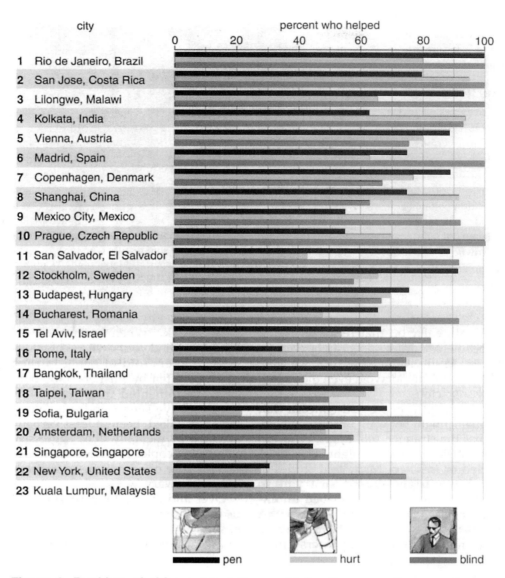

Figure 3. Ranking of cities around the world (by the same three measures show in Figure 2) places Rio first and Kuala Lampur last. It is, however, unlikely that these results reflect any real variation in human nature from country to country. Rather, the author posits, people are more or less likely to offer help to a stranger depending on the place they happen to be in at that moment.

most of his career as a leading scholar at universities in the most helpful city of all, Rio. Rodrigues was not surprised by our results. "There is an important word in Brazil: 'simpático,' " Rodrigues explains. "The term has no equivalent in English. It refers to a range of desirable social qualities—to be friendly, nice, agreeable and good-natured, a person who is fun to be with and pleasant to deal with. Mind you, simpático doesn't mean that a person is necessarily honest or moral. It is a social quality. Brazilians, especially the Cariocas of Rio, want very much to be seen as simpático. And going out of one's way to as-

sist strangers is part of this image." This Brazilian social script also extends to the Hispanic cultures in our study, where a simpático personality is held in equally high regard.

There were other notable trends, although each had its exceptions. Helping rates tended to be high in countries with low economic productivity (low gross domestic product per capita—that is, less purchasing power for each citizen), in cities with a slow pace of life (as measured by pedestrian walking speeds) and in cultures that emphasize the value of social harmony. This city "personality" is con-

sistent with the simpático hypothesis. People in communities where social obligations take priority over individual achievement tend to be less economically productive, but they show more willingness to assist others. This trend did not, however, hold for all of the cities in our study. Pedestrians in the fast-paced, first-world cities of Copenhagen and Vienna, for example, were very kind to strangers, whereas their counterparts in slower-paced Kuala Lumpur were not helpful at all. These exceptions make clear that even city dwellers with a fast pace of life and a focus on economic achievement are capable of finding time for strangers in need and that a slow pace of life is no guarantee that people will invest their leisure time in practicing social ideals.

Start Spreading the News

New York may not have ranked lowest in our global study, as it had in our earlier tests of helpful acts in various U.S. cities, but it came close. Overall, New Yorkers placed 22nd in our list of 23. They ranked 22nd on tests of whether people would retrieve a dropped pen and of whether they would assist someone with a hurt leg. They came out a little below the average (13th) when it came to helping a blind person to cross the street.

We also learned that there may be a difference between helping and civility. In places where people walked fast, they were less likely to be civil even when they did offer assistance. In New York, helping gestures often had a particularly hard edge. During the dropped-pen experiment, for example, helpful New Yorkers would typically call to the experimenter that he had dropped his pen, then quickly move on in the opposite direction. In contrast, helpers in laid-back Rio—where a leisurely gait and *simpático* personality are ways of life—were more likely to return the pen personally, sometimes running to catch up with the experimenter. In the blind-person trials, helpful New Yorkers would often wait until the light turned green, tersely announce that it was safe to cross and then quickly walk ahead. In the friendlier cities, helpers were more likely to offer to walk the experimenter across the street, and they sometimes asked if he then needed further assistance. Indeed, one of our experimenters' problems in these place was how to separate from particularly caring strangers.

In general, it seemed as though New Yorkers are willing to offer help only when they could do so with the assurance of no further contact, as if to say "I'll meet my social obligation but, make no mistake, this is as far as we go together." How much of this attitude is motivated by fear and how much by simply not wanting to waste time is hard to know. But in more helpful cities, like Rio, it often seemed to us that human contact is the very motive for helping. People were

more likely to give aid with a smile and to welcome the "thank you" our experimenter returned.

Perhaps the most dramatic example of uncivil helping involved one of the tests we attempted and then abandoned, the lost-letter experiment. In many cities, I received envelopes that had clearly been opened. In almost all of these cases, the finder had then resealed it or mailed it in a new envelope. Sometimes they attached notes, usually apologizing for opening our letter. Only from New York did I receive an envelope which had its entire side ripped and left open. On the back of the letter the helper had scribbled, in Spanish: "Hijo de puta ir[r]esposable"—which I discovered when it was translated for me, makes a very nasty accusation about my mother. Below that was added a straightforward English-language expletive, which I could readily understand. It is interesting to picture this angry New Yorker, perhaps cursing my irresponsibility all the while he was walking to the mailbox, yet for some reason feeling compelled to take the time to perform his social duty for a stranger he already hated. Ironically, this rudely returned letter counted in the helping column in scoring New York. A most *antipático* test subject, as the Brazilians would say.

Compare this response to those in Tokyo, where several finders hand-delivered the letters to their addressees. Or, consider a note I received on the back of a returned letter from the most helpful city in our earlier study of U.S. cities, Rochester, New York:

> Hi. I found this on my windshield where someone put it with a note saying they found it next to my car. I thought it was a parking ticket. I'm putting this in the mailbox 11/19. Tell whoever sent this to you it was found on the bridge near/across from the library and South Ave. Garage about 5 p.m. on 11/18.

> P. S. Are you related to any Levines in New Jersey or Long Island? L. L.

A Special Attitude?

Do our results mean that New Yorkers are less kind people—less caring on the *inside*—than city dwellers in more helpful places? Not at all. The New Yorkers to whom we spoke gave many good reasons for their reluctance to help strangers. Most, like me, had been taught early on that reaching out to people you don't know can be dangerous. To survive in New York, we were told, you should avoid even the vaguely suspicious.

Some also expressed concern that others might not want unsolicited help, that the stranger, too, might be afraid of outside contact or might feel patronized or insulted. Many told stories of being outright abused for trying to help. One woman described an encounter with a frail, elderly man with a red-tipped cane who appeared unable to manage crossing an intersection. When she gently offered assistance, he barked back, "When I want help I'll ask for it. Mind your own f---ing business." Others told of being burned once too often by hustlers. One nonhelper commented that "most New Yorkers have seen blindness faked, lameness faked, been at least verbally accosted by mentally ill or aggressive homeless people. This does not necessarily make one immune or callous, but rather, wary."

Over and again, New Yorkers told us they cared deeply about the needs of strangers, but that the realities of city living prohibited their reaching out. People spoke with nostalgia for the past, when they would routinely pick up hitchhikers or arrange a meal for a hungry stranger. Many expressed frustration—even anger—that life today deprived them of the satisfaction of feeling like good Samaritans.

These explanations may simply be the rationalizations of uncharitable citizens trying to preserve their self-image. But I do not think this is the case. The bulk of the evidence indicates that helping tends to be less dependent on the nature of the local people than it is on the characteristics of the local environment. And investigators have demonstrated that seemingly minor changes in situation can drastically affect helping—above and beyond the personalities or moral beliefs of the people involved. It is noteworthy that studies show the location

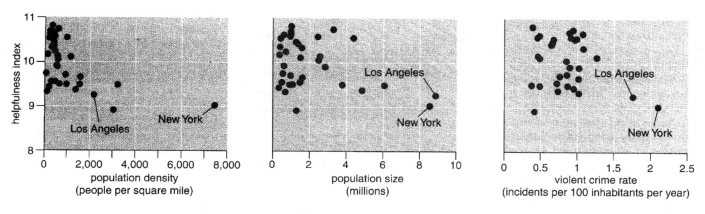

Figure 4. What accounts for the variation in helpfulness? The author's 1994 study of U.S. cities suggests that the key parameter may be population density: Cities having more than about 1,500 people per square mile tend to show comparatively low levels of helpfulness (left). Two of those unfriendly cities, New York and Los Angeles, are also especially large (middle) and have high rates of violent crime (right), factors that might also contribute to the lack of helpfulness one finds on the street. The other cities tested show no obvious correlation between size or crime rate and the prevailing level of helpfulness. Credit: David Schneider/American Scientist.

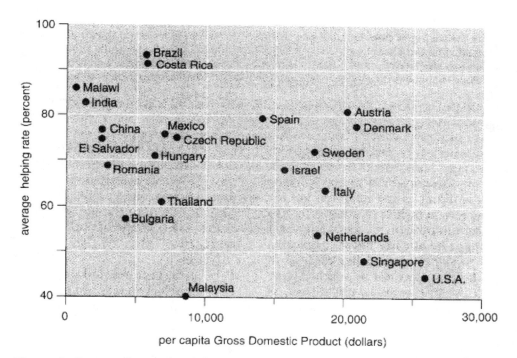

Figure 5. Economic productivity appears to have some influence on the degree of helpfulness one can expect. People generally show the highest level of helpfulness in places with low economic productivity (gauged here by the per-capita Gross Domestic Product after a correction to compensate for relative purchasing power in different countries). Similarly, those in places with high economic productivity typically rank low in measures of helpfulness. The helpfulness values plotted represent the results for one major city in each of these countries. Credit: David Schneider/American Scientist.

where one was raised has less to do with helping than the place one currently lives. In other words, Brazilians and New Yorkers are both more likely to offer help in Ipanema than they are in Manhattan.

Yet the cause of civility in cities like New York and Kuala Lumpur may not be hopeless. Just as characteristics of the situation may operate against helping, there are ways to modify the environment so as to encourage it. Experiments have shown, for example, that reversing the anonymity and diffusion of responsibility that characterize life in some cities—by increasing personal accountability, or simply by getting people to address one another by name—boosts helping. In a 1975 experiment at a New York beach, Thomas Moriarity, then a social psychologist at New York University, found that only 20 percent of people intervened when a man (actually one of the experimenters) blatantly stole a portable radio off of the temporarily abandoned blanket next to them. But when the owner of the radio simply asked her neighbors to keep an eye on the radio while she was gone, 95 percent of those who agreed stepped in to stop the snatcher.

Inducing a bit of guilt—by making people aware that they could be doing more—also seems to make a difference. Perhaps most promising is the observation that helping can be effectively taught. Psychologists have found, for example, that children who are exposed to altruistic characters on television tend to mimic them. And, because prosocial exemplars in real life often induce others to follow suit, any increases in helping are potentially self-perpetuating.

Might a kinder environment eventually raise the level of helpfulness in New York? This city is leading a nationwide trend and currently enjoying a wave of crime reduction. (Statistics indicate that fewer New Yorkers are doing each other injury today than in the recent past.) Could diminished worries over street crime free more people to step forth and

New Yorkers earned a reputation for callousness in 1964 when Catherine ("Kitty") Genovese was killed on this street in Kew Gardens, Queens, while making her way home from her job. Dozens of people in the surrounding buildings heard her screams as she was repeatedly attacked over an interval of 32 minutes, but none came to her aid and she died of stab wounds. This tragic episode inspired much self-analysis among the city's residents. The author's interviews of New Yorkers who proved unwilling to help in simple experiments suggest some of the factors that prevent well-meaning people from aiding strangers.

offer one another aid, strangers included? Our experiments do not address variations over time, but I suspect that little will change. After all, the reduction in the number of harm-doers does not necessarily imply that there will be greater quantity of altruism practiced. And there is little doubt that the drunk man I watched people sidestep when I was six would be even less likely to receive help from a passing stranger today.

A little more than a century ago, author John Habberton may have had New Yorkers in mind when he wrote that "nowhere in the world are there more charitable hearts with plenty of money behind them than in large cities, yet nowhere else is there more suffering." Perhaps good Samaritans are indeed living in New York in large numbers but are hiding behind protective screens. To strangers in need of help, it would make little difference, thoughts being less important than actions. The bottom line: One's prospects for being helped by a stranger are bleaker in New York than they are in Rio, Mexico City or Shanghai. Indeed, you're more likely to receive assistance from someone you don't know just about anywhere else in world.

Bibliography

Clark, M. S. (ed.) 1991. *Prosocial Behavior*. Newbury Park, Calif.: Sage.

Levine, R. V. 1990. The pace of life. *American Scientist* 78:450–459.

Levine, R. 1997. *A Geography of Time*. New York: BasicBooks.

Levine, R. V., T. S. Martinez, G. Brase and K. Sorenson. 1994. Helping in 36 U.S. Cities. *Journal of Personality and Social Psychology* 67:69–82.

Levine, R. V., and A. Norenzayan. 1999. The pace of life in 31 countries. *Journal of Cross-cultural Psychology* 30:178–205.

Levine, R. V., A. Norenzayan and K. Philbrick. 2001. Cross-cultural differences in helping strangers. *Journal of Cross-cultural Psychology* 32:543–560.

Milgram, S. 1970. The experience of living in cities. *Science* 167:1461–1468.

Moriarity, T. 1975. Crime, commitment, and the responsive bystander: Two field experiments. *Journal of Personality and Social Psychology* 31:370–376.

Links to Internet resources for further exploration of "The Kindness of Strangers" are available on the *American Scientist* Web site: http://www.americanscientist.org/articles/05articles/levine.html

Robert V. Levine received his doctorate from New York University in 1974. Except for brief visiting appointments in Brazil, Japan and Sweden, he has spent the past three decades working at California State University in Fresno, where he teaches and does research in the Department of Psychology. In addition to numerous scholarly articles, Levine has authored two popular books, the most recent being The Power of Persuasion: How We're Bought and Sold *(John Wiley & Sons, 2003). Address: Department of Psychology, 5310 N. Campus Drive, M/S PH11, California State University, Fresno, CA 93740-8019. Internet: robertle@csufresno.edu*

The Mountain People

Colin M. Turnbull

In what follows, there will be much to shock, and the reader will be tempted to say, "how primitive, how savage, how disgusting," and, above all, "how inhuman." The first judgments are typical of the kind of ethno- and egocentricism from which we can never quite escape. But "how inhuman" is of a different order and supposes that there are certain values inherent in humanity itself, from which the people described here seem to depart in a most drastic manner. In living the experience, however, and perhaps in reading it, one finds that it is oneself one is looking at and questioning; it is a voyage in quest of the basic human and a discovery of his potential for inhumanity, a potential that lies within us all.

Just before World War II the Ik tribe had been encouraged to settle in northern Uganda, in the mountainous northeast corner bordering on Kenya to the east and Sudan to the north. Until then they had roamed in nomadic bands, as hunters and gatherers, through a vast region in all three countries. The Kidepo Valley below Mount Morungole was their major hunting territory. After they were confined to a part of their former area, Kidepo was made a national park and they were forbidden to hunt or gather there.

The concept of family in a nomadic society is a broad one; what really counts most in everyday life is community of residence, and those who live close to each other are likely to see each other as effectively related, whether there is any kinship bond or not. Full brothers, on the other hand, who live in different parts of the camp may have little concern for each other.

It is not possible, then, to think of the family as a simple, basic unit. A child is brought up to regard any adult living in the same camp as a parent, and age-mate as a brother or sister. The Ik had this essentially social attitude toward kinship, and it readily lent itself to the rapid and disastrous changes that took place following the restriction of their movement and hunting activities. The family simply ceased to exist.

It is a mistake to think of small-scale societies as "primitive" or "simple." Hunters and gatherers, most of all, appear simple and straightforward in terms of their social organization, yet that is far from true. If we can learn about the nature of society from a study of small-scale societies, we can also learn about human relationships. The smaller the society, the less emphasis there is on the formal system and the more there is on interpersonal and intergroup relations. Security is seen in terms of these relationships, and so is survival. The result, which appears so deceptively simple, is that hunters frequently display those characteristics that we find so admirable in man: kindness, generosity, consideration, affection, honesty, hospitality, compassion, charity. For them, in their tiny, close-knit society, these are necessities for survival. In our society anyone possessing even half these qualities would find it hard to survive, yet we think these virtues are inherent in man. I took it for granted that the Ik would possess these same qualities. But they were as unfriendly, uncharitable, inhospitable and generally mean as any people can be. For those positive qualities we value so highly are no longer functional for them; even more than in our own society they

spell ruin and disaster. It seems that, far from being basic human qualities, they are luxuries we can afford in times of plenty or are mere mechanisms for survival and security. Given the situation in which the Ik found themselves, man has no time for such luxuries, and a much more basic man appears, using more basic survival tactics.

Turnbull had to wait in Kaabong, a remote administration outpost, for permission from the Uganda government to continue to Pirre, the Ik water hole and police post. While there he began to learn the Ik language and became used to their constant demands for food and tobacco. An official in Kaabong gave him, as a "gift," 20 Ik workers to build a house and a road up to it. When they arrived at Pirre, however, wages for the workers were negotiated by wily Atum, "the senior of all the Ik on Morungole."

The police seemed as glad to see me as I was to see them. They hungrily asked for news of Kaabong, as though it were the hub of the universe. They had a borehole and pump for water, to which they said I was welcome, since the water holes used by the Ik were not fit for drinking or even for washing. The police were not able to tell me much about the Ik, because every time they went to visit an Ik village, there was nobody there. Only in times of real hunger did they see much of the Ik, and then only enough to know that they were hungry.

The next morning I rose early, but even though it was barely daylight, by the time I had washed and dressed, the Ik were already outside. They were sitting silently, staring at the Land Rover. As impassive as they seemed, there was an air of expectancy, and I was reminded that these were, after all, hunters, and the likelihood was that I was their morning's prey. So I left the Land Rover curtains closed and as silently as possible prepared a frugal breakfast.

Atum was waiting for me. He said that he had told all the Ik that Iciebam [friend of the Ik] had arrived to live with them and that I had given the workers a "holiday" so they could greet me. They were waiting in the villages. They were very hungry, he added, and many were dying. That was probably one of the few true statements he ever made, and I never even considered believing it.

There were seven villages in all. Village Number One was built on a steep slope, and even the houses tilted at a crazy angle. Atum rapped on the outer stockade with his cane and shouted a greeting, but there was no response. This was Giriko's village, he said, and he was one of my workers.

"But I thought you told them to go back to their villages," I said.

"Yes, but you gave them a holiday, so they are probably in their fields," answered Atum, looking me straight in the eye.

At Village Number Two there was indisputably someone inside, for I could hear loud singing. The singing stopped, a pair of hands gripped the stockade and a craggy head rose into view, giving me an undeniably welcoming smile. This was Lokelea. When I asked him what he had been singing about, he answered, "Because I'm hungry."

Village Number Three, the smallest of all, was empty. Village Number Four had only 8 huts, as against the 12 or so in Lokelea's village and the 18 in Giriko's. The outer stockade was broken in one section, and we walked right in. We ducked through a low opening and entered a compound in which a woman was making pottery. She kept on at her work but gave us a cheery welcome and laughed her head off when I tried to speak in Icietot. She willingly showed me details of her work and did not seem unduly surprised at my interest. She said that everyone else had left for the fields except old Nangoli, who, on hearing her name mentioned, appeared at a hole in the stockade shutting off the next compound. Nangoli mumbled toothlessly at

Losike, who told Atum to pour her some water.

As we climbed up to his own village, Number Five, Atum said that Losike never gave anything away. Later I remembered that gift of water to Nangoli. At the time I did not stop to think that in this country a gift of water could be a gift of life.

Atum's village had nearly 50 houses, each within its compound within the stout outer stockade. Atum did not invite me in.

A hundred yards away stood Village Number Six. Kauar, one of the workers, was sitting on a rocky slab just outside the village. He had a smile like Losike's, open and warm, and he said he had been waiting for me all morning. He offered us water and showed me his own small compound and that of his mother.

Coming up from Village Number Seven, at quite a respectable speed, was a blind man. This was Logwara, emaciated but alive and remarkably active. He had heard us and had come to greet me, he said, but he added the inevitable demand for tobacco in the same breath. We sat down in the open sunlight. For a brief moment I felt at peace.

After a short time Atum said we should start back and called over his shoulder to his village. A muffled sound came from within, and he said, "That's my wife, she is very sick—and hungry." I offered to go and see her, but he shook his head. Back at the Land Rover I gave Atum some food and some aspirin, not knowing what else to give him to help his wife.

I was awakened well before dawn by the lowing of cattle. I made an extra pot of tea and let Atum distribute it, and then we divided the workers into two teams. Kauar was to head the team building the house, and Lokelatom, Losike's husband, was to take charge of the road workers.

While the Ik were working, their heads kept turning as though they were expecting something to happen. Every now and again one would stand up and peer into the distance and then take off into the bush for an hour or so. On one such occasion, after the person had been gone two hours, the others started drifting off. By then I knew them better; I

looked for a wisp of smoke and followed it to where the road team was cooking a goat. Smoke was a giveaway, though, so they economized on cooking and ate most food nearly raw. It is a curious hangover from what must once have been a moral code that Ik will offer food if surprised in the act of eating, though they now go to enormous pains not to be so surprised.

I was always up before dawn, but by the time I got up to the villages they were always deserted. One morning I followed the little *oror* [gulley] up from *oror a pirre'i* [Ravine of Pirre] while it was still quite dark, and I met Lomeja on his way down. He took me on my first illicit hunt in Kidepo. He told me that if he got anything he would share it with me and with anyone else who managed to join us but that he certainly would not take anything back to his family. "Each one of them is out seeing what he can get for himself, and do you think they will bring any back for me?"

Lomeja was one of the very few Ik who seemed glad to volunteer information. Unlike many of the others, he did not get up and leave as I approached. Apart from him, I spent most of my time, those days, with Losike, the potter. She told me that Nangoli, the old lady in the adjoining compound, and her husband, Amuarkuar, were rather peculiar. They helped each other get food and water, and they brought it back to their compound to eat together.

I still do not know how much real hunger there was at that time, for most of the younger people seemed fairly well fed, and the few skinny old people seemed healthy and active. But my laboriously extracted genealogies showed that there were quite a number of old people still alive and allegedly in these villages, though they were never to be seen. Then Atum's wife died.

Atum told me nothing about it but kept up his demands for food and medicine. After a while the beady-eyed Lomongin told me that Atum was selling the medicine I was giving him for his wife. I was not unduly surprised and merely remarked that that was too bad for his wife. "Oh no," said Lomongin, "she has been dead for weeks."

It must have been then that I began to notice other things that I suppose I had chosen to ignore before. Only a very few of the Ik helped me with the language. Others would understand when it suited them and would pretend they did not understand when they did not want to listen. I began to be forced into a similar isolationist attitude myself, and although I cannot say I enjoyed it, it did make life much easier. I even began to enjoy, in a peculiar way, the company of the silent Ik. And the more I accepted it, the less often people got up and left as I approached. On one occasion I sat on the *di* [sitting place] by Atum's rain tree for three days with a group of Ik, and for three days not one word was exchanged.

The work teams were more lively, but only while working. Kauar always played and joked with the children when they came back from foraging. He used to volunteer to make the two-day walk into Kaabong and the even more tiring two-day climb back to get mail for me or to buy a few things for others. He always asked if he had made the trip more quickly than the last time.

Then one day Kauar went to Kaabong and did not come back. He was found on the last peak of the trail, cold and dead. Those who found him took the things he had been carrying and pushed his body into the bush. I still see his open, laughing face, see him giving precious tidbits to the children, comforting some child who was crying, and watching me read the letters he carried so lovingly for me. And I still think of him probably running up that viciously steep mountainside so he could break his time record and falling dead in his pathetic prime because he was starving.

Once I settled down into my new home, I was able to work more effectively. Having recovered at least some of my anthropological detachment, when I heard the telltale rustling of someone at my stockade, I merely threw a stone. If when out walking I stumbled during a difficult descent and the Ik shrieked with laughter, I no longer even noticed it.

Anyone falling down was good for a laugh, but I never saw anyone actually trip anyone else. The adults were content to let things happen and then enjoy them; it was probably conservation of energy.

The children, however, sought their pleasures with vigor. The best game of all, at this time, was teasing poor little Adupa. She was not so little—in fact she should have been an adult, for she was nearly 13 years old—but Adupa was a little mad. Or you might say she was the only sane one, depending on your point of view. Adupa did not jump on other people's play houses, and she lavished enormous care on hers and would curl up inside it. That made it all the more jump-on-able. The other children beat her viciously.

Children are not allowed to sleep in the house after they are "put out," which is at about three years old, four at the latest. From then on they sleep in the open courtyard, taking what shelter they can against the stockade. They may ask for permission to sit in the doorway of their parents' house but may not lie down or sleep there. "The same thing applies to old people," said Atum, "if they can't build a house of their own and, of course, *if* their children let them stay in their compounds."

I saw a few old people, most of whom had taken over abandoned huts. For the first time I realized that there really was starvation and saw why I had never known it before: it was confined to the aged. Down in Giriko's village the old ritual priest, Lolim, confidentially told me that he was sheltering an old man who had been refused shelter by his son. But Lolim did not have enough food for himself, let alone his guest; could I... I liked old Lolim, so, not believing that Lolim had a visitor at all, I brought him a double ration that evening. There was rustling in the back of the hut, and Lolim helped ancient Lomeraniang to the entrance. They shook with delight at the sight of the food.

When the two old men had finished eating, I left; I found a hungry-looking and disapproving little crowd clustered outside. They muttered to each other about wasting food. From then on I brought food daily, but in a very short time Lomeraniang was dead, and his son refused to come down from the village above to bury him. Lolim scratched a hole and covered the body with a pile of stones he carried himself, one by one.

Hunger was indeed more severe than I knew, and, after the old people, the children were the next to go. It was all quite impersonal—even to me, in most cases, since I had been immunized by the Ik themselves against sorrow on their behalf. But Adupa was an exception. Her madness was such that she did not know just how vicious humans could be. Even worse, she thought that parents were for loving, for giving as well as receiving. Her parents were not given to fantasies. When she came for shelter, they drove her out; and when she came because she was hungry, they laughed that Icien laugh, as if she had made them happy.

Adupa's reactions became slower and slower. When she managed to find food—fruit peels, skins, bits of bone, half-eaten berries—she held it in her hand and looked at it with wonder and delight. Her playmates caught on quickly; they put tidbits in her way and watched her simple drawn little face wrinkle in a smile. Then as she raised her hand to her mouth, they set on her with cries of excitement, fun and laughter, beating her savagely over the head. But that is not how she died. I took to feeding her, which is probably the cruelest thing I could have done, a gross selfishness on my part to try to salve my own rapidly disappearing conscience. I had to protect her, physically, as I fed her. But the others would beat her anyway, and Adupa cried, not because of the pain in her body but because of the pain she felt at the great, vast, empty wasteland where love should have been.

It was *that* that killed her. She demanded that her parents love her. Finally they took her in, and Adupa was happy and stopped crying. She stopped crying forever because her parents went away and closed the door tight behind them, so tight that weak little Adupa could never have moved it.

The Ik seem to tell us that the family is not such a fundamental unit as we usually suppose, that it is not essential to social life. In the crisis of survival facing the Ik, the family was one of the first institutions to go, and the Ik as a society have survived.

The other quality of life that we hold to be necessary for survival—love—the Ik dismiss as idiotic and highly dangerous. But we need to see more of the Ik before their absolute lovelessness becomes truly apparent.

In this curious society there is one common value to which all Ik hold tenaciously. It is *ngag*, "food." That is the one standard by which they measure right and wrong, goodness and badness. The very word for "good" is defined in terms of food. "Goodness" is "the possession of food," or the "*individual* possession of food." If you try to discover their concept of a "good man," you get the truly Icien answer: one who has a full stomach.

We should not be surprised, then, when the mother throws her child out at three years old. At that age a series of *rites de passage* begins. In this environment a child has no chance of survival on his own until he is about 13, so children from age bands. The junior band consists of children between three and seven, the senior of eight- to twelve-year-olds. Within the band each child seeks another close to him in age for defense against the older children. There friendships are temporary, however, and inevitably there comes a time when each turns on the one that up to then had been the closest to him; that is the *rite de passage*, the destruction of that fragile bond called friendship. When this has happened three or four times, the child is ready for the world.

The weakest are soon thinned out, and the strongest survive to achieve leadership of the band. Such a leader is eventually driven out, turned against by his fellow band members. Then the process starts all over again; he joins the senior age band as its most junior member.

The final *rite de passage* is into adulthood, at the age of 12 or 13. By then the candidate has learned the wisdom of acting on his own, for his own good, while acknowledging that on occasion it is profitable to associate temporarily with others.

One year in four the Ik can count on a complete drought. About this time it began to be apparent that there were going to be two consecutive years of drought and famine. Men as well as women took to gathering what wild fruits and berries they could find, digging up roots, cutting grass that was going to seed, threshing and eating the seed.

Old Nangoli went to the other side of Kidepo, where food and water were more plentiful. But she had to leave her husband, Amuarkuar, behind. One day he appeared at my *odok* and asked for water. I gave him some and was going to get him food when Atum came storming over and argued with me about wasting water. In the midst of the dispute Amuarkuar quietly left. He wandered over to a rocky outcrop and lay down there to rest. Nearby was a small bundle of grass that evidently he had cut and had been dragging painfully to the ruins of his village to make a rough shelter. The grass was his supreme effort to keep a home going until Nangoli returned. When I went over to him, he looked up and smiled and said that my water tasted good. He lay back and went to sleep with a smile on his face. That is how Amuarkuar died, happily.

There are measures that can be taken for survival involving the classical institutions of gift and sacrifice. These are weapons, sharp and aggressive. The object is to build up a series of obligations so that in times of crisis you have a number of debts you can recall; with luck one of them may be repaid. To this end, in the circumstances of Ik life, considerable sacrifice would be justified, so you have the odd phenomenon of these otherwise singularly self-interested people going out of their way to "help" each other. Their help may very well be resented in the extreme, but is done in such a way that it cannot be refused, for it has already been given. Someone may hoe another's field in his absence or rebuild his stockade or join in the building of a house.

The danger in this system was that the debtor might not be around when collection was called for and, by the same token, neither might the creditor. The future was too uncertain for this to be anything but one additional survival measure, though some developed it to a fine technique.

There seemed to be increasingly little among the Ik that could by any stretch of the imagination be called social life, let alone social organization. The family does not hold itself together; economic interest is centered on as many stomachs as there are people; and cooperation is merely a device for furthering an interest that is consciously selfish. We often do the same thing in our so-called "altruistic" practices, but we tell ourselves it is for the good of others. The Ik have dispensed with the myth of altruism. Though they have no centralized leadership or means of physical coercion, they do hold together with remarkable tenacity.

In our world, where the family has also lost much of its value as a social unit and where religious belief no longer binds us into communities, we maintain order only through coercive power that is ready to uphold a rigid law and through an equally rigid penal system. The Ik, however, have learned to do without coercion, either spiritual or physical. It seems that they have come to a recognition of what they accept as man's basic selfishness, of his natural determination to survive as an individual before all else. This they consider to be man's basic right, and they allow others to pursue that right without recrimination.

In large-scale societies such as our own, where members are individual beings rather than social beings, we rely on law for order. The absence of both a common law and a common belief would surely result in lack of any community of behavior; yet Ik society is not anarchical. One might well expect religion, then, to play a powerful role in Icien life, providing a source of unity.

The Ik, as may be expected, do not run true to form. When I arrived, there were still three ritual priests alive. From them and from the few other old people, I learned something of the Ik's belief and practice as they had been before their world was so terribly changed. There had been a powerful unity of belief in Didigwari—a sky god—and a body of ritual practice reinforcing secular behavior that was truly social.

Didigwari himself is too remote to be of much practical significance to the Ik. He created them and abandoned them and retreated into his domain somewhere in the sky. He never came down to earth, but the *abang* [ancestors] have all known life on earth; it is only against them that one can sin and only to them that one can turn for help, through the ritual priest.

While Morungole has no legends attached to it by the Ik, it nonetheless figures in their ideology and is in some ways regarded by them as sacred. I had noticed this by the almost reverential way in which they looked at it—none of the shrewd cunning and cold appraisal with which they regarded the rest of the world. When they talked about it, there was a different quality to their voices. They seemed incapable of talking about Morungole in any other way, which is probably why they talked about it so very seldom. Even that weasel Lomongin became gentle the only time he talked about it to me. He said, "If Atum and I were there, we would not argue. It is a good place." I asked if he meant that it was full of food. He said yes. "Then why do Ik never go there?" "They do go there." "But if hunting is good there, why not live there?" "We don't hunt there, we just go there." "Why?" "I told you, it is a good place." If I did not understand him, that was my fault; for once he was doing his best to communicate something to me. With others it was the same. All agreed that it was "a good place." One added, "That is the Place of God."

Lolim, the oldest and greatest of the ritual priests, was also the last. He was not much in demand any longer, but he was still held in awe, which means kept at a distance. Whenever he approached a *di*, people cleared a space for him, as far away from themselves as possible. The Ik rarely called on his services, for they had little to pay him with, and he had equally little to offer them. The main things they did try to get out of him were certain forms of medicine, both herbal and magical.

Lolim said that he had inherited his power from his father. His father had taught him well but could not give him the power to hear the *abang*—that had to come from the *abang* themselves. He had wanted his oldest son to inherit and had taught him everything he could. But his son, Longoli, was bad, and the *abang* refused to talk to him. They talked instead to his oldest daughter, bald Nangoli. But there soon came the time when all the Ik needed was food in their stomachs, and Lolim could not supply that. The time came when Lolim was too weak to go out and collect the medicines he

needed. His children all refused to go except Nangoli, and then she was jailed for gathering in Kidepo Park.

Lolim became ill and had to be protected while eating the food I gave him. Then the children began openly ridiculing him and teasing him, dancing in front of him and kneeling down so that he would trip over them. His grandson used to creep up behind him and with a pair of hard sticks drum a lively tattoo on the old man's bald head.

I fed him whenever I could, but often he did not want more than a bite. Once I found him rolled up in his protective ball, crying. He had had nothing to eat for four days and no water for two. He had asked his children, who all told him not to come near them.

The next day I saw him leaving Atum's village, where his son Longoli lived. Longoli swore that he had been giving his father food and was looking after him. Lolim was not shuffling away; it was almost a run, the run of a drunken man, staggering from side to side. I called to him, but he made no reply, just a kind of long, continuous and horrible moan. He had been to Longoli to beg him to let him into his compound because he knew he was going to die in a few hours, Longoli calmly told me afterward. Obviously Longoli could not do a thing like that: a man of Lolim's importance would have called for an enormous funeral feast. So he refused. Lolim begged Longoli then to open up Nangoli's *asak* for him so that he could die in *her* compound. But Longoli drove him out, and he died alone.

Atum pulled some stones over the body where it had fallen into a kind of hollow. I saw that the body must have lain parallel with the *oror*. Atum answered without waiting for the question: "He was lying looking up at Mount Meraniang."

Insofar as ritual survived at all, it could hardly be said to be religious, for it did little or nothing to bind Icien society together. But the question still remained: Did this lack of social behavior and communal ritual or religious expression mean that there was no community of belief?

Belief may manifest itself, at either the individual or the communal level, in

what we call morality, when we behave according to certain principles supported by our belief even when it seems against our personal interest. When we call ourselves moral, however, we tend to ignore that ultimately our morality benefits us even as individuals, insofar as we are social individuals and live in a society. In the absence of belief, law takes over and morality has little role. If there was such a thing as an Icien morality, I had not yet perceived it, though traces of a moral past remained. But it still remained a possibility, as did the existence of an unspoken, unmanifest belief that might yet reveal itself and provide a basis for the reintegration of society. I was somewhat encouraged in this hope by the unexpected flight of old Nangoli, widow of Amuarkuar.

When Nangoli returned and found her husband dead, she did an odd thing: she grieved. She tore down what was left of their home, uprooted the stockade, tore up whatever was growing in her little field. Then she fled with a few belongings.

Some weeks later I heard that she and her children had gone over to the Sudan and built a village there. This migration was so unusual that I decided to see whether this runaway village was different.

Lojieri led the way, and Atum came along. One long day's trek got us there. Lojieri pulled part of the brush fence aside, and we went in and wandered around. He and Atum looked inside all the huts, and Lojieri helped himself to tobacco from one and water from another. Surprises were coming thick and fast. That households should be left open and untended with such wealth inside… That there should have been such wealth, for as well as tobacco and jars of water there were baskets of food, and meat was drying on racks. There were half a dozen or so compounds, but they were separated from each other only by a short line of sticks and brush. It was a village, and these were homes, the first and last I was to see.

The dusk had already fallen, and Nangoli came in with her children and grandchildren. They had heard us and came in with warm welcomes. There was no hunger here, and in a very short time each kitchen hearth had a pot of food cooking. Then we sat around the central fire and talked until late, and it was another universe.

There was no talk of "how much better it is here than there"; talk revolved around what had happened on the hunt that day. Loron was lying on the ground in front of the fire as his mother made gentle fun of him. His wife, Kinimei, whom I had never seen even speak to him at Pirre, put a bowl of fresh-cooked berries and fruit in front of him. It was all like a nightmare rather than a fantasy, for it made the reality of Pirre seem all the more frightening.

The unpleasantness of returning was somewhat alleviated by Atum's suffering on the way up the stony trail. Several times he slipped, which made Lojieri and me laugh. It was a pleasure to move rapidly ahead and leave Atum gasping behind so that we could be sitting up on the *di* when he finally appeared and could laugh at his discomfort.

The days of drought wore on into weeks and months and, like everyone else, I became rather bored with sickness and death. I survived rather as did the young adults, by diligent attention to my own needs while ignoring those of others.

More and more it was only the young who could go far from the village as hunger became starvation. Famine relief had been initiated down at Kasile, and those fit enough to make the trip set off. When they came back, the contrast between them and the others was that between life and death. Villages were villages of the dead and dying, and there was little difference between the two. People crawled rather than walked. After a few feet some would lie down to rest, but they could not be sure of ever being able to sit up again, so they mostly stayed upright until they reached their destination. They were going nowhere, these semianimate bags of skin and bone; they just wanted to be with others, and they stopped whenever they met. Perhaps it was the most important demonstration of sociality I ever saw among the Ik. Once they met, they neither spoke nor did anything together.

Early one morning, before dawn, the village moved. In the midst of a hive of activity were the aged and crippled, soon to be abandoned, in danger of being trampled but seemingly unaware of it. Lolim's widow, Lo'ono, whom I had

never seen before, also had been abandoned and had tried to make her way down the mountainside. But she was totally blind and had tripped and rolled to the bottom of the *oror a pirre'i;* there she lay on her back, her legs and arms thrashing feebly, while a little crowd laughed.

At this time a colleague was with me. He kept the others away while I ran to get medicine and food and water, for Lo'ono was obviously near dead from hunger and thirst as well as from the fall. We treated her and fed her and asked her to come back with us. But she asked us to point her in the direction of her son's new village. I said I did not think she would get much of a welcome there, and she replied that she knew it but wanted to be near him when she died. So we gave her more food, put her stick in her hand and pointed her the right way. She suddenly cried. She was crying, she said, because we had reminded her that there had been a time when people had helped each other, when people had been kind and good. Still crying, she set off.

The Ik up to this point had been tolerant of my activities, but all this was too much. They said that what we were doing was wrong. Food and medicine were for the living, not the dead. I thought of Lo'ono. And I thought of other old people who had joined in the merriment when they had been teased or had a precious morsel of food taken from their mouths. They knew that it was silly of them to expect to go on living, and, having watched others, they knew that the spectacle really was quite funny. So they joined in the laughter. Perhaps if we had left Lo'ono, she would have died laughing. But we prolonged her misery for no more than a few brief days. Even worse, we reminded her of when things had been different, of days when children had cared for parents and parents for children. She was already dead, and we made her unhappy as well. At the time I was sure we were right, doing the only "human" thing. In a way we *were*—we were making life more comfortable for ourselves. But now I wonder if the Ik way was not right, if I too should not have laughed as Lo'ono flapped about, then left her to die.

Ngorok was a man at 12. Lomer, his older brother, at 15 was showing signs of

strain; when he was carrying a load, his face took on a curious expression of pain that was not physical pain. Giriko, at 25 was 40, Atum at 40 was 65, and the very oldest, perhaps a bare 50, were centenarians. And I, at 40, was younger than any of them, for I still enjoyed life, which they had learned was not "adult" when they were 3. But they retained their will to survive and so offered grudging respect to those who had survived for long.

Even in the teasing of the old there was a glimmer of hope. It denoted a certain intimacy that did not exist between adjacent generations. This is quite common in small-scale societies. The very old and the very young look at each other as representing the future and the past. To the child, the aged represent a world that existed before their own birth and the unknown world to come.

And now that all the old are dead, what is left? Every Ik who is old today was thrown out at three and has survived, and in consequence has thrown his own children out and knows that they will not help him in his old age any more than he helped his parents. The system has turned one full cycle and is now self-perpetuating; it has eradicated what we know as "humanity" and has turned the world into a chilly void where man does not seem to care even for himself, but survives. Yet into this hideous world Nangoli and her family quietly returned because they could not bear to be alone.

For the moment abandoning the very old and the very young, the Ik as a whole must be searched for one last lingering trace of humanity. They appear to have disposed of virtually all the qualities that we normally think of as differentiating us from other primates, yet they survive without seeming to be greatly different from ourselves in terms of behavior. Their behavior is more extreme, for we do not start throwing our children out until kindergarten. We have shifted responsibility from family to state, the Ik have shifted it to the individual.

It has been claimed that human beings are capable of love and, indeed, are dependent upon it for survival and sanity. The Ik offer us an opportunity for testing this cherished notion that love is essential to survival. If it is, the Ik should have it.

Love in human relationships implies mutuality, a willingness to sacrifice the self that springs from a consciousness of identity. This seems to bring us back to the Ik, for it implies that love is self-oriented, that even the supreme sacrifice of one's life is no more than selfishness, for the victim feels amply rewarded by the pleasure he feels in making the sacrifice. The Ik, however, do not value emotion above survival, and they are without love.

But I kept looking, for it was the one thing that could fill the void their survival tactics had created; and if love was not there in some form, it meant that for humanity love is not a necessity at all, but a luxury or an illusion. And if it was not among the Ik, it meant that mankind can lose it.

The only possibility for any discovery of love lay in the realm of interpersonal relationships. But they were, each one, simply alone, and seemingly content to be alone. It was this acceptance of individual isolation that made love almost impossible. Contact, when made, was usually for a specific practical purpose having to do with food and the filling of a stomach, a single stomach. Such contacts did not have anything like the permanence or duration required to develop a situation in which love was possible.

The isolation that made love impossible, however, was not completely proof against loneliness, I no longer noticed normal behavior, such as the way people ate, running as they gobbled, so as to have it all for themselves. But I did notice that when someone was making twine or straightening a spear shaft, the focus of attention for the spectators was not the person but the action. If they were caught watching by the one being watched and their eyes met, the reaction was a sharp retreat on both sides.

When the rains failed for the second year running, I knew that the Ik as a society were almost certainly finished and that the monster they had created in its place, that passionless, feelingless association of individuals, would spread like a fungus, contaminating all it touched. When I left, I too had been contaminated. I was not upset when I said good-bye to old Loiangorok. I told him I had left a sack of *posho* [ground corn meal] with

the police for him, and I said I would send money for more when that ran out. He dragged himself slowly toward the *di* every day, and he always clutched a knife. When he got there, or as far as he could, he squatted down and whittled at some wood, thus proving that he was still alive and able to do things. The *posho* was enough to last him for months, but I felt no emotion when I estimated that he would last one month, even with the *posho* in the hands of the police. I underestimated his son, who within two days had persuaded the police that it would save a lot of bother if he looked after the *posho*. I heard later that Loiangorok died of starvation within two weeks.

So, I departed with a kind of forced gaiety, feeling that I should be glad to be gone but having forgotten how to be glad. I certainly was not thinking of returning within a year, but I did. The following spring I heard that rain had come at last and that the fields of the Ik had never looked so prosperous, nor the country so green and fertile. A few months away had refreshed me, and I wondered if my conclusions had not been excessively pessimistic. So, early that summer, I set off to be present for the first harvests in three years.

I was not surprised too much when two days after my arrival and installation at the police post I found Logwara, the blind man, lying on the roadside bleeding, while a hundred yards up other Ik were squabbling over the body of a hyena. Logwara had tried to get there ahead of the others to grab the meat and had been trampled on.

First I looked at the villages. The lush outer covering concealed an inner decay. All the villages were like this to some extent, except for Lokelea's. There the tomatoes and pumpkins were carefully pruned and cleaned, so that the fruits were larger and healthier. In what had been my own compound the shade trees had been cut down for firewood, and the lovely hanging nests of the weaver birds were gone.

The fields were even more desolate. Every field without exception had yielded in abundance, and it was a new sensation to have vision cut off by thick crops. But every crop was rotting from sheer neglect.

The Ik said that they had no need to bother guarding the fields. There was so much food they could never eat it all, so why not let the birds and baboons take some? The Ik had full bellies; they were good. The *di* at Atum's village was much the same as usual, people sitting or lying about. People were still stealing from each other's fields, and nobody thought of saving for the future.

It was obvious that nothing had really changed due to the sudden glut of food except that interpersonal relationships had deteriorated still further and that Icien individualism had heightened beyond what I thought even Ik to be capable of.

The Ik had faced a conscious choice between being humans and being parasites and had chosen the latter. When they saw their fields come alive, they were confronted with a problem. If they reaped the harvest, they would have to store grain for eating and planting, and every Ik knew that trying to store anything was a waste of time. Further, if they made their fields look too promising, the government would stop famine relief. So the Ik let their fields rot and continued to draw famine relief.

The Ik were not starving any longer; the old and infirm had all died the previous year, and the younger survivors were doing quite well. But the famine relief was administered in a way that was little short of criminal. As before, only the young and well were able to get down from Pirre to collect the relief; they were given relief for those who could not come and told to take it back. But they never did—they ate it themselves.

The facts are there, though those that can be read here form but a fraction of what one person was able to gather in under two years. There can be no mistaking the direction in which those facts point, and that is the most important thing of all, for it may affect the rest of mankind as it has affected the Ik. The Ik have "progressed," one might say, since the change that has come to them came with the advent of civilization to Africa. They have made of a world that was alive a world that is dead—a cold, dispassionate world that is without ugliness because it is without beauty, without hate because it is without love, and without any realization of truth even, because it simply is. And the symptoms of change in our own society indicate that we are heading in the same direction.

Those values we cherish so highly may indeed be basic to human society but not to humanity, and that means that the Ik show that society itself is not indispensable for man's survival and that man is capable of associating for purposes of survival without being social. The Ik have replaced human society with a mere survival system that does not take human emotion into account. As yet the system i[s] imperfect, for although survival is assured, it is at a minimal level and there is still competition between individuals. With our intellectual sophistication and advanced technology we should be able to perfect the system and eliminate competition, guaranteeing survival for a given number of years for all, reducing the demands made upon us by a social system, abolishing desire and consequently that ever-present and vital gap between desire and achievement, treating us, in a word, as individuals with one basic individual right—the right to survive.

Such interaction as there is within this system is one of mutual exploitation. That is how it already is with the Ik. In our own world the mainstays of a society based on a truly social sense of mutuality are breaking down, indicating that perhaps society as we know it has outworn its usefulness and that by clinging to an outworn system we are bringing about our own destruction. Family, economy, government and religion, the basic categories of social activity and behavior, no

longer create any sense of social unity involving a shared and mutual responsibility among all members of our society. At best they enable the individual to survive as an individual. It is the world of the individual, as is the world of the Ik.

The sorry state of society in the civilized world today is in large measure due to the fact that social change has not kept up with technological change. This mad, senseless, unthinking commitment to technological change that we call progress may be sufficient to exterminate the human race in a very short time even without the assistance of nuclear warfare. But since we have already become individualized and desocialized, we say that extermination will not come in our time, which shows about as much sense of family devotion as one might expect from the Ik.

Even supposing that we can avert nuclear holocaust or the almost universal famine that may be expected if population keeps expanding and pollution remains unchecked, what will be the cost if not the same already paid by the Ik? They too were driven by the need to survive, and they succeeded at the cost of their humanity. We are already beginning to pay the same price, but we not only still have the choice (though we may not have the will or courage to make it), we also have the intellectual and technological ability to avert an Icien end. Any change as radical as will be necessary is not likely to bring material benefits to the present generation, but only then will there be a future.

The Ik teach us that our much vaunted human values are not inherent in human-

ity at all but are associated only with a particular form of survival called society and that all, even society itself, are luxuries that can be dispensed with. That does not make them any less wonderful, and if man has any greatness, it is surely in his ability to maintain these values, even shortening an already pitifully short life rather than sacrifice his humanity. But that too involves choice, and the Ik teach us that man can lose the will to make it. That is the point at which there is an end to truth, to goodness and to beauty, an end to the struggle for their achievement, which gives life to the individual and strength and meaning to society. The Ik have relinquished all luxury in the name of individual survival, and they live on as a people without life, without passion, beyond humanity. We pursue those trivial, idiotic technological encumbrances, and all the time we are losing our potential for social rather than individual survival, for hating as well as loving, losing perhaps our last chance to enjoy life with all the passion that is our nature.

Anthropologist Colin M. Turnbull, author of The Forest People *and* The Lonely Africans, *went to study the Ik of Uganda, who he believed were still primarily hunters, in order to compare them with other hunting-and-gathering societies he had studied in totally different environments. He was surprised to discover that they were no longer hunters but primarily farmers, well on their way to starvation and something worse in a drought-stricken land.*

THE ATROPHY
OF SOCIAL LIFE

D. Stanley Eitzen

Harvard political scientist Robert Putnam has written a provocative book entitled *Bowling Alone*, in which he argues that we Americans are becoming increasingly disengaged from each other. That is, we are less likely than Americans of a generation or two ago to belong to voluntary associations such as the Rotary Club, to play bridge on a regular basis to participate in a bowling league, to belong to the P.T.A., or to vote. In short, Putnam maintains that in the past 50 years or so social life has changed dramatically throughout the United States as various social trends isolate us more and more from each other. The effect, he suggests, is that the bonds of civic cement are disintegrating as we become increasing separated from each other, from our communities and from society. Consequently, the social glue that once held communities together and gave meaning to individual lives is now brittle, as people have become more and more isolated.

I am a sociologist. We sociologists focus on things social the most fundamental of which is social interaction. This is the basic building block of intimate relationships, small groups, formal organizations, communities, and societies. I am concerned and I believe we should all be concerned by some disturbing trends in our society that hinder or even eliminate social interaction, and that indicate a growing isolation as individuals become increasingly separated from their neighbors, their co-workers, and even their family members.

Moving Away

Ours is a mobile society. We move, on average about every five years. We change jobs (14 percent of workers in a typical year leave their jobs voluntarily) or we lose jobs involuntarily (a recent survey indicated that 36 percent of Americans answered "yes" to the question: "Has anyone in your immediate family lost a job in the last three years?"). It's important to note here that the bond between workers and employers is badly frayed as employees are no longer loyal to our employers and employers are clearly not loyal, to their employees as they downsize locally and outsource their jobs and operations to low-wage economies.

We are also moving away from intimate relationships. With 1.25 million divorces occurring annually in the U.S. 2.5 million move away from their spouses. Immigration has the same consequence, creating transnational families, where families are separated with some members living in the U. S. and one or more members back home in another country.

When we move out of relationships or to new geographical areas, or to new kinds of work, we leave behind our relationships with former neighbors. co-workers, and friends. If we anticipate moving, we act like temporary residents, not making the effort to join local organizations, to become acquainted with our neighbors, and invest our time and money to improve the community.

Living Alone

In 1930, 2 percent of the U. S. population lived alone. In 2000, some 10 percent (27.2 million) of the nation's 105 million households were occupied by single people without children, roommates, or other people. People are living longer and the elderly, especially older women, are most likely to live alone. Divorce, by definition, initiates living alone, with 2.5 million former spouses annually moving into separate living arrangements. Another source for living alone is the phenomenon of commuter marriage—an arrangement where wives and husbands maintain separate households as a way of solving the dilemmas of dual-career marriages.

Technology and Isolation

Modern technology often encourages isolation. Consider the isolating consequences of air conditioning, certainly a welcome and necessary technology in many places. Before air conditioning, people spent leisure time outside increasing the likelihood of interaction with neighbors and friends. Now they are inside their homes with doors and windows shut enjoying the cool air, but isolating themselves from their neighbors. Television, too, along with VCRs, DVDs, and video games entice us to stay in our homes more and more.

Before refrigerators, shopping was done every day. This meant that people would see the same shop proprietors and their fellow shoppers daily. This created a daily rhythm, a set of interactions, and the sharing of information, gossip, and mutual concerns. Thus, refrigerators, while reducing the spoilage of food and the necessity of going to the store every day, changed interaction patterns.

Because of computers and telecommunications there is a growing trend for workers to work at home. At last count 28 million Americans worked out of their homes, using computers or telephony instead of face-to-face interaction. While home-based work allows flexibility and independence not found in most jobs, these workers are separated from the rich social networks that often give rise to numerous friendships and make working life enjoyable or at least tolerable.

With the new communications technology, you don't even have to go to a funeral to pay your respects. A new company is now broadcasting funerals on the Internet and you can even sign an electronic guest book and e-mail condolences to the family. Similarly, one can take college courses without attending classes, just using the Internet to communicate with their instructors. Missing, of course, is the face-to-face interaction with fellow students and professors.

Paradoxically, the current communications revolution increases interaction while reducing intimacy. Curt Suplee, science and technology writer for the *Washington Post*, says that we have seen tenfold increases in "communication" by electronic means, and tenfold reductions in person-to-person contact. The more time people spend online, the less they can spare for real-life relationships with family and friends. In effect, as we are increasingly alone before a computer screen, we risk what former U. S. Secretary State Warren Christopher has called "social malnutrition." John L. Locke, a professor of communications, makes a convincing argument in his book, *The De-Voicing of Society*, that e-mail, voice mail, fax machines, beepers, and Internet chat rooms are robbing us of ordinary social talking. Talking, he says, like the grooming of apes and monkeys, is the way we build and maintain social relationships. In his view, it is only through intimate conversation that we can know others well enough to trust them and work with them harmoniously. Most face-to-face communication is nonverbal. Phone communication reduces the nonverbal clues, and e-mail eliminates them entirely. So the new information technologies only create the illusion of communication and intimacy. The result, according to Locke, is that we are becoming an autistic society, communicating messages electronically but without really connecting. In short, these incredible communication devices that combine to network us in so many dazzling ways also separate us increasingly from intimate relationships. Sometimes we even use the technology to avoid the live interaction for whatever reason. Jeffrey Kagan, a telecom industry analyst, sums up the problem: "We are becoming a society that finds it easier, and even preferable to hide behind our computer screens and chat with a raceless, nameless stream of words from across the country or across the globe rather than deal with people face to face and all the complexities, good and bad, of the human relationship."

Geography and Isolation

There is a strong pattern of social homogeneity by place. Cities are arranged into neighborhoods by social class and race. This occurs because of choice, economic means, and the discriminatory behaviors by neighbors, realtors, and lending institutions. Among multiracial societies, only South Africa exceeds our rate of segregation—a problem that concentrates poverty, social disorder, and dysfunctional schools as well as diminishing social cohesion. The degree of racial/ethnic segregation by neighborhood is higher now than in 1990. A Harvard University study found that about 2.3 million African American and Latino children attend "apartheid" schools, where virtually all students are minorities. Similarly, some neighborhoods are segregated by age. Some retirement communities, for example, limit their inhabitants to persons over 55 and those without minor children. Some 6 million households are in neighborhoods that have controlled-entry systems with guards and electric gates. These gated communities wall the residents off physically and socially from "others." Regarding this exclusiveness, sociologist Philip Slater said that we need heterogeneous neighborhoods: "A community that does not have old people and children, white-collar and blue-collar, eccentric and conventional, and so on, is not a community at all, but [a] kind of truncated and deformed monstrosity…"

Even in non-gated communities, we isolate ourselves. One in three Americans has never spent an evening with a neighbor. The affluent often belong to exclusive clubs and send their children to private schools. Two million children are home schooled, which isolates them from their peers. Some people exercise on motorized treadmills and use other home exercise equipment instead of running through their neighborhoods or working out with others.

The suburbs are especially isolating. Rather than walking to the corner grocery or nearby shop and visiting with the clerks and their neighbors, suburbanites drive somewhere away from their immediate neighborhood to shop among strangers. Or they may not leave their home at all, working, shopping, banking, and paying their bills by computer. For suburban teenagers and children almost everything is away—practice fields, music lessons, friends, jobs, schools, and the malls. Thus, a disconnect from those nearby. Suburban neighborhoods in particular are devoid of meeting places. The lack of community

and common meeting places in our cities and especially in the suburbs compounds the isolation of those who have experienced a divorce or the death of a spouse.

Isolation within Families

An especially disturbing trend is the separation of family members from each other. Many spouses are either absent or too self-absorbed to pay very much attention to their children or each other. A recent cover story in Newsweek noted that many dual-income couples no longer or rarely have sex because they are too exhausted and too stressed. On average, parents today spend 22 fewer hours a week with their children than parents did in the 1960s. Part of this is because both parents are working outside the home. But it also results from children being overscheduled with outside-the-home activities. These children have little time for play with other children and their activities replace parent-child interaction. To amplify the last point, American children spend more than half of their waking hours in supervised, child-centered environments. This causes economist Ellen Frank to ask: "What happens to parents, to children, and to the rest of us when children arc stored out of sight?"

Although living in the same house, parents and children may tune each other out emotionally, or by using earphones, or by engaging in other solitary activities. A survey by the Kaiser Family Foundation found that the average child spends five and one-half hours a day alone watching television, on the Internet, playing video games, or reading. Some 30 percent of children under 3 have a television in their bedroom. Some older children even have their own rooms equipped with a telephone, television, VCR, microwave, refrigerator, and computer, which while convenient, isolates them from other family members. Many families rarely eat together in an actual sit-down meal. Family members are often too busy and too involved with their individual schedules to spend quality time together as a family. These homes may be full of people but they are really empty.

The Architecture of Isolation

Another contemporary trend—the increased number of megahouses in the suburbs—results in what we might call the architecture of isolation. These huge houses, built, ironically, at the very time that family size is declining, tend to isolate their inhabitants from outsiders and from other family members. They provide all of the necessities for comfort and recreation, thus glorifying the private sphere over public places. Moreover, the number and size of the rooms encourages each family member to have their own space rather than shared spaces. Thus, the inverse correlation between house size and family interaction.

Contemporary house and landscape design focuses interaction in the backyard, surrounded by privacy fences, some of which make our homes and lots to resemble medieval fortresses. Back yards are inviting with grass and flowerbeds, barbeque pits, swimming pools, jungle gyms, and trampolines. The front of the house no longer has a porch. In the past, families spent time on the porch, relaxing and visiting with neighbors. The front yard, too, is less inviting than the back, often with rock instead of grass. It is important to note that the more affluent we are, the more likely our homes and consumer goods promote social isolation.

Consumerism and Isolation

Sociologist George Ritzer in his recent book, *The Globalization of Nothing*, argues that the social world, particularly in the realm of consumption, is increasingly characterized by "nothing," which he defines as a social form that is generally centrally conceived and controlled and comparatively devoid of distinctive substance. The "something" that is lost is more than likely, an indigenous custom or product, a local store, a familiar gathering place, or simply personalized interaction. Corporations provide standardized, mass-produced products for us to consume and become like other consumers in what we wear, what we eat, and what we desire. We purchase goods in chain stores and restaurants (Dillard's, McDonalds) that are efficient but devoid of distinctive content. A mall in one part of the world may be structured much the same in another location. We bank at ATMs anywhere in the world, but without social interaction. The same is true with shopping on the Internet.

Increasingly, Ritzer says, adults go through their daily routines without sharing stories, gossip, and analyses of events with friends on a regular basis at work, at a coffee shop, neighborhood tavern, or at the local grain elevator. These places of conversation with friends have been replaced by huge stores (Wal-Mart, Home Depot) where we don't know the clerks and other shoppers. The locally owned café has been replaced by chain restaurants. In the process we lose the intimacy of local stores, cafes, and hardware stores, which give their steady customers sense of community and the comfort of meaningful connections with others. Sociologist Philip Slater said that "community life exists when one can go daily to a given location at a given time and see many of the people one knows."

Implications for Society

There are several important implications of increasing social isolation for society. First, the disengaged do not participant in elections, leaving a minority to elect our leaders as occurred in the 2000 presidential election when George Bush was elected with 24 percent of the votes of those eligible. This means that, the voices of outsiders will be faint if heard at all while the voices of the affluent and their money arc heard all the more. All of these consequences support the conservative agenda, as sociologist Paul Starr notes: "These trends could hardly please anyone who cares about the republic, but they have been particularly disturbing to liberals. The most intense periods of liberal reform during the past century—the Progressive era, the New Deal, and the 1960s—were all times when the public was actively engaged, and new forms of civic action and participation emerged. Reforms in that tradition are unlikely to succeed again without the same heightened public arousal, which not only elects candidates but also forces them to pay attention once they are in office."

Second, the breakdown in social connections shows up in everyday sociability, with pernicious effects for social relations as people are less and less civil in schools, at work, in traffic, and in public places.

Third, when people focus only on themselves and people like themselves, they insulate themselves from "others" and from their problems. Thus, we favor dismantling the welfare state and safely net for the less fortunate. We oppose, for example, equity in school funding, allowing rich districts to have superior schools while the disadvantaged have inferior schools. We allow this unraveling of community bonds at our peril, as the walls become thicker between the "haves" and the "have-nots," crime will increase and hostility and fear will reign.

Implications for Individuals

As for individuals, the consequences of this accelerating social isolation are dire. More and more Americans are lonely, bitter, alienated, anomic, and disconnected. This situation is conducive to alcohol and drug abuse, depression, anxiety, and violence. The lonely and disaffected are ripe candidates for membership in cults, gangs, and militias where they find a sense of belonging and a cause to believe in, but in the process they may become more paranoid and, perhaps, even become willing terrorists or mass murderers as were the two alienated adolescents who perpetrated the massacre at Columbine High School in a Denver suburb. At a less extreme level, the alienated will disengage further from society by shunning voluntary associations, by home schooling their children, and by voting against higher taxes for the public good. In short, they will become increasingly self-absorbed, caring only about themselves and ignoring the needs of their neighbors and communities. This translates into the substitution of accumulating things rather than cultivating relationships. In this regard, we should take seriously, the admonition by David Wann the coauthor of *Affluenza: The All-Consuming Epidemic*, who says "We need to acknowledge—as individuals and as a culture—that the best things in life really aren't things. The best things are bonus with people…"

What to Do?

I am not a Luddite. I appreciate the wonders of technology. I welcome change. There are good reasons to move and to change careers and to live in nice houses. But we must recognize the unintended consequences of societal trends that deprive us of our shared humanity. Once we have identified the downside of these trends and our complicity in them, what can we do to reverse their negative effects? I don't have all the answers, but I believe that a few structural changes will help to reduce their negative consequences. As a start, we need to rethink urban design. We must reverse urban sprawl, increasing urban density so that people live near their work, near their neighbors, and within walking distance of stores and recreation. Second, as a society we need to invest in the infrastructure that facilitate public activities such as neighborhood schools, walking and biking trails, parks, the arts, libraries, and community recreation centers. Third, communities need to provide activities that bring people together such as public concerts, fairs, recreational sports for people of all ages, and art festivals. And, fourth, since U. S. society is becoming more diverse, we need to break down the structural barriers that isolate us from "others." We need to affirm affirmative action in legislation and deed, eliminate predatory lending practices and other forms of discrimination, and improve our schools so that equality of educational opportunity actually occurs rather than the present arrangement whereby school systems are rigged in favor of the already privileged. You will note that these proposals are opposite from current policy at the community, state, and federal levels, resulting in a descending spiral toward social atomization. We allow this to occur at our own peril.

At a personal level, we need to recognize what is happening to us and our families and work to counteract these isolating trends. Each of us can think of changes in our lives that will enhance human connections. To those changes, may I suggest the following: Engage in public activities. Have meaningful face-to-face conversations with friends on a regular basis. Get to know your neighbors, co-workers, and the people, who provide services for you. Join with others who share a common interest. Work to improve your community. Become an activist, joining with others to

bring about social change. And, most of all, we need to moderate our celebration of individualism and our tendency toward self-absorption and develop instead a moral obligation to others, to our neighbors (broadly defined) and their children, to those unlike us as well as those similar to us, and to future generations. If not, then our humanity is compromised and our quality of life diminished.

SUGGESTED FURTHER READINGS

Kane, Hal. 2001. *Triumph of the Mundane: The Unseen Trends that Shape Our Lives and Environment*. Washington, D. C.: Island Press.

Locke, John L. 1998. *The De-Voicing of Society: Why We Don't Talk to Each Other*. New York: Simon and Schuster.

Oldenburg, Ray. 1997. *The Great Good Place: Cafes, Coffee Shops, Community Centers, Beauty Parlors, General Stores Bars, Hangouts, and How They Get You Through the Day*. New York: Marlowe.

Putnam, Robert D. 2000. *Bowling Alone: The Collapse and Revival of American Community*. New York: Simon and Schuster.

Ritzer, George. 2004. *The Globalization of Nothing*. Thousand Oaks. CA: Pine Forge Press.

Slater, Philip. 1970. *The Pursuit, of Loneliness: American Culture at the Breaking Point*. Boston: Beacon Press.

D. Stanley Eitzen is a Professor Emeritus in sociology, Colorado State University. He is the author or co-author of nineteen books on various social problems, crime, and sport. This article is a revised version of a speech delivered at Angelo State University, San Angelo, Texas (October 16, 2003). This speech was reprinted in Vital Speeches of the Day (December 15, 2003).

SELF-RELIANCE
THOSE RUGGED INDIVIDUALS

BY JOANNIE FISCHER

No ideal may be held more sacred in America, or be more coveted by others, than the principle of individual freedom. Given the chance to pursue the heart's desires, our utopian vision claims, each of us has the ability—and the right—to make our dreams come true. This extraordinary individualism has prevailed as the core doctrine of the New World through four centuries, bringing with it an unrelenting pressure to prove one's self. The self-made man has been America's durable icon, whether personified by the prairie homesteader or the high-tech entrepreneur.

Yet, from the beginning, the idea of a community of rugged individualists struck many as an oxymoron. In the 1830s, Alexis de Tocqueville warned that the tendency of Americans to do their own thing could very likely doom the country. The Founding Fathers beseeched people to remain involved in community affairs. And today, a chorus of critics worries that the philosophy of individualism has slipped its original moorings, threatening the well-being of the nation and, ironically, individuals themselves.

When the United States first came into being, most people had never even heard the word *individualism*. "Our fathers only knew about egoism," said Tocqueville, who helped coin the term to capture the new way of life in the fledgling nation. Europe, where caste systems determined so much of one's fate, had never had much practical use for individualism. Born of the Protestant Reformation, the ethos was carried across the Atlantic by the Puritans, who believed that each person received marching orders directly from God. In their new society, the reformers decided, people would interact as equals, and God would reward the just. Their reasoning appealed to other groups landing in the New World, and over time, says Harvard political scientist Samuel Huntington, "The Puritan legacy became the American essence."

The first American individualists were thoroughly steeped in a one-for-all mentality on the assumption that all moral persons would devote themselves to the good of the group. Just before landing in Salem Harbor, John Winthrop, the soon-to-be governor of Massachusetts, reminded parishioners: "We must … make others' conditions our own … always having before our eyes our community as members of the same body." And even

as Thomas Jefferson wrote of the right to liberty and the pursuit of happiness, he pictured a nation of independent yeomen who, after tending their land all day, would gladly participate in community meetings.

Singing solo. Not until the mid-1800s did the pursuit of individual fulfillment come to connote a retreat from the group. Ralph Waldo Emerson first preached the concept in his 1841 essay "Self-Reliance." "Society everywhere is in conspiracy against the manhood of every one of its members," he declared. "Whoso would be a man must be a nonconformist." For him, the self was more important, more interesting, than the group. "I have only one doctrine," he wrote: "the infinitude of the private man." Emerson's friend Henry David Thoreau went further, deeming it necessary for him to physically part with society to develop his own integrity. And Walt Whitman, in poems such as "Song of Myself," introduced to the country what Berkeley sociologist Robert Bellah calls "expressive individualism," the valuing of personal pleasures such as sensuality and leisure above all else—something that would have been anathema in the religion-dominated Colonies.

RECONCILING OUR TREASURED FREEDOM WITH THE DEMANDS OF THE LARGER GROUP

This new preoccupation with private experience came at a time when the nation's urban areas were growing more crowded and dangerous and the ideal of universal self-employment was being eroded by a burgeoning underclass. Unlike Winthrop, who went broke from giving away so much of his own money, Emerson cursed himself for parting with the occasional coin, asking, "Are they *my* poor?" It was in this atmosphere that Horatio Alger pumped out more than 100 "rags-to-riches" tales of destitute orphans transformed into wealthy successes by ceaseless effort, ingenuity, and integrity. The moral of the story: Prosperity is possible for anyone willing to try hard enough. Even the day's most generous philanthropists bought into the notion. Andrew Carnegie, himself a rags-to-riches success, who later gave nearly $400 million to fund the arts and libraries, preached that money should never be "wasted" on the poor.

THE SELF-MADE MODEL

"**G**od helps them that help themselves" was a maxim Benjamin Franklin not only touted but lived, perhaps more than any other American ever. The very model of the poor boy who makes good, Franklin rose by initiative and talent to become one of the world's most beloved Americans. Not only did he wow the intellectuals of Europe, convincing them that the new philosophy of individualism was to be taken seriously, but he also provided a stunning example of just how much is possible when self-reliance hitches its wagon to liberty.

Born the 15th child of a poor candle maker, Franklin received only three years of formal schooling. So while other future Founding Fathers, like Thomas Jefferson and John Adams, were receiving the best educations money could buy, an 11-year-old Ben set about educating himself—and never stopped. For starters, he taught himself Latin, French, Spanish, Italian, and German and used them all with flair. Then, having learned to play the harp, violin, and guitar, he delved into science, math, and philosophy. He devoured every book he could find, from Plutarch's *Lives* to John Bunyan's *Pilgrim's Progress*. He learned the publishing business and became one of the world's most successful writers, authoring bestsellers such as *Poor Richard's Almanack*. In 1748, at the age of 42, Franklin had amassed so much wealth that he could retire and devote the rest of his life to his multifarious interests.

Busy. He became even more industrious in "retirement," however, inventing things like bifocals and the lightning rod. Like a modern workaholic, he admonished, "Be always asham'd to catch thy self idle."

But unlike today's typical overachiever, Franklin was devoted to public service. In his home city of Philadelphia, he helped to start the first public library, public museum, college, hospital, and patent office. "When you're good to others," he quipped, "you are best to yourself." With a more serious tone, upon signing the Declaration of Independence, he warned, "We must all hang together or assuredly, we shall all hang separately." Words of wisdom that seem just as apt in today's America. —J.F.

This by-your-bootstraps mentality didn't soften until the Great Depression left a quarter of the nation unemployed, a harsh reality check on the naive belief that nothing could block the truly motivated individual. Since then the nation has created a vast safety net of financial aid. We still prize self-reliance, but we are a relatively generous people, with 3 out of 4 households donating to charity.

Lone heroes. Not only did insistence on a strict self-reliance soften as the 20th century progressed, but many came to fear our rugged individualism was melting into a mediocre conformity. With the 1950s came mass media, tract housing, the organization man, and the concept of the mainstream middle class. In a lightning-rod book, *The Lonely Crowd*, sociologist David Riesman described a shift from the self-reliant personality of the 19th century to the "other-directed" corporate worker of the new service economy. Many used his work to send an alarmist call for the revival of individualism. Out of this sentiment were born heroes like the Lone Ranger, James Dean in *Rebel Without a Cause*, and Beat poets like Jack Kerouac and Allen Ginsberg.

TOCQUEVILLE WARNED THAT OUR TENDENCY TO DO OUR THING COULD DOOM THE NATION.

The 70 million baby boomers soon to come of age would be dubbed the "me generation" for indulging in an obsessive self-interest that critics blamed for everything from rising crime and divorce rates to child abuse and urban decay. In his 1979 *Culture of Narcissism*, Christopher Lasch argued that many Americans could now perceive others only as a mirror of the self. More sympathetically, in *Habits of the Heart: Individualism and Commitment in American Life*, Bellah argued that Americans wanted to transcend their self-absorption but had become trapped by the language of individualism into seeing no point in trying to reconnect with others.

But that's exactly what we *must* do, say today's communitarians, not just for the health of our democracy but for ourselves. In *Bowling Alone*, Harvard public-policy Prof. Robert Putnam documents a huge drop in all forms of public life since the late 1960s and a corresponding rise in measures of malaise, from the use of antidepressants to suicide rates. Medical studies confirm that individuals are sicker and die sooner in direct proportion to the degree that they are isolated from others. Fortunately, says Putnam in his sequel *Better Together*, Americans *are* finding ways to reform meaningful groups, such as using the Internet to create "virtual" communities.

Americans will no doubt continue to assume as a birthright the freedom to forge their own destinies. But a growing consensus also holds that individuals—and democracies—are far better off when people feel part of a larger whole, when they heed Jefferson's directive to "love your neighbor as yourself, and your country more than yourself."

What's So Great About America?

By Dinesh D'Souza

The newcomer who sees America for the first time typically experiences emotions that alternate between wonder and delight. Here is a country where *everything works*: The roads are paper-smooth, the highway signs are clear and accurate, the public toilets function properly, when you pick up the telephone you get a dial tone. You can even buy things from the store and then take them *back* if you change your mind. For the Third World visitor, the American supermarket is a marvel to behold: endless aisles of every imaginable product, 50 different types of cereal, multiple flavors of ice cream, countless unappreciated inventions like quilted toilet paper, fabric softener, roll-on deodorant, disposable diapers.

The immigrant cannot help noticing that America is a country where the poor live comparatively well. This fact was dramatized in the 1980s, when CBS television broadcast an anti-Reagan documentary, "People Like Us," which was intended to show the miseries of the poor during an American recession. The Soviet Union also broadcast the documentary, with the intention of embarrassing the Reagan administration. But it had the opposite effect. Ordinary people across the Soviet Union saw that the poorest Americans had television sets and cars. They arrived at the same conclusion that I witnessed in a friend of mine from Bombay who has been trying unsuccessfully to move to the United States for nearly a decade. I asked him, "Why are you so eager to come to America?" He replied, "Because I really want to live in a country where the poor people are fat."

The point is that the United States is a country where the ordinary guy has a good life. This is what distinguishes America from so many other countries. Everywhere in the world, the rich person lives well. Indeed, a good case can be made that if you are rich, you live better in countries other than America, because you enjoy the pleasures of aristocracy. In India, where I grew up, the wealthy have innumerable servants and toadies groveling before them and attending to their every need.

In the United States, on the other hand, the social ethic is egalitarian, regardless of wealth. For all his riches, Bill Gates could not approach a homeless person and say, "Here's a $100 bill. I'll give it to you if you kiss my feet."

Most likely the homeless guy would tell Gates to go to hell. The American view is that the rich guy may have more money, but he isn't in any fundamental sense better than you are. The American janitor or waiter sees himself as performing a service, but he doesn't see himself as inferior to those he serves. And neither do the customers see him that way: They are generally happy to show him respect and appreciation on a plane of equality. America is the only country in the world where we call the waiter "Sir," as if he were a knight.

The moral triumph of America is that it has extended the benefits of comfort and affluence, traditionally enjoyed by very few, to a large segment of society. Very few people in America have to wonder where their next meal is coming from. Even sick people who don't have money or insurance will receive medical care at hospital emergency rooms. The poorest American girls are not humiliated by having to wear torn clothes. Every child is given an education, and most have the chance to go on to college. The common man can expect to live long enough and have enough free time to play with his grandchildren.

Ordinary Americans not only enjoy security and dignity, but also comforts that other societies reserve for the elite. We now live in a country where construction workers regularly pay $4 for a cappuccino, where maids drive nice cars, where plumbers take their families on vacation to Europe. As Irving Kristol once observed, there is virtually no restaurant in America to which a CEO can go to lunch with the absolute assurance that he will not find his secretary also dining there. Given the standard of living of the ordinary American, it is no wonder that socialist or revolutionary schemes have never found a wide constituency in the United States. As Werner Sombart observed, all socialist utopias in America have come to grief on roast beef and apple pie.

Thus it is entirely understandable that people would associate the idea of America with a better life. For them, money is not an end in itself; money is the means to a longer, healthier, and fuller life. Money allows them to purchase a level of security, dignity, and comfort not available in other countries. Money also frees up time for family life, community involvement, and spiritual pursuits, and so provides moral as well as material gains.

Yet even this offers an incomplete picture of why America is so appealing to so many outsiders. Let me illustrate with the example of my own life. Not long ago, I asked myself: What would my existence have been like had I never come to the United States, if I had stayed in India? Materially, my life has improved, but not in a fundamental sense. I grew up in a middle-class family in Bombay. My father was a chemical engineer; my mother, an office secretary. I was raised without great luxury, but neither did I lack for anything. My standard of living in America is higher, but it is not a radical difference. My life has changed far more dramatically in other ways.

Had I remained in India, I would probably have lived my entire existence within a one-mile radius of where I was born. I would undoubtedly have married a woman of my identical religious, socioeconomic, and cultural background. I would almost certainly have become a medical doctor, an engineer, or a software programmer. I would have socialized within my ethnic community and had few real friends outside that group. I would have a whole set of opinions that could be predicted in advance; indeed, they would not be very different from what my father believed, or his father before him. In sum, my destiny would to a large degree have been given to me.

Instead, I came to Arizona in 1978 as a high-school exchange student, then a year later enrolled at Dartmouth College. There I fell in with a group of students who were actively involved in politics; soon I had switched my major from economics to English literature. My reading included books like Plutarch's *Moralia*; Hamilton, Madison, and Jay's *Federalist Papers*; and Evelyn Waugh's *Brideshead Revisited*. They transported me to places a long way from home and implanted in my mind ideas that I had never previously considered. By the time I graduated, I decided that I should become a writer. America permits many strange careers: This is a place where you can become, say, a comedian. That is very different from most places.

If there is a single phrase that encapsulates life in the Third World, it is that "birth is destiny." A great deal of importance is attached to what tribe you come from, whether you are male or female, and whether you are the eldest son or not. Once your tribe, caste, sex and family position have been established at birth, your life takes a course that is largely determined for you.

In America, by contrast, you get to write the script of your own life. When your parents say to you, "What do you want to be when you grow up?" the question is open ended, it is you who supply the answer. Your parents can advise you: "Have you considered law school?" "Why not become the first doctor in the family?" It is considered very improper, however, for them to try to force your decision. Indeed, American parents typically send their teenage children away to college where they live on their own and learn independence. This is part of the process of forming your mind, choosing a field of interest for yourself, and developing your identity.

It is not uncommon in the United States for two brothers who come from the same gene pool and were raised in similar circumstances to do quite different things: The eldest becomes a gas station attendant, the younger moves up to be vice president at Oracle; the eldest marries his high-school sweetheart and raises four kids; the youngest refuses to settle down; one is the Methodist that he was raised to be, the other becomes a Christian Scientist. What to be, where to live, whom to marry, what to believe, what religion to practice—these are all decisions that Americans make for themselves.

In America your destiny is not prescribed; it is constructed. Your life is like a blank sheet of paper and you are the artist. This notion of being the architect of your own destiny is the incredibly powerful idea that is behind the worldwide appeal of America. Young people especially find the prospect of authoring their own lives irresistible. The immigrant discovers that America permits him to break free of the constraints that have held him captive, so that the future becomes a landscape of his own choosing.

If there is a single phrase that captures this, it is "the pursuit of happiness." As writer V. S. Naipaul notes, "much is contained" in that simple phrase: "the idea of the individual, responsibility, choice, the life of the intellect, the idea of vocation, perfectibility, and achievement. It is an immense human idea. It cannot be reduced to a fixed system. It cannot generate fanaticism. But it is known [around the world] to exist; and because of that, other more rigid systems in the end blow away."

But where did the "pursuit of happiness" come from? And why has it come in America to mean something much more than simple selfishness? America's founders were religious men. They believed that political legitimacy derives from God. Yet they were determined not to permit theological differences to become the basis for political conflict.

The American system refused to establish a national church, instead recognizing all citizens as free to practice their own religion. From the beginning the United States was made up of numerous sects. The Puritans dominated in Massachusetts, the Anglicans in Virginia, the Catholics were concentrated in Maryland, so it was in every group's interest to "live and let live." The ingenuity of the American solution is evident in Voltaire's remark that where there is one religion, you have tyranny; where there are two, you have religious war; but where they are many, you have freedom.

One reason the American founders were able to avoid religious oppression and conflict is that they found a way to channel people's energies away from theological quarrels and into commercial activity. The American system is founded on property rights and trade, and *The Federalist* tells us that protection of the obtaining of property is "the first object of government." The founders reasoned that people who are working assiduously to better their condition are not likely to go around spearing their neighbors.

Capitalism gives America a this-worldly focus that allows death and the afterlife to recede from everyday view. Along with their heavenly aspirations, the gaze of the people is shifted to earthly progress. This "lowering of the sights" convinces many critics that American capitalism is a base, degraded system and that the energies that drive it are crass and immoral.

These modern critiques draw on some very old prejudices. In the ancient world, labor was generally despised. The Greeks looked down on merchants and traders as low-lifes. "The gentleman understands what is noble," Confucius writes in his *Analects*, "the small man understands what is profitable." In the Indian caste system the *vaisya* or trader occupies nearly the lowest rung of the ladder—one step up from the despised "untouchable." The Muslim historian Ibn Khaldun suggests that even gain by conquest is preferable to gain by trade, because conquest embodies the virtues of courage and manliness. In these traditions, the honorable life is devoted to philosophy or the priesthood or military valor. "Making a living" was considered a necessary, but undignified, pursuit. Far better to rout your adversary, kill the men, enslave the women and children, and make off with a bunch of loot than to improve your lot by buying and selling stuff.

Drawing on the inspiration of philosophers like John Locke and Adam Smith, the American founders altered this moral hierarchy. They argued that trade based on consent and mutual gain was preferable to plunder. The founders established a regime in which the self-interest of entrepreneurs and workers would be directed toward serving the wants and needs of others. In this view, the ordinary life, devoted to production, serving the customer, and supporting a family, is a noble and dignified endeavor. Hard work, once considered a curse, now becomes socially acceptable, even honorable. Commerce, formerly a degraded thing, now becomes a virtue.

Of course the founders recognized that in both the private and the public sphere, greedy and ambitious people can pose a danger to the well-being of others. Instead of trying to outlaw these passions, the founders attempted a different approach. As the fifty-first book of *The Federalist* puts it, "Ambition must be made to counteract ambition." In a free society, "the security for civil rights [consists] in the multiplicity of interests." The framers of the Constitution reasoned that by setting interests against each other, by making them compete, no single one could become strong enough to imperil the welfare of the whole.

In the public sphere the founders took special care to devise a system that would minimize the abuse of power. They established limited government, in order that the power of the state would remain confined. They divided authority between the national and state governments. Within the national framework, they provided for separation of powers, so that the legislature, executive, and judiciary would each have its own domain of authority. They insisted upon checks and balances, to enhance accountability.

The founders didn't ignore the importance of virtue, but they knew that virtue is not always in abundant supply. According to Christianity, the problem of the bad person is that his will is corrupted, a fault endemic to human nature. America's founders knew they could not transform human nature, so they devised a system that would thwart the schemes of the wicked and channel the energies of flawed persons toward the public good.

The experiment that the founders embarked upon more than two centuries ago has largely succeeded in achieving its goals. Tribal and religious battles such as we see in Lebanon, Mogadishu, Kashmir, and Belfast don't happen here. Whites and African Americans have lunch together. Americans of Jewish and Palestinian descent collaborate on software problems and play racquetball after work. Hindus and Muslims, Serbs and Croats, Turks and Armenians, Irish Catholics and British Protestants, all seem to have forgotten their ancestral differences and joined the vast and varied American parade. Everybody wants to "make it," to "get ahead," to "hit it big." And even as they compete, people recognize that somehow they are all in this together, in pursuit of some great, elusive American dream. In this respect America is a glittering symbol to the world.

America's founders solved two great problems which are a source of perennial misery and conflict in many other societies—the problem of scarcity, and the problem of religious and tribal conflict. They invented a new regime in which citizens would enjoy a wide range of freedoms—economic freedom, political freedom, and freedom of speech and religion—in order to shape their own lives and pursue happiness. By protecting religion and government from each other, and by directing the energies of the citizens toward trade and commerce, the American founders created a rich, dynamic, and peaceful society. It is now the hope of countless millions all across the world.

Dinesh D'Souza, Rishwain Fellow at the Hoover Institution, is author of What's So Great About America, *from which this is adapted.*

UNIT 2

Socialization and Social Control

Unit Selections

Key Points to Consider

- What are the major natural differences between males and females and how are they socialized differently?

- How can the ways in which children are socialized in America be improved?

- What are the principal factors that make people what they are?

- Why has crime declined in the U.S. in the past two decades?

- What are the differences between street crime and white collar crime? Which has more harmful effects? What are the differences in the severity of the punishments for the two types of criminals? Explain these differences.

 **Links: www.dushkin.com/online/**
These sites are annotated in the World Wide Web pages.

Center for Leadership Studies
http://www.situational.com
Crime Times
http://www.crime-times.org
Ethics Updates/Lawrence Hinman
http://ethics.acusd.edu
National Institute on Drug Abuse (NIDA)
http://165.112.78.61/

Why do we behave the way we do? Three forces are at work: biology, socialization, and the human will or internal decision maker. The focus in sociology is on socialization, which is the conscious and unconscious process whereby we learn the norms and behavior patterns that enable us to function appropriately in our social environment. Socialization is based on the need to belong, because the desire for acceptance is the major motivation for internalizing the socially approved attitudes and behaviors. Fear of punishment is another motivation. It is utilized by parents and institutionalized in the law enforcement system. The language we use, the concepts we apply in thinking, the images we have of ourselves, our gender roles, and our masculine and feminine ideals are all learned through socialization. Socialization may take place in many contexts. The most basic socialization takes place in the family, but churches, schools, communities, the media, and workplaces also play major roles in the process.

The first subsection deals with issues concerning the basic influences on the development of our character and behavior patterns. First, Matt Ridley reviews the latest science on the nature versus nurture debate. It is clear that both are important and now we are learning that there is an interaction between genes and the environment. Ridley explains that "genes are not static blueprints that dictate our destiny. How they are expressed—where and when they are turned on or off and for how long—is affected by changes in the womb, by the environment and by other factors." In the next article, Hara Estroff Marano reviews the literature on the genetic differences between men and women, including mental, sexual, health, emotional, and psychological differences. For example, did you know that women have more gray brain matter and men have more white brain matter? Gray matter provides concentrated processing power and more thought linking capability. White matter helps spatial reasoning and allows a single mindedness. Ridley also explains many other differences.

The next subsection deals with crime, law enforcement, and social control—major concerns today because crime and violence seem to be out of control. In the first article in this subsection, Gene Stephens describes crime trends throughout the world but focuses on the United States. Overall crime rates in the United States were the highest in the Western world in 1980 but have fallen in the

United States and increased in many other nations so that several Western countries now have higher rates. Nevertheless, the U.S. murder rate is still the highest. Stephens presents three competing explanations for the crime decline in the U.S.: 1) greater success of the justice system in catching and locking up criminals, 2) the lowering of the percent of the population in the high crime ages, 3) the greater prevalence and success of community based approaches.

In the next article Jennifer Roback Morse argues that "for some people, prisons are a substitute for parents ... [for] without parents—two of them, married to each other, working together as a team—a child is more likely to end up in the criminal justice system." A key role of parents is to help a child develop a conscience and self-control, and two loving married parents do this job the best. Morse shows that dealing with criminals is very costly for society and indirectly the failure of many marriages contributes substantially to these costs. In the final article, David A. Anderson tries to put into monetary terms the impacts of various types of crimes in the United States. The results produce some surprises. First, when he includes many costs that are seldom taken into account—such as the costs of law enforcement, security measures, and lost time at work— the total bill is over $1 trillion or over $4000 per person. Another surprise is the relative costs of white collar crime versus street crime. Fraud and cheating on taxes costs Americans over 20 times the costs of theft, burglary, and robbery.

WHAT MAKES YOU WHO YOU ARE

Which is stronger—nature or nurture?
The latest science says genes and your
experience interact for your whole life

By MATT RIDLEY

THE PERENNIAL DEBATE ABOUT NATURE AND NURTURE—which is the more potent shaper of the human essence?—is perennially rekindled. It flared up again in the London *Observer* of Feb. 11, 2001. REVEALED: THE SECRET OF HUMAN BEHAVIOR, read the banner headline. ENVIRONMENT, NOT GENES, KEY TO OUR ACTS. The source of the story was Craig Venter, the self-made man of genes who had built a private company to read the full sequence of the human genome in competition with an international consortium funded by taxes and charities. That sequence—a string of 3 billion letters, composed in a four-letter alphabet, containing the complete recipe for building and running a human body—was to be published the very next day (the competition ended in an arranged tie). The first analysis of it had revealed that there were just 30,000 genes in it, not the 100,000 that many had been estimating until a few months before.

Details had already been circulated to journalists under embargo. But Venter, by speaking to a reporter at a biotechnology conference in France on Feb. 9, had effectively broken the embargo. Not for the first time in the increasingly bitter rivalry over the genome project, Venter's version of the story would hit the headlines before his rivals'. "We simply do not have enough genes for this idea of biological determinism to be right," Venter told the *Observer*. "The wonderful diversity of the human species is not hard-wired in our genetic code. Our environments are critical."

In truth, the number of human genes changed nothing. Venter's remarks concealed two whopping nonsequiturs: that fewer genes implied more environmental influences and that 30,000 genes were too few to explain human nature, whereas 100,000 would have been enough. As one scientist put it to me a few weeks later, just 33 genes, each coming in two varieties (on or off), would be enough to make every human being in the world unique. There are more than 10 billion combinations that could come from flipping a coin 33 times, so 30,000 does not seem such a small number after all. Besides, if fewer genes meant more free will, fruit flies would be freer than we are, bacteria freer still and viruses the John Stuart Mill of biology.

Fortunately, there was no need to reassure the population with such sophisticated calculations. People did not weep at the humiliating news that our genome has only about twice as many genes as a worm's. Nothing had been hung on the number 100,000, which was just a bad guess.

But the human genome project—and the decades of research that preceded it—did force a much more nuanced understanding of how genes work. In the early days, scientists detailed how genes encode the various proteins that make up the cells in our bodies. Their more sophisticated and ultimately more satisfying discovery—that gene expression can be modified by experience—has been gradually emerging since the 1980s. Only now is it dawning on scientists what a big and general idea it implies: that learning itself consists of nothing more than switching genes on and off. The more we lift the lid on the genome, the more vulnerable to experience genes appear to be.

This is not some namby-pamby, middle-of-the-road compromise. This is a new understanding of the fundamental building blocks of life based on the discovery that genes are not immutable things handed down from our parents like Moses' stone tablets but are active participants in our lives, designed to take their cues from everything that happens to us from the moment of our conception.

Early Puberty
Girls raised in FATHERLESS HOUSE-HOLDS experience puberty earlier. Apparently the change in timing is the reaction of a STILL MYSTERIOUS set of genes to their ENVIRONMENT. Scientists don't know how many SETS OF GENES act this way

For the time being, this new awareness has taken its strongest hold among scientists, changing how they think about everything from the way bodies develop in the womb to how new species emerge to the inevitability of homosexuality in some people. (More on all this later.) But eventually, as the general population becomes more attuned to this interdependent view, changes may well occur in areas as diverse as education, medicine, law and religion. Dieters may learn precisely which combination of fats, carbohydrates and proteins has the greatest effect on their individual waistlines. Theologians may develop a whole new theory of free will based on the observation that learning expands our capacity to choose our own path. As was true of Copernicus's observation 500 years ago that the earth orbits the sun, there is no telling how far the repercussions of this new scientific paradigm may extend.

To appreciate what has happened, you will have to abandon cherished notions and open your mind. You will have to enter a world in which your genes are not puppet masters pulling the strings of your behavior but puppets at the mercy of your behavior, in which instinct is not the opposite of learning, environmental influences are often less reversible than genetic ones, and nature is designed for nurture.

Fear of snakes, for instance, is the most common human phobia, and it makes good evolutionary sense for it to be instinctive. Learning to fear snakes the hard way would be dangerous. Yet experiments with monkeys reveal that their fear of snakes (and probably ours) must still be acquired by watching another individual react with fear to a snake. It turns out that it is easy to teach monkeys to fear snakes but very difficult to teach them to fear flowers. What we inherit is not a fear of snakes but a predisposition to learn a fear of snakes—a nature for a certain kind of nurture.

Before we dive into some of the other scientific discoveries that have so thoroughly transformed the debate, it helps to understand how deeply entrenched in our intellectual history the false dichotomy of nature vs. nurture became. Whether human nature is born or made is an ancient conundrum discussed by Plato and Aristotle. Empiricist philosophers such as John Locke and David Hume argued that the human mind was formed by experience; nativists like Jean-Jacques Rousseau and Immanuel Kant held that there was such a thing as immutable human nature.

It was Charles Darwin's eccentric mathematician cousin Francis Galton who in 1874 ignited the nature-nurture controversy in its present form and coined the very phrase (borrowing the alliteration from Shakespeare, who had lifted it from an Elizabethan schoolmaster named Richard Mulcaster). Galton asserted that human personalities were born, not made by experience. At the same time, the philosopher William James argued that human beings have more instincts than animals, not fewer.

In the first decades of the 20th century, nature held sway over nurture in most fields. In the wake of World War I, however, three men recaptured the social sciences for nurture: John B. Watson, who set out to show how the conditioned reflex, discovered by Ivan Pavlov, could explain human learning; Sigmund Freud, who sought to explain the influence of parents and early experiences on young minds; and Franz Boas, who argued that the origin of ethnic differences lay with history, experience and circumstance, not physiology and psychology.

Homosexuality
GAY MEN are more likely to have OLDER BROTHERS than either gay women or heterosexual men. It may be that a FIRST MALE FETUS triggers an immune reaction in the mother, ALTERING THE EXPRESSION of key gender genes

Galton's insistence on innate explanations of human abilities had led him to espouse eugenics, a term he coined. Eugenics was enthusiastically adopted by the Nazis to justify their campaign of mass murder against the disabled and the Jews. Tainted by this association, the idea of innate behavior was in full retreat for most of the middle years of the century. In 1958, however, two men began the counterattack on behalf of nature. Noam Chomsky, in his review of a book by the behaviorist B.F. Skinner, argued that it was impossible to learn human language by trial and error alone; human beings must come already equipped with an innate grammatical skill. Harry Harlow did a simple experiment that showed that a baby monkey prefers a soft, cloth model of a mother to a hard, wire-frame mother, even if the wire-frame mother provides it with all its milk; some preferences are innate.

Fast-forward to the 1980s and one of the most stunning surprises to greet scientists when they first opened up animal genomes: fly geneticists found a small group of genes called the hox genes that seemed to set out the body plan of the fly during its early development—telling it roughly where to put the head, legs, wings and so on. But then colleagues studying mice found the same hox genes, in the same order, doing the same job in Mickey's world—telling the mouse where to put its various parts. And when scientists looked in our genome, they found hox genes there too.

Hox genes, like all genes, are switched on and off in different parts of the body at different times. In this way, genes can have subtly different effects, depending on where, when and how they are switched on. The switches that control this process—stretches of DNA upstream of genes—are known as promoters.

Small changes in the promoter can have profound effects on the expression of a hox gene. For example, mice have short necks and long bodies; chickens have long necks and short bodies. If you count the vertebrae in the necks and thoraxes of mice and chickens, you will find that a mouse has seven neck and 13 thoracic vertebrae, a chicken 14 and seven, respectively. The source of this difference lies in the promoter attached to HoxC8, a hox gene that helps shape the thorax of the body. The promoter is a 200-letter paragraph of DNA, and in the two species it differs by just a handful of letters. The effect is to alter the expression of the HoxC8 gene in the development of the chicken embryo. This means the chicken makes thoracic vertebrae in a different part of the body than the mouse. In the python, HoxC8 is expressed right from the head and goes on being expressed for most of the body. So pythons are one long thorax; they have ribs all down the body.

Divorce
If a **FRATERNAL TWIN** gets divorced, there's a **30% CHANCE** that his or her twin will get divorced as well. If the twins are **IDENTICAL**, however, one sibling's divorce **BOOSTS THE ODDS** to 45% that the other will split

To make grand changes in the body plan of animals, there is no need to invent new genes, just as there's no need to invent new words to write an original novel (unless your name is Joyce). All you need do is switch the same ones on and off in different patterns. Suddenly, here is a mechanism for creating large and small evolutionary changes from small genetic differences. Merely by adjusting the sequence of a promoter or adding a new one, you could alter the expression of a gene.

In one sense, this is a bit depressing. It means that until scientists know how to find gene promoters in the vast text of the genome, they will not learn how the recipe for a chimpanzee differs from that for a person. But in another sense, it is also uplifting, for it reminds us more forcefully than ever of a simple truth that is all too often forgotten: bodies are not made, they grow. The genome is not a blueprint for constructing a body. It is a recipe for baking a body. You could say the chicken embryo is marinated for a shorter time in the HoxC8 sauce than the mouse embryo is. Likewise, the development of a certain human behavior takes a certain time and occurs in a certain order, just as the cooking of a perfect souffle requires not just the right ingredients but also the right amount of cooking and the right order of events.

How does this new view of genes alter our understanding of human nature? Take a look at four examples.

LANGUAGE Human beings differ from chimpanzees in having complex, grammatical language. But language does not spring fully formed from the brain; it must be learned from other language-speaking human beings. This capacity to learn is written into the human brain by genes that open and close a critical window during which learning takes place. One of those genes, FoxP2, has recently been discovered on human chromosome 7 by Anthony Monaco and his colleagues at the Wellcome Trust Centre for Human Genetics in Oxford. Just having the FoxP2 gene, though, is not enough. If a child is not exposed to a lot of spoken language during the critical learning period, he or she will always struggle with speech.

Crime Families

GENES may influence the way people respond to a "crimogenic" ENVIRONMENT. How else to explain why the BIOLOGICAL children of criminal parents are more likely than their ADOPTED children to break the LAW?

LOVE Some species of rodents, such as the prairie vole, form long pair bonds with their mates, as human beings do. Others, such as the montane vole, have only transitory liaisons, as do chimpanzees. The difference, according to Tom Insel and Larry Young at Emory University in Atlanta, lies in the promoter upstream of the oxytocin- and vasopressin-receptor genes. The insertion of an extra chunk of DNA text, usually about 460 letters long, into the promoter makes the animal more likely to bond with its mate. The extra text does not create love, but perhaps it creates the possibility of falling in love after the right experience.

ANTISOCIAL BEHAVIOR It has often been suggested that childhood maltreatment can create an antisocial adult. New research by Terrie Moffitt of London's Kings College on a group of 442 New Zealand men who have been followed since birth suggests that this is true only for a genetic minority. Again, the difference lies in a promoter that alters the activity of a gene. Those with high-active monoamine oxidase A genes were virtually immune to the effects of mistreatment. Those with low-active genes were much more antisocial if maltreated, yet—if anything—slightly less antisocial if not maltreated. The low-active, mistreated men were responsible for four times their share of rapes, robberies and assaults. In other words, maltreatment is not enough; you must also have the low-active gene. And it is not enough to have the low-active gene; you must also be maltreated.

HOMOSEXUALITY Ray Blanchard at the University of Toronto has found that gay men are more likely than either lesbians or heterosexual men to have older brothers (but not older sisters). He has since confirmed this observation in 14 samples from many places. Something about occupying a womb that has held other boys occasionally results in reduced birth weight, a larger placenta and a greater probability of homosexuality. That something, Blanchard suspects, is an immune reaction in the mother, primed by the first male fetus, that grows stronger with each male pregnancy. Perhaps the immune response affects the expression of key genes during brain development in a way that boosts a boy's attraction to his own sex. Such an explanation would not hold true for all gay men, but it might provide important clues into the origins of both homosexuality and heterosexuality.

TO BE SURE, EARLIER SCIENTIFIC DISCOVERIES HAD HINTED AT the importance of this kind of interplay between heredity and environment. The most striking example is Pavlovian conditioning. When Pavlov announced his famous experiment a century ago this year, he had apparently discovered how the brain could be changed to acquire new knowledge of the world—in the case of his dogs, knowledge that a bell foretold the arrival of food. But now we know how the brain changes: by the real-time expression of 17 genes, known as the CREB genes. They must be switched on and off to alter connections among nerve cells in the brain and thus lay down a new long-term memory. These genes are at the mercy of our behavior, not the other way around. Memory is in the genes in the sense that it uses genes, not in the sense that you inherit memories.

In this new view, genes allow the human mind to learn, remember, imitate, imprint language, absorb culture and express instincts. Genes are not puppet masters or blueprints, nor are they just the carriers of heredity. They are active during life; they switch one another on and off; they respond to the environment. They may direct the construction of the body and brain in the womb, but then almost at once, in response to experience, they set about dismantling and rebuilding what they have made. They are both the cause and the consequence of our actions.

Will this new vision of genes enable us to leave the nature-nurture argument behind, or are we doomed to reinvent it in every generation? Unlike what happened in previous eras, science is explaining in great detail precisely how genes and their environment—be it the womb, the classroom or pop culture—interact. So perhaps the pendulum swings of a now demonstrably false dichotomy may cease.

It may be in our nature, however, to seek simple, linear, cause-and-effect stories and not think in terms of circular causation, in which effects become their own causes. Perhaps the idea of nature via nurture, like the ideas of quantum mechanics and relativity, is just too counterintuitive for human minds. The urge to see ourselves in terms of nature versus nurture, like our instinctual ability to fear snakes, may be encoded in our genes.

ANCIENT QUARREL

How much of who we are is learned or innate is an argument with a fruitful but fractious pedigree

Nature We may be destined to be bald, mourn our dead, seek mates, fear the dark	**Nurture** But we can also learn to love tea, hate polkas, invent alphabets and tell lies
IMMANUEL KANT His philosophy sought a native morality in the mind	**JOHN LOCKE** Considered the mind of an infant to be a tabula rasa, or blank slate
FRANCIS GALTON Math geek saw mental and physical traits as innate	**IVAN PAVLOV** Trained dogs to salivate at the sound of the dinner bell
KONRAD LORENZ Studied patterns of instinctive behavior in animals	**SIGMUND FREUD** Felt we are formed by mothers, fathers, sex, jokes and dreams
NOAM CHOMSKY Argued that human beings are born with a capacity for grammar	**FRANZ BOAS** Believed chance and environs are key to cultural variation

Matt Ridley is an Oxford-trained zoologist and science writer whose latest book is Nature via Nurture *(HarperCollins)*

The New Sex Scorecard

TALKING OPENLY ABOUT SEX DIFFERENCES IS NO LONGER AN EXERCISE IN POLITICAL INCORRECTNESS; IT IS A NECESSITY IN FIGHTING DISEASE AND FORGING SUCCESSFUL RELATIONSHIPS. AT 109 AND COUNTING, *PT* EXAMINES THE TALLY.

By Hara Estroff Marano

Assumes female/male biological distinction is clear and absolute

Get out the spittoon. Men produce twice as much saliva as women. Women, for their part, learn to speak earlier, know more words, recall them better, pause less and glide through tongue twisters.

Put aside Simone de Beauvoir's famous dictum, "One is not born a woman but rather becomes one." Science suggests otherwise, and it's driving a whole new view of who and what we are. Males and females, it turns out, are different from the moment of conception, and the difference shows itself in every system of body and brain.

It's safe to talk about sex differences again. Of course, it's the oldest story in the world. And the newest. But for a while it was also the most treacherous. Now it may be the most urgent. The next stage of progress against disorders as disabling as depression and heart disease rests on cracking the binary code of biology. Most common conditions are marked by pronounced gender differences in incidence or appearance.

Although sex differences in brain and body take their inspiration from the central agenda of reproduction, they don't end there. "We've practiced medicine as though only a woman's breasts, uterus and ovaries made her unique—and as though her heart, brain and every other part of her body were identical to those of a man," says Marianne J. Legato, M.D., a cardiologist at Columbia University who spearheads the new push on gender differences. Legato notes that women live longer but break down more.

Do we need to explain that difference doesn't imply superiority or inferiority? Although sex differences may provide ammunition for David Letterman or the Simpsons, they unfold in the most private recesses of our lives, surreptitiously molding our responses to everything from stress to space to speech. Yet there are some ways the sexes are becoming more alike—they are now both engaging in the same kind of infidelity, one that is equally threatening to their marriages.

Everyone gains from the new imperative to explore sex differences. When we know why depression favors women two to one, or why the symptoms of heart disease literally hit women in the gut, it will change our understanding of how our bodies and our minds work.

The Gene Scene

Whatever sets men and women apart, it all starts with a single chromosome: the male-making Y, a puny thread bearing a paltry 25 genes, compared with the lavish female X, studded with 1,000 to 1,500 genes. But the Y guy trumps. He has a gene dubbed Sry, which, if all goes well, instigates an Olympic relay of development. It commands primitive fetal tissue to become testes, and they then spread word of masculinity out to the provinces via their chief product, testosterone. The circulating hormone not only masculinizes the body but affects the developing brain, influencing the size of specific structures and the wiring of nerve cells.

25%
of females experience daytime sleepiness, versus 18% of males

But sex genes themselves don't cede everything to hormones. Over the past few years, scientists have come to believe that they too play ongoing roles in gender-flavoring the brain and behavior.

Females, it turns out, appear to have backup genes that protect their brains from big trouble. To level the genetic playing field between men and women, nature normally shuts off one of the two X chromosomes in every cell in females. But about 19 percent of genes escape inactivation; cells get a double dose of some X genes. Having fall-back genes may explain why females are far less subject than males to mental disorders from autism to schizophrenia.

What's more, which X gene of a pair is inactivated makes a difference in the way female and male brains respond to things, says neurophysiologist Arthur P. Arnold, Ph.D., of the University of California at Los Angeles. In some cases, the X gene donated by Dad is nullified; in other cases it's the X from Mom. The parent from whom a woman gets her working genes determines how robust her genes are. Paternal genes ramp up the genetic volume, maternal genes tune it down. This is known as genomic imprinting of the chromosome.

For many functions, it doesn't matter which sex genes you have or from whom you get them. But the Y chromosome itself spurs the brain to grow extra dopamine neurons, Arnold says. These nerve cells are involved in reward and motivation, and dopamine release underlies the pleasure of addiction and novelty seeking. Dopamine neurons also affect motor skills and go awry in Parkinson's disease, a disorder that afflicts twice as many males as females.

XY makeup also boosts the density of vasopressin fibers in the brain. Vasopressin is a hormone that both abets and minimizes sex differences; in some circuits it fosters parental behavior in males; in others it may spur aggression.

Social context to this, rather than biological.

Sex on the Brain

Ruben Gur, Ph.D., always wanted to do the kind of psychological research that when he found something new, no one could say his grandmother already knew it. Well, "My grandmother couldn't tell you that women have a higher percentage of gray matter in their brains," he says. Nor could she explain how that discovery resolves a long-standing puzzle.

99%
of girls play with dolls at age 6, versus 17% of boys

Gur's discovery that females have about 15 to 20 percent more gray matter than males suddenly made sense of another major sex difference: Men, overall, have larger brains than women (their heads and bodies are larger), but the sexes score equally well on tests of intelligence.

Gray matter, made up of the bodies of nerve cells and their connecting dendrites, is where the brain's heavy lifting is done. The female brain is more densely packed with neurons and dendrites, providing concentrated processing power—and more thought-linking capability.

The larger male cranium is filled with more white matter and cerebrospinal fluid. "That fluid is probably helpful," says Gur, director of the Brain Behavior Laboratory at the University of Pennsylvania. "It cushions the brain, and men are more likely to get their heads banged about."

White matter, made of the long arms of neurons encased in a protective film of fat, helps distribute processing throughout the brain. It gives males superiority at spatial reasoning. White matter also carries fibers that inhibit "information spread" in the cortex. That allows a single-mindedness that spatial problems require, especially difficult ones. The harder a spatial task, Gur finds, the more circumscribed the right-sided brain activation in males, but not in females. The white matter advantage of males, he believes, suppresses activation of areas that could interfere with work.

The white matter in women's brains is concentrated in the corpus callosum, which links the brain's hemispheres, and enables the right side of the brain to pitch in on language tasks. The more difficult the verbal task, the more global the neural participation required—a response that's stronger in females.

Women have another heady advantage—faster blood flow to the brain, which offsets the cognitive effects of aging. Men lose more brain tissue with age, especially in the left frontal cortex, the part of the brain that thinks about consequences and provides self-control.

"You can see the tissue loss by age 45, and that may explain why midlife crisis is harder on men," says Gur. "Men have the same impulses but they lose the ability to consider long-term consequences." Now, there's a fact someone's grandmother may have figured out already.

Come on; it has nothing to do with social power >>

Minds of Their Own

The difference between the sexes may boil down to this: dividing the tasks of processing experience. Male and female minds are innately drawn to different aspects of the world around them. And there's new evidence that testosterone may be calling some surprising shots.

Women's perceptual skills are oriented to quick—call it intuitive—people reading. Females are gifted at detecting the feelings and thoughts of others, inferring intentions, absorbing contextual clues and responding in emotionally appropriate ways. They empathize. Tuned to others, they more readily see alternate sides of an argument. Such empathy fosters communication and primes females for attachment.

Women, in other words, seem to be hard-wired for a top-down, big-picture take. Men might be programmed to look at things from the bottom up (no surprise there).

Men focus first on minute detail, and operate most easily with a certain detachment. They construct rules-based analyses of the natural world, inanimate objects and events. In the coinage of Cambridge University psychologist Simon Baron-Cohen, Ph.D., they systemize.

The superiority of males at spatial cognition and females' talent for language probably subserve the more basic difference of systemizing versus empathizing. The two mental styles manifest in the toys kids prefer (humanlike dolls versus mechanical trucks); verbal impatience in males (ordering rather than negotiating); and navigation (women personalize space by finding landmarks; men see a geometric system, taking directional cues in the layout of routes).

26%
of males say they have extramarital sex without being emotionally involved, versus 3% of females

Almost everyone has some mix of both types of skills, although males and females differ in the degree to which one set predominates, contends Baron-Cohen. In his work as director of Cambridge's Autism Research Centre, he finds that children and adults with autism, and its less severe variant Asperger syndrome, are unusual in both dimensions of perception. Its victims are "mindblind," unable to recognize people's feelings. They also have a peculiar talent for systemizing, obsessively focusing on, say, light switches or sink faucets.

Autism overwhelmingly strikes males; the ratio is ten to one for Asperger. In his new book, *The Essential Difference: The Truth About the Male and Female Brain*, Baron-Cohen argues that autism is a magnifying mirror of maleness.

The brain basis of empathizing and systemizing is not well understood, although there seems to be a "social brain," nerve circuitry dedicated to person perception. Its key components lie on the left side of the brain, along with language centers generally more developed in females.

Baron-Cohen's work supports a view that neuroscientists have flirted with for years: Early in development, the male hormone testosterone slows the growth of the brain's left hemisphere and accelerates growth of the right.

Testosterone may even have a profound influence on eye contact. Baron-Cohen's team filmed year-old children at play and measured the amount of eye contact they made with their mothers, all of whom had undergone amniocentesis during pregnancy. The researchers looked at various social factors—birth order, parental education, among others—as well as the level of testosterone the child had been exposed to in fetal life.

Baron-Cohen was "bowled over" by the results. The more testosterone the children had been exposed to in the womb, the less able they were to make eye contact at 1 year of age. "Who would have thought that a behavior like eye contact, which is so intrinsically social, could be in part shaped by a biological factor?" he asks. What's more, the testosterone level during fetal life also influenced language skills. The higher the prenatal testosterone level, the smaller a child's vocabulary at 18 months and again at 24 months.

Lack of eye contact and poor language aptitude are early hallmarks of autism. "Being strongly attracted to systems, together with a lack of empathy, may be the core characteristics

of individuals on the autistic spectrum," says Baron-Cohen. "Maybe testosterone does more than affect spatial ability and language. Maybe it also affects social ability." And perhaps autism represents an "extreme form" of the male brain.

Depression: Pink—and Blue, Blue, Blue

This year, 19 million Americans will suffer a serious depression. Two out of three will be female. Over the course of their lives, 21.3 percent of women and 12.7 percent of men experience at least one bout of major depression.

The female preponderance in depression is virtually universal. And it's specific to unipolar depression. Males and females suffer equally from bipolar, or manic, depression. However, once depression occurs, the clinical course is identical in men and women.

The gender difference in susceptibility to depression emerges at 13. Before that age, boys, if anything, are a bit more likely than girls to be depressed. The gender difference seems to wind down four decades later, making depression mostly a disorder of women in the child-bearing years.

As director of the Virginia Institute for Psychiatric and Behavioral Genetics at Virginia Commonwealth University, Kenneth S. Kendler, M.D., presides over "the best natural experiment that God has given us to study gender differences"—thousands of pairs of opposite-sex twins. He finds a significant difference between men and women in their response to low levels of adversity. He says, "Women have the capacity to be precipitated into depressive episodes at lower levels of stress."

Adding injury to insult, women's bodies respond to stress differently than do men's. They pour out higher levels of stress hormones and fail to shut off production readily. The female sex hormone progesterone blocks the normal ability of the stress hormone system to turn itself off. Sustained exposure to stress hormones kills brain cells, especially in the hippocampus, which is crucial to memory.

It's bad enough that females are set up biologically to internally amplify their negative life experiences. They are prone to it psychologically as well, finds University of Michigan psychologist Susan Nolen-Hoeksema, Ph.D.

Women ruminate over upsetting situations, going over and over negative thoughts and feelings, especially if they have to do with relationships. Too often they get caught in downward spirals of hopelessness and despair.

It's entirely possible that women are biologically primed to be highly sensitive to relationships. Eons ago it might have helped alert them to the possibility of abandonment while they were busy raising the children. Today, however, there's a clear downside. Ruminators are unpleasant to be around, with their oversize need for reassurance. Of course, men have their own ways of inadvertently fending off people. As pronounced as the female tilt to depression is the male excess of alcoholism, drug abuse and antisocial behaviors.

The Incredible Shrinking Double Standard

Nothing unites men and women better than sex. Yet nothing divides us more either. Males and females differ most in mating psychology because our minds are shaped by and for our reproductive mandates. That sets up men for sex on the side and a more casual attitude toward it.

Twenty-five percent of wives and 44 percent of husbands have had extramarital intercourse, reports Baltimore psychologist Shirley Glass, Ph.D. Traditionally for men, love is one thing and sex is . . . well, sex.

90%
of males and females agree
that infidelity is always wrong,
20–25% of all marital fights
are about jealousy

In what may be a shift of epic proportions, sexual infidelity is mutating before our very eyes. Increasingly, men as well as women are forming deep emotional attachments before they even slip into an extramarital bed together. It often happens as they work long hours together in the office.

"The sex differences in infidelity are disappearing," says Glass, the doyenne of infidelity research. "In my original 1980 study, there was a high proportion of men who had intercourse with almost no emotional involvement at all—nonrelational sex. Today, more men are getting emotionally involved."

One consequence of the growing parity in affairs is greater devastation of the betrayed spouse. The old-style strictly sexual affair never impacted men's marital satisfaction. "You could be in a good marriage and still cheat," reports Glass.

Liaisons born of the new infidelity are much more disruptive—much more likely to end in divorce. "You can move away from just a sexual relationship but it's very difficult to break an attachment," says Rutgers University anthropologist Helen Fisher, Ph.D. "The betrayed partner can probably provide more exciting sex but not a different kind of friendship."

It's not that today's adulterers start out unhappy or looking for love. Says Glass: "The work relationship becomes so rich and the stuff at home is pressurized and child-centered. People get involved insidiously without planning to betray."

Any way it happens, the combined sexual-emotional affair delivers a fatal blow not just to marriages but to the traditional male code. "The double standard for adultery is disappearing," Fisher emphasizes. "It's been around for 5,000 years and it's changing in our lifetime. It's quite striking. Men used to feel that they had the right. They don't feel that anymore."

LEARN MORE ABOUT IT:

Eve's Rib: The New Science of Gender-Specific Medicine and How It Can Save Your Life. Marianne J. Legato, M.D. (*Harmony Books, 2002*).

Not "Just Friends": Protect Your Relationship from Infidelity and Heal the Trauma of Betrayal. Shirley P. Glass, Ph.D. (*The Free Press, 2003*).

Male, Female: The Evolution of Human Sex Differences. David C. Geary, Ph.D. (*American Psychological Association, 1998*).

How to explain this if it's all psych biological??)

The smoking gun!

THE CRIMINAL MENACE
SHIFTING GLOBAL TRENDS

GENE STEPHENS

Crime in the United States is bottoming out after a steep slide downward during the past decade. But crime in many other nations—particularly in eastern and parts of western Europe—has continued to climb. In the United States, street crime overall remains near historic lows, prompting some analysts to declare life in the United States safer than it has ever been. In fact, statistics show that, despite terrorism, the world as a whole seems to be becoming safer. This is in sharp contrast to the perceptions of Americans and others, as polls indicate they believe the world gets more dangerous every day.

CURRENT CRIME RATES
AROUND THE WORLD

Although the United States still has more violent crime than other industrialized nations and still ranks high in overall crime, the nation has nevertheless been experiencing a decline in crime numbers. Meanwhile, a number of European countries are catching up; traditionally low-crime societies, such as Denmark and Finland, are near the top in street crime rates today. Other countries that weren't even on the crime radar—such as Japan—are also experiencing a rise in crime.

Comparing crime rates across countries is difficult. Different definitions of crimes, among other factors, make official crime statistics notoriously unreliable. However, the periodic World Crime Survey, a UN initiative to track global crime rates, may offer the most reliable figures currently available:

• *Overall crime (homicide, rape, major assault, robbery) and property crime.* The United States in 1980 clearly led the Western world in overall crime and ranked particularly high in property crime. A decade later, statistics show a marked decline in U.S. property crime. By 2000, overall crime rates for the U.S.

dropped below those of England and Wales, Denmark, and Finland, while U.S. property-crime rates also continued to decline.

• *Homicide.* The United States had consistently higher homicide rates than most Western nations from 1980 to 2000. In the 1990s, the U.S. rate was cut almost in half, but the 2000 rate of 5.5 homicides per 100,000 people was still higher than all nations except those in political and social turmoil. Colombia, for instance, had 63 homicides per 100,000 people; South Africa, 51.

• *Rape.* In 1980 and 1990, U.S. rape rates were higher than those of any Western nation, but by 2000, Canada took the lead. The lowest reported rape rates were in Asia and the Middle East.

• *Robbery* has been on a steady decline in the United States over the past two decades. As of 2000, countries with more reported robberies than the United States included England and Wales, Portugal, and Spain. Countries with fewer reported robberies include Germany, Italy, and France, as well as Middle Eastern and Asian nations.

• *Burglary,* usually considered the most serious property crime, is lower in the United States today than it was in 1980. As of 2000, the United States had lower burglary rates than Australia, Denmark, Finland, England and Wales, and Canada. It had higher reported burglary rates than Spain, Korea, and Saudi Arabia.

• *Vehicle theft* declined steadily in the United States from 1980 to 2000. The 2000 figures show that Australia, England and Wales, Denmark, Norway, Canada, France, and Italy all have higher rates of vehicle theft.

Overall, the United States has experienced a downward trend in crime while other Western nations, and even industrialized non-Western nations, are witnessing higher numbers. What's behind the U.S. decreases? Some analysts believe that tougher laws, enforcement, and incarceration policies have lowered crime in the United States. They point to "three-strikes" legislation, mandatory incarceration for offenses such as drug possession and domestic violence, and tougher street-level enforcement. The reason many European countries are suffering higher crime rates, analysts argue, is because of their fewer laws and more-lenient enforcement and sentencing.

Other analysts argue that socioeconomic changes—such as fewer youth in the crime-prone 15- to 25-year old age group, a booming economy, and more community care of citizens—led to the drop in U.S. crime. They now point out that the new socioeconomic trends of growing unemployment, stagnation of wages, and the growing numbers in the adolescent male population are at work in today's terror-wary climate and may signal crime increases ahead.

Still other analysts see community-oriented policing (COP) problem-oriented policing (POP), and restorative justice (mediation, arbitration, restitution, and community service instead of criminal courts and incarceration) as the nexus of recent and future crime control successes.

U.S. CRIME TREND

Just which crime fighting tactics have effected this U.S. crime trend is a matter of debate. Three loose coalitions offer their views:

Getting tough works. "There is, in fact, a simple explanation for America's success against crime: The American justice system now does a better job of catching criminals and locking them up," writes Eli Lehrer, senior editor of *The American Enterprise.* Lehrer says local control of policing was probably what made a critical difference between the United States and European countries where regional and national systems predominate. He holds that local control allowed police to use enforcement against loitering and other minor infractions to keep the streets clean of potential lawbreakers. He acknowledges that "positive loitering"—stickers or a pat on the back for well-behaved juveniles—was the other side of the successful effort. In addition, more people have since been imprisoned for longer periods of time, seen by "get-tough" advocates as another factor in safer streets today.

Demographics rule. Some criminologists and demographers see the crime decrease as a product of favorable socioeconomic population factors in the mid- through late-1990s. High employment rates, with jobs in some sectors going unfilled for lack of qualified candidates, kept salaries growing. Even the unemployed went back to school to gain job skills. By the end of the decade the older students filled the college classrooms, taking up the slack left by the lower numbers in the traditional student age group. In such times, both violent and property crimes have usually dropped, as economic need decreased and frustration and anger subsided.

"Get-tough" theorists hold that 200 crimes a year could be prevented for each criminal taken off the streets but criminologist Albert Reiss counters that most offenders work in groups and are simply replaced when one leaves.

If demographic advocates are right, then the next few years could see a boom in street crime in the United States due to a combination of growing unemployment, stagnant wages, and

state and local governments so strapped for funds that social programs and even education are facing major cutbacks.

Community-based approaches succeed. Whereas the "get-tough" advocates mention community policing as a factor in the crime decrease, this third group sees the service aspects (rather than strict enforcement) of COP combined with the emerging restorative-justice movement as being the catalyst for success in crime prevention and control.

More criminologists believe street crime is a product of socioeconomic conditions interacting on young people, primarily adolescent males. Usually their crimes occur in interaction with others in gangs or groups, especially when law-abiding alternatives (youth athletic programs, tutors, mentors, community centers, social clubs, after-school programs) are not available. Thus, any chance of success in keeping crime rates low on a long-term basis depends on constant assessment of the community and its needs to maintain a nurturing environment.

COP and POP coordinate community cohesion by identifying problems that will likely result in crime and by simply improving the quality of life in the neighborhoods. The key: partnerships among police, citizens, civic and business groups, public and private social-service agencies, and government agencies. Combined with an ongoing needs analysis in recognition of constantly changing community dynamics, the partnerships can quickly attack any problem or situation that arises.

A restorative-justice movement has grown rapidly but stayed below the radar screen in the United States. In many communities, civil and criminal incidents are more likely to be handled through mediation or arbitration, restitution, community service, and reformation/reintegration than in civil or criminal courts. The goal, besides justice for all, is the development of a symbolic relationship and reconciliation within the community, since more than 90% of all street offenders return to the same community.

LESSONS FOR THE FUTURE OF CRIME PREVENTION AND CONTROL

All schools of thought on why street crime is decreasing have a commonality: proactive prevention rather than reactive retribution. Even the method to achieve this goal is not really in question—only the emphasis.

Since the 1980s, progressive police agencies in the United States have adhered to the "Broken Windows" and "Weed and Seed" philosophies taken from the work of criminologists James Q. Wilson and George L. Keeling. Broken windows are a metaphor for failure to establish and maintain acceptable standards of behavior in the community. The blame, according to Wilson and Keeling, lay primarily in the change in emphasis by police from being peace officers who seek to capture criminals. They argue that, in healthy communities, informal but widely understood rules were maintained by citizens and police, often using extralegal ("move on") or arrest for minor infractions (vagrancy, loitering, pandering). It was, then, this citizen-police partnership that worked to stem community deterioration and disorder, which unattended, would lead to crime.

"Weeding" involved using street-sweeping ordinances to clean the streets of the immediate problems (drunks, drug addicts, petty thieves, panhandlers). "Seeding" involved taking a breather while these offenders were in jail and establishing "opportunity" programs designed to make the community viable and capable of self-regulating its behavioral controls (job training, new employers, day care nurseries in schools, after-school programs, tutors and mentors, civic pride demonstrations, tenant management of housing projects). In the early years, the "weed" portion was clearly favored; in the early 1990s, "seed" programs based on analysis of the specific needs of the individual community were developed and spread—about the time the crime rates began to plunge.

The Weed and Seed programs in the United States imparted the following lessons:

- Proactive prevention must be at the core of any successful crime-control strategy.
- Each community must have an ongoing needs assessment carried out by a police-citizen partnership.
- A multitude of factors—from laws and neighborhood standards to demographics and socioeconomic needs—must be considered in the assessment process.
- Weed and seed must be balanced according to specific needs—somewhat different in each community.
- When crime does occur, community-based restorative justice should be used to provide restitution to victims and community while reforming and then reintegrating the offender as a law-abiding citizen of the community.

NEW APPROACHES FOR THE EMERGING CRIME LANDSCAPE

Twenty-first-century crime is going to require new approaches to prevention and control. Street crime dominated the attention of the justice system in the twentieth century, but recent excesses of corporations, costing stockholders and retirees literally billions of dollars, do not fit into the street-crime paradigm. Nor do political or religious-motivated terrorism, Internet fraud, deception, theft, harassment, pedophilia, and terrorism on an information highway without borders, without ownership, and without jurisdiction. Now attention must—and will—be paid to white-collar crimes, infotech and biotech crimes, and terrorism.

Surveys find that a large majority of corporations have been victims of computer-assisted crimes. Polls of citizens find high rates of victimization by Internet offenses ranging from identity theft to fraud, hacking to harassment. U.S. officials have maintained since the late 1990s that it is just a matter of time until there is a "Pearl Harbor" on the Internet (such as shutting down medical services networks, power grids, or financial services nationwide or even worldwide).

DOOMSDAY SCENARIOS
Following the attacks by terrorists on September 11, 2001, and later strikes abroad, doomsday scenarios have abounded, with release of radio-active or biological toxins being the most frightening. Attempts to shoot down an Israeli commercial airliner with a shoulder-held missile launcher further increased anxiety.

Clearly these crimes against victims generally unknown to the attacker and often chosen randomly cannot be stopped by community policing alone, although vigilant community partners often can spot suspicious activity and expose possible criminals and terrorists. Early response to this dilemma was to pass more laws, catch more offenders, and thus deter future incidents. This is the same response traditionally taken to street crime—the one being abandoned in preference to proactive prevention methods (COP and restorative justice.) Clearly, prevention has to be the first and most important strategy for dealing with the new threats.

Two major approaches will evolve over the next few years. First, national and international partnerships will be necessary to cope with crimes without borders. In 2000, a task force of agents from 32 U.S. communities, the federal government, and 13 other nations conducted the largest-ever crackdown on child pornography exchanged internationally over the Internet. Coordinated by the U.S. Customs Service, the raid resulted in shutting down an international child-pornography ring that used secret Internet chat rooms and sophisticated encryption to exchange thousands of sexually explicit images of children as young as 18 months. It is this type of coordinated transnational effort that will be necessary to cope with infotech and biotech crime and terrorism.

Second, the focus of prevention must change from opportunity reduction to desire reduction. Crime-prevention specialists have long used the equation, Desire + Opportunity = Crime. Prevention programs have traditionally focused on reducing opportunity through target hardening. Locks, alarms, high-intensity lighting, key control, and other methods have been used, along with neighborhood crime watches and citizen patrols.

Little attention has been paid to desire reduction, in large part because of the atomistic approach to crime. Specifically, an offender's criminal behavior is viewed as a result of personal choice. Meanwhile, criminologists and other social scientists say crime is more likely to be a product of the conditions under which the criminal was reared and lived—yet there were no significant efforts to fix this root of the problem. Instead, the criminal-justice system stuck to target hardening, catching criminals, and exacting punishment.

Quashing conditions that lead to a desire to commit crime is especially necessary in light of the apparent reasons terrorists and international criminals attack: religious fervor heightened by seeing abject poverty, illiteracy, and often homelessness and hunger all around while also seeing others live in seeming splendor.

The opportunity to reduce crime and disorder is at hand. The strategies outlined above will go a long way toward that lofty goal as will new technologies. A boom in high-tech development has brought about new surveillance and tracking gadgetry, security machines that see through clothing and skin, cameras and listening devices that see and hear through walls and ceilings, "bugs" that can be surreptitiously placed on individuals and biometric scanners that can identify suspects in large crowds. On the other hand, there are also the technologies that could take away our freedom, particularly our freedom of speech and movement. Some in high government positions believe loss of privacy and presumption of innocence is the price we must pay for safety.

For many it is too high a price. One group that urges judicious use of technology within the limitations of civil liberties protected by the U.S. Constitution is the Society of Police Futurists International (PFI)—a collection primarily of police officials from all over the world dedicated to improving the professional field of policing by taking a professional futurist's approach to preparing for the times ahead. While definitely interested in staying on the cutting edge of technology and even helping to guide its development, PFI debates the promises and perils of each new innovation on pragmatic and ethical grounds. Citizens need to do the same.

Mr. Stephens is a professor emeritus in the Department of Criminology and Criminal Justice at the University of South Carolina. From "Global Trends in Crime," by Gene Stephens, The Futurist, *May–June 2003, pages 40–46.*

Parents or Prisons

By JENNIFER ROBACK MORSE

FOR SOME PEOPLE, prisons are a substitute for parents. This apparent overstatement is shorthand for two more precise points. First, without parents—two of them, married to each other, working together as a team—a child is more likely to end up in the criminal justice system at some point in his life. Without parents, prison becomes a greater probability in the child's life. Second, if a child finds himself in the criminal justice system, either in his youth or adulthood, the prison will perform the parental function of supervising and controlling that person's behavior.

Of course, prison is a pathetic substitute for genuine parents. Incarceration provides extreme, tightly controlled supervision that children typically outgrow in their toddler years and does so with none of the love and affection that characterize normal parental care of small children. But that is what is happening: The person has failed to internalize the self-command necessary for living in a reasonably free and open society at the age most people do. Since he cannot control himself, someone else must control him. If he becomes too much for his parents, the criminal justice system takes over.

These necessary societal interventions do not repair the loss the child has sustained by the loss of a relationship with his parents. By the time the penal system steps in, the state is engaged in damage control. A child without a conscience, a child without self-control, is a lifelong problem for the rest of society.

A child without a conscience or self-control is a lifelong problem for the rest of society.

A free society needs people with consciences. The vast majority of people must obey the law voluntarily. If people don't conform themselves to the law, someone will either have to compel them to do so or protect the public when they do not. It costs a great deal of money to catch, convict, and incarcerate lawbreakers—not to mention that the surveillance and monitoring of potential criminals tax everybody's freedom if habitual lawbreakers comprise too large a percentage of the population.

The basic self-control and reciprocity that a free society takes for granted do not develop automatically. Conscience development takes place in childhood. Children need to develop empathy so they will care whether they hurt someone or whether they treat others fairly. They need to develop self-control so they can follow through on these impulses and do the right thing even if it might benefit them to do otherwise.

All this development takes place inside the family. Children attach to the rest of the human race through their first relationships with their parents. They learn reciprocity, trust, and empathy from these primal relationships. Disrupting those foundational relations has a major negative impact on children as well as on the people around them. In particular, children of single parents—or completely absent parents—are more likely to commit crimes.

Without two parents, working together as a team, the child has more difficulty learning the combination of empathy, reciprocity, fairness, and self-command that people ordinarily take for granted. If the child does not learn this at home, society will have to manage his behavior in some other way. He may have to be rehabilitated, incarcerated, or otherwise restrained. In this case, prisons will substitute for parents.

The observation that there are problems for children growing up in a disrupted family may seem to be old news. Ever since Barbara Defoe Whitehead famously pronounced "Dan Quayle Was Right" (*Atlantic Monthly*, April 1993), the public has become more aware that single motherhood is not generally glamorous in the way it is sometimes portrayed on television. David Blankenhorn's *Fatherless America* (Basic Books, 1995) depicted a country that is fragmenting along family lines. Blankenhorn argued, and continues to argue in his work at the Institute for American Values, that the primary determinant of a person's life chances is whether he grew up in a household with his own father.

Since these seminal works, it has become increasingly clear that the choice to become a single parent is not strictly a private choice. The decision to become an unmarried mother or the decision to disrupt an existing family does not meet the economist's definition of "private." These choices regarding family structure have significant spillover effects on other people. We can no longer deny that such admittedly very personal decisions have an impact on people other than the individuals who choose.

There are two parts to my tale. The first concerns the impact of being raised in a single-parent household on the children. The second involves the impact that those children have on the rest of society.

Current events

THE TWO PARTS of my story were juxtaposed dramatically on the local page of the *San Diego Union-Tribune* one Wednesday morning at the end of January. "Dangling Foot Was Tip-Off," explained the headline. A security guard caught two teenaged boys attempting to dump their "trash" into the dumpster of the gated community he was responsible for guarding. The guard noticed what looked like a human foot dangling out of the bag. He told the boys he wanted to see what was in it. They refused. As a private security guard, he had no authority to arrest or detain the pair. He took their license plate number and a description of the duo and called authorities.

The "trash" proved to be the dismembered body of the boys' mother. They had strangled her, chopped off her head and hands, and ultimately dumped her body in a ravine in Orange County. The boys were half-brothers. The elder was 20 years old. His father had committed suicide when the boy was an infant. The younger boy was 15. His father had abandoned their mother. As of this writing, the older boy, Jason Bautista, was being held in lieu of $1 million bail. The younger, Matthew Montejo, was being held in juvenile hall.

At first glance, the second news item seems unrelated to the first. On the same page of the newspaper, a headline read, "Mayor Wants 20% Budget Cuts." This particular mayor presides over the city of Oceanside, the same city where the brothers tried to dump their mother's body. In nearby Vista, the mayor's "State of the City Address Warns of Possible Deep Cuts." In Carlsbad, one freeway exit to the south, the city's finances were "Called Good Now, Vulnerable in Future." All these mayors were tightening their cities' belts in response to severe budget cuts proposed by California Governor Gray Davis. The governor expects to reduce virtually every budget category in the state budget except one: the Department of Corrections.

Therein lies the tale: These stories are connected by more than just the date and time of their reportage. The increase in serious crimes by younger and younger offenders is absorbing a greater percentage of state resources, necessarily crowding out other services. The Bautista brothers and others like them do have something to do with the budget woes of state and local governments.

Several other high-profile cases of juvenile crime fit this pattern. Alex and Derek King, aged 12 and 13 respectively, bludgeoned their sleeping father to death with a baseball bat and set fire to the house to hide the evidence. The mother of the King brothers had not lived with them for the seven years prior to the crime. Derek had been in foster care for most of those years until his behavior, including a preoccupation with fire, became too difficult for his foster parents to handle. The murder took place two months after Derek was returned to his father's custody.

John Lee Malvo, the youthful assistant in the Beltway Sniper case, came to the United States with his mother from Jamaica. His biological father has not seen him since 1998. His mother evidently had a relationship with John Allen Mohammed, who informally adopted her son. Mohammed himself, probably the mastermind if not the triggerman in the serial sniper case, was also a fatherless child. According to one of his relatives, Mohammed's mother died when he was young; his grandfather and aunt raised him because his dad was not around.

While these high-profile cases dramatize the issues at stake, excessive focus on individual cases like these can be a distraction. As more information about the Bautista family comes in, for instance, a variety of mitigating or confounding circumstances might emerge to suggest that factors other than living in a single-parent home accounted for the horrible crime. A family history of mental illness, perhaps, or maybe a history of child abuse by the mother toward the children may surface as contributing factors. And indeed, many of the most gruesome crimes are committed not by fatherless children in single-mother households, but by motherless boys, growing up in a father-only household. Some, such as John Lee Malvo, had essentially no household at all. But these confounding factors should not distract us from the overwhelming evidence linking single parents or absent parents to the propensity to commit crimes.

The statistical evidence

THIS RESULT HAS been found in numerous studies. The National Fatherhood Initiative's *Father Facts*, edited in 2002 by Wade Horn and Tom Sylvester, is the best one-stop shopping place for this kind of evidence. Of the many studies reviewed there, a representative one was reported in the *Journal of Marriage and the Family* in May 1996. Researchers Chris Couglin and Samuel Vuchinich found that being in stepparent or single-parent households more than doubled the risk of delinquency by age 14. Similarly, a massive 1993 analysis of the underclass by M. Anne Hill and June O'Neill, published by Baruch College's Center for the Study of Business and Government, found that the likelihood that a young male will engage in criminal activity increases substantially if he is raised without a father.

These studies, like most in this area, attempted to control for other, confounding factors that might be correlated with living in a single-parent household. If single mothers have less money than married mothers, then perhaps poverty is the fundamental problem for their children. But even taking this possibility into account, the research still shows that boys who grew up outside of intact marriages were, on average, more likely than other boys to end up in jail.

Another set of studies found that the kids who are actually in the juvenile justice system disproportionately come from disrupted families. The Wisconsin Department of Health and Social Services, in a 1994 report entitled "Family Status of Delinquents in Juvenile Correctional Facilities in Wisconsin," found that only 13 percent came from families in which the biological mother and father were married to each other. By contrast, 33 percent had parents who were either divorced or separated, and 44 percent had parents who had never married. The 1987 *Survey of Youth in Custody*, published by the U.S. Bureau of Justice Statistics, found that 70 percent of youth in state reform institutions across the U.S. had grown up in single- or no-parent situations.

Causal links

THERE ARE SEVERAL plausible links between single parenthood and criminal behavior. The internal dynamic of a one-parent household is likely to be rather different from that of a two-parent household. Two parents can supervise the child's behavior more readily than one. Misbehavior can continue undetected and uncorrected for longer periods of time until it becomes more severe and more difficult to manage.

Likewise, the lowered level of adult input partially accounts for the lowered educational attainments of children of single parents. Such families report parents spending less time supervising homework and children spending less time doing homework. Not surprisingly, kids in these families have inferior grades and drop out of school more frequently. Leaving school increases the likelihood of a young person becoming involved in criminal behavior. It is similarly no surprise that adolescents who are left home alone to supervise themselves after school find more opportunities to get into trouble. Finally, the percentage of single-parent families in a neighborhood is one of the strongest predictors of the neighborhood's crime rate. In fact, Wayne Osgood and Jeff Chambers, in their 2000 article in the journal *Criminology*, find that father absence is more significant than poverty in predicting the crime rate.

These kinds of factors are easy enough to understand. A more subtle connection between the fractured family and criminal behavior is the possibility that the child does not form strong human attachments during infancy. A child obviously cannot attach to an absent parent. If the one remaining parent is overwhelmed or exhausted or preoccupied, the child may not form a proper attachment even to that parent. Full-fledged attachment disorder is often found among children who have spent a substantial fraction of their infancy in institutions or in foster care. (Think of Derek King.)

An attachment-disordered child is the truly dangerous sociopath, the child who doesn't care what anyone thinks, who does whatever he can get away with. Mothers and babies ordinarily build their attachments by being together. When the mother responds to the baby's needs, the baby can relax into her care. The baby learns to trust. He learns that human contact is the great good that ensures his continued existence. He learns to care about other people. He comes to care where his mother is and how she responds to him. Eventually, he will care what his mother thinks of him.

> *Usually, the parents win the race between the growth of the child's body and that of his conscience.*

This process lays the groundwork for the development of the conscience; caring what she thinks of him allows him to internalize her standards of good conduct. As he gets older, bigger, and stronger, his mother can set limits on his behavior without physically picking him up and carrying him out of trouble. Mother's raised eyebrow from across the room can be a genuine deterrent against misbehavior. As he matures, she doesn't even need to be present. He simply remembers what she wants him to do. Ultimately, he doesn't explicitly think about his parents' instructions. Without even considering punishments or approval, his internal voice reminds him, "We don't do that sort of thing." He has a conscience.

In most families, the parents win the race between the growth of the child's body and that of his conscience. By the time a child is too large and strong to muscle around, he had better have some self-command. If he doesn't, somebody will have to monitor his behavior all the time. He'll lie and steal and sneak. Punishments won't have much impact. He will become more sophisticated at calculating what he wants to try to get away with.

If the parents weren't abusive to begin with, they can become so at this point. They may keep trying to step up the penalties without realizing that the penalties aren't the point. The problem is that the child isn't listening to any inner voice of conscience. The child shouldn't even be thinking about the severity of penalties. The child ought to be thinking, "I am not the kind of person who even considers doing that."

Mental illness and genetics

ONE ALTERNATIVE hypothesis is that a family history of mental illness provides the causal relationship between crime and family structure. People who have a family history of certain kinds of mental illness may also have a higher propensity to become single parents. The same mental instability that contributes to a higher propensity to commit crimes may also make it more difficult for the person to form and sustain long-term relationships such as marriage.

A number of studies examine the relationship between single parenthood and some kinds of mental and emotional problems. A Swedish study by Gunilla Ringback Weitoft, Anders Hjern, Bengt Haglund, and Mans Rosen, released in January 2003 in the British medical journal *Lancet*, considered the impact of single-parent households on adolescents. This study explicitly took account of the family's history of mental illness. The Swedish adolescent children of single-parent households were twice as likely to abuse drugs or alcohol, twice as likely to attempt suicide, and about one and a half times as likely to suffer from a psychiatric illness. Parental history of mental illness accounted for very little of the variation in these various adolescent problems.

An extensive study of British data, reported by Andrew Cherlin and colleagues in the April 1998 issue of the *American Sociological Review*, also establishes a link between living in a single-parent household and some kinds of emotional problems over the child's entire lifetime. These researchers found that having divorced parents increases the likelihood of a wide range of problems, including depression, anxiety, phobias, and obsessions, over the entire lifetime. In addition, these children are more likely to be aggressive and disobedient during childhood.

The increased likelihood of aggressive behavior is confirmed in a variety of American studies, including Michael Workman and John Beer's 1992 study in *Psychological Reports* and Nancy Vaden-Kiernan's 1995 study in the *Journal of Abnormal Child Psychology*. Not every instance of aggressive behavior is criminal behavior, of course, but it is fair to say that something that increases the likelihood of aggression probably raises the possibility of some kinds of crime.

The cost of controlling people

PEOPLE WHO DO not control themselves have to be controlled by outside forces. This very costly business may, for a while, be hidden from the public eye. The family absorbs the costs. A single mother, for instance, may try to enlist the help of her parents or other extended family members if she has a truly out-of-control child. The family, however it is structured, rearranges itself to protect itself from the child who is disruptive, defiant, or violent. The family has to provide extremely tight supervision or else bear the brunt of the child's behavior.

If the behavior gets serious enough, the criminal justice system will be called into action. People outside the family then have to manage the child's behavior. These people might include some combination of police officers, prison guards, social workers, psychiatrists, judges, and parole officers, depending on the child's age and the seriousness of his crimes. All these people have to be paid, either by the family or by the taxpayers. When the public sector gets involved, the costs become visible to the rest of society.

> *When the public sector gets involved, the costs become visible to the rest of society.*

These costs add up. In California, for instance, the corrections budget has doubled since the 1960s as a percentage of the state's budget. By 2002–03, the prison system accounted for about 6 percent of the state budget, or more than $5.2 billion, an amount greater than what the state spends on transportation. Despite the current California budget crisis forcing cutbacks in most areas, the Department of Corrections is gaining a small boost of $40 million.

Some critics have claimed that these increases are political paybacks: The California Correctional Peace Officers Association has been one of the governor's biggest campaign contributors. This charge has some plausibility, since most of the increases in the department's budget are going to personnel costs. But being a prison guard is not a particularly pleasant job, and somebody, as they say, has to do it. Many of the facilities are in remote, unattractive parts of the state where attracting workers presents a continuing challenge. For instance, the Pelican Bay maximum-security prison in the far north of California is considered, if I may use the term, "godforsaken." The all-male facility recently had to use an ob-gyn as a primary care physician due to the difficulty of attracting an internal medicine doctor there.

While it may be easy for some to conclude that Davis is courting favor with his contributors, the teachers unions are also powerful political players in California, and education faces unprecedented cuts. The Department of Corrections spends $26,700 per adult inmate per year. Nobody seriously wants the governor to empty the prisons to save money.

Other critics claim that California's prison costs have escalated because the system is too tough on criminals. These critics cite the "Three Strikes" law, which requires a lifetime of incarceration for criminals with three offenses, no matter how trivial. Because of the law, an unprecedented number of relatively young people will spend the rest of their lives in prison at taxpayer expense.

Although such a law seems harsh, we should remember why we have a Three Strikes law in the first place: Richard Allen Davis. The sociopathic, unrepentant killer of Polly Klaas had a long history of criminal behavior. He had been recently released from prison when he stole Polly from her own bedroom and killed her. In the courtroom, he not only showed no remorse for his crime, he shouted obscenities at her parents. The people of California were sickened by the thought that a person so obviously dangerous should ever have been released.

As it happens, Richard Allen Davis was part of a disrupted family. His parents divorced when he was nine years old. He had virtually no contact with his mother after that. His father was often absent from the home and would leave his children with his own mother or with his different wives.

> *Think how much the state would save for every young person who can go on to create a life of his own.*

We could pose the question of costs to the taxpayer in this way: Suppose the kids in the juvenile justice system were functioning well enough that they could be a reasonably normal part of society. They could then be in the educational system instead of in the juvenile justice system. Look at the per-person cost of incarceration for a year, compared with the cost of education.

The California Youth Authority is the juvenile branch of California's criminal justice system. The system works with youngsters in a variety of settings, including camps, schools, and residential treatment facilities. According to the state Legislative Analysts Office, the state spends approximately $49,200 per year per person on these programs.

If that same young person could function normally in society, he would cost taxpayers about $8,568 per year while in K–12 education. If he went on to the community college system, he would cost about $4,376—or about a tenth of the cost of a year under the jurisdiction of the Youth Authority. If he went to the prestigious University of California system, he would cost the state $17,392. Think how much the state would save for every young person who can go on to create a life of his own rather than have to have his every move controlled or monitored by someone else.

The educational system represents an investment; the state's expenditures are likely to be repaid over the years by its graduates when they become productive citizens. By contrast, the money spent on incarceration has little prospect of turning the individual into a more productive citizen. These expenditures merely neutralize the negative impact on society of an individual who can't or won't control himself.

Statistics and probabilities

SOME MIGHT RESPOND that they personally are acquainted with many wonderful children of single parents. The parents are loving and giving; the children are thriving. But these anecdotal cases are not decisive. For every such story, we could produce a counter-story of a struggling single-parent family that fits the more distressing profile. The mother is a lovely person who did her best, but the boy got out of hand in his teenage years. Or the mother started out as a lovely person, but she became preoccupied with her new boyfriend or her job troubles. Her parents are heartbroken because they can see that their grandchildren are headed for trouble.

Besides, it is important to understand what statistical evidence does and does not prove. To say that a child of a single mother is twice as likely to commit a crime as the child of married parents is not to say that each and every child of every unwed mother will commit crimes or that no child of married parents will ever commit crimes. It is simply to say that growing up with unmarried parents is a significant risk factor.

Nor does saying that single-parent households are a risk factor diminish the possibility that some propensity for criminal activity might be genetically determined. Some individuals may well have a genetic propensity for aggression or for mental instability—or even for sociopathic behavior. These individuals are surely at higher than average risk for criminal activity, whether their parents are married or not. But the claim that some sociopaths are born does not preclude the possibility that some sociopaths are made. It makes sense to minimize the risk factors over which we can exercise a reasonable amount of control.

Some of the causal links between single-parent households and criminal behavior are better established than others. The causal connection between dropping out of school and higher probability of criminal behavior seems pretty straightforward and is well-documented. The link from single-parent households to attachment disorder is a weaker causal connection with a lower probability. But because a lifetime without a conscience is such a serious problem, it makes sense to try to lower the risk.

Look at it this way: When the evidence linking smoking with lung cancer first came to light, many people wanted to minimize that link. People with a serious addiction felt it was impossible for them to give up smoking. They didn't necessarily welcome the arrival of accurate information about a ship that had already sailed. "I know someone who smoked for a lifetime and never had cancer," skeptics replied. And indeed, that could be true. Smokers do not all die of smoking-related illness.

However, looking at the vast sweep of the evidence, enough people do die of smoking-related illnesses that smoking can safely be classified as a serious risk factor. And it is a choice-related risk factor, unlike genetic predispositions toward disease that might increase the likelihood of contracting lung cancer. It makes sense to have public health campaigns to educate the public about the risks associated with smoking, even though people irredeemably addicted to smoking might prefer not to be afflicted with this guilt- and anxiety-provoking information. Similarly, there is now enough evidence about the risks associated with growing up in a single-parent household that people are entitled to accurate information about those risks.

What to do?

No SERIOUS PERSON would claim that the government can or should take over marriage as a matter for "public" regulation and control, even if there are significant externalities to some behaviors. At a minimum, though, the government ought to refrain from counterproductive policies that discourage family formation or encourage family dissolution. The current regime of no-fault divorce, for example, really amounts to unilateral divorce.

Divorce imposes large costs on children. A unilateral divorce also imposes costs on the person who wants to preserve the marriage. Such people are willing to exert effort to stay married, but they don't even have the opportunity to state this case in court. These injured parties, adults and children alike, can never be made fully whole as the law would ordinarily require in a tort. It is a distortion of the idea of freedom to claim that no-fault divorce is the only policy consistent with individual liberty. Even a purely economic theory suggests that the imposition of costs on third parties should not be allowed to occur willy-nilly. Common decency requires that people who impose costs on others at least offer an account of themselves. The law should do no less.

But real policy recommendations have to go well beyond the reach of the law. In matters relating to the family, the dichotomy between "private" and "public," so familiar in policymaking circles, does not really work; these are not mutually exhaustive categories. We need an additional analytical category: "social."

Family matters are first and foremost social matters because a family is a little society. The larger society is built in crucial ways upon the little society of the family. The family is more than a collection of individuals who make quasi-market exchanges with each other. And families are not miniature political institutions. The label of "social" also points us in the right direction for solutions. The most important tools for building up the family are not primarily economic and political, but social and cultural. Accurate information is a necessary educational tool in reversing the culture of despair around the institution of marriage.

A young woman needs to know that the decision to have a child by herself is a decision that exposes her and her child to a lifetime of elevated risks: of poverty, of lower education, of depression, and of prison. Getting and staying married may seem formidable to a young pregnant woman because marriage is filled with a hundred irritations and difficulties. She might think it simpler to strike out alone rather than to put up with the innumerable adjustments and accommodations that are inevitable in married life. And it is easier for us to remain uninvolved in such a decision. But we are not doing the young person any favors by acting as if we are ignorant of the likely consequences of her choices. The time-honored American ethos of "live and let live" has metamorphosed into a categorical imperative to keep our mouths shut.

For years we have heard that single parenthood is an alternative lifestyle choice that doesn't affect anyone but the person who chooses it. We have been instructed that society should loosen the stigma against it in order to promote individual freedom of choice. We have been scolded for being insufficiently sensitive to the plight of single mothers if we utter any criticism of their decisions. At the urging of various activist groups, the government and society at large have been developing a posture of neutrality among family arrangements. There are no better or worse forms of family, we are told. There are no "broken families," only "different families."

The premise behind this official posture of neutrality is false. The decision to become a single parent or to disrupt an existing family does affect people outside the immediate household. These words may seem harsh to adults who have already made crucial life decisions, but it is time to be candid. We need to create a vocabulary for lovingly, but firmly and without apology, telling young people what we know. Surely, telling the truth is no infringement on anyone's liberty. Young people need to have accurate information about the choices they face. For their own sake—and for ours.

Jennifer Roback Morse is a research fellow at the Hoover Institution, Stanford University. She is the author of Love and Economics: Why the Laissez-Faire Family Doesn't Work (*Spence Publishing, 2001*).

The Aggregate Burden of Crime

David A. Anderson

Introduction

Distinct from previous studies that have focused on selected crimes, regions, or outcomes, this study attempts an exhaustively broad estimation of the crime burden....

Overt annual expenditures on crime in the United States include $47 billion for police protection, $36 billion for corrections, and $19 billion for the legal and judicial costs of state and local criminal cases. (Unless otherwise noted, all figures are adjusted to reflect 1997 dollars using the Consumer Price Index.) Crime victims suffer $876 million worth of lost workdays, and guns cost society $25 billion in medical bills and lost productivity in a typical year. Beyond the costs of the legal system, victim losses, and crime prevention agencies, the crime burden includes the costs of deterrence (locks, safety lighting and fencing, alarm systems and munitions), the costs of compliance enforcement (non-gendarme inspectors and regulators), implicit psychic and health costs (fear, agony, and the inability to behave as desired), and the opportunity costs of time spent preventing, carrying out, and serving prison terms for criminal activity.

This study estimates the impact of crime taking a comprehensive list of the repercussions of aberrant behavior into account. While the standard measures of criminal activity count crimes and direct costs, this study measures the impact of crimes and includes indirect costs as well. Further, the available data on which crime cost figures are typically based is imprecise. Problems with crime figures stem from the prevalence of unreported crimes, inconsistencies in recording procedures among law enforcement agencies, policies of recording only the most serious crime in events with multiple offenses, and a lack of distinction between attempted and completed crimes. This research does not eliminate these problems, but it includes critical crime-prevention and opportunity costs that are measured with relative precision, and thus places less emphasis on the imprecise figures used in most other measures of the impact of crime....

Previous Studies

Several studies have estimated the impact of crime; however, none has been thorough in its assessment of the substantial indirect costs of crime and the crucial consideration of private crime prevention expenditures. The FBI Crime Index provides a measure of the level of crime by counting the acts of murder, rape, robbery, aggravated assault, burglary, larceny, motor vehicle theft, and arson each year. The FBI Index is purely a count of crimes and does not attempt to place weights on various criminal acts based on their severity. If the number of acts of burglary, larceny, motor vehicle theft, or arson decreases, society might be better off, but with no measure of the severity of the crimes, such a conclusion is necessarily tentative. From a societal standpoint what matters is the extent of damage inflicted by these crimes, which the FBI Index does not measure.

Over the past three decades, studies of the cost of crime have reported increasing crime burdens, perhaps more as a result of improved understanding and accounting for the broad repercussions of crime than due to the increase in the burden itself. Table 1 summarizes the findings of eight previous studies....

The Effects of Crime

The effects of crime fall into several categories depending on whether they constitute the allocation of resources due to crime that could otherwise be used more productively, the production of ill-favored commodities, transfers from victims to criminals, opportunity costs, or implicit costs associated with risks to life and health. This section examines the meaning and ramifications of each of these categories of crime costs.

Crime-Induced Production

Crime can result in the allocation of resources towards products and activities that do not contribute to society except in their association with crime. Examples include the production of personal protection devices, the trafficking of drugs, and the operation of correctional facilities. In the absence of crime, the time, money, and material resources absorbed by the provision of these goods and services could be used for the creation of benefits rather than the avoidance of harm. The foregone benefits from these alternatives represent a real cost of crime to society. (Twenty dollars spent on a door lock is twenty dollars that cannot be spent on groceries.) Thus, expenditures on crime-related products are treated as a loss to society.

Table 1

Previous Study	Focus	Not Included	$ (billions)
Colins (1994)	General	Opportunity Costs, Miscellaneous Indirect Components	728
Cohen, Miller, and Wiersema (1995)	Victim Costs of Violent and Property Crimes	Prevention, Opportunity, and Indirect Costs	472
U.S. News (1974)	General	Opportunity Costs, Miscellaneous Indirect Components	288
Cohen, Miller, Rossman (1994)	Cost of Rape, Robbery, and Assault	Prevention, Opportunity, and Indirect Costs	183
Zedlewski (1985)	Firearms, Guard Dogs, Victim Losses, Commercial Security	Residential Security, Opportunity Costs, Indirect Costs	160
Cohen (1990)	Cost of Personal and Household Crime to Victims	Prevention, Opportunity, and Indirect Costs	113
President's Commission on Law Enforcement (1967)	General	Opportunity Costs, Miscellaneous Indirect Components	107
Klaus (1994)	National Crime and Victimization Survey Crimes	Prevention, Opportunity, and Indirect Costs	19

Crimes against property also create unnecessary production due to the destruction and expenditure of resources, and crimes against persons necessitate the use of medical and psychological care resources. In each of these cases, crime-related purchases bid-up prices for the associated items, resulting in higher prices for all consumers of the goods. In the absence of crime, the dollars currently spent to remedy and recover from crime would largely be spent in pursuit of other goals, bidding-up the prices of alternative categories of goods. For this reason, the *net* impact of price effects is assumed to be zero in the present research.

Opportunity Costs

As the number of incarcerated individuals increases steadily, society faces the large and growing loss of these potential workers' productivity.… Criminals are risk takers and instigators—characteristics that could make them contributors to society if their entrepreneurial talents were not misguided. Crimes also take time to conceive and carry out, and thus involve the opportunity cost of the criminals' time regardless of detection and incarceration. For many, crime is a full-time occupation. Society is deprived of the goods and services a criminal would have produced in the time consumed by crime and the production of "bads" if he or she were on the level. Additional opportunity costs arise due to victims' lost workdays, and time spent securing assets, looking for keys, purchasing and installing crime prevention devices, and patrolling neighborhood-watch areas.

The Value of Risks to Life and Health

The implicit costs of violent crime include the fear of being injured or killed, the anger associated with the inability to behave as desired, and the agony of being a crime victim. Costs associated with life and health risks are perhaps the most difficult to ascertain, although a considerable literature is devoted to their estimation. The implicit values of lost life and injury are included in the list of crime costs below; those not wishing to consider them can simply subtract these estimates from the aggregate figure.

Transfers

One result of fraud and theft is a transfer of assets from victim to criminal.…

Numerical Findings

Crime-Induced Production

… Crime-induced production accounts for about $400 billion in expenditures annually. Table 2 presents the costs of goods and services that would not have to be produced in the absence of crime. Drug trafficking accounts for an estimated $161 billion in expenditure. With the $28 billion cost of prenatal drug exposure and almost $11 billion worth of federal, state, and local drug control efforts (including drug treatment, education, interdiction, research, and intelligence), the combined cost of drug-related activities is about $200 billion. Findings that over half of the arrestees in 24 cities tested positive for recent drug use and about one-third of offenders reported being under the influence of drugs at the time of their offense suggest that significant portions of the other crime-cost categories may result indirectly from drug use.

About 682,000 police and 17,000 federal, state, special (park, transit, or county) and local police agencies account for $47 billion in expenditures annually. Thirty-six billion dollars is dedicated each year to the 895 federal and state prisons, 3,019 jails, and 1,091 state, county, and local juvenile detention centers. Aside from guards in correctional institutions, private expenditure on guards amounts to more than $18 billion annually. Security guard agencies employ 55 percent of the 867,000 guards in the U.S.; the remainder are employed in-house. While guards are expected and identifiable at banks and military complexes, they have a less conspicuous presence at railroads, ports, golf courses, laboratories, factories, hospitals, retail stores, and other places of business. The figures in this paper do not include receptionists, who often play a duel role of monitoring unlawful entry into a building and providing information and assistance.…

Table 2

Crime-Induced Production	$ (millions)
Drug Trafficking	160,584
Police Protection	47,129
Corrections	35,879
Prenatal Exposure to Cocaine and Heroin	28,156
Federal Agencies	23,381
Judicial and Legal Services—State & Local	18,901
Guards	17,917
Drug Control	10,951
DUI Costs to Driver	10,302
Medical Care for Victims	8,990
Computer Viruses and Security	8,000
Alarm Systems	6,478
Passes for Business Access	4,659
Locks, Safes, and Vaults	4,359
Vandalism (except Arson)	2,317
Small Arms and Small Arms Ammunition	2,252
Replacements due to Arson	1,902
Surveillance Cameras	1,471
Safety Lighting	1,466
Protective Fences and Gates	1,159
Airport Security	448
Nonlethal weaponry, e.g., Mace	324
Elec. Retail Article Surveillance	149
Theft Insurance (less indemnity)	96
Guard Dogs	49
Mothers Against Drunk Driving	49
Library Theft Detection	28
Total	397,395

Opportunity Costs

In their study of the costs of murder, rape, robbery, and aggravated assault, Cohen, Miller, and Rossman estimate that the average incarcerated offender costs society $5,700 in lost productivity per year. Their estimate was based on the observation that many prisoners did not work in the legal market prior to their offense, and the opportunity cost of those prisoners' time can be considered to be zero. The current study uses a higher estimate of the opportunity cost of incarceration because unlike previous studies, it examines the relative savings from a *crime-free* society. It is likely that in the absence of crime including drug use, some criminals who are not presently employed in the legal workforce would be willing and able to find gainful employment. This assumption is supported by the fact that many criminals are, in a way, motivated entrepreneurs whose energy has taken an unfortunate focus. In the absence of more enticing underground activities, some of the same individuals could apply these skills successfully in the legal sector....

Table 3

The Value of Risks to Life and Health	$ (millions)
Value of Lost Life	439,880
Value of Injuries	134,515
Total	**574,395**

The Value of Risks to Life and Health

Table 3 presents estimates of the implicit costs of violent crime. The value of life and injury estimates used here reflect the amounts individuals are willing to accept to enter a work environment in which their health state might change. The labor market estimates do not include losses covered by workers' compensation, namely health care costs (usually provided without dollar or time limits) and lost earnings (within modest bounds, victims or their spouses typically receive about two thirds of lost earnings for life or the duration of the injury). The values do capture perceived risks of pain, suffering, and mental distress associated with the health losses. If the risk of involvement in violent crime evokes more mental distress than the risk of occupational injuries and fatalities, the labor market values represent conservative estimates of the corresponding costs of crime. Similar estimates have been used in previous studies of crime costs....

The average of 27 previous estimates of the implicit value of human life as reported by W. Kip Viscusi is 7.1 million. Removing two outlying estimates of just under $20 million about which the authors express reservation, the average of the remaining studies is $6.1 million. Viscusi points out that the majority of the estimates fall between $3.7 and $8.6 million ($3 and $7 million in 1990 dollars), the average of which is again $6.1 million. The $6.1 million figure was multiplied by the 72,111 crime-related deaths to obtain the $440 billion estimate of the value of lives lost to crime. Similarly, the average of 15 studies of the implicit value of non-fatal injuries, $52,637, was multiplied by the 2,555,520 reported injuries resulting from drunk driving and boating, arson, rape, robbery, and assaults to find the $135 billion estimate for the implicit cost of crime-related injuries.

Transfers

More than $603 billion worth of transfers result from crime. After the $204 billion lost to occupational fraud and the $123 billion in unpaid taxes, the $109 billion lost to health insurance fraud represents the greatest transfer by more than a factor of two, and the associated costs amount to almost ten percent of the nations' health care expenditures. Robberies, perhaps the classic crime, ironically generate a smaller volume of transfers ($775 million) than any other category of crime. The transfers of goods and money resulting from fraud and theft do not necessarily impose a net burden on society, and may in fact increase social welfare to the extent that those on the receiving end value the goods more than those losing them. Nonetheless, as Table 4 illustrates, those on the losing side bear a $603 billion annual burden....

Table 4

Transfers	$ (millions)
Occupational Fraud	203,952
Unpaid Taxes	123,108
Health Insurance Fraud	108,610
Financial Institution Fraud	52,901
Mail Fraud	35,986
Property/Casualty Insurance Fraud	20,527
Telemarketing Fraud	16,609
Business Burglary	13,229
Motor Vehicle Theft	8,913
Shoplifting	7,185
Household Burglary	4,527
Personal Theft	3,909
Household Larceny	1,996
Coupon Fraud	912
Robbery	775
Total	603,140

Table 5

The Aggregate Burden of Crime	$ (billions)
Crime-Induced Production	397
Opportunity Costs	130
Risks to Life and Health	574
Transfers	603
Gross Burden	**$1,705**
Net of Transfers	**$1,102**
Per Capita (in dollars)	**$4,118**

There are additional cost categories that are not included here, largely because measures that are included absorb much of their impact. Nonetheless, several are worth noting. Thaler, Hellman and Naroff, and Rizzo estimate the erosion of property values per crime. An average of their figures, $2,024, can be multiplied by the total number of crimes reported in 1994, 13,992, to estimate an aggregate housing devaluation of $28 billion. Although this figure should reflect the inability to behave as desired in the presence of crime, it also includes psychic and monetary costs imposed by criminal behavior that are already included in this [article].

Julie Berry Cullen and Stephen D. Levitt discuss urban flight resulting from crime. They report a nearly one-to-one relationship between serious crimes and individuals parting from major cities. The cost component of this is difficult to assess because higher commuting costs must be measured against lower property costs in rural areas, and the conveniences of city living must be compared with the amenities of suburbia. Several other categories of crime costs receive incomplete representation due to insufficient data, and therefore make the estimates here conservative. These include the costs of unreported crimes (although the National Crime Victimization Survey provides information beyond that reported to the police), lost taxes due to the underground economy, and restrictions of behavior due to crime.

When criminals' costs are estimated implicitly as the value of the assets they receive through crime, the gross cost of crime (including transfers) is estimated to exceed $2,269 billion each year, and the net cost is an estimated $1,666 billion. When criminals' costs are assumed to equal the value of time spent planning and committing crimes and in prison, the estimated annual gross and net costs of crime are $1,705 and $1,102 billion respectively. Table 5 presents the aggregate costs of crime based on the more conservative, time-based estimation method. The disaggregation of this and the previous tables facilitates the creation of customized estimates based on

marized in Table 1 included transfers, so the appropriate comparison is to the gross cost estimate in the current study. As the result of a more comprehensive treatment of repercussions, the cost of crime is now seen to be more than twice as large as previously recognized.

Conclusion

Previous studies of the burden of crime have counted crimes or concentrated on direct crime costs. This paper calculates the aggregate burden of crime rather than absolute numbers, includes indirect costs, and recognizes that transfers resulting from theft should not be included in the net burden of crime to society. The accuracy of society's perspective on crime costs will improve with the understanding that these costs extend beyond victims' losses and the cost of law enforcement to include the opportunity costs of criminals' and prisoners' time, our inability to behave as desired, and the private costs of crime deterrence.

As criminals acquire an estimated $603 billion dollars worth of assets from their victims, they generate an additional $1,102 billion worth of lost productivity, crime-related expenses, and diminished quality of life. The net losses represent an annual per capita burden of $4,118. Including transfers, the aggregate burden of crime is $1,705 billion. In the United States, this is of the same order of magnitude as life insurance purchases ($1,680 billion), the outstanding mortgage debt to commercial banks and savings institutions ($1,853 billion), and annual expenditures on health ($1,038 billion).

As the enormity of this negative-sum game comes to light, so, too, will the need for countervailing efforts to redefine legal policy and forge new ethical standards. Periodic estimates of the full cost of crime could speak to the success of national strategies to encourage decorum, including increased expenditures on law enforcement, new community strategic approaches, technological innovations, legal reform, education, and the development of ethics curricula. Economic theory dictates that resources should be devoted to moral enhancement until the benefits from marginal efforts are surpassed by their costs. Programs that decrease the burden of crime by more than the cost of implementation should be continued, while those associated with negligible or positive net increments in the cost of crime should be altered to better serve societal goals.

UNIT 3

Groups and Roles in Transition

Unit Selections

Key Points to Consider

- Is the family in America in crisis? What indicators of family health have worsened and what indicators have improved?

- What factors are influencing women's roles today? How are they changing women's lives?

- How do you explain the high divorce rate in America?

- Do you think that gay marriages should be legally treated as equal to heterosexual marriages?

- What factors create community? How can they be brought into being under today's conditions? What are the impediments to community? What are the consequences of weak communities? Does the Internet strengthen community?

 **Links: www.dushkin.com/online/**
These sites are annotated in the World Wide Web pages.

The Gallup Organization
 http://www.gallup.com

Marriage and Family Therapy
 http://www.aamft.org/index_nm.asp

The North-South Institute
 http://www.nsi-ins.ca/ensi/index.html

PsychNet/American Psychological Association
 http://www.apa.org/topics/homepage.html

SocioSite: Feminism and Woman Issues
 http://www.pscw.uva.nl/sociosite/TOPICS/Women.html

Primary groups are small, intimate, spontaneous, and personal. In contrast, secondary groups are large, formal, and impersonal. Primary groups include the family, couples, gangs, cliques, teams, and small tribes or rural villages. Primary groups are the main sources that the individual draws upon in developing values and an identity. Secondary groups include most of the organizations and bureaucracies in a modern society and carry out most of its instrumental functions. Often primary groups are formed within secondary groups such as a factory, school, or business.

Urbanization, geographic mobility, centralization, bureaucratization, and other aspects of modernization have had an impact on the nature of groups, the quality of the relationships between people, and individuals' feelings of belonging. The family, in particular, has undergone radical transformation. The greatly increased participation of women in the paid labor force and their increased careerism have led to severe conflicts for women between their work and family roles.

The first subsection of this unit deals with marriage and family in the context of dramatic changes in the culture and the economy. Everyone seems to agree that the family is in trouble, but Stephanie Coontz challenges this viewpoint in the first article in this subsection. She takes issue with the data presented for the decline of marriage and the family thesis and offers evidence that marriage is strong today even though divorce is common. In fact, she argues that today's families are better than families of a century ago in many ways. According to Coontz "the biggest problem facing most families … is not that our families have changed too much but that our institutions have changed too little."

The next two articles look at current marriage issues. The first reviews the recent research on the benefits of marriage, which are many. The title summarizes the findings in one sentence: if you want a better life you should get married. Marrieds have better sex lives, better physical and mental health, better material conditions and finances, and of course the children are better off. The second article by Polly Shulman presents some sophisticated practical advice for married people. Social changes have reduced the factors binding marriages together. "Today the only cohesive force holding marriages together is the quality of the relationship between the spouses." Seven myths lead to unrealistic expectations that lead spouses to give up too quickly on their marriage. This article corrects the following myths: 1) "all you need is love," 2) "people don't really change," 3) "my spouse just doesn't know how to listen," 4) we start off fresh and divorced from old family baggage, 5) "egalitarian marriage is easier than traditional marriage," 6) "children solidify a marriage," and 7) "the sexual revolution has made great sex easier than ever."

The next subsection focuses on sexual behavior and gender roles. In the first article, John Cloud provides an overview of the current hot topic of gay marriage. The Massachusetts Supreme Court ruled that it is unconstitutional to deny gay couples marriage licences. This has spurred President Bush to sponsor a constitutional amendment defining marriage as limited to heterosexual couples and eleven states passing resolutions to this effect. Cloud presents the history of this issue and various views on it. In the next article Claudia Wallis discusses how mothers are resolving the pull of the workplace and the pull of child rearing. Increasingly women are staying home with the kids. She cites research that supports this decision and she tells the stories of how it worked out for several women who have stayed home.

The last subsection of unit 3 looks at cities and communities. The first article in the unit speculates on what might happen when, within a half century, no group will be a majority in America. Today this is true of Sacramento, California. The authors examine how this situation works out in America's most integrated city. Twenty percent of babies are multiracial and though racial tensions exist, they are relatively minor. In the second article, Amitai Etzioni describes the trends toward greater inequality and diversity in the United States and asks whether these trends threaten the integration of American society. Since the 1960s identity politics have succeeded in reducing past injustices but also have divided the nation along group lines. Then he draws on sociological theory to propose ways to build community by reducing inequalities, increasing bonds, and generating stronger value commitments.

THE AMERICAN FAMILY

New research about an old institution challenges the conventional wisdom that the family today is worse off than in the past. Essay by Stephanie Coontz

As the century comes to an end, many observers fear for the future of America's families. Our divorce rate is the highest in the world, and the percentage of unmarried women is significantly higher than in 1960. Educated women are having fewer babies, while immigrant children flood the schools, demanding to be taught in their native language. Harvard University reports that only 4 percent of its applicants can write a proper sentence.

Things were worse at the turn of the last century than they are today. Most workers labored 10 hours a day, six days a week, leaving little time for family life.

There's an epidemic of sexually transmitted diseases among men. Many streets in urban neighborhoods are littered with cocaine vials. Youths call heroin "happy dust." Even in small towns, people have easy access to addictive drugs, and drug abuse by middle-class wives is skyrocketing. Police see 16-year-old killers, 12-year-old prostitutes, and gang members as young as 11.

America at the end of the 1990s? No, America at the end of the 1890s.

The litany of complaints may sound familiar, but the truth is that many things were worse at the start of this century than they are today. Then, thousands of children worked full-time in mines, mills and sweatshops. Most workers labored 10 hours a day, often six days a week, which left them little time or energy for family life. Race riots were more frequent and more deadly than those experienced by recent generations. Women couldn't vote, and their wages were so low that many turned to prostitution.

Photograph courtesy of Thomas L. Gavin.

© 1900 A Couple and their eight children sit for a family portrait. Wth smaller families today, mothers are able to spend twice as much time with each child.

In 1900 a white child had one chance in three of losing a brother or sister before age 15, and a black child had a fifty-fifty chance of seeing a sibling die. Children's-aid groups reported widespread abuse and neglect by parents. Men who deserted or divorced their wives rarely paid child support. And only 6 percent of the children graduated from high school, compared with 88 percent today.

Photograph courtesy of Kathryn M. Gavin.

On the 1940s family farm, fathers out working the fields had less time to spend with their families.

Why do so many people think American families are facing worse problems now than in the past? Partly it's because we compare the complex and diverse families of the 1990s with the seemingly more standard-issue ones of the 1950s, a unique decade when every long-term trend of the 20th century was temporarily reversed. In the 1950s, for the first time in 100 years, the divorce rate fell while marriage and fertility rates soared, crating a boom in nuclear-family living. The percentage of foreign-born individuals in the country decreased. And the debates over social and cultural issues that had divided Americans for 150 years were silenced, suggesting a national consensus on family values and norms.

Some nostalgia for the 1950s is understandable: Life looked pretty good in comparison with the hardship of the Great Depression and World War II. The GI Bill gave a generation of young fathers a college education and a subsidized mortgage on a new house. For the first time, a majority of men could support a family and buy a home without pooling their earnings with those of other family members. Many Americans built a stable family life on these foundations.

But much nostalgia for the 1950s is a result of selective amnesia—the same process that makes childhood memories of summer vacations grow sunnier with each passing year. The superficial sameness of 1950s family life was achieved through censorship, coercion and discrimination. People with unconventional beliefs faced governmental investigation and arbitrary firings. African Americans and Mexican Americans were prevented from voting in some states by literacy tests that were not administered to whites. Individuals who didn't follow the rigid gender and sexual rules of the day were ostracized.

Leave It to Beaver did not reflect the real-life experience of most American families. While many moved into the middle class during the 1950s, poverty remained more widespread than in the worst of our last three recessions. More children went hungry, and poverty rates for the elderly were more than twice as high as today's.

Even in the white middle class, not every woman was as serenely happy with her lot as June Cleaver was on TV. Housewives of the 1950s may have been less rushed than today's working mothers, but they were more likely to suffer anxiety and depression. In many states, women couldn't serve on juries or get loans or credit cards in their own names.

And not every kid was as wholesome as Beaver Cleaver, whose mischievous antics could be handled by Dad at the dinner table. In 1955 alone, Congress discussed 200 bills aimed at curbing juvenile delinquency. Three years later, LIFE reported that urban teachers were being terrorized by their students. The drugs that were so freely available in 1900 had been outlawed, but many children grew up in families ravaged by alcohol and barbiturate abuse.

Rates of unwed childbearing tripled between 1940 and 1958, but most Americans didn't notice because unwed mothers generally left town, gave their babies up for adoption and returned home as if nothing had happened. Troubled youths were encouraged to drop out of high school. Mentally handicapped children were warehoused in institutions like the Home for Idiotic and Imbecilic Children in Kansas, where a woman whose sister had lived there for most of the 1950s once took me. Wives routinely told pollsters that being disparaged or ignored by their husbands was a normal part of a happier than-average marriage.

Many of our worries today reflect how much better we want to be, not how much better we used to be.

Denial extended to other areas of life as well. In the early 1900s, doctors refused to believe that the cases of gonorrhea and syphilis they saw in young girls could have been caused by sexual abuse. Instead, they reasoned, girls could get these diseases from toilet seats, a myth that terrified generations of mothers and daughters. In the 1950s, psychiatrists dismissed incest reports as Oedipal fantasies on the part of children.

Spousal rape was legal throughout the period and wife beating was not taken seriously by authorities. Much of what we now label child abuse was accepted as a normal part of parental discipline. Physicians saw no reason to question parents who claimed that their child's broken bones had been caused by a fall from a tree.

American Mirror

Muncie, Ind. (pop. 67,476), calls itself America's Hometown. But to generations of sociologists it is better known as America's Middletown—the most studied place in the 20th century American landscape. "Muncie has nothing extraordinary about it," says University of Virginia professor Theodore Caplow, which is why, for the past 75 years, researchers have gone there to observe the typical American family. Muncie's averageness first drew sociologists Robert and Helen Lynd in 1924. They returned in 1935 (their follow-up study was featured in a LIFE photo essay by Margaret Bourke-White). And in 1976, armed with the Lynds' original questionnaires, Caplow launched yet another survey of the town's citizens.

Caplow discovered that family life in Muncie was much healthier in the 1970s than in the 1920s. No only were husbands and wives communicating more, but unlike married couples in the 1920s, they were also shopping, eating out, exercising and going to movies and concerts together. More than 90 percent of Muncie's couples characterized their marriages as "happy" or "very happy." In 1929 the Lynds had described partnerships of a drearier kind, "marked by sober accommodation of each partner to his share in the joint undertaking of children, paying off the mortgage and generally 'getting on.'"

Caplow's five-year study, which inspired a six-part PBS series, found that even though more moms were working outside the home, two thirds of them spent at least two hours a day with their children; in 1924 fewer than half did. In 1924 most children expected their mothers to be good cooks and housekeepers, and wanted their fathers to spend time with them and respect their opinions. Fifty years later, expectations of fathers were unchanged, but children wanted the same—time and respect—from their mothers.

This year, Caplow went back to survey the town again. The results (and another TV documentary) won't be released until December 2000.

—*Sora Song*

There are plenty of stresses in modern family life, but one reason they seem worse is that we no longer sweep them under the rug. Another is that we have higher expectations of parenting and marriage. That's a good thing. We're right to be concerned about inattentive parents, conflicted marriages, antisocial values, teen violence and child abuse. But we need to realize that many of our worries reflect how much better we *want* to be, not how much better we *used* to be.

Fathers in intact families are spending more time with their children than at any other point in the past 100 years. Although the number of hours the average woman spends at home with her children has declined since the early 1900s, there has been a decrease in the number of children per family and an increase in individual attention to each child. As a result, mothers today, including working moms, spend almost twice as much time with each child as mothers did in the 1920s. People who raised children in the 1940s and 1950s typically report that their own adult children and grandchildren communicate far better with their kids and spend more time helping with homework than they did—even as they complain that other parents today are doing a worse job than in the past.

Despite the rise in youth violence from the 1960s to the early 1990s, America's children are also safer now than they've ever been. An infant was four times more likely to die in the 1950s than today. A parent then was three times more likely than a modern one to preside at the funeral of a child under the age of 15, and 27 percent more likely to lose an older teen to death.

If we look back over the last millennium, we can see that families have always been diverse and in flux. In each period, families have solved one set of problems only to face a new array of challenges. What works for a family in one economic and cultural setting doesn't work for a family in another. What's helpful at one stage of a family's life may be destructive at the next stage. If there is one lesson to be drawn from the last millennium of family history, it's that families are always having to play catch-up with a changing world.

Take the issue of working mothers. Families in which mothers spend as much time earning a living as they do raising children are nothing new. They were the norm throughout most of the last two millennia. In the 19th century, married women in the United States began a withdrawal from the workforce, but for most families this was made possible only by sending their children out to work instead. When child labor was abolished, married women began reentering the workforce in ever large numbers.

For a few decades, the decline in child labor was greater than the growth of women's employment. The result was an aberration: the male-breadwinner family. In the 1920s, for the first time, a bare majority of American children grew up in families where the husband provided all the income, the wife stayed home full-time, and they and their siblings went to school instead of work. During the 1950s, almost two thirds of children grew up in such families, an all-time high. Yet that same decade saw an acceleration of workforce participation by wives and mothers that soon made the dual-earner family the norm, a trend not likely to be reversed in the next century.

What's new is not that women make half their families' living, but that for the first time they have substantial control over their own income, along with the social freedom

© Getty Images/Index Stock

In the 1950s, life looked pretty good in comparison with the hardships of the Great Depression and World War II.

to remain single or to leave an unsatisfactory marriage. Also new is the declining proportion of their lives that people devote to rearing children, both because they have fewer kids and because they are living longer. Until about 1940, the typical marriage was broken by the death of one partner within a few years after the last child left home. Today, couples can look forward to spending more than two decades together after the children leave.

The growing length of time partners spend with only each other for company has made many individuals less willing to put up with an unhappy marriage, while women's economic independence makes it less essential for them to do so. It is no wonder that divorce has risen steadily since 1900. Disregarding a spurt in 1946, a dip in the 1950s and another peak around 1980, the divorce rate is just where you'd expect to find it, based on the rate of increase from 1900 to 1950. Today, 40 percent of all marriages will end in divorce before a couple's 40th anniversary. Yet despite this high divorce rate, expanded life expectancies mean that more couples are reaching that anniversary than ever before.

Families and individuals in contemporary America have more life choices than in the past. That makes it easier for some to consider dangerous or unpopular options. But it also makes success easier for many families that never would have had a chance before—interracial, gay or lesbian, and single-mother families, for example. And it expands horizons for most families.

Women's new options are good not just for themselves but for their children. While some people say that women who choose to work are selfish, it turns out that maternal self-sacrifice is not good for children. Kids do better when their mothers are happy with their lives, whether their satisfaction comes from being a full-time homemaker or from having a job.

Largely because of women's new roles at work, men are doing more at home. Although most men still do less housework than their wives, the gap has been halved since the 1960s. Today, 49 percent of couples say they share childcare equally, compared with 25 percent of 1985.

Men's greater involvement at home is good for their relationships with their parents, and also good for their children. Hands-on fathers make better parents than men who let their wives do all the nurturing and childcare: They raise sons who are more expressive and daughters who are more likely to do well in school, especially in math and science.

The biggest problem is not that our families have changed too much but that our institutions have changed too little.

In 1900, life expectancy was 47 years, and only 4 percent of the population was 65 or older. Today, life expectancy is 76 years, and by 2025, about 20 percent of Americans will be 65 or older. For the first time, a generation of adults must plan for the needs of both their parents and their children. Most Americans are responding with remarkable grace. One in four households gives the equivalent of a full day a week or more in unpaid care to an aging relative, and more than half say they expect to do so in the next 10 years. Older people are less likely to be impoverished or incapacitated by illness than in the past, and they have more opportunity to develop a relationship with their grandchildren.

Even some of the choices that worry us the most are turning out to be manageable. Divorce rates are likely to remain high, but more non-custodial parents are staying in touch with their children. Child-support receipts are up. And a lower proportion of kids from divorced families are exhibiting problems than in earlier decades. Stepfamilies are learning to maximize children's access to supportive adults rather than cutting them off from one side of the family.

Out-of-wedlock births are also high, however, and this will probably continue because the age of first marriage for women has risen to an all-time high of 25, almost five years above what it was in the 1950s. Women who marry at an older age are less likely to divorce, but they have more years when they are at risk—or at choice—for a nonmarital birth.

Nevertheless, births to teenagers have fallen from 50 percent of all nonmarital births in the late 1970s to just 30 percent today. A growing proportion of women who have a nonmarital birth are in their twenties and thirties and usually have more economic and educational resources than unwed mothers of the past. While two involved parents are generally better than one, a mother's personal maturity, along with her educational and economic status, is a better predictor of how well her child will turn out than her marital status. We should no longer assume that children raised by single parents face debilitating disadvantages.

As we begin to understand the range of sizes, shapes and colors that today's families come in, we find that the differences *within* family types are more important than the differences *between* them. No particular family form guarantees success, and no particular form is doomed to fail. How a family functions on the inside is more important than how it looks from the outside.

The biggest problem facing most families as this century draws to a close is not that our families have changed too much but that our institutions have changed too little. America's work policies are 50 years out of date, designed for a time when most moms weren't in the workforce and most dads didn't understand the joys of being involved in childcare. Our school schedules are 150 years out of date, designed for a time when kids needed to be home to help with the milking and haying. And many political leaders feel they have to decide whether to help parents stay home longer with their kids or invest in better childcare, preschool and afterschool programs, when most industrialized nations have long since learned it's possible to do both.

So America's social institutions have some Y2K bugs to iron out. But for the most part, our families are ready for the next millennium.

LIVING BETTER
GET WED

AMY M. BRAVERMAN

While pundits, politicians, and moralists weigh the pros and cons of gay marriage, Linda Waite is still focused on traditional American couples, countering messages from the "antimarriage" culture and championing marriage's benefits: specifically, that marriage itself is good for your physical and mental health, good for your financial stability, good for your sex life, good for your kids—good for almost every aspect of what many Americans consider a happy life.

And Waite, the Lucy Flower professor in Sociology, is spreading the word. Her book, *The Case for Marriage: Why Married People Are Happier, Healthier, and Better Off Financially* (Doubleday, 2000), cowritten by Maggie Gallagher of the Institute of American Values, has sold 25,000 copies. Although its title sounds like a socially conservative missive, its coauthor is a conservative columnist, and its message helped to inform President George W. Bush's marriage initiative for welfare recipients, the book is not, Waite says, a right-wing tract. Waite, in fact, describes herself as a liberal Democrat. "I come at this from a researcher's perspective." What the slim, 55-year-old with a short, no-nonsense haircut means is, she didn't create the facts, she's just reporting them.

Those facts refute much conventional wisdom. They show that married men, rather than trading their libidos for lawnmowers, have more sex than single men. And married women are less depressed than single women, contrary to feminist sociologist Jessie Bernard's explosive 1972 book arguing that wives were more phobic, depressed, dependent, and passive—findings that have shaped cultural conceptions, ever since. More recently, Waite has shown that divorce does not make unhappily married people any happier. In a study released in July 2002, she and five colleagues analyzed data from the University of Wisconsin's National Survey of Family and Households. When the adults who said they were unhappily married in the late 1980s were interviewed again five years later, those who had divorced were on average still unhappy or even *less* happy, while those who stayed in their marriages on average had moved past the bad times and were at a happier stage. After controlling for race, age, gender, and income, Waite's group found that divorce usually did not reduce symptoms of depression, raise self esteem, or. increase a sense of mastery over one's life.

"The general pattern," Waite says, "is that people who stay in an unhappy marriage are at least as well off as those who divorce, so there's no benefit to leaving a marriage you're unhappy with." That argument—that people who at some point are unhappy with their marriage later become happy in the same marriage—is the subject of Waite and Gallagher's forthcoming book, *The Case for Staying Married*, under contract with Oxford University Press.

Not that Waite's exchanging her sociological expertise for a counseling certificate. "I don't give advice," she says. "All we can say is, the suggestion is that a lot of things that make people unhappy don't stay." She may not counsel couples, but she actively promotes her findings, organizing several conferences on marriage, sitting on the research board for the National Marriage Project, whose mission is to "strengthen the institution of marriage" through research and education, and advising the University's Religion, Culture, and Family Project. *The Case for Marriage*, Waite says, is more than anything else a public health argument. "It's like exercise," she says. "Studies show that, on average, people who exercise experience health benefits. The next step is to say that you should exercise." Similarly, "a consistent body of work suggests to me that an OK marriage, one that isn't terrible, causes improvements" in general well-being. And those studies, she notes, point to marriage not only as a sign of a longer, healthier life, higher income, and better sex, but also as a cause.

A 1990 study, for example, showed that unmarried women have a 50 percent higher mortality rate than married women; single men 250 percent higher than married men. Husbands' greater health benefit, Waite and Gallagher write, "appears to flow from the fact that single men behave in particularly unhealthy, risky ways that single women typically do not," such as drinking, smoking, and reckless driving—"stupid bachelor tricks" that, Waite notes, divorced and widowed men often return to. Wives tend to track their husbands' health, scheduling doctor's appointments and providing direct care. And husbands benefit from wives' emotional support, making them more likely than single men to recover from a serious illness or to manage a chronic illness.

Wives also experience health gains, including their mental health, It's true that married women with young children generally report feeling more "overburdened" than single, childless women, but studies have found that married women—and men—have better mental health than singles. Although women are more prone to depression than men, marriage doesn't account for the gap.

FINANCIAL BENEFITS

For women the biggest marriage benefit, however, is not health but finances. With the higher incomes men often contribute to a relationship, married women can access better housing, safer neighborhoods, and often the security of owning their own homes. They're more likely to have private health insurance—only half of divorced, widowed, and never-married women do, according to one study. Married men benefit financially as well—they make at least 10 percent more than single men do, Waite and Gallagher write, and perhaps as much as 40 percent more. Economic theory suggests that husbands earn more money because they are freer to specialize in money-making—while wives typically specialize in housework and child care. (But it does not necessarily follow, Waite and Gallagher note, that men make more money because they do less housework. "While time spent on housework does affect the earnings of wives, some evidence suggests that husbands who spend more hours on household tasks do not earn less money as a result."

Skeptics may wonder if it's really marriage that makes the difference. Perhaps people who are happier and healthier to begin with are more likely to get married. Perhaps the divorced are sicker and die younger because marriages are more likely to break up from the stress of an illness. Perhaps men who make more money are more likely to attract (and keep) a wife. Certain "selection mechanisms," Waite and Gallagher admit, do play a role in explaining married people's better health and higher incomes. But in addition, they believe, marriage itself creates better lives. Accounting for initial health status, the married live longer. "Even sick people who marry live longer than their counterparts who don't," they write. And selection alone doesn't explain married men's higher earnings; "their wages actually rise faster while they are married" than single men's wages do—even when occupation, industry, hours and weeks worked, and tenure are factored in.

Meanwhile, living together, or cohabiting, "does not confer the same protection as being married," they write. "The big health difference is between married people and the nonmarried, not between people who live alone and those who don't," Waite's own research of people in their 50s and 60s showed that single adults, "whether living alone, with children, or with others, described their emotional health more negatively than did the married people." Those who divorce or are widowed regain many of marriage's benefits if they remarry, and cohabitation provides some of marriage's emotional benefits, but for a shorter term. Breakups are more likely with live-in couples than with married ones, and cohabitors, Waite and Gallagher write, are generally less happy and less satisfied with their sex lives than the wed. In fact, the National Sex Survey led by Chicago

professors Edward Laumann and Robert Michael and another large sex study by University of Denver psychologists showed that married people have more sex than single people do, and they enjoy it more, both physically and emotionally.

Of course, not all marriages are happy, and Waite isn't suggesting that victims of domestic violence or chronic infidelity should stay married. Rather, she's targeting the relatively quick, no-fault divorces—people unhappy because one spouse works long hours, because they're taking care of a sick child, because they have money problems, those who wonder if something better is out there, if they could be more satisfied, if the thrill from their newly married days could be rekindled with a new partner. Those are the kinds of issues, Waite and Gallagher learned in focus groups they held to complement Waite's statistical analysis, that couples can move past if they decide to work on their marriages.

"Maybe by demanding perfection we're setting our standards too high," Waite says. "The very intense emotion people feel when they fall in love is physiologically by definition, fleeting. To think that another relationship will make you feel that way forever dooms you because it's not possible."

ANTIMARRIAGE CULTURE

The proclivity to leave results from the antimarriage culture. Waite believes, perpetuated by television and movies, athletes and other media stars, friends and relatives. If a struggling spouse heard "Hang in there, you're doing the right thing" more often than "You don't need to put up with this," Waite says, "at the margin somebody's going to listen." But instead friends encourage each other to leave, "and then it's easier for other people to leave because they have a role model."

NO-FAULT DIVORCE

No-fault divorce, which California instituted in 1969 and all states have in some form today, has made it easier to leave a marriage for less-than-dire reasons, In a no-fault divorce a spouse does not have to prove the other's wrongdoing, such as adultery, but only that there is no reasonable prospect of reconciliation. A spouse can receive a no-fault divorce even if the other spouse doesn't want it, and the couple may divorce out of court. Advocates see the process as a boon for women who want to leave abusive marriages without paying court fees, while critics such as Waite views no-fault as another cause of society's carefree attitude toward divorce. Then there's Barbara Dafoe Whitehead, AM'71, PhD'76, who codirects the National Marriage Project and writes extensively on family and child welfare. Although no-fault divorce "has unintentionally led to a legal system of divorce on demand," Whitehead wrote in the August/September 1997 *First Things: The Journal of Religion and Public Life*, a point/counterpoint piece in which she squared off with Waite coauthor Gallagher, she does not believe it should be eliminated as legislators in some states have attempted. Restoring a fault requirement, rather than forcing couples to work harder on their marriages, Whitehead wrote, would among other consequences deter "socially isolated and timorous women, often battered wives, from seeking divorce."

But no-fault, Whitehead concedes, has contributed to a culture more comfortable with divorce than it used to be. A 1998 *American Economic Review* study, Waite and Gallagher note in their book, showed that no-fault raised divorce rates by about 6.5 percent, accounting for 17 percent of the increase between 1968 and 1988. Today the chance that a marriage will end after 15 years—the figure widely cited as the "divorce rate"—is 43 percent, according to the National Center for Health Statistics' provisional 2001 numbers. While legislators in states such as Iowa and New Mexico have introduced measures to eliminate no-fault, in 1997 Louisiana became the first state to institute optional "covenant marriages," more binding unions that require premarital counseling, forgo the no-fault divorce option, and mandate up to a two-year cooling-off period before a divorce. That waiting period is something Waite advocates. Rather than running to divorce lawyers, she suggests, couples should first try counseling, or—because many men in her focus groups didn't like the idea of paying someone they weren't sure was committed to saving their marriage—seek out a religious leader or a marriage class.

After arguing so heavily for marriage and against divorce, it's more than a bit surprising to learn that—years before she began research on the subject Waite was divorced herself. Married as Michigan State undergraduates, she and her first husband split after four years. "We realized we wanted to live different kinds of lives," she says. Which may sound like one of those flippant reasons to divorce, but for people married a short time who have no children, she argues, "it's very different. You're not leaving somebody who's financially dependent, you haven't built years of friendships, you don't have kids, you're not as much a working single unit as people who are married for a long time." It's what demographer Pamela Paul would call a "starter marriage," which she defines in *The Starter Marriage and the Future of Matrimony* (Villard, 2002) as a union lasting live years or less and producing no children. Census Bureau statistics show that in 1998 more than 3 million 18- to 29-year-olds were divorced. In 1962, Paul notes, there were 253,000 divorced 25- to 29-year-olds, In fact, a 2001 Center for Disease Control and Prevention report shows, 20 percent of first-marriage divorces now occur within five years.

PARENTAL CONFLICT

Many of those marriages, like Waite's first, are childless. But once spouses have children, the divorce outlook changes. Researchers disagree whether children of unhappily married couples are better off if the parents stay together or divorce. After analyzing the studies, Waite and Gallagher conclude that children are usually *not* better off when unhappy spouses divorce. Marital dissatisfaction, they write, "is probably not in and of itself psychologically damaging for children: what count, is whether, how often, and how intensely parents fight in front of their children both before and after divorce." And while divorce may end marital conflict for adults, it doesn't stop "what really

bothers kids: parental conflict," they write. Children of divorce also have less money, live in poorer neighborhoods, go to poorer schools, and do worse in school than children of married parents—even if those marriages have a high degree of conflict. Divorce-for-the-children advocates point to a 1991 study showing that kids with mental health problems, such as anxiety or depression, are usually affected more by home conflict before the divorce than after it. But study author Andrew Cherlin, of Johns Hopkins University, re-examined the issue in two later studies and concluded, Waite and Gallagher write, that "the divorce itself does have additional long-term negative effects on children's psychological well-being." Twenty-three-year-olds whose parents divorced before they turned 16, Cherlin found, had poorer mental health than children from intact families.

Waite has two children with her second husband of 30 years, Chicago sociology professor Ross Stolzenberg, who does research on the effects of work, and is the editor of *Sociological Methodology*, the research methods journal of the American Sociological Association. Their 24-year-old daughter is married, lives in Israel, and has a two-year-old child. Their 18-year-old daughter lives at home and has cerebral palsy, which has strained the family at times. "When it was terrible we all had emotional responses," Waite says, "but everybody has times like that."

Waite didn't begin promoting marriage because of an underlying ideology. She actually stumbled upon the topic. In the early 1990s she and a colleague studied the relationship between marital status and mortality for the National Institutes of health. Controlling for age, they found that when both men and women became divorced or widowed, they were more likely to die than if they were married. Before writing up the study for a scientific journal Waite reviewed existing literature to see "what it might be about marriage that increases chances for living." She found a lot of material on physical and emotional health related to marriage. Then in 1995 Waite was elected president of the Population Association of America, a society of professionals using population data, and was asked to give a "big picture" address to the group. By then she was researching sexual behavior in different kinds of unions—couples dating, cohabiting, married. At the same time a colleague from the RAND Corporation, whose Population Research Center Waite had directed, was studying marriage and health issues, and Waite read additional studies showing that married men had higher earnings than other men. "I put all this stuff together and realized that the people working on wages don't know anything about the sex stuff and so on," she says. "There's a general pattern here that nobody's noticed. All of the big things in life—good outcomes for children, health, long life—depend on marriage." So marriage's many rewards became her talk, which was published in *Demography*, the association's journal. A Harvard University Press editor proposed she turn it into a book called *The Case for Marriage*.

AN APOLITICAL BOOK

A colleague suggested Gallagher as a cowriter, someone to help make the research accessible to lay readers. Waite had read

Gallagher's work and was "impressed by how carefully and accurately she represented the social-science research." During the writing, Gallagher "always deferred to me on the facts," Waite says, and because of their differing politics they kept certain topics, such as gay marriage, out of the book altogether. "In some sense I was naive to think others would just listen to the arguments and evidence," Waite says. "But some people inferred from [Gallagher's] other life"—that is, as a conservative writer and activist—"that the book was political. But I wrote it, and I'm [professionally] apolitical."

Then Wade Horn, assistant secretary for children and families in the U.S. Department of Health and Human Services, read the book. Horn, a Ph.D. in clinical psychology and past president of the National Fatherhood Initiative, which promotes responsibility and marriage, says Waite's empirical research helped to provide a nonideological basis for Bush's "healthy marriage" initiative for welfare recipients. "Linda's research made the case that marriage matters for the community and for children." Horn says. "Now we have to figure out what we're going to do about it." Bush's measure, part of the welfare-reform package approved by the House and still winding through Senate committees in mid-September, would provide money to slate or community governments or organizations for marriage-strengthening projects, such as conflict-management or marriage courses. Although it's been portrayed as an effort to impose marriage on welfare recipients to solve their problems, the initiative, Horn says, would actually target people already considering marriage. More than two-thirds of unmarried urban couples with children are "actively considering marriage," says Horn, "but we never ask them" about it and point them to resources that might help them get there. Funding different approaches in different places, Horn hopes some ideas prove successful and in time a good model might emerge.

So how does Waite feel about providing conservatives with more fuel for their traditional-family arguments? To Waite, it just so happens that a specific political movement has found in her a researcher whose message they like. As Horn puts it. "Marriage is not an institution that's the sole purview of any aspect of the political spectrum. As a real empiricist [Waite] didn't set out to prove an ideological point. She looked at the evidence and made a conclusion."

LOOKING FORWARD

Those pro-family conclusions have taken her far. Besides *The Case for Marriage* and its forthcoming sequel, she and fellow Chicago sociologist Barbara Schneider will soon publish a book on the Sloan 500 Family Study, which examined 500 American families—married and working parents with either adolescents or kindergartners. "Doing things with the family made parents more cheerful, friendly, and cooperative," Waite told the *Chicago Tribune*. "Parents who spend less time with the kids and spouse are stressed, anxious, and angry."

Again, the message seems plain. The benefits of family life, like those of marriage, are significant but require work. It's a lesson Waite hopes, through her research, that couples will hear.

Ms. Braverman is an associate editor of the University of Chicago Magazine. From "Healthy, Wealthy, & Wed," by Amy M. Braverman, University of Chicago Magazine, *October 2003, pages 32–39.*

Great Expectations

By: Polly Shulman

Summary: Has the quest to find the perfect soul mate done more harm than good? Psychologists provide insight into how the never-ending search for ideal love can keep you from enjoying a marriage or a healthy relationship that you already have.

Q: How do you turn a good relationship sour?

A: Pursue your inalienable right to happiness, hot sex, true love and that soul mate who must be out there somewhere.

Marriage is dead! The twin vises of church and law have relaxed their grip on matrimony. We've been liberated from the grim obligation to stay in a poisonous or abusive marriage for the sake of the kids or for appearances. The divorce rate has stayed constant at nearly 50 percent for the last two decades. The ease with which we enter and dissolve unions makes marriage seem like a prime-time spectator sport, whether it's Britney Spears in Vegas or bimbos chasing after the Bachelor.

Long live the new marriage! We once prized the institution for the practical pairing of a cash-producing father and a home-building mother. Now we want it all—a partner who reflects our taste and status, who sees us for who we are, who loves us for all the "right" reasons, who helps us become the person we want to be. We've done away with a rigid social order, adopting instead an even more onerous obligation: the mandate to find a perfect match. Anything short of this ideal prompts us to ask: Is this all there is? Am I as happy as I should be? Could there be somebody out there who's better for me? As often as not, we answer yes to that last question and fall victim to our own great expectations.

Nothing has produced more unhappiness than the concept of the soul mate.

That somebody is, of course, our soul mate, the man or woman who will counter our weaknesses, amplify our strengths and provide the unflagging support and respect that is the essence of a contemporary relationship. The reality is that few marriages or partnerships consistently live up to this ideal. The result is a commitment limbo, in which we care deeply for our partner but keep one stealthy foot out the door of our hearts. In so doing, we subject the relationship to constant review: Would I be happier, smarter, a better person with someone else? It's a painful modern quandary. "Nothing has produced more unhappiness than the concept of the soul mate," says Atlanta psychiatrist Frank Pittman.

Consider Jeremy, a social worker who married a businesswoman in his early twenties. He met another woman, a psychologist, at age 29, and after two agonizing years, left his wife for her. But it didn't work out—after four years of cohabitation, and her escalating pleas to marry, he walked out on her, as well. Jeremy now realizes that the relationship with his wife was solid and workable but thinks he couldn't have seen that 10 years ago, when he left her. "There was always someone better around the corner—and the safety and security of marriage morphed into boredom and stasis. The allure of willing and exciting females was too hard to resist," he admits. Now 42 and still single, Jeremy acknowledges, "I hurt others, and I hurt myself."

Like Jeremy, many of us either dodge the decision to commit or commit without fully relinquishing the right to keep looking—opting for an arrangement psychotherapist Terrence Real terms "stable ambiguity." "You park on the border of the relationship, so you're in it but not of it," he says. There are a million ways to do that: You can be in a relationship but not be sure it's really the right one, have an eye open for a better deal or something on the side, choose someone impossible or far away.

Yet commitment and marriage offer real physical and financial rewards. Touting the benefits of marriage may sound like conservative policy rhetoric, but nonpartisan sociological research backs it up: Committed partners have it all over singles, at least on average. Married people are more financially stable, according to Linda Waite, a sociologist at the University of Chicago and a coauthor of The Case for Marriage: Why Married People are Happier, Healthier and Better Off. Both married men and married women have more assets on average than singles; for women, the differential is huge.

We're in commitment limbo: We care deeply for our partner but keep one stealthy foot out the door of our heart.

The benefits go beyond the piggy bank. Married people, particularly men, tend to live longer than people who aren't married. Couples also live better: When people expect to stay together, says Waite, they pool their resources, increasing their individual standard of living. They also pool their expertise—in cooking, say, or financial management. In general, women improve men's health by putting a stop to stupid bachelor tricks and bugging their husbands to exercise and eat their vegetables. Plus, people who aren't comparing their partners to someone else in bed have less trouble performing and are more emotionally satisfied with sex. The relationship doesn't have to be wonderful for life to get better, says Waite: The statistics hold true for mediocre marriages as well as for passionate ones.

The pragmatic benefits of partnership used to be foremost in our minds. The idea of marriage as a vehicle for self-fulfillment and happiness is relatively new, says Paul Amato, professor of sociology, demography and family studies at Penn State University. Surveys of high school and college students 50 or 60 years ago found that most wanted to get married in order to have children or own a home. Now, most report that they plan to get married for love. This increased emphasis on emotional fulfillment within marriage leaves couples ill-prepared for the realities they will probably face.

Because the early phase of a relationship is marked by excitement and idealization, "many romantic, passionate couples expect to have that excitement forever," says Barry McCarthy, a clinical psychologist and coauthor—with his wife, Emily McCarthy—of Getting It Right the First Time: How to Build a Healthy Marriage. Longing for the charged energy of the early days, people look elsewhere or split up.

Flagging passion is often interpreted as the death knell of a relationship. You begin to wonder whether you're really right for each other after all. You're comfortable together, but you don't really connect the way you used to. Wouldn't it be more honest—and braver—to just admit that it's not working and call it off? "People are made to feel that remaining in a marriage that doesn't make you blissfully happy is an act of existential cowardice," says Joshua Coleman, a San Francisco psychologist.

Coleman says that the constant cultural pressure to have it all—a great sex life, a wonderful family—has made people ashamed of their less-than-perfect relationships and question

whether such unions are worth hanging on to. Feelings of dissatisfaction or disappointment are natural, but they can seem intolerable when standards are sky-high. "It's a recent historical event that people expect to get so much from individual partners," says Coleman, author of Imperfect Harmony, in which he advises couples in lackluster marriages to stick it out—especially if they have kids. "There's an enormous amount of pressure on marriages to live up to an unrealistic ideal."

Michaela, 28, was drawn to Bernardo, 30, in part because of their differences: She'd grown up in European boarding schools, he fought his way out of a New York City ghetto. "Our backgrounds made us more interesting to each other," says Michaela. "I was a spoiled brat, and he'd been supporting himself from the age of 14, which I admired." Their first two years of marriage were rewarding, but their fights took a toll. "I felt that because he hadn't grown up in a normal family, he didn't grasp basic issues of courtesy and accountability," says Michaela. They were temperamental opposites: He was a screamer, and she was a sulker. She recalls, "After we fought, I needed to be drawn out of my corner, but he took that to mean that I was a cold bitch." Michaela reluctantly concluded that the two were incompatible.

In a society hell-bent on individual achievement and autonomy, working on a difficult relationship may get short shrift.

In fact, argue psychologists and marital advocates, there's no such thing as true compatibility.

"Marriage is a disagreement machine," says Diane Sollee, founder of the Coalition for Marriage, Family and Couples Education. "All couples disagree about all the same things. We have a highly romanticized notion that if we were with the right person, we wouldn't fight." Discord springs eternal over money, kids, sex and leisure time, but psychologist John Gottman has shown that long-term, happily married couples disagree about these things just as much as couples who divorce.

"There is a mythology of 'the wrong person,'" agrees Pittman. "All marriages are incompatible. All marriages are between people from different families, people who have a different view of things. The magic is to develop binocular vision, to see life through your partner's eyes as well as through your own."

The realization that we're not going to get everything we want from a partner is not just sobering, it's downright miserable. But it is also a necessary step in building a mature relationship, according to Real, who has written about the subject in How Can I Get Through to You: Closing the Intimacy Gap Between Men and Women. "The paradox of intimacy is that our ability to stay close rests on our ability to tolerate solitude inside a relationship," he says. "A central aspect of grown-up love is grief. All of us long for—and think we deserve—perfection." We can hardly be blamed for striving for bliss and self-fulfillment in our romantic lives—our inalienable right to the pursuit of happiness is guaranteed in the first blueprint of American society.

This same respect for our own needs spurred the divorce-law reforms of the 1960s and 1970s. During that era, "The culture shifted to emphasize individual satisfaction, and marriage was part of that," explains Paul Amato, who has followed more than 2,000 families for 20 years in a long-term study of marriage and divorce. Amato says that this shift did some good by freeing people from abusive and intolerable marriages. But it had an unintended side effect: encouraging people to abandon relationships that may be worth salvaging. In a society hell-bent on individual achievement and autonomy, working on a difficult relationship may get short shrift, says psychiatrist Peter Kramer, author of Should You Leave?

We get the divorce rate that we deserve as a culture, says Peter Kramer.

"So much of what we learn has to do with the self, the ego, rather than giving over the self to things like a relationship," Kramer says. In our competitive world, we're rewarded for our individual achievements rather than for how we help others. We value independence over cooperation, and sacrifices for values like loyalty and continuity seem foolish. "I think we get the divorce rate that we deserve as a culture."

The steadfast focus on our own potential may turn a partner into an accessory in the quest for self-actualization, says Maggie Robbins, a therapist in New York City. "We think that this person should reflect the beauty and perfection that is the inner me—or, more often, that this person should compensate for the yuckiness and mess that is the inner me," says Robbins. "This is what makes you tell your wife, 'Lose some weight—you're making me look bad,' not 'Lose some weight, you're at risk for diabetes.'"

Michaela was consistently embarrassed by Bernardo's behavior when they were among friends. "He'd become sullen and withdrawn—he had a shifty way of looking off to the side when he didn't want to talk. I felt like it reflected badly on me," she admits. Michaela left him and is now dating a wealthy entrepreneur. "I just thought there had to be someone else out there for me."

The urge to find a soul mate is not fueled just by notions of romantic manifest destiny. Trends in the workforce and in the media create a sense of limitless romantic possibility. According to Scott South, a demographer at SUNY-Albany, proximity to potential partners has a powerful effect on relationships. South and his colleagues found higher divorce rates among people living in communities or working in professions where they encounter lots of potential partners—people who match them in age, race and education level. "These results hold true not just for unhappy marriages but also for happy ones," says South.

The temptations aren't always living, breathing people. According to research by psychologists Sara Gutierres and Douglas Kenrick, both of Arizona State University, we find reasonably attractive people less appealing when we've just seen a hunk or a hottie—and we're bombarded daily by images of gorgeous models and actors. When we watch Lord of the Rings, Viggo Mortensen's kingly mien and Liv Tyler's elfin charm can make our husbands and wives look all too schlumpy.

Kramer sees a similar pull in the narratives that surround us. "The number of stories that tell us about other lives we could lead—in magazine articles, television shows, books—has increased enormously. We have an enormous reservoir of possibilities," says Kramer.

And these possibilities can drive us to despair. Too many choices have been shown to stymie consumers, and an array of alternative mates is no exception. In an era when marriages were difficult to dissolve, couples rated their marriages as more satisfying than do today's couples, for whom divorce is a clear option, according to the National Opinion Research Center at the University of Chicago.

While we expect marriage to be "happily ever after," the truth is that for most people, neither marriage nor divorce seem to have a decisive impact on happiness. Although Waite's research shows that married people are happier than their single counterparts, other studies have found that after a couple years of marriage, people are just about as happy (or unhappy) as they were before settling down. And assuming that marriage will automatically provide contentment is itself a surefire recipe for misery.

"Marriage is not supposed to make you happy. It is supposed to make you married," says Pittman. "When you are all the way in your marriage, you are free to do useful things, become a better person." A committed relationship allows you to drop pretenses and seductions, expose your weaknesses, be yourself—and know that you will be loved, warts and all. "A real relationship is the collision of my humanity and yours, in all its joy and limitations," says Real. "How partners handle that collision is what determines the quality of their relationship."

Such a down-to-earth view of marriage is hardly romantic, but that doesn't mean it's not profound: An authentic relationship with another person, says Pittman, is "one of the first steps toward connecting with the human condition—which is necessary if you're going to become fulfilled as a human being." If we accept these humble terms, the quest for a soul mate might just be a noble pursuit after all.

Polly Shulman is a freelance writer in New York City.

THE BATTLE OVER GAY MARRIAGE

**IT'S OFFICIAL: GAYS CAN MARRY IN MASSACHUSETTS COME MAY.
A TIME REPORT ON HOW IT HAPPENED, WHAT IT MEANS—
AND HOW IT MAY PLAY OUT IN THE RACE FOR THE WHITE HOUSE**

By John Cloud

OUR MARRIAGES OFTEN PROVOKE us to throw the china and utter the unforgivables. The context is usually personal, not political, but either way, passions run high. In May, barring some unforeseen procedural hindrance, gay couples will wed for the first time ever in the U.S. They will have that opportunity by order of the Massachusetts Supreme Judicial Court, which ruled last week that it is unconstitutional to deny them marriage licenses. Gays and lesbians across the country celebrated. Hundreds of gay people have already called or e-mailed town clerk Doug Johnstone in Provincetown, Mass., to ask when they can marry. One of the licenses Johnstone's office will issue will be his own. After 25 years together, he and his partner will finally have the chance to say their vows before the commonwealth.

Many other Americans are worried that even though a freedom has been granted, an institution has been threatened. "If we have homosexual marriage mainstream, I can't even describe to you what our culture will be like," warns Sandy Rios, president of Concerned Women for America, one of the leading anti-gay-marriage organizations. Many conservatives object that such a monumental social change was sanctioned by

such a small group—four of seven judges on the Massachusetts court. "We're hearing from people throughout the country," says a hoarse Glenn Stanton, spokesman for Focus on the Family, a conservative group in Colorado Springs, Colo. "They don't know which to be more outraged at—the death of marriage or the death of democracy."

Marriage may or may not be dead, but democracy is doing fine. The court decision has intensified efforts to pass a U.S. constitutional amendment banning gay marriage. One version of the amendment already has more than 100 cosponsors in Congress. (Two-thirds of both houses will be required to pass the amendment, which will then have to be ratified by at least three-quarters—38—of the states.) Conservative activists will make sure that voters hear a lot about gay marriage between now and November since the likely Democratic nominee for President, Senator John Kerry, comes from Massachusetts. By unhappy coincidence, the Democrats will also hold their convention in Boston this summer. "It could be like Chicago 1968," says gay-marriage foe Ray Flynn, a former Democratic mayor of Boston and ambassador to the Vatican, who is now president of Your Catholic Voice.

"The country will see the party as taken over by the radical left."

Last Thursday, at various campaign stops, Kerry was forced to say—over and over, to the point of understandable exasperation—that he opposes gay marriage and disagrees with his state's court ruling. But he also favors civil unions for gay couples and would vote against a U.S. constitutional amendment. You can find a consistent line here: Kerry thinks the matter should be left to states. But in a debate as raw as the one over same-sex unions, President Bush's simple position—marriage should be between a man and a woman—will be easier to explain, not least because a clear majority of Americans also hold it. In a TIME/CNN poll conducted last week, 62% of respondents said they oppose the legalization of same-sex marriage; less than a third favor it.

But the President remembers the lessons of 1992, when moderate voters punished his father for a G.O.P. convention loaded with extremist declamations on the culture wars. Bush the son is careful to avoid coarse language about gays and lesbians. As Air Force One flew to South Carolina last week, the President made clear his opposition to gay marriage but added, "I'm not

Gay Marriage: A History

1901 Murray Hall, a prominent Tammany Hall politician, masquerades as a man over a 30-year period and twice marries a woman. Not until death comes, in 1901, is it discovered that Hall is a woman.

1969 The Rev. Troy Perry of the Metropolitan Community Church, a Los Angeles–based church founded for gay, bisexual and transgender people, begins conducting same-sex marriage ceremonies that he calls holy unions.

1971 Jack Baker and his partner, James McConnell, both 28, unsuccessfully sue for a marriage license in Minnesota. A judge lets them acquire a legal relationship by allowing McConnell to adopt Baker.

1989 Denmark becomes the first country to recognize same-sex unions, allowing couples to register as partners.

1991 Three same-sex couples in Hawaii sue the state for the right to get married. Before the courts can issue a final ruling, the voters in 1998 amend the state constitution to ensure marriage is limited to couples of the opposite sex.

1994 IKEA airs a groundbreaking television commercial in the U.S. that features a gay male couple shopping together for furniture.

1994 Two characters on the TV show *Northern Exposure,* innkeepers Ron and Erick, are married. But prime time is not ready for everything: the two men do not kiss as the ceremony ends.

1996 Two characters on NBC's *Friends,* Ross's ex-wife and her girlfriend, get married. Newt Gingrich's sister Candace performs the TV ceremony.

1996 President Clinton signs the Defense of Marriage Act, denying federal recognition of same-sex marriage.

1998 In response to a court case brought by a male couple seeking to marry, Alaska amends its constitution to ban same-sex marriage.

2000 Governor Howard Dean of Vermont signs a law permitting civil unions between same-sex partners. Vermont is the first state to legally recognize same-sex unions.

2000 The Netherlands is the first country to allow same-sex couples the right to marry, providing the benefits that come with a civil marriage. The first couples marry in April 2001.

2002 The first same-sex union is announced in the *New York Times*. The partners are Daniel Andrew Gross and Steven Goldstein, and their civil-union ceremony takes place in Vermont.

2003 Belgium joins the Netherlands in recognizing marriage between same-sex couples.

2003 Two Canadian provinces, Ontario and British Columbia, permit same-sex marriage.

2003 *Bride's* magazine runs a one-page article on same-sex weddings. This is the first time that a major bridal magazine has published a piece on the subject.

2003 The Supreme Judicial Court of Massachusetts rules that the commonwealth's constitution protects the right of homosexual couples to marry.

2004 The Massachusetts court rules that mere civil unions are discriminatory, thereby paving the way for same-sex marriages to start taking place in May.

against anybody," according to Jim De-Mint, a Republican Congressman who was aboard. "If some people want to have a contract, that's O.K., but marriage is the foundation of society."

Though it was an offhand comment, the idea that Bush might favor some kind of "contract" for gay couples—presumably a type of state recognition—is astonishing when you look back at the brief history of the gay-marriage debate. As recently as 1993, when the Hawaii Supreme Court issued the first appellate-court ruling in favor of gay marriage (a ruling that never took effect because Hawaiians voted to amend their constitution), even domestic partnerships were still considered radical. Only a few liberal municipalities offered them—Berkeley and West Hollywood in California, for example—and they didn't cover much. You could get a certificate suitable for framing and the assurance that a hospital within city limits would let you visit a sick partner. That was about it. FORTUNE 500 companies were only be-

ginning to allow partners of gay and lesbian employees to buy into health insurance plans. Most big cities didn't offer their employees such arrangements; in 1993 plans to extend health benefits to same-sex partners of city employees in Atlanta and Seattle caused great public consternation.

Today municipalities routinely invite partners of gay employees to join health plans. Kansas City, Kans., became the latest to do so just last week. The website of the Human Rights Campaign, the nation's largest gay political group, now lists 7,414 U.S. employers that offer domestic-partner benefits. And New Jersey, Hawaii, California and Vermont have established statewide registries for gay couples. Until last week, Vermont's law was the most famous (thanks to former Governor Howard Dean) as well as the most sweeping. That state's civil unions go well beyond the limited package of benefits usually associated with domestic partnerships and offer everything except the word marriage—inherit-

ance rights, joint state-tax filings, joint adoptions, the whole show. But not the word marriage.

Which is where things stood until last week. The Massachusetts decision laid out the case for why, in the majority's opinion, everything but marriage is not enough. The state senate had asked the court if it could establish civil unions to meet the constitutional requirement of equality for gay couples set forth in an earlier ruling. "The answer," the court replied, "is 'No.'" Why not? "Because the proposed law [establishing civil unions] by its express terms forbids same-sex couples entry into civil marriage [and therefore] continues to relegate same-sex couples to a different status ... The history of our nation has demonstrated that separate is seldom, if ever, equal."

But in her dissent, Justice Martha Sosman pointed out that even if Massachusetts allowed gay marriages, those marriages would still not be fully equal since "differences in Federal law and the law of other States will frustrate the goal of complete equality." What she meant is that even after Zach and Brad marry in Massachusetts, the couple will not be married in, say, Alaska, which has a constitutional amendment prohibiting same-sex marriages. (In all, 39 states have laws or amendments restricting marriage to straight couples.) What's more, the couple will not be married in the eyes of the Federal Government, which enacted a law in 1996—supporters called it the Defense of Marriage Act—defining marriage as "only a legal union between one man and one woman." Zach will not be able to take advantage of the Family and Medical Leave Act to care for Brad when he is ill, nor will he be eligible for the surviving-spouse benefit offered by the Social Security Administration if Brad dies. In fact, Zach and Brad will not enjoy any of the 1,049 benefits and protections afforded to married couples by federal statutes.

Sosman wrote that "once the euphoria of [the case] subsides, the reality of the still less than truly equal status of same-sex couples will emerge." With all the practical differences between straight and gay unions, she argued, "it is eminently reasonable to give a different name to the legal status being conferred on same-sex couples by the proposed bill." But the majority dismissed that reasoning. It countered that federal and other states' laws were "irrelevant … Courts define what is constitutionally permissible, and the Massachusetts Constitution does not permit this type of labeling."

For gay-rights lawyers, the language was gratifying. They have tried to persuade Americans for years that they were not arguing for a "special right" called *gay* marriage but rather for simple equality. Exclusion from marriage was discrimination, they argued—even if it was a cushy, Vermont-syrup discrimination. For those attorneys, civil unions were, as the court itself said, a "type of labeling." The Massachusetts lawyers wanted no half measures: "It was always about marriage," says lead attorney Mary Bonauto of Gay and Lesbian Advocates and Defenders.

But it wasn't always about marriage. As recently as the early '90s, bringing marriage cases was considered foolish in gay legal circles. At least six court cases

arguing that gays should have the right to marry were filed in the 1970s, and all had promptly failed. None were filed in the 1980s, and by the early 1990s only a few gay intellectuals, like Andrew Sullivan, then editor of the *New Republic*, a center-left magazine of policy and politics based in Washington, were arguing for marriage. In the rest of the gay community, there was division, uncertainty, even among the attorneys at Lambda Legal, the leading gay legal group. Gay radicals felt that marriage was a patriarchal, retro institution that gays should avoid altogether. Others felt that pressing for gay marriage was a strategic mistake— "too much, too soon," in the words of a gay lawyer familiar with the battles.

It was in this environment that Lambda declined to represent three couples who in 1991 sued Hawaii for the right to marry. By 1993 that case had quietly made its way to the state supreme court, and in May of that year the court startled the gay-rights movement—and drew international attention—when it ruled that barring gay people from getting married amounted to discrimination based on sex. (The court sent the case back to trial, but by 1998 the state constitutional amendment had passed, and no gay couples ever wed in the Aloha State.)

After the Hawaii ruling, Lambda reversed course. One of its top attorneys, Evan Wolfson, began traveling the country to speak on gay marriage. Both gay and straight audiences needed convincing that it wasn't a distant fantasy. "I spoke in churches, gay organizations, the Federalist Society. I spoke in almost every state in the country. This went on for years. And the real thing that started to make the big difference is when we started to believe it could happen," says Wolfson, 47, who now runs his own project called Freedom to Marry. "And once that happened—after Hawaii, after this was being debated in California and Vermont—we saw a surge of people who had not been particularly active in the movement now come into it." High-profile losses in California and other states were eventually followed by a halfway win in Vermont and then, of course, a full victory last week in Massachusetts.

AS WOLFSON WAS TRYING TO PROMOTE same-sex marriage, Matt Daniels was becoming convinced that it would damage the institution of the family. Daniels, 40, runs the Alliance for Marriage, which wrote the Federal Marriage Amendment now before Congress. Daniels comes to the issues of marriage and family breakdown from a very personal place. His father walked out when he was 2, leaving his mom to work as a secretary. One night when Daniels was in third grade, she was assaulted on her way home. "She ends up with a broken back, disabled, on welfare, depressed," says Daniels, trailing off. "So I was basically raised on welfare."

Daniels got a scholarship to Dartmouth, but after college he had to return home to care for his mother, who was dying of congestive heart failure. (She passed away in 1990.) During that period, he began volunteering in homeless shelters, where he says he saw the consequences of family breakdown, including welfare dependency and youth crime. "And it's about that time that we began to see the court activity in Vermont," he recalls. "Already we had seen it in Hawaii." Daniels was deeply troubled by the prospect of gay marriage, he says, "because of the unique combination of gifts that the two genders bring to the raising of children. The family—defined as built on the union of male and female—from my perspective is the foundation of society. The United States could survive without ideologies on left and right, without the Democratic Party or the Republican Party, but if you look at social-science data, we cannot thrive if we continue to see the disintegration of the unit of the family."

By the late '90s, Daniels was working for the Boston-based Massachusetts Family Institute, an independent conservative group loosely affiliated with Focus on the Family. In Boston, he became friendly with the Rev. Dr. Ray Hammond, a physician turned pastor who had won national plaudits for helping inner-city youths in Boston. Eventually Daniels—with the help of Hammond and several other minority ministers—founded the Alliance for Marriage.

Although the alliance has a modest budget of $900,000 a year, compared

MAINLINE CHURCHES
Not Quite as Liberal as They Look

Readers of newspaper "Vows" columns, which have lately blossomed to include gay and lesbian ceremonies, may think that although the Catholic and evangelical churches regard same-sex wedlock as ungodly, *somebody* must be churning out gay marriages wholesale. In fact, no major church offers a ritual for full-fledged gay marriage. True, the old liberal Protestant mainline churches have over decades, bestow on thousands of couples alternative sanctions called union ceremonies or same-sex blessings. But even these are ferociously debated. Controversy over them—along with a new argument about whether to enter the national fight over marriage in its civil form—may soon rival the gay-ordination issue as liberal Protestantism's worst headache.

Mainline churches are sometimes more liberal regarding society at large than they are about themselves. Last November, for instance, Bishop Susan Hassinger, the top United Methodist Church official in New England, sent out a pastoral letter about the Massachusetts Supreme Judicial Court's initial ruling allowing gay civil marriages. She made two points. One was that the Methodists' Social Principles explicitly promote "basic human rights and civil liberties … for homosexual persons" and so should "imply support" for the civil decision. The other was that since the Principles define marriage *within the church* as being between a man and a women, "at this point in our denomination's common life, the covenant of marriage is reserved for heterosexual couples."

Many fellow Methodists may not even concede her first assertion. Among mainline churches, theirs have proved the least tolerant of any sort of gay commitment. Four years ago at a bitter denominational meeting, delegates emphatically sustained a ban on gay union ceremonies by Methodist ministers, one of whom had been defrocked when he went ahead anyway. At the Methodists' next conference in April, emboldened conservatives hope to pass some statement that not just Methodist marriages but all marriages should be hetero-only. "It's a timely, front-burner issue," says James Heidinger, publisher of the traditionalist magazine *Good News*.

In June the precise opposite may occur at the convention of the Presbyterian Church (U.S.A.). Unlike the Methodists, the Presbyterians upheld holy-union ceremonies back in 2001, and this June the denomination's pro-gay-rights faction will press for a liberal stance regarding the world at large.

The meetings of both churches will be heated, yet the combative mood may be tempered by the recent history of the Episcopal Church USA, where the gay-blessings fracas proved costly. The rites were commonly practiced in the church, and Episcopal bishops voted last August to designate communities that celebrate them as "within the bounds of our common life." That approval, along with the enthronement of openly gay bishop Gene Robinson, sparked a movement by conservatives to disassociate their dioceses from the main church leadership, which may result in something, like a schism. If they can, the other mainline denominations will try to avoid letting things go quite that far.

—By David Van Biema.
With reporting by Jill Underwood/Los Angeles

with $120 million for Focus on the Family, it has influence beyond its means. Just as Wolfson was promoting gay marriage when gays wouldn't listen, Daniels was suggesting a constitutional amendment to ban gay marriage when conservatives wouldn't listen. When the alliance held a press conference to announce the idea in the summer of 2001, Daniels says, "there wasn't any debate going on about a marriage amendment." But by the following May, the alliance had lined up a Congressman—a Democrat, actually—to introduce the Federal Marriage Amendment. Today it has 109 co-sponsors in the House and five in the Senate.

The amendment would limit marriage to opposite-sex couples, but it would not outlaw civil unions, which Daniels believes should be available to states. His moderation on that point is considered

apostasy on the right, and Daniels has had to battle more powerful groups that want the amendment to go further, explicitly banning not only gay marriages but any state's recognition of gay relationships. For the past few months, about 20 serious movement conservatives—stalwarts like former presidential candidate Gary Bauer, Louis Sheldon of the Traditional Values Coalition and Don Wildmon of the American Family Association—have strategized on how to toughen the language. Daniels, who says one conservative leader told him his multicultural alliance "looks like the bar scene from *Star Wars*," has not been invited.

Calling themselves the Arlington group because they first met last summer in that Washington suburb, these conservatives feel that "ideally," as Bauer said last week, "we would like an amendment that would make it unconstitutional to

have gay marriage or fake marriage, the civil unions." Realistically, however, they have concluded that such a sweeping amendment probably won't pass. It's very early in the process, but the White House seems to be leaning toward the more flexible language.

THE PROPOSED AMENDMENT GOT A BIG PUSH last week, and it is likely to get another in May, when pictures of lesbians kissing their brides will be broadcast round the world. (One caveat: there is still a slim chance that gay-marriage opponents in the Bay State—including G.O.P. Governor Mitt Romney—will find a way to stop the marriages before May. But the state's highest court is not likely to approve any delays, so stopping gay weddings would probably mean outright defiance of the court. Most observers don't think Romney would risk his future on an Orval Faubus ploy.)

By May the Bush machine will be in high gear. You can expect that if Kerry is the nominee, plenty of television commercials accusing Kerry of being a Massachusetts liberal will air during breaks from newscasts about the latest gay wedding. Another problem for Kerry may lie across the continent in California, a state any Democrat must carry to win the White House. This week assemblyman Mark Leno is expected to introduce a bill in the California legislature that would legalize gay marriage. Gay activists plan an all-out battle. "Our goal is to be the first state in the nation to [legalize gay marriage] through the democratic process as opposed to the courts," says Toni Broaddus of Equality California, the state's leading gay-advocacy group. The last thing the Democrats want in California is a conservative base energized by a bloody gay-marriage fight over the summer.

But it gets worse. Because of Massachusetts, other states will be considering constitutional amendments to ban same-sex marriage. In fact, some 20 states have already introduced (or are expected to introduce) such amendments, according to the Human Rights Campaign. "I fear all this will create a backlash so much more powerful than our community is prepared to handle," says Matt Foreman of the National Gay and Lesbian Task Force.

For now, Kerry's advisers say they aren't worried their candidate will be mauled in the showdown. "The court has decided one thing, and Kerry has said he disagrees," says a senior Kerry adviser. Every time the Republicans bring up the issue, they give Kerry "the opportunity to highlight that his view isn't the traditional Massachusetts-liberal view." Kerry himself snapped last week, "I have the same position that Vice President Dick Cheney has. [The Republicans] ought to talk to Dick Cheney ... before they start playing games with this. And we'll find out just how political and how craven they are." Kerry was referring to Cheney's statement during the 2000 campaign that he believes the issue of rights for gay couples "is regulated by the states. I think different states are likely to come to different conclusions, and that's appropriate." Cheney's daughter is a lesbian, and many gays hoped he would openly support same-sex marriage. But last month Cheney told the Denver *Post* that he will support whatever position the President takes, even if that means backing a ban on gay marriages.

The gay-marriage debate, because it touches the emotional and social fabric that makes up family, can be brutal. Last March in Nebraska, the attorney general issued an opinion saying that under the state's constitution, gay people do not have the right to make burial arrangements for their partners. The generally civil members of the Massachusetts court were barely civil to one another by the time they issued their second opinion. In her ruling, Chief Justice Margaret Marshall said Justice Sosman, who had dissented, "so clearly misses the point that further discussion appears to be useless." It is a small sign that tempers are likely to flare when the national debate begins.

The Case for Staying Home

Caught between the pressures of the workplace and the demands of being a mom, more women are sticking with the kids

By Claudia Wallis

It's 6:35 in the morning, and Cheryl Nevins, 34, dressed for work in a silky black maternity blouse and skirt, is busily tending to Ryan, 2 1/2, and Brendan, 11 months, at their home in the leafy Edgebrook neighborhood of Chicago. Both boys are sobbing because Reilly, the beefy family dog, knocked Ryan over. In a blur of calm, purposeful activity, Nevins, who is 8 months pregnant, shoves the dog out into the backyard, changes Ryan's diaper on the family-room rug, heats farina in the microwave and feeds Brendan cereal and sliced bananas while crooning *Open, Shut Them* to encourage the baby to chew. Her husband Joe, 35, normally out the door by 5:30 a.m. for his job as a finance manager for Kraft Foods, makes a rare appearance in the morning muddle. "I do want to go outside with you," he tells Ryan, who is clinging to his leg, "but Daddy has to work every day except Saturdays and Sundays. That stinks."

At 7:40, Vera Orozco, the nanny, arrives to begin her 10 1/2-hour shift at the Nevinses'. Cheryl, a labor lawyer for the Chicago board of education, hands over the baby and checks her e-mail from the kitchen table. "I almost feel apprehensive if I leave for work without logging on," she confesses. Between messages, she helps Ryan pull blue Play-Doh from a container, then briefs Orozco on the morning's events: "They woke up early. Ryan had his poop this morning, this guy has not." Throughout the day, Orozco will note every meal and activity on a tattered legal pad on the kitchen counter so Nevins can stay up to speed.

Suddenly it's 8:07, and the calm mom shifts from cruise control into hyperdrive. She must be out the door by 8:10 to make the 8:19 train. Once on the platform, she punches numbers into her cell phone, checks her voice mail and then leaves a message for a co-worker. On the train, she makes more calls and proofreads documents. "Right now, work is crazy," says Nevins, who has been responsible for negotiating and administering seven agreements between the board and labor unions.

Nevins is "truly passionate" about her job, but after seven years, she's about to leave it. When the baby arrives, she will take off at least a year, maybe two, maybe five. "It's hard. I'm giving up a great job that pays well, and I have a lot of respect and authority," she says. The decision to stay home was a tough one, but most of her working-mom friends have made the same choice. She concludes, "I know it's the right thing."

TEN, 15 YEARS AGO, IT ALL SEEMED SO doable. Bring home the bacon, fry it up in a pan, split the second shift with some sensitive New Age man. But slowly the snappy, upbeat work-life rhythm has changed for women in high-powered posts like Nevins. The U.S. workweek still averages around 34 hours, thanks in part to a sluggish manufacturing sector. But for those in financial services, it's 55 hours; for top executives in big corporations, it's 60 to 70, says Catalyst, a research and consulting group that focuses on women in business. For dual-career couples with kids under 18, the combined work hours have grown from 81 a week in 1977 to 91 in 2002, according to the Families and Work Institute. E-mail, pagers and cell phones promised to allow execs to work from home. Who knew that would mean that home was no longer a sanctuary? Today BlackBerrys sprout on the sidelines of Little League games. Cell phones vibrate at the school play. And it's back to the e-mail after *Goodnight Moon*. "We are now the workaholism capital of the world, surpassing the Japanese," laments sociologist Arlie Hochschild, author of *The Time Bind: When Work Becomes Home and Home Becomes Work*.

Meanwhile, the pace has quickened on the home front, where a mother's job has expanded to include managing a packed schedule of child-enhancement activities. In their new book *The Mommy Myth*, Susan Douglas, a professor of communication studies at the University of Michigan, and Meredith Michaels, who teaches philosophy at Smith College, label the phenomenon the New Momism. Nowadays, they write, our culture insists that "to be a remotely decent mother, a woman has to devote her entire physical, psychological, emotional, and intellectual being, 24/7, to her children." It's a standard of success that's "impossible to meet," they argue. But that sure doesn't stop women from trying.

For most mothers—and fathers, for that matter—there is little choice but to persevere on both fronts to pay the bills. Indeed, 72% of mothers with children under 18 are in the work force—a figure that is up sharply from 47% in 1975 but has held steady since 1997. And thanks in part to a dodgy economy, there's growth in another category, working women whose husbands are unemployed, which has risen to 6.4% of all married couples.

But in the professional and managerial classes, where higher incomes permit more choices, a reluctant revolt is under way. Today's women execs are less willing to play the jug-

gler's game, especially in its current high-speed mode, and more willing to sacrifice paychecks and prestige for time with their family. Like Cheryl Nevins, most of these women are choosing not so much to drop out as to stop out, often with every intention of returning. Their mantra: You can have it all, just not all at the same time. Their behavior, contrary to some popular reports, is not a June Cleaver–ish embrace of old-fashioned motherhood but a new, nonlinear approach to building a career and an insistence on restoring some kind of sanity. "What this group is staying home from is the 80-hour-a-week job," says Hochschild. "They are committed to work, but many watched their mothers and fathers be ground up by very long hours, and they would like to give their own children more than they got. They want a work-family balance."

Because these women represent a small and privileged sector, the dimensions of the exodus are hard to measure. What some experts are zeroing in on is the first-ever drop-off in workplace participation by married mothers with a child less than 1 year old. That figure fell from 59% in 1997 to 53% in 2000. The drop may sound modest, but, says Howard Hayghe, an economist at the Bureau of Labor Statistics, "that's huge," and the figure was roughly the same in 2002. Significantly, the drop was mostly among women who were white, over 30 and well educated.

Census data reveal an uptick in stay-at-home moms who hold graduate or professional degrees—the very women who seemed destined to blast through the glass ceiling. Now 22% of them are home with their kids. A study by Catalyst found that 1 in 3 women with M.B.A.s are not working full-time (it's 1 in 20 for their male peers). Economist and author Sylvia Ann Hewlett, who

teaches at Columbia University, says she sees a brain drain throughout the top 10% of the female labor force (those earning more than $55,000). "What we have discovered in looking at this group over the last five years," she says, "is that many women who have any kind of choice are opting out."

Other experts say the drop-out rate isn't climbing but is merely more visible now that so many women are in high positions. In 1971 just 9% of medical degrees, 7% of law degrees and 4% of M.B.A.s were awarded to women; 30 years later, the respective figures were 43%, 47% and 41%.

■ THE GENERATION FACTOR

FOR AN OLDER GROUP OF FEMALE PROFESSIONALS who came of age listening to Helen Reddy roar, the exodus of younger women can seem disturbingly regressive. Fay Clayton, 58, a partner in a small Chicago law firm, watched in dismay as her 15-person firm lost three younger women who left after having kids, though one has since returned part time. "I fear there is a generational split and possibly a step backwards for younger women," she says.

Others take a more optimistic view. "Younger women have greater expectations about the work-life balance," says Joanne Brundage, 51, founder and executive director of Mothers & More, a mothers' support organization with 7,500 members and 180 chapters in the U.S. While boomer moms have been reluctant to talk about their children at work for fear that "people won't think you're a professional," she observes, younger women "feel more entitled to ask for changes and advocate for themselves." That sense of confidence is reflected in the evolution of

THE PROPORTION OF WORKING MARRIED MOTHERS WITH CHILDREN UNDER AGE 3 DROPPED FROM 61% IN 1997 TO 58% IN 2002 her organization's name. When Brundage founded it in Elmhurst, Ill., 17 years ago, it was sheepishly called FEMALE, for Formerly Employed Mothers at Loose Ends.

Brundage may be ignoring that young moms can afford to think flexibly about life and work while pioneering boomers first had to prove they could excel in high-powered jobs. But she's right about the generational difference. A 2001 survey by Catalyst of 1,263 men and women born from 1964 to 1975 found that Gen Xers "didn't want to have to make the kind of trade-offs the previous generation made. They're rejecting the stresses and sacrifices," says Catalyst's Paulette Gerkovich. "Both women and men rated personal and family goals higher than career goals."

A newer and larger survey, conducted late last year by the Boston-area marketing group Reach Advisors, provides more evidence of a shift in attitudes. Gen X (which it defined as those born from 1965 to 1979) moms and dads said they spent more time on child rearing and household tasks than did boomer parents (born from 1945 to 1964). Yet Gen Xers were much more likely than boomers to complain that they wanted more time. "At first we thought, Is this just a generation of whiners?" says Reach Advisors president James Chung. "But they really wish they had more time with their kids." In the highest household-income bracket ($120,000 and up), Reach Advisors found that 51% of Gen X moms were home full time, compared with 33% of boomer moms. But the younger stay-at-home moms were much more likely to say they intended to return to work: 46% of Gen Xers expressed that goal, compared with 34% of boomers.

Chung and others speculate that the attitude differences can be explained in part by forces that shaped each generation. While boomer women sought career opportunities that were unavailable to their mostly stay-at-home moms, Gen Xers were

the latchkey kids and the children of divorce. Also, their careers have bumped along in a roller-coaster, boom-bust economy that may have shaken their faith in finding reliable satisfaction at work.

Pam Pala, 35, of Salt Lake City, Utah, is in some ways typical. She spent years building a career in the heavily male construction industry, rising to the position of construction project engineer with a big firm. But after her daughter was born 11 months ago, she decided to stay home to give her child the attention Pala had missed as a kid. "I grew up in a divorced family. My mom couldn't take care of us because she had to work," she says. "We went to baby-sitters or stayed home alone and were scared and hid under the bathroom counter whenever the doorbell rang." Pala wants to return to work when her daughter is in school, and she desperately hopes she won't be penalized for her years at home. "I have a feeling that I'll have to start lower on the totem pole than where I left," she says. "It seems unfair."

■ **MATERNAL DESIRE AND DOUBTS**

DESPITE SUCH MISGIVINGS, MOST WOMEN who step out of their careers find expected delights on the home front, not to mention the enormous relief of no longer worrying about shortchanging their kids. Annik Miller, 32, of Minneapolis, Minn., decided not to return to her job as a business-systems consultant at Wells Fargo Bank after she checked out day-care options for her son Alex, now 11 months. "I had one woman look at me honestly and say she could promise that my son would get undivided attention eight times each day—four bottles and four diaper changes," says Miller. "I appreciated her honesty, but I knew I couldn't leave him."

Others appreciate a slower pace and being there when a child asks a tough question. In McLean, Va., Oakie Russell's son Dylan, 8, re-

cently inquired, out of the blue, "Mom, who is God's father?" Says Russell, 45, who gave up a dream job at PBS: "So, you're standing at the sink with your hands in the dishwater and you're thinking, 'Gee, that's really complicated. But I'm awfully glad I'm the one you're asking.'"

Psychologist Daphne de Marneffe speaks to these private joys in a new book, *Maternal Desire* (Little Brown). De Marneffe argues that feminists and American society at large have ignored the basic urge that most mothers feel to spend meaningful time with their children. She decries the rushed fragments of quality time doled out by working moms trying to do it all. She writes, "Anyone who has tried to 'fit everything in' can attest to how excruciating the five-minute wait at the supermarket checkout line becomes, let alone a child's slow-motion attempt to tie her own shoes when you're running late getting her to school." The book, which puts an idyllic gloss on staying home, could launch a thousand resignations.

What de Marneffe largely omits is the sense of pride and meaning that women often gain from their work. Women who step out of their careers can find the loss of identity even tougher than the loss of income. "I don't regret leaving, but a huge part of me is gone," says Bronwyn Towle, 41, who surrendered a demanding job as a Washington lobbyist to be with her two sons. Now when she joins her husband Raymond, who works at the U.S. Chamber of Commerce, at work-related dinners, she feels sidelined. "Everyone will be talking about what they're doing," says Towle, "and you say, 'I'm a stay-at-home mom.' It's conference-buzz kill."

Last year, after her youngest child went to kindergarten, Towle eased back into the world of work. She found a part-time job in a forward-thinking architectural firm but hopes to return to her field eventually. "I wish there was more part-time or job-sharing work," she says. It's a wish expressed by countless formerly working moms.

■ BUILDING ON-RAMPS

HUNTER COLLEGE SOCIOLOGIST Pamela Stone has spent the past few years interviewing 50 stay-at-home mothers in seven U.S. cities for a book on professional women who have dropped out. "Work is much more of a culprit in this than the more rosy view that it's all about discovering how great your kids are," says Stone. "Not that these mothers don't want to spend time with their kids. But many of the women I talked to have tried to work part time or put forth job-sharing plans, and they're shot down. Despite all the family-friendly rhetoric, the workplace for professionals is extremely, extremely inflexible."

That's what Ruth Marlin, 40, of New York City found even at the family-friendly International Planned Parenthood Federation. After giving birth to her second child, 15 months ago, she was allowed to ease back in part time. But Marlin, an attorney and a senior development officer, was turned down when she asked to make the part-time arrangement permanent. "With the job market contracted so much, the opportunities just aren't there anymore," says Marlin, who hates to see her $100,000 law education go to waste. "Back in the dotcom days, people just wanted employees to stay. There was more flexibility. Who knows? Maybe the market will change."

There are signs that in some corners it is changing. In industries that depend on human assets, serious work is being done to create more part-time and flexible positions. At PricewaterhouseCoopers, 10% of the firm's female partners are on a part-time schedule, according to the accounting firm's chief diversity of-ficer, Toni Riccardi. And, she insists, it's not career suicide: "A three-day week might slow your progress, but it won't prohibit you" from climbing the career ladder. The company has also begun to address the e-mail ball and chain. In December PWC shut down for 11 days over the holidays for the first time ever. "We realize people do need to rejuvenate," says Riccardi. "They don't, if their eye is on the BlackBerry and their hand is on a keyboard."

PWC is hardly alone. Last month economist Hewlett convened a task force of leaders from 14 companies and four law firms, including Goldman Sachs and Pfizer, to discuss what she calls the hidden brain drain of women and minority professionals. "We are talking about how to create off-ramps and on-ramps, slow lanes and acceleration ramps" so that workers can more easily leave, slow down or re-enter the work force, she explains.

"This is a war for talent," says Carolyn Buck Luce, a partner at the accounting firm Ernst & Young, who co-chairs the task force. Over the past 20 years, half of new hires at Ernst & Young have been women, she notes, and the firm is eager not only to keep them but to draw back those who have left to tend their children. This spring Deloitte Touche Tohmatsu will launch a Personal Pursuits program, allowing above-average performers to take up to five years of unpaid leave for personal reasons. Though most benefits will be suspended, the firm will continue to cover professional licensing fees for those on leave and will pay to send them for weeklong annual training sessions to keep their skills in shape. Such efforts have spawned their own goofy jargon. Professionals who return to their ex-employers are known as boomerangs, and the effort to reel them back in is called alumni relations.

One reason businesses are getting serious about the brain drain is demographics. With boomers nearing retirement, a shortfall of perhaps 10 million workers appears likely by 2010. "The labor shortage has a lot to do with it," says Melinda Wolfe, managing director and head of Goldman Sachs' global leadership and diversity.

Will these programs work? Will part-time jobs really be part time, as opposed to full-time jobs paid on a partial basis? Will serious professionals who shift into a slow lane be able to pick up velocity when their kids are grown? More important, will corporate culture evolve to a point where employees feel genuinely encouraged to use these options? Anyone who remembers all the talk about flex time in the 1980s will be tempted to dismiss the latest ideas for making the workplace family-friendly. But this time, perhaps, the numbers may be on the side of working moms—along with many working dads who are looking for options.

On-ramps, slow lanes, flexible options and respect for all such pathways can't come soon enough for mothers eager to set examples and offer choices for the next generation. Terri Laughlin, 38, a stay-at-home mom and former psychology professor at the University of Nebraska at Lincoln, was alarmed a few weeks ago when her daughters Erin, 8, and Molly, 6, announced their intentions to marry men "with enough money so we can stay at home." Says Laughlin: "I want to make sure they realize that although it's wonderful staying at home, that's only one of many options. What I hope to show them is that at some point I can re-create myself and go back to work."

An Inner-City Renaissance

The nation's ghettos are making surprising strides. Will the gains last?

Take a stroll around Harlem these days, and you'll find plenty of the broken windows and rundown buildings that typify America's ghettos. But you'll also see a neighborhood blooming with signs of economic vitality. New restaurants have opened on the main drag, 125th Street, not far from a huge Pathmark supermarket, one of the first chains to offer an alternative to overpriced bodegas when it moved in four years ago. There's a Starbucks—and nearby, Harlem U.S.A., a swank complex that opened in 2001 with a nine-screen Magic Johnson Theatres, plus Disney and Old Navy stores and other retail outlets. Despite the aftermath of September 11 and a sluggish economy, condos are still going up and brownstones are being renovated as the middle classes—mostly minorities but also whites—snap up houses that are cheap by Manhattan standards.

It's not just Harlem, either. Across the U.S., an astonishing economic trend got under way in the 1990s. After half a century of relentless decline, many of America's blighted inner cities have begun to improve. On a wide range of economic measures, ghettos and their surrounding neighborhoods actually outpaced the U.S. as a whole, according to a new study of the 100 largest inner cities by Boston's Initiative for a Competitive Inner City, a group founded in 1994 by Harvard University management professor Michael E. Porter.

Consider this: Median inner-city household incomes grew by 20% between 1990 and 2000, to a surprising $35,000 a year, the ICIC found, while the national median gained only 14%, to about $57,000. Inner-city poverty fell faster than poverty did in the U.S. as a whole, housing units and homeownership grew more quickly, and even the share of the population with high school degrees increased more. Employment growth didn't outdo the national average, with jobs climbing 1% a year between 1995 and 2001, vs. 2% nationally. Still, the fact that inner cities, which are 82% minority, created any jobs at all after decades of steady shrinkage is something of a miracle.

SCENT OF OPPORTUNITY

NOR ARE THE GAINS just the byproduct of the superheated economy of the late 1990s. Rather, they represent a fundamental shift in the economics of the inner city as falling crime rates and crowded suburbs lure the middle-class back to America's downtowns. After decades of flight out of inner cities, companies as diverse as Bank of America, Merrill Lynch, and Home Depot have begun to see them as juicy investment opportunities. National chains are opening stores, auto dealerships, and banks to tap into the unfulfilled demand of inner cities.

Wall Street, too, is jumping in, making loans and putting up equity for local entrepreneurs. "Smart businesspeople gravitate toward good opportunities, and it has become clear that inner cities are just that," says David W. Tralka, chairman of Merrill Lynch & Co.'s Business Financial Services group. In 2002, his group, which caters to small business, began formally targeting inner cities. It now offers financing and commercial mortgages for hundreds of inner-city entrepreneurs around the country.

Is it possible that America at last has started to solve one of its most intractable social ills? True, the progress so far is minuscule compared with the problems created by decades of capital flight, abysmal schools, and drug abuse. And some inner cities, like Detroit's, have made little sustained progress. Ghettos also have been hit by the joblessness of this latest recovery. The national poverty rate has jumped by nearly a percentage point since 2000, to 12.1% last year, so it almost certainly did likewise in inner cities, which the ICIC defined as census tracts with poverty rates of 20% or more.

But as the economy recovers, a confluence of long-term trends is likely to continue to lift inner cities for years. The falling crime rate across the country has been a key factor, easing fears that you take your life in your hands by setting foot in an inner city. At the same time, larger demographic shifts—aging boomers turned empty nesters, more gays and nontraditional households without children, homeowners fed up with long commutes—have propelled Americans back into cities. When they arrive, slums suddenly look like choice real estate at bargain prices.

BEYOND PHILANTHROPY

POLITICAL AND CIVIC LEADERS helped lay the groundwork, too. After floundering for decades following the exodus of factories to the suburbs in the 1950s, many cities finally found new economic missions in the 1990s, such as tourism, entertainment, finance, and services. This has helped boost the geographic desirability of inner-city areas. New state and federal policies brought private capital back, too, by putting teeth into anti-redlining laws and by switching housing subsidies from public projects to tax breaks for builders. As a result, neighborhoods like the predominantly African-American Leimert Park in South Central Los Angeles are becoming thriving enclaves.

The outcome has been a burst of corporate and entrepreneurial activity that already has done more to transform inner

Inner Cities and Their Residents ...

The Boston-based Initiative for a Competitive Inner City has completed the first-ever analysis of the 100-largest inner cities in the U.S. and finds the once-dismal picture brightening

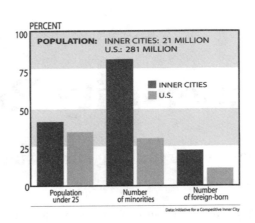

PERCENT

POPULATION: INNER CITIES: 21 MILLION
U.S.: 281 MILLION

■ INNER CITIES
■ U.S.

Population under 25 | Number of minorities | Number of foreign-born

Data: Initiative for a Competitive Inner City

...Did Better than the Nation As a Whole in the 90s...

Change between 1990 and 2000 Census data

	INNER CITIES	U.S.
Population	24%	13%
Household income	20%	14%
Housing unit growth	20%	13%
High school graduates*	55 to 61%	75 to 80%
College graduates*	10 to 13%	20 to 24%
Home ownership	29 to 32%	64 to 66%
Poverty rate	34 to 30%	13 to 12%

*Of those 25 and over

...Although There's Still A Long Way to Go

2000 Census data

	INNER CITIES	U.S.
High school graduates*	61%	80%
College graduates*	13%	24%
Poverty rate	31%	11.3%
Unemployment rate	12.8%	5.8%
Home ownership rate	32%	66%
Average household income	$34,755	$56,600
Aggregate household income	$250 billion	$6 trillion

Data: Initiative for a Competitive Inner City

cities than have decades of philanthropy and government programs. "What we couldn't get people to do on a social basis they're willing to do on an economic basis," says Albert B. Ratner, co-chairman of Forest City Enterprises Inc., a $5 billion real estate investment company that has invested in dozens of inner-city projects across the country.

EMERGING MARKETS

THE NEW VIEW OF GHETTOS began to take hold in the mid-1990s, when people such as Bill Clinton and Jesse Jackson started likening them to emerging markets overseas. Porter set up the ICIC in 1994 as an advocacy group to promote inner cities as overlooked investment opportunities. Since then, it has worked with a range of companies, including BofA, Merrill Lynch, Boston Consulting Group, and PricewaterhouseCoopers to analyze just how much spending power exists in inner cities.

The new study, due to be released on Oct. 16, uses detailed census tract data to paint the first comprehensive economic and demographic portrait of the 21 million people who live in the 100 largest inner cities. The goal, says Porter, "is to get market forces to bring inner cities up to surrounding levels."

Taken together, the data show an extraordinary renaissance under way in places long ago written off as lost causes. America's ghettos first began to form early in the last century, as blacks left Southern farms for factory jobs in Northern cities. By World War II, most major cities had areas that were up to 80% black, according to the 1993 book *American Apartheid*, co-authored by University of Pennsylvania sociology professor Douglas S. Massey and Nancy A. Denton, a sociology professor at the State University of New York at Albany. Ghettos grew faster after World War II as most blacks and Hispanics who could follow manufacturing jobs to the suburbs did so, leaving behind the poorest and most

un-employable. Immigrants poured in, too, although most tended to leave as they assimilated.

In this context, the solid gains the ICIC found in the 1990s represent an extraordinary shift in fortunes. One of the biggest changes has come in housing. As cities have become desirable places to live again, the number of inner-city housing units jumped by 20% in the 1990s, vs. 13% average for the U.S. as a whole.

A number of companies were quick to see the change. BofA, for example, has developed a thriving inner-city business since it first began to see ghettos as a growth market six years ago. In 1999 it pulled together a new unit called Community Development Banking, which focuses primarily on affordable housing for urban, mostly inner-city, markets, says CDB President Douglas B. Woodruff. His group's 300 associates are on track this year to make $1.5 billion in housing loans in 38 cities, from Baltimore to St. Louis.

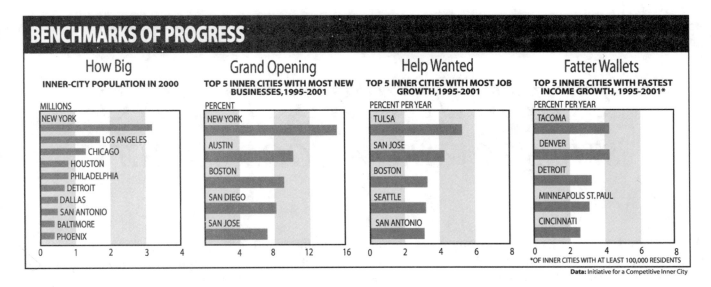

BENCHMARKS OF PROGRESS

How Big
INNER-CITY POPULATION IN 2000

MILLIONS
NEW YORK
LOS ANGELES
CHICAGO
HOUSTON
PHILADELPHIA
DETROIT
DALLAS
SAN ANTONIO
BALTIMORE
PHOENIX
0 1 2 3 4

Grand Opening
TOP 5 INNER CITIES WITH MOST NEW BUSINESSES, 1995-2001

PERCENT
NEW YORK
AUSTIN
BOSTON
SAN DIEGO
SAN JOSE
4 8 12 16

Help Wanted
TOP 5 INNER CITIES WITH MOST JOB GROWTH, 1995-2001

PERCENT PER YEAR
TULSA
SAN JOSE
BOSTON
SEATTLE
SAN ANTONIO
0 2 4 6 8

Fatter Wallets
TOP 5 INNER CITIES WITH FASTEST INCOME GROWTH, 1995-2001*

PERCENT PER YEAR
TACOMA
DENVER
DETROIT
MINNEAPOLIS ST. PAUL
CINCINNATI
0 2 4 6 8
*OF INNER CITIES WITH AT LEAST 100,000 RESIDENTS

Data: Initiative for a Competitive Inner City

They will do an additional $550 million in equity investments, mostly real estate.

SHELLED OUT

PENSION FUNDS AND other large investors are putting in cash, too. The Los Angeles County Employee Retirement Assn. has sunk $210 million into urban real estate since 2000, including $87 million in August for a bankrupt, 2,496-room apartment complex in Brooklyn, N.Y. The plan is to do things like fix the broken elevators, hire security guards, and kick out nonpaying tenants. "We believe there are opportunities that weren't there before or that we weren't aware of," says board member Bruce Perelman.

One question is whether the ICIC's findings represent not so much progress by the poor as their displacement by middle-class newcomers. In other words, inner-city incomes could be rising simply because affluent new home buyers jack up the average. But experts think gentrification explains only a small part of what's going on. "It's certainly a local phenomenon, but if you aggregate 100 inner cities, gentrification is a small trend," says ICIC research director Alvaro Lima, who spearheaded the study.

In Chicago, for instance, a $65 million redevelopment of the notorious Cabrini-Green housing project has replaced three slummy high-rises with mixed-income units. The area has a new library, new schools, and a new retail center featuring a major grocery store, Starbucks, and Blockbuster (BBI)—all staffed by scores of local residents. "The goal is not gentrification, it's to integrate the classes," says Phyllis L. Martin, the head of a local committee that's trying to lure more than $50 million in private capital to help the city replace 3,245 public housing units in another blighted area, Bronzeville.

"We're just beginning to undo all the damage"

Despite the brightening picture, the decay of most inner cities is so advanced that half a dozen years of progress makes only a dent. The degree of poverty—a measure of how many poor people there are in a census tract—fell 11% in 60 large cities in the 1990s, according to an analysis by U Penn's Massey that parallels ICIC's approach. While that's a significant decline, it only begins to offset the doubling of poverty concentrations in prior decades, he found. "The gains are the first positive news since at least the 1950s, but we're just beginning to undo all the damage," says Massey.

BADGE OF SHAME

WHAT'S MORE, too many inner cities remain untouched. More than a third of the ICIC's 100 cities lost jobs between 1995 and 2001. Detroit's ghetto has seen little new development and shed one-fifth of its jobs over this period. Residents did gain from the booming auto industry, which hired many locals and pushed up their median incomes at a 3.2% annual pace in the 1990s—the third highest increase of the ICIC 100. But with auto makers now shedding jobs again, those gains are likely to be short-lived. More broadly, improving inner cities won't come close to wiping out poverty in the U.S. While the inner-city poverty rate of 31% is nearly three times the national average, the 6.5 million poor people who live there represent less than a fifth of the country's 34.6 million poor.

Still, America's ghettos have been a national badge of shame for so long that any real gain is news. The change in perspective also seems to be an enduring one, not just a 1990s blip. For evidence, consider Potamkin Auto Group, which owns 70 dealerships around the country and will break ground in Harlem in late October on a $50 million development that will include Cadillac, Chevrolet, Hummer, and Saturn dealers. Potamkin also has a project in another inner city and is mulling a national expansion. "We see opportunities there," says Robert Potamkin, president of the family-owned company. This view, that inner cities can be a good place to do business, may be the most hopeful news about the country's urban blight in decades.

—By Aaron Bernstein in Washington, with Christopher Palmeri in Los Angeles and Roger O. Crockett in Chicago

COMMUNITY BUILDING
STEPS TOWARD A GOOD SOCIETY

AMITAI ETZIONI

Well-formed national societies are not composed of millions of individuals but are constituted as communities of communities. These societies provide a framework within which diverse social groups as well as various subcultures find shared bonds and values. When this framework falls apart, we find communities at each other's throats or even in vicious civil war, as we sadly see in many parts of the world. (Arthur Schlesinger Jr. provides an alarming picture of such a future for our society in his book, *The Disuniting of America*.)

Our community of communities is particularly threatened in two ways that ought to command more of our attention in the next years. First, our society has been growing more diverse by leaps and bounds over recent decades, as immigration has increased and Americans have become more aware of their social and cultural differences. Many on the left celebrate diversity because they see it as ending white European hegemony in our society. Many on the right call for "bleaching out" ethnic differences to ensure a united, homogenous America.

A second challenge to the community of communities emanates from the fact that economic and social inequality has long been rising. Some see a whole new divide caused by the new digital technologies, although others believe that the Internet will bridge these differences. It is time to ask how much inequality the community of communities can tolerate while still flourishing. If we are exceeding these limits, what centrist corrections are available to us?

DIVERSITY WITHIN UNITY

As a multiethnic society, America has long debated the merit of unity versus pluralism, of national identity versus identity politics, of assimilation of immigrants into mainstream culture versus maintaining their national heritages. All of these choices are incompatible with a centrist, communitarian approach to a good society. Assimilation is unnecessarily homogenizing, forcing people to give up important parts of their selves; unbounded racial, ethnic, and cultural diversity is too conflict-prone for a society in which all are fully respected. The concept of a community of communities provides a third model.

The community of communities builds on the observation that loyalty to one's group, to its particular culture and heritage, is compatible with sustaining national unity as long as the society is perceived not as an arena of conflict but as a society that has some community-like features. (Some refer to a community of communities as an imagined community.) Members of such a society maintain layered loyalties. "Lower" commitments are to one's immediate community, often an ethnic group; "higher" ones are to the community of communities, to the nation as a whole. These include a commitment to a democratic way of life, to a constitution and more generally to a government by law, and above all to treating others—not merely the members of one's group—as ends in themselves and not merely as instruments. Approached this way, one realizes that up to a point, *diversity can avoid being the opposite of unity and can exist within it*.

Moreover, sustaining a particular community of communities does not contradict the gradual development of still more encompassing communities, such as the European Union, a North American community including Canada and Mexico, or, one day, a world community.

During the last decades of the 20th century, the U.S. was racked by identity politics that, in part, have served to partially correct past injustices committed against women and minorities, but have also divided the nation along group lines. Other sharp divisions have appeared between the religious right and much of the rest of the country. One of the merits of the centrist, communitarian approach has been that it has combined efforts to expand the common ground and to cool intergroup rhetoric. Thus communitarians helped call off the "war" between the genders, as Betty Friedan—who was one of the original endorsers of the Communitarian Platform—did in 1997.

New flexibility in involving faith-based groups in the provision of welfare, health care, and other social services, and even allowing some forms of religious activities in public schools, has defused some of the tension between the religious right and the rest of society. The national guidelines on religious expression in public schools, first released by the U.S. Department of Education on the directive of President Clinton in August of 1995, worked to this end. For example, in July of 1996, these guidelines spurred the St. Louis School Board to implement a clearly defined, districtwide policy on school prayer. This policy helped allay the confusion—and litigation—that had previously plagued the role of religion in this school district.

The tendency of blacks and whites not to dialogue openly about racial issues, highlighted by Andrew Hacker, has to some degree been overcome. The main, albeit far from successful, effort in this direction has been made by President Clinton's Advisory Board on Race. And for the first time in U.S. history, a Jew was nominated by a major political party for the post of vice president.

In the next years, intensified efforts are called for to balance the legitimate concerns and needs of various communities that constitute the American society on one hand, and the need to shore up our society as a community of communities on the other. Prayers truly initiated by students might be allowed in public schools as long as sufficient arrangements are made for students who do not wish to participate to spend time in other organized activities. There are no compelling reasons to oppose "after hours" religious clubs establishing themselves in the midst of numerous secular programs. Renewed efforts for honest dialogues among the races are particularly difficult and needed. None of these steps will cause the differences among various communities—many of which serve to enrich our culture and social life—to disappear. But they may go a long way toward reinforcing the framework that keeps American society together while it is being recast.

UNIFYING INEQUALITY

Society cannot long sustain its status as a community of communities if general increases in well-being, even including those that trickle down to the poorest segments of the society, keep increasing the economic distance between the elites and the common people. Fortunately, it seems that at least by some measures, economic inequality has not increased in the United States between 1996 and 2000. And by several measures, the federal income tax has grown surprisingly progressive. (The opposite must be said about rising payroll taxes.) About a third of those who filed income tax returns in 2000 paid no taxes or even got a net refund from the Internal Revenue Service (IRS). However, the level of inequality in income at the end of the 20th century was substantially higher than it was in earlier periods. Between 1977 and 1999, the after-tax income of the top 1 percent of the U.S. population increased by 115 percent, whereas the after-tax income of the U.S. population's lowest fifth decreased by 9 per-

cent. There is little reason to expect that this trend will not continue.

SOCIAL JUSTICE

We may debate what social justice calls for; however, there is little doubt about what community requires. If some members of a community are increasingly distanced from the standard of living of most other members, they will lose contact with the rest of the community. The more those in charge of private and public institutions lead lives of hyper-affluence—replete with gated communities and estates, chauffeured limousines, servants and personal trainers—the less in touch they are with other community members. Such isolation not only frays social bonds and insulates privileged people from the moral cultures of the community, but it also blinds them to the realities of the lives of their fellow citizens. This, in turn, tends to cause them to favor unrealistic policies ("let them eat cake") that backfire and undermine the trust of the members of the society in those who lead and in the institutions they head.

The argument has been made that for the state to provide equality of outcomes undermines the motivation to achieve and to work, stymies creativity and excellence, and is unfair to those who do apply themselves. It is also said that equality of outcomes would raise labor costs so high that a society would be rendered uncompetitive in the new age of global competition. Equality of opportunity has been extolled as a substitute. However, to ensure equality of opportunity, some equality of outcome must be provided. As has often been pointed out, for all to have similar opportunities, they must have similar starting points. These can be reached only if all are accorded certain basics. Special education efforts such as Head Start, created to bring children from disadvantaged backgrounds up to par, and training for workers released from obsolescent industries are examples of programs that provide some equality of results to make equality of opportunity possible.

Additional policies to further curb inequality can be made to work at both ends of the scale. Policies that ensure a rich basic minimum serve this goal by lifting those at the lower levels of the economic pyramid. Reference is often made to education and training programs that focus on those most in need of catching up. However, these work very slowly. Therefore, in the short run more effects will be achieved by raising the Earned Income Tax Credit and the minimum wage, and by implementing new inter-community sharing initiatives.

The poor will remain poor no matter how much they work as long as they own no assets. This is especially damaging because people who own assets, especially a place of residence (even if only an apartment), are most likely to "buy" into a society—to feel and be part of a community. By numerous measures, homeowners are more involved in the life of their communities, and their children are less likely to drop out of school. Roughly one-third of Americans do not own their residence; 73 percent of whites do, compared to 47 percent of African Americans and Hispanics.

MORTGAGES

Various provisions allowing those with limited resources to get mortgages through federally chartered corporations like Fannie Mae, which helps finance mortgages for many lower-income people, have been helpful in increasing ownership. More needs to be done on this front, especially for those of little means. This might be achieved by following the same model used in the Earned Income Tax Credit in the U.S. and the Working Families Tax Credit in the United Kingdom: providing people who earn below a defined income level with "earned interest on mortgages," effectively granting them two dollars for every dollar set aside to provide seed money for a mortgage. And sweat equity might be used as the future owner's contribution—for instance, if they work on their own housing site. (Those who benefit from the houses that Habitat for Humanity builds are required to either make some kind of a financial contribution themselves or help in the construction of their homes.) Far from implausible, various ideas along these lines were offered by both George W. Bush and Al Gore during the 2000 election campaign, as well as by various policy researchers.

Reducing hard core unemployment by trying to bring jobs to poor neighborhoods (through "enterprise zones") or by training the long-unemployed in entrepreneurial skills is often expensive and slow, and is frequently unsuccessful. The opposite approach, moving people from poor areas to places where jobs are, often encounters objections by the neighborhoods into which they are moved, as well as by those poor who feel more comfortable living in their home communities. A third approach should be tried much more extensively: providing ready transportation to and from places of employment.

Measures to cap the higher levels of wealth include progressive income taxes, some forms of inheritance tax, closing numerous loopholes in the tax codes, and ensuring that tax on capital is paid as it is on labor. Given that several of these inequality curbing measures cannot be adopted on a significant scale if they seriously endanger the competitive state of a country, steps to introduce many of them should be undertaken jointly with other Organization for Economic Cooperation and Development (OECD) countries, or better yet, among all the nations that are our major competitors and trade partners.

One need not be a liberal—one can be a solid communitarian—and still be quite dismayed to learn that the IRS audits the poor (defined as income below $25,000) more than the rich (defined as income above $100,000). In 1999, the IRS audited 1.36 percent of poor taxpayers, compared to 1.15 percent of rich taxpayers. In 1988, the percentage for the rich was 11.4. In one decade, there was thus a decline of about 90 percent in auditing the rich. This occurred because Congress did not authorize the necessary funds, despite the General Accounting Office's finding that the rich are more likely to evade taxes than are the poor. This change in audit patterns also reflects the concern of Republican members of Congress that the poor will abuse the Earned Income Tax Credit that the Clinton administration has introduced. It should not take a decade to correct this imbalance.

Ultimately, this matter and many others will not be properly attended to until there is a basic change in the moral culture of the society and in the purposes that animate it. Without such a change, a major reallocation of wealth can be achieved only by force, which is incompatible with a democratic society and will cause a wealth flight and other damage to the economy. In contrast, history from early Christianity to Fabian socialism teaches us that people who share progressive values will be inclined to share their wealth voluntarily. A good society seeks to promote such values through a grand dialogue rather than by dictates.

THE NEW GRAND DIALOGUE

The great success of the economy in the 1990s made Americans pay more attention to the fact that there are numerous moral and social questions of concern to the good society that capitalism has never aspired to answer and that the state should not promote. These include moral questions such as what we owe our children, our parents, our friends, and our neighbors, as well as people from other communities, including those in far away places. Most important, we must address this question: What is the ultimate purpose our personal and collective endeavors? Is ever greater material affluence our ultimate goal and the source of meaning? When is enough—enough? What are we considering the good life? *Can a good society be built on ever increasing levels of affluence? Or should we strive to center it around other values, those of mutuality and spirituality?*

The journey to the good society can benefit greatly from the observation, supported by a great deal of social science data, that ever increasing levels of material goods are not a reliable source of human well-being or contentment—let alone the basis for a morally sound society. To cite but a few studies of a large body of findings: Frank M. Andrews and Stephen B. Withey found that the level of one's socioeconomic status had meager effects on one's "sense of well-being" and no significant effect on "satisfaction with life-as-a-whole." Jonathan L. Freedman discovered that levels of reported happiness did not vary greatly among the members of different economic classes, with the exception of the very poor, who tended to be less happy than others. David G. Myers reported that although per capita disposable (after-tax) income in inflation-adjusted dollars almost exactly doubled between 1960 and 1990, 32 percent of Americans reported that they were "very happy" in 1993, almost the same proportion as did in 1957 (35 percent). Although economic growth slowed after the mid-1970s, Americans' reported happiness was remarkably stable (nearly always between 30 and 35 percent) across both high-growth and low-growth periods.

HAPPINESS

These and other such data help us realize that the pursuit of well-being through ever higher levels of consumption is Sisyphean. When it comes to material goods, enough is never enough. This is not an argument in favor of a life of sackcloth and ashes, of poverty and self-denial. The argument is that once basic material needs (what Abraham Maslow called "creature comforts") are well sated and securely provided for, additional income does not add to happiness. On the contrary, hard evidence—not some hippie, touchy-feely, LSD-induced hallucination—shows that profound contentment is found in nourishing ends-based relationships, in bonding with others, in community building and public service, and in cultural and spiritual pursuits. Capitalism, the engine of affluence, has never aspired to address the whole person; typically it treats the person as *Homo economicus.* And of course, statist socialism subjugated rather than inspired. It is left to the evolving values and cultures of centrist societies to fill the void.

Nobel laureate Robert Fogel showed that periods of great affluence are regularly followed by what he calls Great Awakenings, and that we are due for one in the near future. Although it is quite evident that there is a growing thirst for a purpose deeper than conspicuous consumption, we may not have the ability to predict which specific form this yearning for spiritual fulfillment will take.

There are some who hold firmly that the form must be a religious one because no other speaks to the most profound matters that trouble the human soul, nor do others provide sound moral guidance. These believers find good support in numerous indicators that there was a considerable measure of religious revival in practically all forms of American religion over the last decades of the 20th century. The revival is said to be evident not merely in the number of people who participate in religious activities and the frequency of their participation in these activities, but also in the stronger, more involving, and stricter kinds of commitments many are making to religion. (Margaret Talbot has argued effectively that conservative Christians, especially fundamentalists, constitute the true counterculture of our age; they know and live a life rich in fulfillment, not centered around consumer goods.) Others see the spiritual revival as taking more secular forms, ranging from New Age cults to a growing interest in applied ethics.

PRIORITIES

Aside from making people more profoundly and truly content individuals, a major and broadly based upward shift on the Maslovian scale is a prerequisite for being able to better address some of the most tantalizing problems plaguing modern societies, whatever form such a shift may take. That is what is required before we can come into harmony with our environment, because these higher priorities put much less demand on scarce resources than do lower ones. And such a new set of priorities may well be the only conditions under which those who are well endowed would be willing to support serious reallocation of wealth and power, as their personal fortunes would no longer be based on amassing ever larger amounts of consumer goods. In addition, transitioning to a knowledge-based economy would free millions of people (one hopes all of them, gradually) to relate to each other mainly as members of families and communities, thus laying the social foundations for a society in which ends-based relationships dominate while instrumental ones are well contained.

The upward shift in priorities, a return to a sort of moderate counterculture, a turn toward voluntary simplicity—these require a grand dialogue about our personal and shared goals. (A return to a counterculture is not a recommendation for more abuse of controlled substances, promiscuity, and self-indulgence—which is about the last thing America needs—but the realization that one can find profound contentment in reflection, friendship, love, sunsets, and walks on the beach rather than in the pursuit of ever more control over ever more goods.) Intellectuals and the media can help launch such a dialogue and model the new forms of behavior. Public leaders can nurse the recognition of these values by moderating consumption at public events and ceremonies, and by celebrating those whose achievements are compatible with a good society rather than with a merely affluent one.

But ultimately, such a shift lies in changes in our hearts and minds, in our values and conduct—what Robert Bellah called the "habits of the heart." We shall not travel far toward a good society unless such a dialogue is soon launched and advanced to a good, spiritually uplifting conclusion.

Mr. Etzioni is editor of The Responsive Community. *From "Next: Three Steps Towards A Good Society," by Amitai Etzioni,* The Responsive Community, *Winter 2000–01, pages 49–58.*

Reprinted from *Current*, January 2001, pp. 29-33. Originally printed in *The Responsive Community*, Vol. II, No. 1, Winter 2000/01, pp. 49-58, which was adapted from the author's book *Next: The Road to the Good Society* (New York: Basic Books, 2001). Copyright © 2000 by Communitarian Network. Reprinted by permission.

UNIT 4

Stratification and Social Inequalities

Unit Selections

Key Points to Consider

- What inequalities do you find unacceptable and what inequalities do you find acceptable?

- Is the current level of income inequality unjust? If so, why? What negative effects does it have on society?

- Why is stratification such an important theme in sociology?

- Which social groups are likely to rise in the stratification system in the next decade? Which groups will fall? Why?

- How does stratification along income lines differ from stratification along racial or gender lines?

- Do you think women and blacks are treated fairly in America? Are changes needed in the policies that deal with discrimination? Why or why not?

- Is affirmative action no longer needed? Is it unjust or just?

 **Links: www.dushkin.com/online/**
These sites are annotated in the World Wide Web pages.

Americans With Disabilities Act Document Center
http://www.jan.wvu.edu/links/adalinks.htm
American Scientist
http://www.amsci.org/amsci/amsci.html
Give Five
http://www.independentsector.org/give5/givefive.html
Joint Center for Poverty Research
http://www.jcpr.org
NAACP Online: National Association for the Advancement of Colored People
http://www.naacp.org

People are ranked in many different ways—by physical strength, education, wealth, or other characteristics. Those who are rated highly often have power over others, special status, and prestige. The differences among people constitute their life chances, the probability that an individual or group will be able to obtain the valued and desired goods in a society. These differences are referred to as stratification, the system of structured inequalities in social relationships.

In most industrialized societies, income is one of the most important divisions among people. Karl Marx described stratification in terms of class rather than income. For him social class referred mainly to two distinct groups: those who control the means of production and those who do not. This section examines the life chances of the rich and the poor and of various disadvantaged groups, which best demonstrates the crucial features of the stratification system in the United States.

The first subsection of this unit deals with income inequality and the hardship of the poor. In his article, "For Richer," Paul Krugman describes the great increase in the inequality of income in the past three decades and explains its causes. He also discusses some rather unpleasant political and social consequences of these inequalities. In the next article, Beth Shulman shows some of the underside of the inequality that Krugman describes. She questions the claim that America is the land of opportunity. In the past America deserved that accolade, but now many hard working Americans "are stuck in low-wage jobs that do not provide the basics for a decent life." Now most Western European countries surpass America on mobility measures. Shulman tells several poignant stories that translate these statistics into life.

The American welfare system is addressed in the second subsection of unit 4. The first article describes the generous welfare system for the rich, and the next describes the effects of the 1996 welfare reform on the poor. First, Donald Barlett and James Steele explain how corporations milk federal, state, and local governments of billions of dollars. It comes as no surprise to a student of society that the political economy is set up to benefit the upper class and the powerful but the extent of that bias, when pointed out, can shock us anyway. The next article evaluates the results of the 1996 welfare reform. It begins by providing facts showing that it was not as bad as it was made out to be. For example, it was not very costly, being less than 5 percent of the costs of social security. Nevertheless, it needed to be reformed and the reform lowered caseloads 57 percent through 2001, and the majority of leavers are working (much of this change was due to the good economy). On the negative side the jobs generally are bad jobs that pay little and are unsteady. Finally, on several counts the new welfare system is more punitive.

The most poignant inequality in America is the gap between blacks and whites. Recently there has been considerable good news that the gap has been closing and many indicators that quality of life has improved for blacks. In the next article Barbara Kantrowitz and Pat Wingert clarify where affirmative action is today. It had a glorious history in the past when it pushed the nation toward fairness. However, what is its proper role today? Is it needed now and is it unfair now? This article clarifies what affir-

mative action is, where it stands legally today, and how universities should handle the issue.

In the next article, the authors demonstrate the prevalence of prejudice and hatred in America and how quickly hatred toward a group can evolve. Since September 11, 2001, hatred toward Muslims has erupted despite calls for tolerance from President George W. Bush and other public leaders. One explanation of hatred and prejudice against entire groups is social identity theory. People have a powerful drive to divide people into groups, identify with one group, and develop negative views of some of the out groups. Fortunately, "people who are concerned about their prejudices have the power to correct them." The following article discusses the problem of integrating different groups in the context of massive immigration into the United States. Can so many newcomers be assimilated into American culture? According to Anne Wortham, the United States has been quite successful in assimilating immigrants, most of whom want what America stands for when they come. They support democracy and other American institutions and are willing to work hard to get ahead. Relatively high and rising intermarriage rates demonstrate increasing assimilation, but continuing housing segregation is one indicator of impediments to assimilation.

The last subsection of unit 4 deals with sex inequalities. In the first article of the section, Joel Wendland reacts to the spate of articles in the media about the new gender gap favoring females. She acknowledges that girls do better than boys in school and have higher graduation rates but she shows that this has not yet closed the true gender gap that still considerably disadvantages women. For example, according to the AFL-CIO the average woman will lose $523,000 in lifetime earnings because of unequal pay. In the next article, Alice Leuchtag describes one of the great evils that is haunting the world today—sex slavery. The sex trade system grows out of poverty and profits. Extreme poverty forces parents to sell their girls into servitude often not knowing that they will become sex slaves. Considerable profits drive the system. The exploitation involved is horrendous making this a worldwide human rights issue.

The articles in this unit portray tremendous differences in wealth and life chances among people. Systems of inequality affect what a person does and how he or she does it. An important purpose of this unit is to help you become more aware of how stratification operates in social life.

For Richer

How the permissive capitalism of the boom destroyed American equality.

By Paul Krugman

I. The Disappearing Middle

When I was a teenager growing up on Long Island, one of my favorite excursions was a trip to see the great Gilded Age mansions of the North Shore. Those mansions weren't just pieces of architectural history. They were monuments to a bygone social era, one in which the rich could afford the armies of servants needed to maintain a house the size of a European palace. By the time I saw them, of course, that era was long past. Almost none of the Long Island mansions were still private residences. Those that hadn't been turned into museums were occupied by nursing homes or private schools.

For the America I grew up in—the America of the 1950's and 1960's—was a middle-class society, both in reality and in feel. The vast income and wealth inequalities of the Gilded Age had disappeared. Yes, of course, there was the poverty of the underclass—but the conventional wisdom of the time viewed that as a social rather than an economic problem. Yes, of course, some wealthy businessmen and heirs to large fortunes lived far better than the average American. But they weren't rich the way the robber barons who built the mansions had been rich, and there weren't that many of them. The days when plutocrats were a force to be reckoned with in American society, economically or politically, seemed long past.

Daily experience confirmed the sense of a fairly equal society. The economic disparities you were conscious of were quite muted. Highly educated professionals—middle managers, college teachers, even lawyers—often claimed that they earned less than unionized blue-collar workers. Those considered very well off lived in split-levels, had a housecleaner come in once a week and took summer vacations in Europe. But they sent their kids to public schools and drove themselves to work, just like everyone else.

But that was long ago. The middle-class America of my youth was another country.

We are now living in a new Gilded Age, as extravagant as the original. Mansions have made a comeback. Back in 1999 this magazine profiled Thierry Despont, the "eminence of excess," an architect who specializes in designing houses for the super-rich. His creations typically range from 20,000 to 60,000 square feet; houses at the upper end of his range are not much smaller than the White House. Needless to say, the armies of servants are back, too. So are the yachts. Still, even J.P. Morgan didn't have a Gulfstream.

As the story about Despont suggests, it's not fair to say that the fact of widening inequality in America has gone unreported. Yet glimpses of the lifestyles of the rich and tasteless don't necessarily add up in people's minds to a clear picture of the tectonic shifts that have taken place in the distribution of income and wealth in this country. My sense is that few people are aware of just how much the gap between the very rich and the rest has widened over a relatively short period of time. In fact, even bringing up the subject exposes you to charges of "class warfare," the " politics of envy" and so on. And very few people indeed are willing to talk about the profound effects—economic, social and political—of that widening gap.

Yet you can't understand what's happening in America today without understanding the extent, causes and consequences of the vast increase in inequality that has taken place over the last three decades, and in particular the astonishing concentration of income and wealth in just a few hands. To make sense of the current wave of corporate scandal, you need to understand how the man in the gray flannel suit has been replaced by the imperial C.E.O. The concentration of income at the top is a key reason that the United States, for all its economic achievements, has more poverty and lower life expectancy than any other major advanced nation. Above all, the growing concentration of wealth has reshaped our political system: it is at the root both of a general shift to the right and of an extreme polarization of our politics.

But before we get to all that, let's take a look at who gets what.

II. The New Gilded Age

The Securities and Exchange Commission hath no fury like a woman scorned. The messy divorce proceedings of Jack Welch, the legendary former C.E.O. of General Electric, have had one unintended benefit: they have given us a peek at the perks of the corporate elite, which are normally hidden from public view. For it turns out that when Welch retired, he was granted for life the use of a Manhattan apartment (including food, wine and laundry), access to corporate jets and a variety of other in-kind benefits, worth at least $2 million a year. The perks were revealing: they illustrated the extent to which corporate leaders now expect to be treated like *ancien régime* royalty. In monetary terms, however, the perks must have meant little to Welch. In 2000, his last full year running G.E., Welch was paid $123 million, mainly in stock and stock options.

> The 13,000 richest families in America now have almost as much income as the 20 million poorest. And those 13,000 families have incomes 300 times that of average families.

Is it news that C.E.O.'s of large American corporations make a lot of money? Actually, it is. They were always well paid compared with the average worker, but there is simply no comparison between what executives got a generation ago and what they are paid today.

Over the past 30 years most people have seen only modest salary increases: the average annual salary in America, expressed in 1998 dollars (that is, adjusted for inflation), rose from $32,522 in 1970 to $35,864 in 1999. That's about a 10 percent increase over 29 years—progress, but not much. Over the same period, however, according to Fortune magazine, the average real annual compensation of the top 100 C.E.O.'s went from $1.3 million—39 times the pay of an average worker—to $37.5 million, more than 1,000 times the pay of ordinary workers.

The explosion in C.E.O. pay over the past 30 years is an amazing story in its own right, and an important one. But it is only the most spectacular indicator of a broader story, the reconcentration of income and wealth in the U.S. The rich have always been different from you and me, but they are far more different now than they were not long ago—indeed, they are as different now as they were when F. Scott Fitzgerald made his famous remark.

That's a controversial statement, though it shouldn't be. For at least the past 15 years it has been hard to deny the evidence for growing inequality in the United States. Census data clearly show a rising share of income going to the top 20 percent of families, and within that top 20 percent to the top 5 percent, with a declining share going to families in the middle. Nonetheless, denial of that evidence is a sizable, well-financed industry. Conservative think tanks have produced scores of studies that try to discredit the data, the methodology and, not least, the motives of those who report the obvious. Studies that appear to refute claims of increasing inequality receive prominent endorsements on editorial pages and are eagerly cited by right-leaning government officials. Four years ago Alan Greenspan (why did anyone ever think that he was nonpartisan?) gave a keynote speech at the Federal Reserve's annual Jackson Hole conference that amounted to an attempt to deny that there has been any real increase in inequality in America.

The concerted effort to deny that inequality is increasing is itself a symptom of the growing influence of our emerging plutocracy (more on this later). So is the fierce defense of the backup position, that inequality doesn't matter—or maybe even that, to use Martha Stewart's signature phrase, it's a good thing. Meanwhile, politically motivated smoke screens aside, the reality of increasing inequality is not in doubt. In fact, the census data understate the case, because for technical reasons those data tend to undercount very high incomes—for example, it's unlikely that they reflect the explosion in C.E.O. compensation. And other evidence makes it clear not only that inequality is increasing but that the action gets bigger the closer you get to the top. That is, it's not simply that the top 20 percent of families have had bigger percentage gains than families near the middle: the top 5 percent have done better than the next 15, the top 1 percent better than the next 4, and so on up to Bill Gates.

Studies that try to do a better job of tracking high incomes have found startling results. For example, a recent study by the nonpartisan Congressional Budget Office used income tax data and other sources to improve on the census estimates. The C.B.O. study found that between 1979 and 1997, the after-tax incomes of the top 1 percent of families rose 157 percent, compared with only a 10 percent gain for families near the middle of the income distribution. Even more startling results come from a new study by Thomas Piketty, at the French research institute Cepremap, and Emmanuel Saez, who is now at the University of California at Berkeley. Using income tax data, Piketty and Saez have produced estimates of the incomes of the well-to-do, the rich and the very rich back to 1913.

The first point you learn from these new estimates is that the middle-class America of my youth is best thought of not as the normal state of our society, but as an interregnum between Gilded Ages. America before 1930 was a society in which a small number of very rich people controlled a large share of the nation's wealth. We became a middle-class society only after the concentration of income at the top dropped sharply during the New Deal, and especially during World War II. The economic historians Claudia Goldin and Robert Margo have dubbed the narrowing of income gaps during those years the Great Compression. Incomes then stayed fairly equally distributed until the 1970's: the rapid rise in incomes during the first postwar generation was very evenly spread across the population.

Since the 1970's, however, income gaps have been rapidly widening. Piketty and Saez confirm what I suspected: by most measures we are, in fact, back to the days of "The Great Gatsby." After 30 years in which the income shares of the top 10 percent of taxpayers, the top 1 percent and so on were far below their levels in the 1920's, all are very nearly back where they were.

And the big winners are the very, very rich. One ploy often used to play down growing inequality is to rely on rather coarse statistical breakdowns—dividing the population into five "quintiles," each containing 20 percent of families, or at most 10 "deciles." Indeed, Greenspan's speech at Jackson Hole relied mainly on decile data. From there it's a short step to denying that we're really talking about the rich at all. For example, a conservative commentator might concede, grudgingly, that there has been some increase in the share of national income going to the top 10 percent of taxpayers, but then point out that anyone with an income over $81,000 is in that top 10 percent. So we're just talking about shifts within the middle class, right?

Wrong: the top 10 percent contains a lot of people whom we would still consider middle class, but they weren't the big winners. Most of the gains in the share of the top 10 percent of taxpayers over the past 30 years were actually gains to the top 1 percent, rather than the next 9 percent. In 1998 the top 1 percent started at $230,000. In turn, 60 percent of the gains of that top 1 percent went to the top 0.1 percent, those with incomes of more than $790,000. And almost half of those gains went to a mere 13,000 taxpayers, the top 0.01 percent, who had an income of at least $3.6 million and an average income of $17 million.

A stickler for detail might point out that the Piketty-Saez estimates end in 1998 and that the C.B.O. numbers end a year earlier. Have the trends shown in the data reversed? Almost surely not. In fact, all indications are that the explosion of incomes at the top continued through 2000. Since then the plunge in stock prices must have put some crimp in high incomes—but census data show inequality continuing to increase in 2001, mainly because of the severe effects of the recession on the working poor and near poor. When the recession ends, we can be sure that we will find ourselves a society in which income inequality is even higher than it was in the late 90's.

So claims that we've entered a second Gilded Age aren't exaggerated. In America's middle-class era, the mansion-building, yacht-owning classes had pretty much disappeared. According to Piketty and Saez, in 1970 the top 0.01 percent of taxpayers had 0.7 percent of total income—that is, they earned "only" 70 times as much as the average, not enough to buy or maintain a mega-residence. But in 1998 the top 0.01 percent received more than 3 percent of all income. That meant that the 13,000 richest families in America had almost as much income as the 20 million poorest households; those 13,000 families had incomes 300 times that of average families.

And let me repeat: this transformation has happened very quickly, and it is still going on. You might think that 1987, the year Tom Wolfe published his novel "The Bonfire of the Vani-

ties" and Oliver Stone released his movie "Wall Street," marked the high tide of America's new money culture. But in 1987 the top 0.01 percent earned only about 40 percent of what they do today, and top executives less than a fifth as much. The America of "Wall Street" and "The Bonfire of the Vanities" was positively egalitarian compared with the country we live in today.

III. Undoing the New Deal

In the middle of the 1980's, as economists became aware that something important was happening to the distribution of income in America, they formulated three main hypotheses about its causes.

The "globalization" hypothesis tied America's changing income distribution to the growth of world trade, and especially the growing imports of manufactured goods from the third world. Its basic message was that blue-collar workers—the sort of people who in my youth often made as much money as college-educated middle managers—were losing ground in the face of competition from low-wage workers in Asia. A result was stagnation or decline in the wages of ordinary people, with a growing share of national income going to the highly educated.

A second hypothesis, "skill-biased technological change," situated the cause of growing inequality not in foreign trade but in domestic innovation. The torrid pace of progress in information technology, so the story went, had increased the demand for the highly skilled and educated. And so the income distribution increasingly favored brains rather than brawn.

Some economists think the New Deal imposed norms of relative equality in pay that persisted for more than 30 years, creating a broadly middle-class society. Those norms have unraveled.

Finally, the "superstar" hypothesis—named by the Chicago economist Sherwin Rosen—offered a variant on the technological story. It argued that modern technologies of communication often turn competition into a tournament in which the winner is richly rewarded, while the runners-up get far less. The classic example—which gives the theory its name—is the entertainment business. As Rosen pointed out, in bygone days there were hundreds of comedians making a modest living at live shows in the borscht belt and other places. Now they are mostly gone; what is left is a handful of superstar TV comedians.

The debates among these hypotheses—particularly the debate between those who attributed growing inequality to globalization and those who attributed it to technology—were many and bitter. I was a participant in those debates myself. But I won't dwell on them, because in the last few years there has been a growing sense among economists that none of these hypotheses work.

I don't mean to say that there was nothing to these stories. Yet as more evidence has accumulated, each of the hypotheses has seemed increasingly inadequate. Globalization can explain part of the relative decline in blue-collar wages, but it can't explain the 2,500 percent rise in C.E.O. incomes. Technology may explain why the salary premium associated with a college education has risen, but it's hard to match up with the huge increase in inequality among the college-educated, with little progress for many but gigantic gains at the top. The superstar theory works for Jay Leno, but not for the thousands of people who have become awesomely rich without going on TV.

The Great Compression—the substantial reduction in inequality during the New Deal and the Second World War—also seems hard to understand in terms of the usual theories. During World War II Franklin Roosevelt used government control over wages to compress wage gaps. But if the middle-class society that emerged from the war was an artificial creation, why did it persist for another 30 years?

Some—by no means all—economists trying to understand growing inequality have begun to take seriously a hypothesis that would have been considered irredeemably fuzzy-minded not long ago. This view stresses the role of social norms in setting limits to inequality. According to this view, the New Deal had a more profound impact on American society than even its most ardent admirers have suggested: it imposed norms of relative equality in pay that persisted for more than 30 years, creating the broadly middle-class society we came to take for granted. But those norms began to unravel in the 1970's and have done so at an accelerating pace.

Exhibit A for this view is the story of executive compensation. In the 1960's, America's great corporations behaved more like socialist republics than like cutthroat capitalist enterprises, and top executives behaved more like public-spirited bureaucrats than like captains of industry. I'm not exaggerating. Consider the description of executive behavior offered by John Kenneth Galbraith in his 1967 book, "The New Industrial State": "Management does not go out ruthlessly to reward itself—a sound management is expected to exercise restraint." Managerial self-dealing was a thing of the past: "With the power of decision goes opportunity for making money.... Were everyone to seek to do so... the corporation would be a chaos of competitive avarice. But these are not the sort of thing that a good company man does; a remarkably effective code bans such behavior. Group decision-making insures, moreover, that almost everyone's actions and even thoughts are known to others. This acts to enforce the code and, more than incidentally, a high standard of personal honesty as well."

Thirty-five years on, a cover article in *Fortune* is titled "You Bought. They Sold." "All over corporate America," reads the blurb, "top execs were cashing in stocks even as their companies were tanking. Who was left holding the bag? You." As I said, we've become a different country.

Let's leave actual malfeasance on one side for a moment, and ask how the relatively modest salaries of top executives 30 years ago became the gigantic pay packages of today. There are two main stories, both of which emphasize changing norms rather than pure economics. The more optimistic story draws an analogy between the explosion of C.E.O. pay and the explosion of baseball salaries with the introduction of free agency. According to this story, highly paid C.E.O.'s really are worth it, because having the right man in that job makes a huge difference. The more pessimistic view—which I find more plausible—is that competition for talent is a minor factor. Yes, a great executive can make a big difference—but those huge pay packages have been going as often as not to executives whose performance is mediocre at best. The key reason executives are paid so much now is that they appoint the members of the corporate board that determines their compensation and control many of the perks that board members count on. So it's not the invisible hand of the market that leads to those monumental executive incomes; it's the invisible handshake in the boardroom.

But then why weren't executives paid lavishly 30 years ago? Again, it's a matter of corporate culture. For a generation after World War II, fear of outrage kept executive salaries in check. Now the outrage is gone. That is, the explosion of executive pay represents a social change rather than the purely economic forces of supply and demand. We should think of it not as a market trend like the rising value of waterfront property, but as something more like the sexual revolution of the 1960's—a relaxation of old strictures, a new permissiveness, but in this case the permissiveness is financial rather than sexual. Sure enough, John Kenneth Galbraith described the honest executive of 1967 as being one who "eschews the lovely, available and even naked woman by whom he is intimately surrounded." By the end of the 1990's, the executive motto might as well have been "If it feels good, do it."

How did this change in corporate culture happen? Economists and management theorists are only beginning to explore that question, but it's easy to suggest a few factors. One was the changing structure of financial markets. In his new book, "Searching for a Corporate Savior," Rakesh Khurana of Harvard Business School suggests that during the 1980's and 1990's, "managerial capitalism"—the world of the man in the gray flannel suit—was replaced by "investor capitalism." Institutional investors weren't willing to let a C.E.O. choose his own successor from inside the corporation; they wanted heroic leaders, often outsiders, and were willing to pay immense sums to get them. The subtitle of Khurana's book, by the way, is "The Irrational Quest for Charismatic C.E.O.'s."

But fashionable management theorists didn't think it was irrational. Since the 1980's there has been ever more emphasis on the importance of "leadership"—meaning personal, charismatic leadership. When Lee Iacocca of Chrysler became a business celebrity in the early 1980's, he was practically alone: Khurana reports that in 1980 only one issue of Business Week featured a C.E.O. on its cover. By 1999 the number was up to 19. And once it was considered normal, even necessary, for a C.E.O. to be famous, it also became easier to make him rich.

Economists also did their bit to legitimize previously unthinkable levels of executive pay. During the 1980's and 1990's a torrent of academic papers—popularized in business magazines and incorporated into consultants' recommendations—argued that Gordon Gekko was right: greed is good; greed works. In order to get the best performance out of executives, these papers argued, it was necessary to align their interests with those of stockholders. And the way to do that was with large grants of stock or stock options.

It's hard to escape the suspicion that these new intellectual justifications for soaring executive pay were as much effect as cause. I'm not suggesting that management theorists and economists were personally corrupt. It would have been a subtle, unconscious process: the ideas that were taken up by business schools, that led to nice speaking and consulting fees, tended to be the ones that ratified an existing trend, and thereby gave it legitimacy.

What economists like Piketty and Saez are now suggesting is that the story of executive compensation is representative of a broader story. Much more than economists and free-market advocates like to imagine, wages—particularly at the top—are determined by social norms. What happened during the 1930's and 1940's was that new norms of equality were established, largely through the political process. What happened in the 1980's and 1990's was that those norms unraveled, replaced by an ethos of "anything goes." And a result was an explosion of income at the top of the scale.

IV. The Price of Inequality

It was one of those revealing moments. Responding to an e-mail message from a Canadian viewer, Robert Novak of "Crossfire" delivered a little speech: "Marg, like most Canadians, you're ill informed and wrong. The U.S. has the longest standard of living—longest life expectancy of any country in the world, including Canada. That's the truth."

But it was Novak who had his facts wrong. Canadians can expect to live about two years longer than Americans. In fact, life expectancy in the U.S. is well below that in Canada, Japan and every major nation in Western Europe. On average, we can expect lives a bit shorter than those of Greeks, a bit longer than those of Portuguese. Male life expectancy is lower in the U.S. than it is in Costa Rica.

Still, you can understand why Novak assumed that we were No. 1. After all, we really are the richest major nation, with real G.D.P. per capita about 20 percent higher than Canada's. And it has been an article of faith in this country that a rising tide lifts all boats. Doesn't our high and rising national wealth translate into a high standard of living—including good medical care—for all Americans?

Well, no. Although America has higher per capita income than other advanced countries, it turns out that that's mainly because our rich are much richer. And here's a radical thought: if the rich get more, that leaves less for everyone else.

That statement—which is simply a matter of arithmetic—is guaranteed to bring accusations of "class warfare." If the accuser gets more specific, he'll probably offer two reasons that it's foolish to make a fuss over the high incomes of a few people at the top of the income distribution. First, he'll tell you that what the elite get may look like a lot of money, but it's still a small share of the total—that is, when all is said and done the rich aren't getting that big a piece of the pie. Second, he'll tell you that trying to do anything to reduce incomes at the top will hurt, not help, people further down the distribution, because attempts to redistribute income damage incentives.

These arguments for lack of concern are plausible. And they were entirely correct, once upon a time—namely, back when we had a middle-class society. But there's a lot less truth to them now.

First, the share of the rich in total income is no longer trivial. These days 1 percent of families receive about 16 percent of total pretax income, and have about 14 percent of after-tax income. That share has roughly doubled over the past 30 years, and is now about as large as the share of the bottom 40 percent of the population. That's a big shift of income to the top; as a matter of pure arithmetic, it must mean that the incomes of less well off families grew considerably more slowly than average income. And they did. Adjusting for inflation, average family income—total income divided by the number of families—grew 28 percent from 1979 to 1997. But median family income—the income of a family in the middle of the distribution, a better indicator of how typical American families are doing—grew only 10 percent. And the incomes of the bottom fifth of families actually fell slightly.

Let me belabor this point for a bit. We pride ourselves, with considerable justification, on our record of economic growth. But over the last few decades it's remarkable how little of that growth has trickled down to ordinary families. Median family income has risen only about 0.5 percent per year—and as far as we can tell from somewhat unreliable data, just about all of that increase was due to wives working longer hours, with little or no gain in real wages. Furthermore, numbers about income don't reflect the growing riskiness of life for ordinary workers. In the days when General Motors was known in-house as Generous Motors, many workers felt that they had considerable job security—the company wouldn't fire them except in extremis. Many had contracts that guaranteed health insurance, even if they were laid off; they had pension benefits that did not depend on the stock market. Now mass firings from long-established companies are commonplace; losing your job means losing your insurance; and as millions of people have been learning, a 401(k) plan is no guarantee of a comfortable retirement.

Still, many people will say that while the U.S. economic system may generate a lot of inequality, it also generates much higher incomes than any alternative, so that everyone is better off. That was the moral Business Week tried to convey in its recent special issue with "25 Ideas for a Changing World." One of those ideas was "the rich get richer, and that's O.K." High incomes at the top, the conventional wisdom declares, are the result of a free-market system that provides huge incentives for performance. And the system delivers that performance, which means that wealth at the top doesn't come at the expense of the rest of us.

A skeptic might point out that the explosion in executive compensation seems at best loosely related to actual performance. Jack Welch was one of the 10 highest-paid executives in the United States in 2000, and you could argue that he earned it. But did Dennis Kozlowski of Tyco, or Gerald Levin of Time Warner, who were also in the top 10? A skeptic might also point out that even during the economic boom of the late

1990's, U.S. productivity growth was no better than it was during the great postwar expansion, which corresponds to the era when America was truly middle class and C.E.O.'s were modestly paid technocrats.

But can we produce any direct evidence about the effects of inequality? We can't rerun our own history and ask what would have happened if the social norms of middle-class America had continued to limit incomes at the top, and if government policy had leaned against rising inequality instead of reinforcing it, which is what actually happened. But we can compare ourselves with other advanced countries. And the results are somewhat surprising.

Many Americans assume that because we are the richest country in the world, with real G.D.P. per capita higher than that of other major advanced countries, Americans must be better off across the board—that it's not just our rich who are richer than their counterparts abroad, but that the typical American family is much better off than the typical family elsewhere, and that even our poor are well off by foreign standards.

But it's not true. Let me use the example of Sweden, that great conservative *bête noire*.

A few months ago the conservative cyberpundit Glenn Reynolds made a splash when he pointed out that Sweden's G.D.P. per capita is roughly comparable with that of Mississippi—see, those foolish believers in the welfare state have impoverished themselves! Presumably he assumed that this means that the typical Swede is as poor as the typical resident of Mississippi, and therefore much worse off than the typical American.

As the rich get richer, they can buy a lot besides goods and services. Money buys political influence; used cleverly, it also buys intellectual influence.

But life expectancy in Sweden is about three years higher than that of the U.S. Infant mortality is half the U.S. level, and less than a third the rate in Mississippi. Functional illiteracy is much less common than in the U.S.

How is this possible? One answer is that G.D.P. per capita is in some ways a misleading measure. Swedes take longer vacations than Americans, so they work fewer hours per year. That's a choice, not a failure of economic performance. Real G.D.P. per hour worked is 16 percent lower than in the United States, which makes Swedish productivity about the same as Canada's.

But the main point is that though Sweden may have lower average income than the United States, that's mainly because our rich are so much richer. The median Swedish family has a standard of living roughly comparable with that of the median U.S. family: wages are if anything higher in Sweden, and a higher tax burden is offset by public provision of health care and generally better public services. And as you move further down the income distribution, Swedish living standards are way ahead of those in the U.S. Swedish families with children that are at the 10th percentile—poorer than 90 percent of the population—

have incomes 60 percent higher than their U.S. counterparts. And very few people in Sweden experience the deep poverty that is all too common in the United States. One measure: in 1994 only 6 percent of Swedes lived on less than $11 per day, compared with 14 percent in the U.S.

The moral of this comparison is that even if you think that America's high levels of inequality are the price of our high level of national income, it's not at all clear that this price is worth paying. The reason conservatives engage in bouts of Sweden-bashing is that they want to convince us that there is no tradeoff between economic efficiency and equity—that if you try to take from the rich and give to the poor, you actually make everyone worse off. But the comparison between the U.S. and other advanced countries doesn't support this conclusion at all. Yes, we are the richest major nation. But because so much of our national income is concentrated in relatively few hands, large numbers of Americans are worse off economically than their counterparts in other advanced countries.

And we might even offer a challenge from the other side: inequality in the United States has arguably reached levels where it is counterproductive. That is, you can make a case that our society would be richer if its richest members didn't get quite so much.

I could make this argument on historical grounds. The most impressive economic growth in U.S. history coincided with the middle-class interregnum, the post-World War II generation, when incomes were most evenly distributed. But let's focus on a specific case, the extraordinary pay packages of today's top executives. Are these good for the economy?

Until recently it was almost unchallenged conventional wisdom that, whatever else you might say, the new imperial C.E.O.'s had delivered results that dwarfed the expense of their compensation. But now that the stock bubble has burst, it has become increasingly clear that there was a price to those big pay packages, after all. In fact, the price paid by shareholders and society at large may have been many times larger than the amount actually paid to the executives.

It's easy to get boggled by the details of corporate scandal—insider loans, stock options, special-purpose entities, mark-to-market, round-tripping. But there's a simple reason that the details are so complicated. All of these schemes were designed to benefit corporate insiders—to inflate the pay of the C.E.O. and his inner circle. That is, they were all about the "chaos of competitive avarice" that, according to John Kenneth Galbraith, had been ruled out in the corporation of the 1960's. But while all restraint has vanished within the American corporation, the outside world—including stockholders—is still prudish, and open looting by executives is still not acceptable. So the looting has to be camouflaged, taking place through complicated schemes that can be rationalized to outsiders as clever corporate strategies.

Economists who study crime tell us that crime is inefficient—that is, the costs of crime to the economy are much larger than the amount stolen. Crime, and the fear of crime, divert resources away from productive uses: criminals spend their time stealing rather than producing, and potential victims spend time and money trying to protect their property. Also, the things people do to avoid becoming victims—like avoiding dangerous districts—have a cost even if they succeed in averting an actual crime.

The same holds true of corporate malfeasance, whether or not it actually involves breaking the law. Executives who devote their time to creating innovative ways to divert shareholder money into their own pockets probably aren't running the real business very well (think Enron, WorldCom, Tyco, Global Crossing, Adelphia…). Investments chosen because they create the illusion of profitability while insiders cash in their stock options are a waste of scarce resources. And if the supply of funds from lenders and shareholders dries up because of a lack of trust, the economy as a whole suffers. Just ask Indonesia.

The argument for a system in which some people get very rich has always been that the lure of wealth provides powerful incentives. But the question is, incentives to do what? As we learn more about what has actually been going on in corporate America, it's becoming less and less clear whether those incentives have actually made executives work on behalf of the rest of us.

V. Inequality and Politics

In September the Senate debated a proposed measure that would impose a one-time capital gains tax on Americans who renounce their citizenship in order to avoid paying U.S. taxes. Senator Phil Gramm was not pleased, declaring that the proposal was "right out of Nazi Germany." Pretty strong language, but no stronger than the metaphor Daniel Mitchell of the Heritage Foundation used, in an op-ed article in The Washington Times, to describe a bill designed to prevent corporations from rechartering abroad for tax purposes: Mitchell described this legislation as the "Dred Scott tax bill," referring to the infamous 1857 Supreme Court ruling that required free states to return escaped slaves.

Twenty years ago, would a prominent senator have likened those who want wealthy people to pay taxes to Nazis? Would a member of a think tank with close ties to the administration have drawn a parallel between corporate taxation and slavery? I don't think so. The remarks by Gramm and Mitchell, while stronger than usual, were indicators of two huge changes in American politics. One is the growing polarization of our politics—our politicians are less and less inclined to offer even the appearance of moderation. The other is the growing tendency of policy and policy makers to cater to the interests of the wealthy. And I mean the wealthy, not the merely well-off: only someone with a net worth of at least several million dollars is likely to find it worthwhile to become a tax exile.

You don't need a political scientist to tell you that modern American politics is bitterly polarized. But wasn't it always thus? No, it wasn't. From World War II until the 1970's—the same era during which income inequality was historically low—political partisanship was much more muted than it is today. That's not just a subjective assessment. My Princeton political science colleagues Nolan McCarty and Howard Rosenthal, together with Keith Poole at the University of Houston, have done a statistical analysis showing that the voting behavior of a congressman is much better predicted by his party affiliation today than it was twenty-five years ago. In fact, the division between the parties is sharper now than it has been since the 1920's.

What are the parties divided about? The answer is simple: economics. McCarty, Rosenthal and Poole write that "voting in Congress is highly ideological—one-dimensional left/right, liberal versus conservative." It may sound simplistic to describe Democrats as the party that wants to tax the rich and help the poor, and Republicans as the party that wants to keep taxes and social spending as low as possible. And during the era of middle-class America that would indeed have been simplistic: politics wasn't defined by economic issues. But that was a different country; as McCarty, Rosenthal and Poole put it, "If income and wealth are distributed in a fairly equitable way, little is to be gained for politicians to organize politics around nonexistent conflicts." Now the conflicts are real, and our politics is organized around them. In other words, the growing inequality of our incomes probably lies behind the growing divisiveness of our politics.

But the politics of rich and poor hasn't played out the way you might think. Since the incomes of America's wealthy have soared while ordinary families have seen at best small gains, you might have expected politicians to seek votes by proposing to soak the rich. In fact, however, the polarization of politics has occurred because the Republicans have moved to the right, not because the Democrats have moved to the left. And actual economic policy has moved steadily in favor of the wealthy. The major tax cuts of the past twenty-five years, the Reagan cuts in the 1980's and the recent Bush cuts, were both heavily tilted toward the very well off. (Despite obfuscations, it remains true that more than half the Bush tax cut will eventually go to the top 1 percent of families.) The major tax increase over that period, the increase in payroll taxes in the 1980's, fell most heavily on working-class families.

The most remarkable example of how politics has shifted in favor of the wealthy—an example that helps us understand why economic policy has reinforced, not countered, the movement toward greater inequality—is the drive to repeal the estate tax. The estate tax is, overwhelmingly, a tax on the wealthy. In 1999, only the top 2 percent of estates paid any tax at all, and half the estate tax was paid by only 3,300 estates, 0.16 percent of the total, with a minimum value of $5 million and an average value of $17 million. A quarter of the tax was paid by just 467 estates worth more than $20 million. Tales of family farms and businesses broken up to pay the estate tax are basically rural legends; hardly any real examples have been found, despite diligent searching.

You might have thought that a tax that falls on so few people yet yields a significant amount of revenue would be politically popular; you certainly wouldn't expect widespread opposition. Moreover, there has long been an argument that the estate tax promotes democratic values, precisely because it limits the ability of the wealthy to form dynasties. So why has there been a powerful political drive to repeal the estate tax, and why was such a repeal a centerpiece of the Bush tax cut?

There is an economic argument for repealing the estate tax, but it's hard to believe that many people take it seriously. More significant for members of Congress, surely, is the question of who would benefit from repeal: while those who will actually benefit from estate tax repeal are few in number, they have a lot of money and control even more (corporate C.E.O.'s can now count on leaving taxable estates behind). That is, they are the sort of people who command the attention of politicians in search of campaign funds.

But it's not just about campaign contributions: much of the general public has been convinced that the estate tax is a bad thing. If you try talking about the tax to a group of moderately prosperous retirees, you get some interesting reactions. They refer to it as the "death tax"; many of them believe that their estates will face punitive taxation, even though most of them will pay little or nothing; they are convinced that small businesses and family farms bear the brunt of the tax.

These misconceptions don't arise by accident. They have, instead, been deliberately promoted. For example, a Heritage Foundation document titled "Time to Repeal Federal Death Taxes: The Nightmare of the American Dream" emphasizes stories that rarely, if ever, happen in real life: "Small-business owners, particularly minority owners, suffer anxious moments wondering whether the businesses they hope to hand down to their children will be destroyed by the death tax bill,... Women whose children are grown struggle to find ways to re-enter the work force without upsetting the family's estate tax avoidance plan." And who finances the Heritage Foundation? Why, foundations created by wealthy families, of course.

The point is that it is no accident that strongly conservative views, views that militate against taxes on the rich, have spread even as the rich get richer compared with the rest of us: in addition to directly buying influence, money can be used to shape public perceptions. The liberal group People for the American Way's report on how conservative foundations have deployed vast sums to support think tanks, friendly media and other institutions that promote right-wing causes is titled "Buying a Movement."

Not to put too fine a point on it: as the rich get richer, they can buy a lot of things besides goods and services. Money buys political influence; used cleverly, it also buys intellectual influence. A result is that growing income disparities in the United States, far from leading to demands to soak the rich, have been accompanied by a growing movement to let them keep more of their earnings and to pass their wealth on to their children.

This obviously raises the possibility of a self-reinforcing process. As the gap between the rich and the rest of the population grows, economic policy increasingly caters to the interests of the elite, while public services for the population at large—above all, public education—are starved of resources. As policy increasingly favors the interests of the rich and neglects the interests of the general population, income disparities grow even wider.

VI. Plutocracy?

In 1924, the mansions of Long Island's North Shore were still in their full glory, as was the political power of the class that owned them. When Gov. Al Smith of New York proposed building a system of parks on Long Island, the mansion owners were bitterly opposed. One baron—Horace Havemeyer, the "sultan of sugar"—warned that North Shore towns would be "overrun with rabble from the city." "Rabble?" Smith said. "That's me you're talking about." In the end New Yorkers got their parks, but it was close: the interests of a few hundred wealthy families nearly prevailed over those of New York City's middle class.

America in the 1920's wasn't a feudal society. But it was a nation in which vast privilege—often inherited privilege—stood in contrast to vast misery. It was also a nation in which the government, more often than not, served the interests of the privileged and ignored the aspirations of ordinary people.

Those days are past—or are they? Income inequality in America has now returned to the levels of the 1920's. Inherited wealth doesn't yet play a big part in our society, but given time—and the repeal of the estate tax—we will grow ourselves a hereditary elite just as set apart from the concerns of ordinary Americans as old Horace Havemeyer. And the new elite, like the old, will have enormous political power.

Kevin Phillips concludes his book "Wealth and Democracy" with a grim warning: "Either democracy must be renewed, with politics brought back to life, or wealth is likely to cement a new and less democratic regime—plutocracy by some other name." It's a pretty extreme line, but we live in extreme times. Even if the forms of democracy remain, they may become meaningless. It's all too easy to see how we may become a country in which the big rewards are reserved for people with the right connections; in which ordinary people see little hope of advancement; in which political involvement seems pointless, because in the end the interests of the elite always get served.

Am I being too pessimistic? Even my liberal friends tell me not to worry, that our system has great resilience, that the center will hold. I hope they're right, but they may be looking in the rearview mirror. Our optimism about America, our belief that in the end our nation always finds its way, comes from the past— a past in which we were a middle-class society. But that was another country.

Paul Krugman is a Times columnist and a professor at Princeton.

Working and Poor in the USA

A VAST IMPOVERISHED POPULATION LANGUISHES IN THE MIDST OF OUR ECONOMY.

Beth Shulman

For generations, Americans shared a tacit understanding that if you worked hard, you could earn a livable income and provide basic security for yourself and your family. That promise has been broken. More than 30 million Americans—one in four workers—are stuck in low-wage jobs that do not provide the basics for a decent life.

As we celebrate the fortieth anniversary of President Johnson's declaration of the War on Poverty, we are reminded that economic growth alone is not sufficient to combat the problem. Today, the war on poverty must be fought not on the margins but in the very mainstream of our economy. It must be a war to restore the promise of work.

While the Democratic presidential contenders are vocal about general economic conditions, ill-advised tax cuts and continuing unemployment, they have only recently begun to point out a fundamental economic failure—the failure of work to meet people's needs.

Finding ways to make sure that people who work hard can take care of their families would put the Democrats on the offensive instead of their customary defensive position on family values. It would have broad appeal to working Americans, as millions of middle-income jobs take on the characteristics of the low-wage economy—layoffs, outsourcing, unaffordable healthcare and vanishing pension benefits. And it would have great potential to help those suffering in low-wage jobs—workers like Cynthia Porter.

Cynthia Porter works full time as a certified nursing assistant at a nursing home in Marion, Alabama. When she comes on duty at 11 PM, she makes rounds, checking the residents for skin tears and helping them go to the toilet or use a bedpan. She has to make sure she turns the bedridden every two hours, or they will get bedsores. And if bedsores are left unattended, she tells me, they can get so bad you can put your fist in them. But there aren't enough people on her shift. Often only two nursing assistants are on duty to take care of forty-five residents. And Cynthia must also wash the wheelchairs, clean up the dining rooms, mop the floors and scrub out the refrigera-

tor, drawers and closets during her shift. Before she leaves, she helps the residents get dressed for breakfast.

For all this, Cynthia makes $350 every two weeks. She is separated from her husband, who gives her no child support. The first two weeks each month she pays her $150 rent. The next two weeks, she pays her water and her electric bills. It is difficult to afford Clorox or shampoo. Insuring that her children are fed properly is a stretch. She is still paying off the bicycles she bought for them last Christmas.

She can't afford a car, so she pays someone to drive her the twenty-five miles to work. There have been a few days when she couldn't find a ride. "I walked at 12 o'clock at night," she said. "I'd rather walk and be a little late than call in. I'd rather make the effort. I couldn't just sit here. I don't want to miss a day—otherwise, I might be fired." No public transportation is available that could take her all the way to work.

Cynthia lives with her three children in a small maroon-colored shack. It is miles from a main road. Inside, the plywood floor is so thin and worn that the ground can be seen below. In the next room, a toilet sinks into the floor. There is no phone. A broken heater sits against the wall; the landlord refuses to fix it.

Keeping her children's clothes clean requires great effort because Cynthia has no washing machine. Instead, she fills her bathtub halfway and gets on her hands and knees to scrub the clothes. Then she hangs them out to dry.

I first met Cynthia at a union meeting. She had a quiet, dignified presence with her dark suit and her hair pulled back in a bun. She and twenty-five others from the nursing home—all eighty of her co-workers are African-American women, like her—gathered in the little brick Masonic building outside of Marion to talk about having a union. None had ever gotten a raise of more than 13 cents an hour. Some who had been there ten years were still making $6 an hour. But ultimately, it was the lack of respect from their employer that motivated these women. They said they often told their supervisors something important about patients, but no one listened. The home offered no promotions either. Cynthia said, "I knew it wouldn't improve without outside help."

Despite the frustration and the difficult conditions, Cynthia beams when she talks about her job. "I like helping people," she says. "I like talking with them, and shampooing their hair. I like old people. If they are down, I can really make them feel better. The patients say, 'Nobody loves me or comes to see me.' Sometimes I help the residents play dominoes. Sometimes their hands shake, but I hold them. It's a lot of fun for them. I tell them 'I love you,' and give them a hug. I like being a CNA. I'm doing what I want to be doing."

In 1962 Michael Harrington stirred the conscience of the nation with the publication of *The Other America*. He reminded a country basking in the glow of postwar prosperity that poverty was alive and well. Harrington revealed the struggles of invisible millions living in passed-over regions of the country and the economy—in Appalachia, the South, in rural America. They were caught in dying towns and industries, shunted off the main tracks of the economy into unemployment, and left to fester in idleness and despair. In a word, they were outlanders, watching as the rest of the country went to work and thrived. The nation spent the remainder of the century wrestling with this sort of jobless poverty, expanding and then contracting the welfare state as it experimented with different ways of dealing with a population cut off from the economic mainstream.

These forms of poverty persist, and the country is still arguing about what to do with its welfare recipients. But the great secret of America is that a vast impoverished population has grown up in our midst. These are not Americans who have been excluded from the world of work; in fact, they make up the core of much of the new economy. And it is estimated that low-wage jobs will make up 30 percent of the economy by the end of this decade.

Thirty million Americans make less than $8.70 an hour, the official US poverty level for a family of four. (Most experts estimate that it takes at least double this level for a family to provide for its basic needs.) Their low-wage, no-benefits jobs translate into billions of dollars in profits, executive pay, high stock prices and low store prices.

Who are they? They are all around us in jobs essential to our lives. Low-wage workers are security guards and childcare givers. They are nursing-home workers and retail clerks. They are hospital orderlies and teachers' assistants. They are hotel workers and pharmacy technicians. They bone the chicken that we eat, clean the office buildings where we work and handle our questions and complaints at call centers.

Yet few express outrage about the plight of these workers. There is a reigning American mythology that blunts any concern: that holding a low-wage job is a temporary situation, that mobility and education and time will solve whatever problem exists.

The evidence, however, contradicts this myth. Most low-wage workers will never move up the ladder into the middle class. Economics professors Peter Gottschalk of Boston College and Sheldon Danziger of the University of Michigan found that about half of those whose family income ranked in the bottom 20 percent in 1968 were still in the same group in 1991. Of those who had moved up, nearly three-fourths remained below the median income. The US economy provides less mobility for low-wage earners, according to an Organization for Economic Co-operation and Development study, than the economies of France, Italy, Britain, Germany, Denmark, Finland and Sweden.

Inadequate wages are only part of the problem. Most of these workers lack basic job benefits. In 1995 less than half of workers making under $20,000 a year were offered health insurance by their employer. Only one in five workers with incomes below $20,000 has pension coverage. For low-wage parents with children under 6, one-third do not get paid vacations or paid holidays. And most low-wage jobs fail to provide sick pay or disability pay. These jobs leave little flexibility to care for a sick child or deal with an emergency at school—let alone the normal appointments and needs of everyday life. Quality childcare is unaffordable for most, and many nighttime shifts and employers' schedule changes make it harder and more expensive to obtain.

Low-wage workplaces are often physically dangerous and emotionally degrading. High injury rates are common. Constant surveillance, time clocks, drug testing and rigid rules reinforce the workers' pervasive sense that employers do not trust them. Fear is the chief motivator: Being five minutes late can mean losing a job. A few minutes too long in the bathroom can bring punishment. It is consistent with this lack of respect from employers that these workers are half as likely to receive employer-sponsored training as workers in higher-wage jobs.

These conditions are no accident. Over the past quarter-century, a variety of political, economic and corporate decisions have undercut the bargaining power of workers, especially those at the lower end of the work force. Those decisions included the push to increase global trade and open global markets, government efforts to deregulate industries that had been highly unionized, tight monetary policies and a corporate ideological shift away from the postwar social contract with employees and toward the principle of maximizing shareholder value. During the same period, the most vulnerable workers were deprived of many of the institutions, laws and political allies that generally helped to counterbalance these forces. Liberal allies who historically had championed their interests mostly sat silent. Unions were in decline. Minimum-wage, fair employment and labor laws were weakened.

Today, Americans can make different choices. Democrats should call for a compact with working Americans that establishes the mutual obligations and responsibilities of employers, workers and government. The compact would have a simple and clear purpose: It would insure that if you work hard you will be treated fairly and have the resources to provide for yourself and your family.

One place to start is raising the minimum wage to $8.70 and indexing it to inflation. The compact should require that industries receiving public funds through contracts, tax abatements or other subsidies provide quality jobs with benefits and living wages. Access to affordable healthcare must be provided to all workers and their families. Workers need to know they can get time off to be with a sick child or an elderly parent without fear of losing their jobs or a day's pay. Quality childcare and early education should be made available to their children. And workers must have the right to organize without fear of intimidation, harassment or being fired.

In the past, we have established standards and rights to insure that older Americans would not be impoverished or go without healthcare, to prevent young children from working and to insure equal opportunity in employment regardless of race, religion, national origin, sex or age. Now we must set standards to protect the well-being of all working families and the integrity of the nation. It is urgent, both morally and politically, for the Democratic candidates to confront this critical issue.

Beth Shulman is a lawyer and consultant focusing on work-related issues. This article is adapted from The Betrayal of Work: How Low-Wage Jobs Fail 30 Million Americans *(New Press).*

CORPORATE WELFARE

A TIME investigation uncovers how hundreds of companies get on the dole—and why it costs every working American the equivalent of two weeks' pay every year

By Donald L. Barlett and James B. Steele

HOW WOULD YOU LIKE TO PAY ONLY A QUARTER OF THE REAL ESTATE TAXES you owe on your home? And buy everything for the next 10 years without spending a single penny in sales tax? Keep a chunk of your paycheck free of income taxes? Have the city in which you live lend you money at rates cheaper than any bank charges? Then have the same city install free water and sewer lines to your house, offer you a perpetual discount on utility bills—and top it all off by landscaping your front yard at no charge?

Fat chance. You can't get any of that, of course. But if you live almost anywhere in America, all around you are taxpayers getting deals like this. These taxpayers are called corporations, and their deals are usually trumpeted as "economic development" or "public-private partnerships." But a better name is corporate welfare. It's a game in which governments large and small subsidize corporations large and small, usually at the expense of another state or town and almost always at the expense of individual and other corporate taxpayers.

Two years after Congress reduced welfare for individuals and families, this other kind of welfare continues to expand, penetrating every corner of the American economy. It has turned politicians into bribery specialists, and smart business people into con artists. And most surprising of all, it has rarely created any new jobs.

While corporate welfare has attracted critics from both the left and the right, there is no uniform definition. By TIME's definition, it is this: any action by local, state or federal government that gives a corporation or an entire industry a benefit not offered to others. It can be an outright subsidy, a grant, real estate, a low-interest loan or a government service. It can also be a tax break—a credit, exemption, deferral or deduction, or a tax rate lower than the one others pay.

The rationale to curtail traditional welfare programs, such as Aid to Families with Dependent Children and food stamps, and to impose a lifetime limit on the amount of aid received, was compelling: the old system didn't work. It was unfair, destroyed incentive, perpetuated dependence and distorted the economy. An 18-month TIME investigation has found that the same indictment, almost to the word, applies to corporate welfare. In some ways, it represents pork-barrel legislation of the worst order. The difference, of course, is that instead of rewarding the poor, it rewards the powerful.

And it rewards them handsomely. The Federal Government alone shells out $125 billion a year in corporate welfare, this in the midst of one of the more robust economic periods in the nation's history. Indeed, thus far in the 1990s, corporate profits have totaled $4.5 trillion—a sum equal to the cumulative paychecks of 50 million working Americans who earned less than $25,000 a year, for those eight years.

During one of the most robust economic periods in our nation's history, the Federal Government has shelled out $125 billion in corporate welfare, equivalent to all the income tax paid by 60 million individuals and families.

That makes the Federal Government America's biggest sugar daddy, dispensing a range of giveaways from tax abatements to price supports for sugar itself. Companies get government money to advertise their products; to help build new plants, offices and stores; and to train their workers. They sell their goods to foreign buyers that make the acquisitions with tax dollars supplied by the U.S. government; engage in foreign transactions that are insured by the government; and are excused from paying a portion of their income tax if they sell products overseas. They pocket lucrative government contracts to carry out ordinary business operations, and government grants to conduct research that will improve their profit margins. They are extended partial tax immunity if they locate in certain geographical areas, and they may write off as business expenses some of the perks enjoyed by their top executives.

The justification for much of this welfare is that the U.S. government is creating jobs. Over the past six years, Congress appropriated $5 billion to run the Export-Import Bank of the United States, which subsidizes companies that sell goods abroad. James A. Harmon, president and chairman, puts it this way: "American workers… have higher-quality, better-paying jobs, thanks to Eximbank's financing." But the numbers at the bank's five biggest beneficiaries—AT&T, Bechtel, Boeing, General Electric and McDonnell Douglas (now a part of Boeing)—tell another story. At these companies, which have accounted for about 40% of all loans, grants and long-term guarantees in this decade, overall employment has fallen 38%, as more than a third of a million jobs have disappeared.

The picture is much the same at the state and local level, where a different kind of feeding frenzy is taking place. Politicians stumble over one another in the rush to arrange special deals for select corporations, fueling a growing economic war among the states. The result is that states keep throwing money at companies that in many cases are not serious about moving anyway. The companies are certainly not reluctant to take the money, though, which is available if they simply utter the word relocation. And why not? Corporate executives, after all, have a fiduciary duty to squeeze every dollar they can from every locality waving blandishments in their face.

State and local governments now give corporations money to move from one city to another—even from one building to another—and tax credits for hiring new employees. They supply funds to train workers or pay part of their wages while they are in training, and provide scientific and engineering assistance to solve workplace technical problems. They repave existing roads and build new ones. They lend money at bargain-basement interest rates to erect plants or buy equipment. They excuse corporations from paying sales and property taxes and relieve them from taxes on investment income.

There are no reasonably accurate estimates on the amount of money states shovel out. That's because few want you to know. Some say they maintain no records. Some say they don't know where the files are. Some say the information is not public. All that's certain is that the figure is in the many billions of dollars each year—and it is growing, when measured against the subsidy per job.

In 1989 Illinois gave $240 million in economic incentives to Sears, Roebuck & Co. to keep its corporate headquarters and 5,400 workers in the state by moving from Chicago to suburban Hoffman Estates. That amounted to a subsidy of $44,000 for each job.

In 1991 Indiana gave $451 million in economic incentives to United Airlines to build an aircraft-maintenance facility that would employ as many as 6,300 people. Subsidy: $72,000 for each job.

In 1993 Alabama gave $253 million in economic incentives to Mercedes-Benz to build an automobile-assembly plant near Tuscaloosa and employ 1,500 workers. Subsidy: $169,000 for each job.

And in 1997 Pennsylvania gave $307 million in economic incentives to Kvaerner ASA, a Norwegian global engineering and construction company, to open a shipyard at the former Philadelphia Naval Shipyard and employ 950 people. Subsidy: $323,000 for each job.

This kind of arithmetic seldom adds up. Let's say the Philadelphia job pays $50,000. And each new worker pays $6,700 in local and state taxes. That means it will take nearly a half-century of tax collections from each individual to earn back the money granted to create his or her job. And that assumes all 950 workers will be recruited from outside Philadelphia and will relocate in the city, rather than move from existing jobs within the city, where they are already paying taxes.

All this is in service of a system that may produce jobs in one city or state, thus fostering the illusion of an uptick in employment. But it does not create more jobs in the nation as a whole. Market forces do that, and that's why 10 million jobs have been created since 1990. But most of those jobs have been created by small- and medium-size companies, from high-tech start-ups to franchised cleaning services. FORTUNE 500 companies, on the other hand, have erased more jobs than they have created this past decade, and yet they are the biggest beneficiaries of corporate welfare.

To be sure, some economic incentives are handed out for a seemingly worthwhile public purpose. The tax breaks that companies receive to locate in inner cities come to mind. Without them, companies might not invest in those neighborhoods. However well intended, these subsidies rarely produce lasting results. They may provide short-term jobs but not long-term employment. And in the end, the costs outweigh any benefits.

And what are those costs? The equivalent of nearly two weekly paychecks from every working man and woman in America—extra money that would stay in their pockets if it didn't go to support some business venture or another.

If corporate welfare is an unproductive end game, why does it keep growing in a period of intensive government cost cutting? For starters, it has good p.r. and an army of bureaucrats working to expand it. A corporate-welfare bureaucracy of an estimated 11,000 organizations and agencies has grown up, with access to city halls, statehouses, the Capitol and the White House. They conduct seminars, conferences and training sessions. They have their own trade associations. They publish their own journals and newsletters. They create attractive websites on the Internet. And they never call it "welfare." They call it "economic incentives" or "empowerment zones" or "enterprise zones."

Whatever the name, the result is the same. Some companies receive public services at reduced rates, while all others pay the full cost. Some companies are excused from paying all or a portion of their taxes due, while all others must pay the full amount imposed by law. Some companies receive grants, low-interest loans and other subsidies, while all others must fend for themselves.

In the end, that's corporate welfare's greatest flaw. It's unfair. One role of government is to help ensure a level playing field for people and businesses. Corporate welfare does just the opposite. It tilts the playing field in favor of the largest or the most politically influential or most aggressive businesses.…

From *Time*, November 9, 1998, pp. 36-39. © 1998 by Time Inc. Magazine Company. Reprinted by permission.

Requiem for Welfare

Evelyn Z. Brodkin

THERE WERE few mourners at welfare's funeral. In fact, its demise was widely celebrated when congressional Republicans teamed up with a majority of their Democratic colleagues and then-president Bill Clinton to enact a new welfare law in 1996. The law ended the sixty-one-year old federal commitment to aid poor families and ushered in a commitment to lower welfare rolls and put recipients to work.

To many politicians and the public, anything seemed preferable to the widely discredited program known as Aid to Families with Dependent Children (AFDC). Conservatives were sure that the new welfare would pull up the poor by their bootstraps and redeem them through the virtues of work. Liberals set aside their misgivings, hoping that work would redeem the poor politically and open opportunities to advance economic equality.

More than six years later, the demise of the old welfare remains largely unlamented. But what to make of the changes that have occurred in the name of reform? Often, laws produce more smoke than fire, intimating big change, but producing little. Not this time. In ways both apparent and not fully appreciated, welfare reform has reconfigured both the policy and political landscape. Some of these changes can evoke nostalgia for the bad old days of welfare unreformed.

Reconsidering Welfare's Fate

An immediate consequence of the new law was to defuse welfare as a hot political issue. There's little attention to it these days—apart from some five million parents and children who rely on welfare to alleviate their poverty (and the policy analysts who pore over mountains of data to calculate how it "works"). Legislators have shown no appetite for restarting the welfare wars of prior years. And is it any wonder? The news about welfare has looked good—at least, superficially. Caseloads have plummeted since implementation of the new welfare, dropping 57 percent between 1997 and 2001. Some smaller states essentially cleared their caseloads, with Wyoming and Idaho proudly announcing reductions of 88.9 percent and 85.1 percent, respectively. Even states with large, urban populations have cut caseloads by one-half to three-quarters.

As an issue, welfare ranked among the top five items of interest to the public in 1995 and 1996. But in recent years, it has almost dropped off the Gallup charts. Other polls show that, among respondents who are aware of welfare reform, more than 60 percent think it's working well. Meanwhile, the nation has moved on to other concerns: terrorism, Iraq, the economy. Why reopen the welfare issue now?

In part, the 1996 law itself spurred reassessment. The law was designed to expire in 2002 unless reauthorized by Congress. With Congress unable to reach agreement before the 2002 election, welfare's reauthorization became one of the many measures to get a temporary extension and a handoff to the 108th Congress.

Beyond reauthorization, welfare merits a close look because battles over welfare policy have often been a bellwether of broader political developments. Welfare policy was near the forefront of sixties social activism, one of the banners under which the urban poor, minorities, and other disaffected groups successfully pressed for greater government intervention on behalf of social and economic equality. For the national Democratic Party, the politics of poverty fit an electoral strategy aimed at mobilizing urban and minority voters. Although the expansion of welfare proved to be temporary and limited, the politics of poverty produced federal initiatives that had broad and lasting impact, among them Medicaid, food stamps, earned income tax credits, and programs to aid schools in poor communities.

Attacks on welfare marked the beginning of a conservative mobilization against the welfare state in the late 1970s. Lurid accounts in George Gilder's *Wealth and Poverty* and Mickey Kaus's *The End of Equality* portrayed welfare and the poor as enemies of the democratic marketplace. President Ronald Reagan picked up these themes and contributed his own colorful anecdotes about welfare cheats and fraud, as he pushed forward cuts in taxes and social welfare programs. These forays into the politics of personal piety fit a Republican electoral strategy aimed at mobilizing the religious right and bringing the white working class into the party fold.

Out with the "Old" Welfare

Reforming welfare assumed new urgency in the 1990s, an urgency grounded less in policy realities than in electoral politics. Alarms were sounded about a crisis of cost, although for three decades, spending on AFDC amounted to less than 2 percent of the federal budget. The $16 billion the federal government allocated to AFDC was dwarfed by spending on Social Security and defense, each costing more than $300 billion per year. Public opinion polls, however, indicated a different perception. Forty percent of respondents believed that welfare was one of the most expensive national programs, even larger than Social Security or defense.

Polls also indicated that much of the public believed welfare recipients had it too easy, although few knew what welfare really provided. In fact, AFDC gave only meager support to poor families. In 1996, the median monthly benefit for a family of three was $366. Even when combined with food stamps, welfare lifted few poor families above the federal poverty line. Even the much-touted crisis of dependency ("dependent" being a term loosely applied to anyone receiving welfare) was not reflected in the evidence. The share of families receiving welfare for extended periods declined between 1970 and 1985 and leveled off after that. Families that received welfare for more than six years constituted only a small minority of the welfare caseload at any point in time.

Although the hue and cry over a supposed welfare crisis was greatly overblown, Bill Clinton clearly appreciated welfare's potent political symbolism. As a presidential candidate, he famously pledged to "end welfare as we know it," a turn of phrase useful in demonstrating that he was a "new Democrat" unburdened by the liberalism of his predecessors. His proposals for reform emphasized neoliberal themes of work and individual responsibility, but coupled demands for work with provision of social services intended to improve individual employment prospects. The Clinton administration's plans also assumed the enactment of universal health insurance that would help underwrite the well-being of the working poor. But that did not happen.

After the Republicans took over Congress in 1994, and Clinton began his fateful descent into personal irresponsibility, the initiative shifted decidedly toward the right. House Majority Leader Newt Gingrich seized the opportunity to turn Clinton's pledge against him, sending the president two welfare measures then thought to be so harsh that they almost begged for a veto. The measures ended the federal guarantee of income support, imposed strict work rules, and set time limits on the provision of benefits. Clinton vetoed them.

But on the eve of his renomination at the 1996 Democratic convention, Clinton signed a measure much like those he had vetoed. There followed a few highly public resignations among indignant staff and a rebuke from the Congressional Black Caucus. But Clinton's decision (advocated by strategist Dick Morris and running mate Al Gore, among others) effectively took the welfare issue away from the Republicans and highlighted Clinton's "new Democratic" appeal to critical swing suburban and blue-collar, crossover voters.

Clinton became the first elected Democratic President since Franklin Roosevelt to win a second term. But Clinton was no Roosevelt. In fact, he redeemed his pledge to "end welfare" by presiding over the destruction of a pillar of the New Deal welfare state.

Enter the "New" Welfare

The Personal Responsibility and Work Opportunity Reconciliation Act of 1996 replaced AFDC with a program aptly named Temporary Assistance to Needy Families (TANF). AFDC had provided an open-ended entitlement of federal funds to states based on the amount of benefits they distributed to poor families. TANF ended that entitlement, establishing a five-year block grant fixed at $16.5 billion annually (based on the amount allocated to AFDC in its last year) that states could draw down to subsidize welfare and related expenditures.

Mistrusting the states' willingness to be tough enough on work, Congress incorporated detailed and coercive provisions. First, it set time limits for assistance, restricting federal aid to a lifetime maximum of sixty months. If states wanted to exceed those limits, they would have to pay for most of it themselves. Second, parents were required to work or participate in so-called work activities after a maximum of two years of welfare receipt. Third, TANF established escalating work quotas. States that wanted to collect their full portion of federal dollars would have to show, by 2002, that 50 percent of adults heading single-parent households were working thirty hours per week. Fourth, it meticulously specified those work "activities" that would enable states to meet their quotas, among them paid work, job search, and unpaid workfare (in which recipients "worked off" their welfare benefits at minimum wage or provided child care for other welfare recipients). It limited the use of education and vocational training as countable activities.

Although the "work" side of TANF was clearly pre-eminent, there were some modest provisions on the "opportunity" side, with Congress providing $2.3 billion to help subsidize child care for working mothers and $3 billion in a block grant for welfare-to-work programs.

Beyond these prominent features, the new welfare also packed some hidden punches. It rewarded states for cutting welfare caseloads, largely without regard to how they did it. States that reduced their caseloads (whether those losing welfare found work or not) received credit against officially mandated quotas. If Congress was worried about states' slacking off from its tough work demands, the law indicated no concern that they might go too far in restricting access to benefits or pushing people off the welfare rolls. Only caseload reductions counted.

Under the banner of devolution, the law also gave states new authority to design their own welfare programs. While the welfare debate highlighted the professed virtues of innovation, less obvious was the license it gave states to craft policies even tougher and more restrictive than those allowed by federal law.

Pushing welfare decision making to the state and local level has never been good for the poor. In many states, poor families and their allies have little political influence. Moreover, constitutional balanced-budget requirements make states structurally unsuited to the task of protecting vulnerable residents against economic slumps. When unemployment goes up and state tax revenue goes down, the downward pressure on social spending intensifies.

The secret triumph of devolution lay, not in the opportunities for innovation, but in the opportunity for a quiet unraveling of the safety net.

The Unfolding Story of Welfare Transformed[1]

What has happened since 1996? For one thing, the new welfare changed a national program of income assistance to an array of state programs, each with its own assortment of benefits, services, restrictions, and requirements. There has always been wide variation in the amount of cash aid states provided, and federal waivers allowed states to deviate from some national rules. But devolution spurred far greater policy inconsistency by allowing states, essentially, to make their own rules. Consequently, what you get (or whether you get anything at all) depends on where you live.

In addition, devolution set off a state "race to the bottom," not by reducing benefit levels as some had predicted, but by imposing new restrictions that limited access to benefits. States across the nation have taken advantage of devolution to impose restrictions tougher than those required by federal law.

For example, although federal law required recipients to work within two years, most states require work within one year, some require immediate work, and others demand a month of job search before they even begin to process an application for assistance. No longer required to exempt mothers with children under three years old from work requirements, most states permit an exemption only for mothers with babies under one year old, and some have eliminated exemptions altogether. In nineteen states, lifetime limits for welfare receipt are set below the federal maximum of sixty months. Other states have imposed so-called family caps that preclude benefits for babies born to mothers already receiving welfare. If federal policymakers secretly hoped that states would do part of the dirty work of cutting welfare for them, they must be pleased with these results.

However, the picture from the states is anything but consistent or uniformly punitive. Many help those recipients accepting low-wage jobs by subsidizing the costs of transportation, child care, and medical insurance (although often only for one year). Twenty-two states try to keep low-wage workers afloat by using welfare benefits to supplement their incomes, "stopping the clock" on time limits for working parents. Significantly, the federal clock keeps ticking, and states adopting this strategy must use their own funds to support working families reaching the five-year lifetime limit. With state budgets increasingly squeezed by recession, it is hard to predict how strong the state commitment to preserve these supports will be.

Many state and local agencies have already cut back work preparation and placement programs funded under a $3 billion federal welfare-to-work block grant. Those funds spurred a short-term boom in contracting to private agencies. But the block grant expired leaving little evidence that states were able to build new systems for supporting work over the long term. In fact, no one knows exactly what all of this contracting produced, as state and local agencies kept limited records and conducted few careful evaluations. A close look at contracting in Illinois, for example, revealed the creation of a diffuse array of short-term programs operating under contract requirements that left many agencies unable to build anything of lasting value.

There is another strange twist to the convoluted welfare story: in their zest for services over support, states actually shifted government funds from the pockets of poor families to the pockets of private service providers. They distributed 76 percent of their AFDC funds in cash aid to the poor in 1996, but gave poor families only 41 percent of their TANF funds in 2000. Substantial portions of the TANF budget were consumed by child care costs, although it is difficult to say exactly how all the TANF funds were used. The General Accounting Office suggests that there is a fair amount of "supplantation" of services previously funded from other budget lines but now paid for by TANF.

Beyond the Caseload Count

The picture becomes still more complicated when one attempts to peer behind the head count in order to assess what actually happened in the purge of welfare caseloads. Exactly how did states push those caseloads down? What has happened to poor families that no longer have recourse to welfare? What kind of opportunities does the lower wage labor market really offer? Research has only begun to illuminate these crucial questions, but the evidence is disheartening.

Finding Good Jobs: There are three ways to lower welfare caseloads. One is by successfully moving recipients into good jobs with stable employment where they can earn enough to maintain their families above poverty (or, at least, above what they could get on welfare). Recipients may find jobs on their own, which many do, or with connections facilitated by welfare agencies and service providers.

Financial supports provided by TANF have allowed some recipients to take jobs where they earn too little to make ends meet on their own. Child-care and transportation subsidies make a difference for those workers. They also benefit from federally funded food stamps that stretch the grocery budget. But food stamp use fell off 40 percent after 1994, although fewer families were receiving welfare and more had joined the ranks of the working poor. Absent external pressures, most states made no effort to assure access to food stamps for those losing welfare. In fact, government studies indicate that administrative hassles and misinformation discouraged low-income families from obtaining benefits.

Taking Bad Jobs: A second way to lower welfare caseloads is to pressure recipients into taking bad jobs. Not all lower wage jobs are bad, but many of those most readily available to former recipients undermine their best efforts to make it as working parents. These jobs are characterized by unstable schedules, limited access to health insurance or pensions, no sick leave, and job insecurity. Because high turnover is a feature of these jobs, at any given moment, many are apt to be available. Indeed, employers seeking to fill these undesirable "high-velocity" jobs, where there is continuous churning of the workforce, are all too eager to use welfare agencies as a hiring hall.

This may partially explain why more than a fifth of those leaving welfare for work return within a year or two. Proponents of the new welfare conveniently blame individual work behavior or attitudes for job churning, but ignore the role of employers who structure jobs in ways that make job loss inevitable. What's a supermarket clerk to do when her manager makes frequent schedule changes, periodically shortens her hours, or asks her to work in a store across town? What happens is that carefully constructed child care arrangements break down, lost pay days break the family budget, and the hours it takes to commute on public transportation become unmanageable. The family-friendly workplace that more sought-after workers demand couldn't be farther from the hard reality of lower wage jobs.

One of the little appreciated virtues of the old welfare is that it served as a sort of unemployment insurance for these lower wage workers excluded from regular unemployment insurance by their irregular jobs. Welfare cushioned the layoffs, turnover, and contingencies that go with the territory. Under the new welfare, these workers face a hard landing because welfare is more difficult to get and offers little leeway to acquire either the time or skills that might yield a job with a future. Over the longer term, low-wage workers may find their access to welfare blocked by time limits. Although the five-year lifetime limit ostensibly targets sustained reliance on welfare, this limit could come back to bite those who cycle in and out of the lower wage labor force. At this point, no one knows how this will play out.

Creating Barriers to Access: A third way to reduce welfare caseloads is by reducing access—making benefits harder to acquire and keep. Some states explicitly try to divert applicants by imposing advance job-search requirements, demanding multiple trips to the welfare office in order to complete the application process, or informally advising applicants that it may not be worth the hassle. In some welfare offices, caseworkers routinely encourage applicants to forgo cash aid and apply only for Medicaid and food stamps.

Benefits are also harder to keep, as caseworkers require recipients to attend frequent meetings either to discuss seemingly endless demands for documentation or to press them on issues involving work. Everyday life in an urban welfare office is difficult to describe and, for many, even harder to believe. There are the hours of waiting in rows of plastic chairs, the repeated requests for paperwork, the ritualized weekly job club lectures about how to smile, shake hands, and show a good attitude to employers. As inspiration, caseworkers leading job club sessions often tell stories from their own lives of rising from poverty to become welfare workers (positions likely to be cut back as caseloads decline). When clients tell their own tales of cycling from bad jobs to worse and ask for help getting a good job, caseworkers are apt to admonish them for indulging in a "pity party."

Access to welfare may also be constrained through a profoundly mundane array of administrative barriers that simply make benefits harder to keep. A missed appointment, misplaced documents (often lost by the agency), delayed entry of personal data—these common and otherwise trivial mishaps can result in a loss of benefits for "non-cooperation."

The Public Benefits Hotline, a call-in center that provides both advice and intervention for Chicago residents, received some ten thousand calls in the four years after welfare reform, most of them involving hassles of this sort.[2] In other parts of the country, these types of problems show up in administrative hearing records and court cases, where judges have criticized welfare agencies for making "excessive" demands for verification documents, conducting "sham assessments" leading to inappropriate imposition of work requirements, and sanctioning clients for missing appointments when they should have helped them deal with child care or medical difficulties.

Is There a Bottom Line?

The new welfare has produced neither the immediate cataclysm its opponents threatened nor the economic and social redemption its proponents anticipated. Opponents had warned that welfare reform would plunge one million children into poverty. In the midst of an unprecedented economic boom, that didn't happen. But, even in the best of times, prospects were not auspicious for those leaving welfare.

According to the Urban Institute, about half of those leaving welfare for work between 1997 and 1999 obtained jobs where they earned a median hourly wage of only $7.15. If the jobs offered a steady forty hours of work a week (which lower wage jobs usually don't), that would provide a gross annual income of $14,872. That places a mother with two children a precarious $1,000 above the formal poverty line for the year 2000 and a two-parent family with two children nearly $3,000 *below* that line. But more than one-fifth of those leaving welfare for work didn't make it through the year—either because they lost their jobs, got sick, or just couldn't make ends meet. The only thing surprising about these figures is that the numbers weren't higher. Others left or lost welfare, but did not find work, with one in seven adults losing welfare reporting no alternative means of support. Their specific fate is unknown, but most big cities have been reporting worrisome increases in homelessness and hunger.

If there is any bottom line, it is that caseloads have been purged. But neither the market for lower wage workers nor the policies put into practice in the name of welfare reform have purged poverty from the lives of the poor. Even in the last years of the economic boom, between 1996 and 1998, the Urban Institute found that three hundred thousand more individuals in single-parent families slipped into extreme poverty. Although they qualified for food stamps that might have stretched their resources a bit further, many did not get them. Government figures indicate that families leaving welfare for work often lose access to other benefits, which states do not automatically continue irrespective of eligibility.

More recently, census figures have begun to show the effects of recession coupled with an eroded safety net. The nation's poverty rate rose to 11.7 percent in 2001, up from 11.3 percent the prior year. More troubling still, inequality is growing and poverty is deepening. In 2001, the "poverty gap," the gap between the official poverty line and the income of poor individuals, reached its highest level since measurements were first taken in 1979. In California, often a harbinger of larger social trends, a startling two in three poor children now live in families where at least one adult is employed. Can the families of lower wage workers live without access to welfare and other government supports? Apparently, they can live, but not very well.

Slouching Toward Reauthorization

"We have to remember that the goal of the reform program was not to get people out of poverty, but to achieve financial independence, to get off welfare." This statement by a senior Connecticut welfare official quoted in the *New York Times* is more candid than most. But it illustrates the kind of political rationale that policymakers use to inoculate themselves against factual evidence of the new welfare's failure to relieve poverty.

With TANF facing reauthorization in the fall of 2002, it was clear that reconsideration of welfare policy would take place on a new playing field. Tough work rules, time limits, and devolution were just the starting point. The Bush administration advanced a reauthorization plan that increased work requirements, cut opportunities for education and training, added new doses of moralism, and extended devolution.

The Republican-controlled House passed a TANF reauthorization bill (later deferred by the Senate) requiring recipients to work forty hours a week and demanding that states enforce these requirements for 70 percent of families receiving welfare by 2007. The bill also created incentives for states to require work within a month of granting welfare benefits and continued to credit states for caseload reductions, regardless of whether families losing welfare had jobs that could sustain them.

Families would face harsh new penalties, simply for running afoul of administrative rules. The House-passed measure required states to impose full family sanctions if caseworkers find a recipient in violation of those rules for sixty days. This makes entire families vulnerable to losing aid if a parent misses a couple of appointments or gets tangled in demands to supply documents verifying eligibility, just the type of problem that crops up routinely in states with complicated rules and outdated record-keeping systems.

One of the least mentioned but most dangerous features of the House bill was a "superwaiver" that would allow the executive branch to release states from social welfare obligations contained in more than a dozen federal poverty programs, in-cluding not only TANF, but also food stamps and Medicaid. This stealth provision would allow the Bush administration to override existing legislation by fiat. The nominal justification for the superwaiver is that it would ease the path of state innovation and experimentation. It would also ease the path for state cuts in social programs beyond all previous experience.

A more visibly contentious feature of the House bill was a provision to spend $300 million dollars per year on programs to induce welfare recipients to marry. This provision is one of the favorites of the religious right, along with the administration's funding for faith-based social services. These moral redemption provisions may be more important for what they signify to the Republican Party's conservative base than for what they do, as many states have resisted these types of things in the past. However, on this point, it is irresistible to quote America's favorite president, the fictional President Josiah Bartlet of the television series *West Wing*, who quipped: "When did the government get into the yenta business?"

Of Poverty, Democracy, and Welfare

The demise of the old welfare marked more than an end to a policy that many believed had outlived its usefulness. It also marked the end of welfare *politics* as we knew it. In the tepid debate over reauthorization in the fall of 2002, the bitter conflicts of earlier years over government's role in addressing poverty were replaced by half-hearted tinkering. Even provisions with the potential to induce hand-to-hand combat—such as those on marriage or the superwaiver—elicited relatively low-intensity challenges.

Is this because the new welfare yielded the benefits that liberals had hoped for, removing a contentious issue from the table and conferring legitimation on the poor, not as recipients, but as workers? Did it satisfy conservatives by clearing caseloads and demanding work? That does not seem to be the case.

If the poor have benefited from a new legitimacy, it is hard to see the rewards. Congress has not rushed to offer extensive new work supports. In fact, the House bill contained $8 to $10 billion less for work supports than the Congressional Budget Office estimated would be needed. In 2002, Congress couldn't even agree to extend unemployment insurance for those outside the welfare system who were felled by recession, corporate collapses, and the high-tech slide. While conservatives celebrated the caseload count, they also savored the opportunity to raise the ante with more onerous work requirements and marriage inducements, and even made a bid to eliminate other social protections through the superwaiver.

In the aftermath of the November 2002 election, a conservative consolidation of power was in the air. In a televised interview with Jim Lehrer, Republican spokesman Grover Norquist dared Democrats to take on the welfare issue. "If the Democrats want to stand up against welfare reform, let them! Two years from now, they'll be in even worse shape in the Senate elections."

Some congressional Democrats did take tentative steps against the tide, suggesting provisions that would fund new welfare-to-work services, provide additional job subsidies, increase the child care allotment, provide alternatives to work for recipients categorized as having work "barriers," and restore benefits to legal immigrants who were cut from welfare in 1996. Maryland Representative Benjamin Cardin was chief sponsor of a bill suggesting that states should be held accountable, not only for caseload reduction, but for poverty reduction. This notion had little traction in the 107th Congress and is likely to have even less in the next. Without the foundation of a politics of poverty to build on, such laudable ideas seem strangely irrelevant, even to the Democrats' agenda.

If welfare is a bellwether of broader political developments, there's little mistaking which way the wind is blowing. It has a decidedly Dickensian chill. The politics of poverty that gave birth to the old welfare has been supplanted by the politics of personal piety that gave birth to the new. This reflects a convergence between a neoliberal agenda of market dominance and a neoconservative agenda of middle-class moralism. In this reconfigured politics, personal responsibility is code for enforcement of the market. The new Calvinism advanced by welfare policy treats inequality as a natural consequence of personal behavior and attitude in an impartial marketplace. It is consistent with a shift in the role of the state from defender of the vulnerable and buffer against the market to one of protector-in-chief of both market and morals. This shift does not favor a small state, but a different state, one capable of enforcing market demands on workers, responding to corporate demands for capital (through public subsidies, bailouts, and tax breaks), and, perhaps more symbolically, regulating morality.

Welfare policy neither created, nor could prevent, these developments. Nor is it a foregone conclusion that government will shirk its social responsibilities. After all, America's growing economic inequality is fundamentally at odds with its commitment to political equality.

In contrast to the United States, the policies of Western European countries suggest that there need not be an absolute conflict between the welfare state and the market. Despite their allegiance to the latter, other nations continue to offer greater social protection to their citizens and worry about the democratic consequences of excluding the disadvantaged from the economy and the polity. U.S. policymakers need to move past stale debates pitting work against welfare and the poor against the nonpoor, if they are to advance policies that promote both social inclusion and economic opportunity.

Welfare, though small in scope, is large in relevance because it is a place where economic, social, and political issues converge. The old welfare acknowledged, in principle, a political commitment to relieve poverty and lessen inequality, even if, in practice, that commitment was limited, benefits were ungenerous, and access uneven. The new welfare dramatically changed the terms of the relationship between disadvantaged citizens and their state. It devolved choices about social protection from the State to the states, and it placed the value of work over the values of family well-being and social equity. As bad as the old welfare may have been, there is reason to lament its demise after all.

Notes

1. The discussion in this section draws, in part, on research conducted for the Project on the Public Economy of Work at the University of Chicago, supported by the Ford Foundation, the National Science Foundation, and the Open Society Institute. The author and Susan Lambert are co-directors.

2. The Hotline is a collaborative effort of the Legal Assistance Foundation of Chicago and community antipoverty advocates.

EVELYN Z. BRODKIN is associate professor at the School of Social Service Administration and lecturer in the Law School of the University of Chicago. She writes widely on poverty and politics.

From *Dissent*, Winter 2003 pp. 29–36. © 2003 by Dissent Magazine. Reprinted by permission. www.dissentmagazine.org

What's At Stake

In the competitive world of college admissions, 'fairness' is often in the eye of the beholder. Here are the facts about affirmative action.

BY BARBARA KANTROWITZ AND PAT WINGERT

In 1978, THE SUPREME COURT opened the doors of America's elite campuses to a generation of minority students when it ruled that universities' admissions policies could take applicants' race into account. But the decision, by a narrowly divided court drawing a hairsplitting distinction between race as a "plus factor" (allowed) and numerical quotas (forbidden), did not end an often bitter and emotional debate. A quarter of a century after the ruling in *Regents of the University of California v. Bakke*, affirmative action is still being challenged by disappointed applicants to selective colleges and graduate schools, and still hotly defended by civil-rights groups. Now that two such cases, both involving the University of Michigan, have reached the Supreme Court, the issue can no longer be evaded: when, if ever, should schools give preferential treatment to minorities, based solely on their race?

4.3%
THE PERCENTAGE OF BLACK PLAYERS ON THE UNIVERSITY OF MICHIGAN FOOTBALL TEAM, 1941

45%
THE PERCENTAGE OF BLACK PLAYERS ON THE UNIVERSITY OF MICHIGAN FOOTBALL TEAM, 2002

7%
THE PERCENTAGE OF YALE UNIVERSITY STUDENTS WHOM ARE BLACK

It's a measure of how far we've come that the desirability of improving opportunities for black and Hispanic students is a given in the debate. But the fundamental question of where "fairness" lies hasn't changed, and the competition keeps growing. Each year, more students apply to the top universities, which by and large have not increased the sizes of their classes in the past 50 years. The court will have to decide who deserves first crack at those

scarce resources. (Right now, about one sixth of blacks get college degrees, compared with 30 percent of whites and 40 percent of Asians.) And if the court allows affirmative action to continue in some form, it will only set the stage for future debate over even more perplexing questions. Do all minorities deserve an edge or just those from disadvantaged backgrounds? What about white students from poor families? And how do you balance the academic records of students from the suburbs and the inner cities? As the controversy heats up, here's a 10-step guide to sorting out the issues at stake:

1 What is affirmative action?

When President Kennedy first used the term in the early 1960s, "affirmative action" simply meant taking extra measures to ensure integration in federally funded jobs. Forty years later, a wide range of programs fall under this rubric, although all are meant to encourage enrollment of underrepresented minorities—generally blacks, Hispanics and Native Americans. Schools vary in how much weight they assign to the student's race. For some, it's a decisive consideration; for others, it's jut one among a number of factors such as test scores, grades, family background, talents and extracurricular activities. After the *Bakke* decision emphasized the importance of campus diversity as a "compelling" benefit to society, colleges quickly responded with efforts not just to attract minorities but to create a broader geographic and socioeconomic mix, along with a range of academic, athletic or artistic talent.

In 2003, the debate over the merits of affirmative action essentially boils down to questions of fairness for both black and white applicants. Critics say it results in "reverse discrimination" against white applicants who are passed over in favor of less well-qualified black students, some of whom suffer when they attend schools they're not prepared for. But Gary Orfield, director of Harvard University's Civil Rights Project, argues that emphasizing diversity has not meant admitting unqualified students. "I have been on the admissions committees of five different

PRO

Diversity Is Essential...
He knew he was in for a fight. But it's a battle the former University of Michigan president believes must be won.

BY LEE C. BOLLINGER

When I became president of the University of Michigan in 1997, affirmative action in higher education was under siege from the right. Buoyed by a successful lawsuit against the University of Texas Law School's admissions policy and by ballot initiatives such as California's Proposition 209, which outlawed race as a factor in college admissions, the opponents set their sights on affirmative-action programs at colleges across the country.

The rumor that Michigan would be the next target in this campaign turned out to be correct. I believed strongly that we had no choice but to mount the best legal defense ever for diversity in higher education and take special efforts to explain this complex issue, in simple and direct language, to the American public. There are many misperceptions about how race and ethnicity are considered in college admissions. Competitive colleges and universities are always looking for a mix of students with different experiences and backgrounds—academic, geographic, international, socioeconomic, athletic, public-service oriented and, yes, racial and ethnic.

It is true that in sorting the initial rush of applications, large universities will give "points" for various factors in the selection process in order to ensure fairness as various officers review applicants. Opponents of Michigan's undergraduate system complain that an applicant is assigned more points for being black, Hispanic or Native American than for having a perfect SAT score. This is true, but it trivializes the real issue: whether, in principle, race and ethnicity are appropriate considerations.

The simple fact about the Michigan undergraduate policy is that it gives overwhelming weight to traditional academic factors—some 110 out of a total of 150 points. After that, there are some 40 points left for other factors, of which 20 can be allocated for race or socioeconomic status.

Race has been a defining element of the American experience. The historic *Brown v. Board of Education* decision is almost 50 years old, yet metropolitan Detroit is more segregated now than it was in 1960. The majority of students who each year arrive on a campus like Michigan's graduated from virtually all-white or all-black high schools. The campus is their first experience living in an integrated environment.

This is vital. Diversity is not merely a desirable addition to a well-rounded education. It is as essential as the study of the Middle Ages, of international politics and of Shakespeare. For our students to better understand the diverse country and world they inhabit, they must be immersed in a campus culture that allows them to study with, argue with and become friends with students who may be different from them. It broadens the mind, and the intellect—essential goals of education.

Reasonable people can disagree about affirmative action. But it is important that we do not lose the sense of history, the compassion and the largeness of vision that defined the best of the civil-rights era, which has given rise to so much of what is good about America today.

BOLLINGER is president of Columbia University.

CON

... But Not at This Cost
Admissions policies like Michigan's focus not on who, but what, you are—perpetuating a culture of victimhood

BY ARMSTRONG WILLIAMS

Back in 1977, when I was a senior in high school, I received scholarship offers to attend prestigious colleges. The schools wanted me in part because of my good academic record—but also because affirmative action mandates required them to encourage more black students to enroll. My father wouldn't let me take any of the enticements. His reasoning was straightforward: scholarship money should go to the economically deprived. And since he could pay for my schooling, he would. In the end, I chose a historically black college—South Carolina State.

What I think my father meant, but was perhaps too stern to say, was that one should always rely on hard work and personal achievement to carry the day—every day. Sadly, this rousing point seems lost on the admissions board at the University of Michigan, which wrongly and unapologetically discriminates on the basis of skin color. The university ranks applicants on a scale that awards points for SAT scores, highschool grades and race. For example, a perfect SAT score is worth 12 points. Being black gets you 20 points. Is there anyone who can look at those two numbers and think they are fair?

Supporters maintain that the quota system is essential to creating a diverse student body. And, indeed, there is some validity to this sort of thinking. A shared history of slavery and discrimination has ingrained racial hierarchies into our national identity, divisions that need to be erased. There is, however, a very real danger that we are

merely reinforcing the idea that minorities are first and foremost victims. Because of this victim status, the logic goes, they are owed special treatment. But that isn't progress, it's inertia.

If the goal of affirmative action is to create a more equitable society, it should be need-based. Instead, affirmative action is defined by its tendency to reduce people to fixed categories: at many universities, it seems, admissions officers look less at who you are than *what* you are. As a result, affirmative-action programs rarely help the least among us. Instead, they often benefit the children of middle- and upper-class black Americans who have been conditioned to feel they are owed something.

This is alarming. We have finally, after far too long, reached a point where black Americans have pushed into the mainstream—and not just in entertainment and sports. From politics to corporate finance, blacks succeed. Yet many of us still feel entitled to special benefits—in school, in jobs, in government contracts.

It is time to stop. We must reach a point where we expect to rise or fall on our own merits. We just can't continue to base opportunities on race while the needs of the poor fall by the wayside. As a child growing up on a farm, I was taught that personal responsibility was the lever that moved the world. That is why it pains me to see my peers rest their heads upon the warm pillow of victim status.

WILLIAMS is a syndicated columnist.

universities," he says, "and I have never seen a student admitted just on the basis of race. [Committees] think about what the class will be like, what kind of educational experience the class will provide." Opponents also say that with the expansion of the black middle class in the past 20 years, these programs should be refocused on kids from low-income homes. "It just doesn't make sense to give preference to the children of a wealthy black businessman, but not to the child of a Vietnamese boat person or an Arab-American who is suffering discrimination," says Curt Levey, director of legal affairs at the Center for Individual Rights, which is representing the white applicants who were turned down by the University of Michigan.

Despite the public perception that affirmative action is rampant on campuses, these programs really only affect a very small number of minority students. It's a legal issue mainly on highly selective public campuses, such as Michigan, Berkeley or Texas. Even at these schools, the actual numbers of minority students are still small—which is why supporters of affirmative action say race should still matter. Blacks account for 11 percent of undergraduates nationally; at the most elite schools the percentage is often smaller. For example, fewer than 7 percent of Harvard's current freshman class is black, compared with 12.9 percent of the overall population.

2 How did the University of Michigan become the test case?

Both sides say it was really a matter of chance more than anything else. "It's not like we studied 1,000 schools and picked them out," says Levey. To have the makings of a test case, the suit had to involve a public university whose admissions information could be obtained under the Freedom of Information Act. It also had to be a very large school that relied on some kind of numerical admissions formula—unlike the more individualized approach generally used by private colleges with large admissions staffs.

In fact, Michigan is just one of a number of public universities that have faced legal challenges in recent years. In 1996, the U.S. Court of Appeals for the Fifth Circuit banned the use of race in admissions at the University of Texas Law School. The Supreme Court declined to hear the law school's appeal, but by that time, the university had changed its admissions procedures anyway. The University of Georgia dropped race as a factor after a similar suit. But when Michigan's admissions policy came under challenge in the mid-1990s, university officials decided to fight back—all the way to the Supreme Court.

3 How does the Michigan system work?

Although President George W. Bush reduced Michigan's complex admissions process to a single sound bite—comparing the relative values given to SAT scores and race—a student's academic record is actually the most important factor. For undergraduate applicants, decisions are made on a point system. Out of a total of 150 possible points, a student can get up to 110 for academics. That includes a

possible 80 points for grades and 12 points for standardized test scores. Admissions counselors then add or subtract points for the rigor of the high school (up to 10) and the difficulty of the curriculum (up to 8 for students who take the toughest courses). Applicants can get up to 40 more points for such factors as residency in underrepresented states (2 points) or Michigan residency (10 points, with a 6-point bonus for living in an underrepresented county). Being from an underrepresented minority group or from a predominantly minority high school is worth 20 points. So is being from a low-income family—even for white students. The same 20 points are awarded to athletes. Students also earn points for being related to an alumnus (up to 4 points), writing a good personal essay (up to 3 points) and participating in extracurricular activities (up to 5 points). Admissions officials say the scale is only a guide; there's no target number that automatically determines whether a student is admitted or rejected. Michigan also has a "rolling" admissions policy, which means that students hear a few months after they apply. The number of spaces available depends on when in this cycle a student applies.

At the law school, there's no point system, but the admissions officers say higher grades and standardized test scores do increase an applicant's chances. Those factors are considered along with the rigor of an applicant's courses, recommendations and essays. The school also says that race "sometimes makes the difference in whether or not a student is admitted."

4 Does the Michigan system create quotas?

This is an issue the court will probably have to decide. Awarding points could amount to a quota if it resulted in routinely filling a fixed number of places. Levey claims that the fact that the number of minority students admitted is relatively stable from year to year proves there is a target Michigan tries to hit. Michigan's president, Mary Sue Coleman, is adamant that that's not the case. "We do not have, and never have had, quotas or numerical targets in either the undergraduate or Law School admissions programs," she said in a statement issued after Bush's speech last week. At the law school, the most recent entering class of 352 students included 21 African-Americans, 24 Latinos and 8 Native Americans. The year before, there were 26 African-Americans, 16 Latinos and 3 Native Americans. The university says that over the past nine years, the number of blacks in the entering class has ranged from 21 to 37. On the undergraduate level, the university says that blacks generally make up between 7 and 9 percent of the entering class.

In general, few outright quota systems exist anymore. "The only legal way to have quotas today is to address a proven constitutional violation," says Orfield. "For instance, if you can prove that a police or fire department intentionally did not hire any blacks for 25 years, and you can prove discrimination, a judge can rule that there can be a quota for the next five years."

Affirmative Action, 25 Years Later

Lawsuits are prompting the Supreme Court to revisit a landmark 1978 decision in favor of race-based college admissions. Affirmative action's legacy, and its uncertain future.

SAT Scores

SAT1: 2002 NAT'L AVERAGE	
White	1060
Black	857
Hispanic	910
Asian/Pac. Islander	1070
Native American	962
SAT1: 2002 UNIV. AVERAGE	
UC Berkeley	1180–1440*
Univ. of Florida (2001)	1229
Univ. of Michigan	1180–1390*
UT Austin	1222

The Case Against Michigan

Plaintiff Barbara Grutter claims she lost her spot at Michigan Law School to less qualified minorities; 100% of blacks with Grutter's ranking were accepted the year she applied, but only 9% of whites.

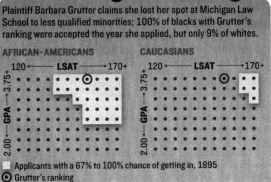

☐ Applicants with a 67% to 100% chance of getting in, 1995
◉ Grutter's ranking

Univ. of Mich. Point System

The university uses a point scale to rate prospective students. Its policy of awarding minorities an extra 20 has stirred protest. Here's how a fictional applicant would score a promising 130:

GPA Score	Points
2.0	40
2.1	42
2.2	44
2.3	46
2.4	48
2.5	50
2.6	52
2.7	54
2.8	56
2.9	58
3.0	60
3.1	62
3.2	64
3.3	66
3.4	68
3.5	**(70)**
3.6	72
3.7	74
3.8	76
3.9	78
4.0	80

HIGH-SCHOOL QUALITY

Score	Points
0	0
1	2
2	4
3	**(6)**
4	8
5	10

DIFFICULTY OF CURRICULUM

Score	Points
-2	-4
-1	-2
0	0
1	2
2	**(4)**
3	6
4	8

TEST SCORES

ACT	SAT1	Points
1–19	400–920	0
20–21	930–1000	6
22–26	1010–1190	**(10)**
27–30	1200–1350	11
31–36	1360–1600	12

Points (maximum of 40)

GEOGRAPHY
- **(10)** Michigan resident
- 6 Underrepresented Michigan county
- 2 Underrepresented state

ALUMNI
- 4 Legacy (parents, stepparents)
- 1 Other (grandparents, siblings)

ESSAY
- 1 Very good
- **(2)** Excellent
- 3 Outstanding

PERSONAL ACHIEVEMENT
- 1 State
- **(3)** Regional
- 5 National

LEADERSHIP AND SERVICE
- 1 State
- 2 Regional
- **(5)** National

MISCELLANEOUS (choose one)
- 20 Socioeconomic disadvantage
- **(20)** Underrepresented racial/ethnic minority identification or education
- 5 Men in nursing
- 20 Scholarship athlete
- 20 Provost's discretion

Race and Higher Education

The number of minorities attending four-year colleges has risen about 85% since the Supreme Court OK'd affirmative action in admissions.

Race/ethnicity
- ▨ White
- ■ Black
- ■ Hispanic
- ■ Asian/Pac. Islander
- ■ Native American
- ☐ Other/Did not answer

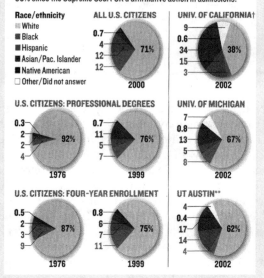

ALL RACES ARE NON-HISPANIC EXCEPT "HISPANIC." NUMBERS DO NOT ADD TO 100 DUE TO ROUNDING. "25TH TO 75TH PERCENTILES. †FRESHMAN ADMITS ONLY. **UNDERGRADUATES. SOURCES: U.S. CENSUS BUREAU, UC BERKELEY, UNIV. OF MICHIGAN, UT AUSTIN, UNIV. OF FLORIDA, THE CENTER FOR INDIVIDUAL RIGHTS, THE COLLEGE BOARD. RESEARCH AND TEXT BY JOSH ULICK. GRAPHIC BY BONNIE SCRANTON.

New Options for Diversity?

Several states have enacted the alternatives to affirmative action that Bush favors. But do they reach an equal number of minorities?

- **CALIFORNIA**: Voters passed Proposition 209 in **1996**. It bans affirmative action in university admissions. The plan promises a state-university spot for the top **4%** of students from every high school, including the most disadvantaged ones. Other factors may be involved, but Berkeley's black undergraduate enrollment has dropped **33%** from **1996** to **2001**.
- **TEXAS**: A **1997** plan ended affirmative action in admissions. High-school students in the top **10%** of their class are guaranteed slots at state schools. Since then, black enrollment has remained relatively stable at UT Austin.
- **FLORIDA**: As of **2000**, state universities no longer consider race in admissions, but promise slots for students in the top **20%** of classes.

AFFIRMATIVE ACCESS

Making the Grade
Bush wants admissions policies to look like his home state's. But in Texas, his plan gets middling marks.

BY LEIF STRICKLAND

Natalie Fogiel, an 18-year-old high-school senior in Dallas, has SAT scores higher than the Ivy League's collective average—she scored 1490 out of 1600. She's a National Merit Scholar semifinalist, and she's active in Student Congress. Fogiel doesn't want to go to Harvard or Yale. She wants to go to the business school at her state university's flagship campus, the University of Texas at Austin. But under Texas's five-year-old "affirmative access" policy—which guarantees admission to any state university for all seniors graduating in the top 10 percent of their classes—Fogiel isn't sure she'll get in. Because she goes to Highland Park High School in Dallas—one of the most competitive public schools in the country—she's only in the top 15 percent.

As the Supreme Court prepares to review the constitutionality of affirmative-action programs, President Bush has been championing programs such as Texas's, which passed when he was governor. But at some of the state's best schools, the policy has been attacked with the same words—"unfair" and "divisive"—that Bush uses to describe affirmative action. "If I had gone anywhere else, I probably would be in the top 1 percent," Fogiel says. While Texas's program prohibits using race as a factor, Texas's many segregated high schools mean the result is much the same. Since the 10 percent plan was implemented, minority enrollment at UT Austin has returned to roughly the same levels as when affirmative action was in effect.

The problem with the 10 percent policy, some Highland Park students say, is that it assumes all high schools are alike. And Highland Park High—with its 97 percent white student population—is clearly unique. Even a student who scores all A's in regular classes for four straight years wouldn't be guaranteed a place in the top quarter of his class. (You'd need to add honors classes to the mix.)

But elsewhere, the policy is playing well. Israel Hernandez is in the top 10 percent of W. H. Adamson High School, which is overwhelmingly Hispanic. He's the first member of his family to go to college; he'll be attending Texas A&M in the fall. "It's like everyone has their hopes and dreams on me," he says. Texas A&M has been to Adamson (average SAT score: 838) more than a dozen times this year touting its Century Scholars program, which specifically targets promising inner-city students like Hernandez.

Texas's plan doesn't just help traditional minorities. "The 10 percent diversifies economically," says Harvard Law professor Lani Guinier. "It benefits rural west Texas, which is primarily white but also very poor."

The policy isn't causing Highland Park students too much hardship—98 percent of its graduates went to college last year. Most of those who applied to UT and didn't get into their preferred programs were admitted to the university nonetheless—either into another school or to a provisional program. For her part, Fogiel says she probably won't go to UT if she isn't accepted to Austin's business program. She'll opt for one of her safeties: Georgetown or Boston College.

With MARK MILLER in Dallas

On campuses, some education experts say that what appear to be quotas may actually just reflect a relatively steady number of minority applicants within a certain state. "I don't know of a public or private institution that uses quotas," says Alexander Astin, director of the Higher Education Research Institute at UCLA. "That's a red herring. There is always a consideration of merit given." Nonetheless, admissions officers at public and private universities admit that they are always very conscious of demography—and work hard to make sure that the number of minority students does not decline precipitously from one year to the next.

5 How can the court rule?

The short answer is: the Supreme Court can do whatever it wants. The options range from leaving the *Bakke* decision intact to barring any use of race in college admissions. Or the court could issue a narrowly tailored opinion, one that would affect only Michigan's point system and perhaps only the number of points the university assigns to race. "I think it's a good guess that they may say that they cannot give minorities a specific number of points, or say points are fine, but they can only award 10," says Levey.

The experts agree that the key vote will belong to Justice Sandra Day O'Connor. Some court watchers predict that she will try to find a very specific solution that will leave affirmative action largely intact. "She probably won't buy anything that's open-ended," says Sheldon Steinbach, general counsel of the American Council on Education, a consortium of the nation's leading research universities. "Maybe she will say that it can be done in some narrowly defined way." Steinbach doesn't think the court will order schools to disregard everything but the supposedly objective criteria of grades and test scores. Such a ruling "would tie the hands of admissions officers from shaping the kind of class they want to fulfill the academic mission of the institution," Steinbach says. Another possibility is that the court will order schools to give preference to students who are economically disadvantaged, which would cover many minority applicants.

6 Will the decision affect private universities and colleges?

The answer really depends on what the justices rule, but legal experts generally agree that private institutions would have to follow the court's guidelines because virtually all receive some federal funding. However, the ruling would have a noticeable impact only at elite institutions since most colleges in this country accept the vast majority of applicants. And the elite schools—no more than several dozen around the country—generally employ multistep admissions procedures that leave plenty of room for subjective judgments. Unlike the numerical formulas used by large public universities, these would be difficult to challenge in court.

Already, several landmark state cases have pushed private schools to make changes. In the wake of the Texas decision, officials at highly selective Rice University in Houston, on the advice of the state attorney general, banned the use of race in all admissions decisions. Clerks were told to strip any reference to a student's race or ethnicity from admissions and financial-aid applications before they were forwarded to the admission committee. Although the proportion of minorities dropped right after the change, it's now back up to the levels before the ruling, officials say—about 7 percent black and 10.5 percent Hispanic. That was accomplished through "significant" recruiting, a Rice spokesman said.

7 How would an anti-affirmative-action ruling affect other preferences for legacies and athletes?

Some educators think legacies (the children or grandchildren of alumni) could become unintended victims of an anti-affirmative-action ruling. On the face of it, providing preferential treatment to these applicants does not violate the Constitution, but as a matter of fairness—and politics—legacies would be hard to defend, since they are usually white and middle class. However, many colleges would probably resist the change because legacies bring a sense of tradition and continuity to the school. (They also are a powerful inducement to alumni donations.) Athletic preferences are a different story. They don't disproportionately favor whites so they're probably not as vulnerable.

8 Whom does affirmative action hurt and whom does it help?

Opponents of affirmative action claim it actually hurts some minority students, particularly those who end up struggling to compete in schools they're not prepared for. And, they say, it unfairly tars well-qualified minority students with the suspicion that they were admitted because of their race. Supporters say that's a spurious argument because race may sometimes be the deciding factor between qualified applicants, but it is never the only reason a student is admitted.

The more obvious potential victims, of course, are white students who have been denied admission—like the plaintiffs in the Michigan suit. But there's no guarantee that these students would have been admitted even if there were no black applicants. In their 1998 book "The Shape of the River," William Bowen and Derek Bok (former presidents of Princeton and Harvard, respectively) analyzed the records of 45,000 students at elite uni-

versities and found that without race-sensitive admissions, white applicants' chances of being admitted to selective universities would have increased only slightly, from 25 to 26.2 percent. But Bowen and Bok also found that black applicants' chances were greatly enhanced by affirmative action, and the vast majority of black students went on to graduate within six years—even at the most selective institutions. The black graduates were more likely to go to graduate or professional school than their white counterparts and more likely to be leaders of community, social service or professional organizations after college.

Supporters of affirmative action say both white and black students benefit from living in a diverse academic environment, one that closely resembles the increasingly diverse workplace. Opponents say schools don't need affirmative action to create a diverse campus; instead they say that other admissions strategies, such as "affirmative access," can accomplish the same goals.

9 What is "affirmative access"?

In the wake of lawsuits, several states have adopted alternative ways to bring minority students to campus. Modern political marketing seems to require a label for everything, and "affirmative access" has emerged as the label for these plans. Each operates differently. In California, the top 4 percent of students at each in-state high school is guaranteed admission to the University of California (although not necessarily to the most prestigious campuses, Berkeley and UCLA). For the University of Texas, it's the top 10 percent, and in Florida, the top 20 percent. The success of these new initiatives varies. California's plan was enacted after the passage of Proposition 209, which forbids using race in admissions. In 1997, the last year before the use of race was banned, 18.8 percent of the class consisted of underrepresented minorities. Last year that number was 19.1 percent systemwide. But some individual campuses, like Berkeley and UCLA, have not returned to pre-1997 levels. At the University of Texas, the percentage of black and Hispanic entering freshmen has remained fairly steady, but officials say the 10 percent law alone isn't enough. "You have to add some targeted procedures that work in tandem with the law," says University of Texas president Larry Faulkner. "And for us that's been pretty aggressive recruiting programs aimed at top 10 percent students in areas where minority students live, and carefully tailored scholarship programs aimed at students in areas or schools that have not historically attended UT."

Opponents of affirmative access like lawyer Martin Michaelson, who specializes in higher-education cases, say these programs rest on the dubious premise that "residential segregation patterns are a better method for choosing a college class than the judgment of educators" and create, in effect, a built-in constituency for continued segregation. Critics also worry that a program that mixes schools of widely different qualities may reward less-

What Merit Really Means

JONATHAN ALTER

ANYONE WITH HALF A BRAIN KNOWS THAT GRADES AND TEST scores aren't the only way to define "merit" in college admissions. Sometimes a good jump shot or batting average is "merit." Or a commitment to a soup kitchen. Or the ability to overcome an obstacle in life. Conscientious admissions officers take a wide variety of factors into account and make rounded, subtle judgments about the composition of the incoming class. The debate over affirmative action in education boils down to whether universities should be free to make that judgment or be told by the government how to choose.

The problem with affirmative action is not, as some conservatives suggest, that it has eroded standards and dumbed down elite institutions. The level of academic achievement among freshmen at, say, Yale is far higher than it was when George W. Bush entered in 1964. With his highschool record, he probably wouldn't be admitted today, even if he were black. No, what's wrong with affirmative action is that it has too often been routinized and mechanized, and has thus begun to resemble the very thinking it was supposed to replace.

Conservatives, trying to stand on principle, argue that affirmative action is simply reverse discrimination. In certain realms, like the awarding of federal contracts, that may be true. But college is different. The college experience is partly about preparing students for adult life, which increasingly means learning to deal with people of many different backgrounds. To hear the Bill Bennetts of the world, whites and Asian-Americans rejected by the colleges of their choice are like blacks rejected by the lunch counters of their choice in the Jim Crow South. It's a lame analogy. Lunch counters (and other public facilities) have no right to discriminate; neither do nonselective colleges, about 80 percent of the total. But exclusive institutions, by definition, must exclude.

The basis on which they do so should at least be consistent. You either favor weighing immutable nonacademic "preferences" or you don't. Some conservatives want to continue preferences for alumni children and end those for minorities. Some liberals want the reverse—to keep affirmative action but end legacies. Both sides ace their hypocrisy boards. Personally, I go for preferences, within limits, because I want the smart alumni kid from Pacific Palisades to sit in the dining hall and get to know the smart poor kid from Camden. Neither the University of Michigan policy nor the Bush administration challenge to it are likely to take us closer to that end.

The larger problem is that exclusive colleges too often use that worn-out crutch of a word—"diversity"—to cover for their lack of genuine integration (in dorms, for instance), and a lack of progress on socioeconomic affirmative action. Only 3 percent of students in top universities come from the poorest quarter of the American population. A Harvard study last year found that colleges are too often "recyclers of privilege" instead of "engines of upward mobility." Harvard itself falls short on this score, with fewer than 9 percent of its students coming from families eligible for Pell grants (i.e., the modest means). Princeton and Notre Dame are among those that don't do discernibly better.

Ironically, colleges like these with nice-sounding "needs-blind admission" policies consistently admit fewer poorer kids because, as a James Irvine Foundation report discovered, "they feel like they're off the hook." They're so proud of themselves for not calculating students' ability to pay in making admissions decisions that they do less than they could to recruit poorer students—and thus fail to take enough "affirmative action" (in its original, beating-the-bushes sense) to redress socioeconomic disparities. It's easier to go with familiar, relatively affluent high schools they know will produce kids more likely to succeed.

Recently, Berkeley, UCLA and USC have done twice or three times better than every other elite school in enrolling economically disadvantaged students. Why? Because California has abolished racial preferences, which forced these schools to adopt economic affirmative action. Richard Kahlenberg of The Century Foundation says that's the only way to get more poor kids admitted. A forthcoming study from that foundation will show that substituting economic preferences for race at the top 146 schools would lessen the black and Hispanic representation only two percentage points (from 12 percent currently to 10 percent).

But I still think it makes sense to allow both class and race to be considered—and to let 1,000 other factors bloom, as good colleges do. Just don't make it mechanical. The anti-affirmative-action forces have to abandon the notion that GPAs and SATs add up to some numerical right to admission; the advocates for the status quo have to give up the numerical awarding of points for things like race, because sometimes being African American or Hispanic or Native American should be a big plus, and sometimes it shouldn't. It depends on the kid. All of which means that no matter what happens in the Supreme Court, the University of Michigan and other large schools should spend the money needed for a more subtle and subjective quest for true merit.

qualified students than more-traditional programs. At the University of Texas, Faulkner says no; he believes that class rank is a better predictor of collegiate success than test scores, even at high schools with large numbers of disadvantaged students. But Orfield, who is in the final stages of completing a formal study of these programs, disagrees; he says that less-qualified students are being admitted under the percentage programs. Often, Orfield says, 60 percent of kids at suburban high schools have better credentials than the top 10 percent of kids at inner-city schools (sidebar). The affirmative-access approach would also be hard to apply in nonstate colleges and graduate schools that draw students from all over the country.

Another approach would be to target students from low-income homes, regardless of race. That would eliminate the problem of giving middle-class blacks an edge. But Orfield says that being middle class does not protect black students from the effects of racism, and they are still often at a disadvantage in the admissions process. "Race still matters," he says. "It's fine with me if we apply affirmative action to poor people, but I think we need it for middle-class blacks as well."

10 So what is the most equitable way to select the best-qualified applicants?

In judging admissions policies, it's important to remember that schools aren't just looking to reward past achievement. They want to attract students who will create the richest academic and social communities, and who have the best odds of success in college and later life. As a result, admissions officers say, what they really look for are signs of intellectual energy and personal enthusiasm—qualities that can show up in grades, scores, essays, recommendations, extracurricular activities, or a mix of all these. "Merit" has become particularly difficult to define in an era when elite colleges are getting many more well-qualified applicants than they can possibly accept, and when distrust of standardized admissions tests is growing. And making hard and fast distinctions based on race isn't going to get any easier as the growing trend toward racial mixing increases over the next century and people choose to identify with more than one group. The only thing educators who have struggled with these issues agree on is that there is no magic formula, not even for the Supreme Court.

With VANESSA JUAREZ
and ANA FIGUEROA

WHY WE HATE

We may not admit it, but we are plagued with xenophobic tendencies. Our hidden prejudices run so deep, we are quick to judge, fear and even hate the unknown.

By Margo Monteith, Ph.D. and Jeffrey Winters

BALBIR SINGH SODHI WAS SHOT TO DEATH ON September 15 in Mesa, Arizona. His killer claimed to be exacting revenge for the terrorist attacks of September 11. Upon his arrest, the murderer shouted, "I stand for America all the way." Though Sodhi wore a turban and could trace his ancestry to South Asia, he shared neither ethnicity nor religion with the suicide hijackers. Sodhi—who was killed at the gas station where he worked—died just for being different in a nation gripped with fear.

For Arab and Muslim Americans, the months after the terrorist attacks have been trying. They have been harassed at work and their property has been vandalized. An Arab San Francisco shop owner recalled with anger that his five-year-old daughter was taunted by name-callers. Classmates would yell "terrorist" as she walked by.

Public leaders from President George W. Bush on down have called for tolerance. But the Center for American-Islamic Relations in Washington, D.C., has tallied some 1,700 incidents of abuse against Muslims in the five months following September 11. Despite our better nature, it seems, fear of foreigners or other strange-seeming people comes out when we are under stress. That fear, known as xenophobia, seems almost hardwired into the human psyche.

Researchers are discovering the extent to which xenophobia can be easily—even arbitrarily—turned on. In just hours, we can be conditioned to fear or discriminate against those who differ from ourselves by characteristics as superficial as eye color. Even ideas we believe are just common sense can have deep xenophobic underpinnings. Research conducted this winter at Harvard reveals that even among people who claim to have no bias, the more strongly one supports the ethnic profiling of Arabs

at airport-security checkpoints, the more hidden prejudice one has against Muslims.

But other research shows that when it comes to whom we fear and how we react, we do have a choice. We can, it seems, choose not to give in to our xenophobic tendencies.

THE MELTING POT

America prides itself on being a melting pot of cultures, but how we react to newcomers is often at odds with that self-image. A few years ago, psychologist Markus Kemmelmeier, Ph.D., now at the University of Nevada at Reno, stuck stamped letters under the windshield wipers of parked cars in a suburb of Detroit. Half were addressed to a fictitious Christian organization, half to a made-up Muslim group. Of all the letters, half had little stickers of the American flag.

Would the addresses and stickers affect the rate at which the letters would be mailed? Kemmelmeier wondered. Without the flag stickers, both sets of letters were mailed at the same rate, about 75 percent of the time. With the stickers, however, the rates changed: Almost all the Christian letters were forwarded, but only half of the Muslim letters were mailed. "The flag is seen as a sacred object," Kemmelmeier says. "And it made people think about what it means to be a good American."

In short, the Muslims didn't make the cut.

Not mailing a letter seems like a small slight. Yet in the last century, there have been shocking examples of xenophobia in our own back yard. Perhaps the most famous in American history was the fear of the Japanese during World War II. This particular wave of hysteria lead to the rise of slurs and bigoted depictions in the media, and more alarmingly, the mass internment of 120,000 people of Japanese ancestry beginning in 1942. The internments have become a national embarrassment: Most of the Japanese held were American citizens, and there is little evidence that the imprisonments had any real strategic impact.

Today the targets of xenophobia—derived from the Greek word for *stranger*—aren't the Japanese. Instead, they are Muslim immigrants. Or Mexicans. Or Chinese. Or whichever group we have come to fear.

Just how arbitrary are these xenophobic feelings? Two famous public-school experiments show how easy it is to turn one "group" against another. In the late 1960s, California high school history teacher Ron Jones recruited students to participate in an exclusive new cultural program called "the Wave." Within weeks, these students were separating themselves from others and aggressively intimidating critics. Eventually, Jones confronted the students with the reality that they were unwitting participants in an experiment demonstrating the power of nationalist movements.

Sonam Wangmo:
"Am I fearful of Arab men in turbans? No, I am not. I was born and raised in India, and I am familiar with other races. I have learned to be attuned to different cultures. I find that there are always new, positive things to be learned from other people; it brings out the best in us."

A few years later, a teacher in Iowa discovered how quickly group distinctions are made. The teacher, Jane Elliott, divided her class into two groups—those with blue eyes and those with brown or green eyes. The brown-eyed group received privileges and treats, while the blue-eyed students were denied rewards and told they were inferior. Within hours, the once-harmonious classroom became two camps, full of mutual fear and resentment. Yet, what is especially shocking is that the students were only in the third grade.

SOCIAL IDENTITY

The drive to completely and quickly divide the world into "us" and "them" is so powerful that it must surely come from some deep-seated need. The exact identity of that need, however, has been subject to debate. In the 1970s, the late Henri Tajfel, Ph.D., of the University of Bristol in England, and John Turner, Ph.D., now of the Australian National University, devised a theory to explain the psy-

chology behind a range of prejudices and biases, not just xenophobia. Their theory was based, in part, on the desire to think highly of oneself. One way to lift your self-esteem is to be part of a distinctive group, like a winning team; another is to play up the qualities of your own group and denigrate the attributes of others so that you feel your group is better.

Terry Kalish:
"I am planning a trip to Florida, and I'm nervous about flying with my kids; I'm scared. If an Arab man sat next to me, I would feel nervous. I would wonder, 'Does he have explosives?' But then I feel ashamed to think this way. These poor people must get so scrutinized. It's wrong."

Tajfel and Turner called their insight "social identity theory," which has proved valuable for understanding how prejudices develop. Given even the slenderest of criteria, we naturally split people into two groups—an "in-group" and an "out-group." The categories can be of geopolitical importance—nationality, religion, race, language—or they can be as seemingly inconsequential as handedness, hair color or even height.

Once the division is made, the inferences and projections begin to occur. For one, we tend to think more highly of people in the in-group than those in the out-group, a belief based only on group identity. Also, a person tends to feel that others in the in-group are similar to one's self in ways that—although stereotypical—may have little to do with the original criteria used to split the groups. Someone with glasses may believe that other people who wear glasses are more voracious readers—even more intelligent—than those who don't, in spite of the fact that all he really knows is that they don't see very well. On the other hand, people in the out-group are believed to be less distinct and less complex than are cohorts in the in-group.

Although Tajfel and Turner found that identity and categorization were the root cause of social bias, other researchers have tried to find evolutionary explanations for discrimination. After all, in the distant past, people who shared cultural similarities were found to be more genetically related than those who did not. Therefore, favoring the in-group was a way of helping perpetuate one's genes. Evolutionary explanations seem appealing, since they rely on the simplest biological urges to drive complicated behavior. But this fact also makes them hard to prove. Ironically, there is ample evidence backing up the "softer" science behind social identity theory.

HIDDEN BIAS

Not many of us will admit to having strong racist or xenophobic biases. Even in cases where bias becomes public debate—such as the profiling of Arab Muslims at airport-security screenings—proponents of prejudice claim that they are merely promoting common sense. That reluctance to admit to bias makes the issue tricky to study.

To get around this problem, psychologists Anthony Greenwald, Ph.D., of the University of Washington in Seattle, and Mahzarin Banaji, Ph.D., of Harvard, developed the Implicit Association Test. The IAT is a simple test that measures reaction time: The subject sees various words or images projected on a screen, then classifies the images into one of two groups by pressing buttons. The words and images need not be racial or ethnic in nature—one group of researchers tested attitudes toward presidential candidates. The string of images is interspersed with words having either pleasant or unpleasant connotations, then the participant must group the words and images in various ways—Democrats are placed with unpleasant words, for instance.

Rangr:
"For the months following 9/11, I had to endure my daily walk to work along New York City's Sixth Avenue. It seemed that half the people stared at me with accusation. It became unbearable. Yet others showed tremendous empathy. Friends, co-workers and neighbors, even people I had never met, stopped to say, 'I hope your turban has not caused you any trouble.' At heart, this is a great country."

The differences in reaction time are small but telling. Again and again, researchers found that subjects readily tie in-group images with pleasant words and out-group images with unpleasant words. One study compares such groups as whites and blacks, Jews and Christians, and young people and old people. And researchers found that if you identify yourself in one group, it's easier to pair images of that group with pleasant words—and easier to pair the opposite group with unpleasant imagery. This reveals the underlying biases and enables us to study how quickly they can form.

Really though, we need to know very little about a person to discriminate against him. One of the authors of this story, psychologist Margo Monteith, Ph.D., performed an IAT experiment comparing attitudes toward two sets of made-up names; one set was supposedly "American,"

the other from the fictitious country of Marisat. Even though the subjects knew nothing about Marisat, they showed a consistent bias against it.

While this type of research may seem out in left field, other work may have more "real-world" applications. The Southern Poverty Law Center runs a Web version of the IAT that measures biases based on race, age and gender. Its survey has, for instance, found that respondents are far more likely to associate European faces, rather than Asian faces, with so-called American images. The implication being that Asians are seen as less "American" than Caucasians.

Similarly, Harvard's Banaji has studied the attitudes of people who favor the racial profiling of Arab Muslims to deter terrorism, and her results run contrary to the belief that such profiling is not driven by xenophobic fears. "We show that those who endorse racial profiling also score high on both explicit and implicit measures of prejudice toward Arab Muslims," Banaji says. "Endorsement of profiling is an indicator of level of prejudice."

BEYOND XENOPHOBIA

If categorization and bias come so easily, are people doomed to xenophobia and racism? It's pretty clear that we are susceptible to prejudice and that there is an unconscious desire to divide the world into "us" and "them." Fortunately, however, new research also shows that prejudices are fluid and that when we become conscious of our biases we can take active—and successful—steps to combat them.

Researchers have long known that when observing racially mixed groups, people are more likely to confuse the identity of two black individuals or two white ones, rather than a white with a black. But Leda Cosmides, Ph.D., and John Tooby, Ph.D., of the Center for Evolutionary Psychology at the University of California at Santa Barbara, and anthropologist Robert Kurzban, Ph.D., of the University of California at Los Angeles, wanted to test whether this was innate or whether it was just an artifact of how society groups individuals by race.

To do this, Cosmides and her colleagues made a video of two racially integrated basketball teams locked in conversation, then they showed it to study participants. As reported in the *Proceedings of the National Academy of Sciences*, the researchers discovered that subjects were more likely to confuse two players on the same team, regardless of race, rather than two players of the same race on opposite teams.

Cosmides says that this points to one way of attacking racism and xenophobia: changing the way society imposes group labels. American society divides people by race and by ethnicity; that's how lines of prejudice form. But simple steps, such as integrating the basketball teams, can reset mental divisions, rendering race and ethnicity less important.

This finding supports earlier research by psychologists Samuel Gaertner, Ph.D., of the University of Delaware in Newark, and John Dovidio, Ph.D., of Colgate University in Hamilton, New York. Gaertner and Dovidio have studied how bias changes when members of racially mixed groups must cooperate to accomplish shared goals. In situations where team members had to work together, bias could be reduced by significant amounts.

Monteith has also found that people who are concerned about their prejudices have the power to correct them. In experiments, she told subjects that they had performed poorly on tests that measured belief in stereotypes. She discovered that the worse a subject felt about her performance, the better she scored on subsequent tests. The guilt behind learning about their own prejudices made the subjects try harder not to be biased.

This suggests that the guilt of mistaking individuals for their group stereotype—such as falsely believing an Arab is a terrorist—can lead to the breakdown of the belief in that stereotype. Unfortunately, such stereotypes are reinforced so often that they can become ingrained. It is difficult to escape conventional wisdom and treat all people as individuals, rather than members of a group. But that seems to be the best way to avoid the trap of dividing the world in two—and discriminating against one part of humanity.

READ MORE ABOUT IT:

Nobody Left to Hate: Teaching Compassion After Columbine, Elliot Aronson (W.H. Freeman and Company, 2000)

The Racist Mind: Portraits of American Neo-Nazis and Klansmen, Madonna Kolbenschlag (Penguin Books, 1996)

Margo Monteith, Ph.D., is an associate professor of psychology at the University of Kentucky. Jeffrey Winters is a New York-based science writer.

THE MELTING POT

Part I: Are We There Yet?

Anne Wortham

In the years following the American Revolution the expectation developed that over time the best traditions of Europe would be blended or amalgamated into a dynamic unity; that Englishmen, Germans, Italians, Irishmen, and Russians[1] would all become Americans, a new group that would be different from any of the original groups but also a combination of them all.[2] This was the vision of a young French nobleman, Michel Guillaume Jean de Crèvecoeur (1735–1813), who immigrated to the United States in 1759 and in 1782 published a book on life in America entitled *Letters From an American Farmer.* "What, then, is the American, this new man?" asked Crèvecoeur. "He is neither an European nor the descendant of an European; hence that strange mixture of blood which you will find in no other country.... Here individuals of all nations are melted into a new race of men whose labor and posterity will one day cause great changes in the world."[3]

"What, then, is the American, this new man?" asked Crèvecoeur. "He is neither an European nor the descendant of an European; hence that strange mixture of blood which you will find in no other country.... Here individuals of all nations are melted into a new race of men whose labor and posterity will one day cause great changes in the world."

Crèvecoeur's image of the United States as a melting pot had little basis in fact. For one thing, by restricting his application of the melting pot to whites, he omitted American Indians and Negroes, who made up about 20 percent of the total colonial population. Extensive cultural diversity had been characteristic of the aboriginal North American peoples long before European colonialization.[4] Crèvecoeur's model also ignored the cultural and regional differences among the diverse Europeans who immigrated to the New World in the seventeenth century: they were no more homogeneous than the indigenous people of many cultures who already populated the land.

In contrast to Crèvecoeur's vision, which reflected his romanticized perception of his times, Ralph Waldo Emerson (1803–1882) saw the melting pot as a promise to be fulfilled in the future. Unlike Crèvecoeur, he included Negroes in the mix. For Emerson the United States was the "asylum of all nations," and he predicted that "the energy of Irish, Swedes, Poles, and Cossacks, and all the European tribes—of the Africans, and of the Polynesians, will construct a new race, a new religion, a new state, a new literature, which will be as vigorous as the new Europe which came out of the smelting-pot of the Dark Ages, or that which earlier emerged from Pelasgic and Etruscan barbarism."[5]

MORE MELTING POT VISIONS

Yet another melting-pot vision was promoted by the influential historian Frederick Jackson Turner (1861–1932). In 1893, Turner argued that American identity was not Anglo-Saxon in origin and was forged in the Middle West, which he saw as "a newer and richer civilization" from which "a new product, which held the promise of world brotherhood" had emerged. The frontier had been the catalyst that had already fused the immigrants into a composite new national stock, argued Turner.[6] But his model was an inaccurate depiction of frontier reality. As Vincent Parrillo points out, "The pioneers did adapt to their new environment but the culture remained Anglo-American in form and content. Furthermore, in many areas of the Middle West Turner speaks about, culturally homogeneous settlements of Germans or Scandinavians often maintained distinct subcultures for generations."[7]

Perhaps the most quoted melting-pot idealist is Israel Zangwill (1864–1926), a British-born Jew, whose 1908 play *The Melting Pot* portrayed America as "God's crucible, the great melting pot where all the races of Europe are melting and reforming!" To the immigrants entering Ellis Island, Zangwill's protagonist exhorted: "A fig for your feuds and vendettas! German and Frenchman, Irishman and Englishman, Jews, Russians—into the crucible with you all! God is making the American... He will be the fusion of all the races, the coming superman."[8] The politician William Jennings Bryan (1860–1925) echoed Zangwill's sentiments: "Great has been the Greek, the Latin, the Slav, the Celt, the Teuton, and the Saxon; but greater than any of these is the American, who combines the virtues of them all."[9]

Reflecting on the plausibility of the melting-pot ideal, Milton Gordon notes that, given a population drawn from many nations, "was it not possible then, to think of the evolving American society not simply as a slightly modified England but rather as a totally new blend, culturally and biologically, in which the stocks and folkways of Europe were, figuratively speaking, indiscriminately mixed in the political pot of the emerging nation and melted together by the fires of American influence and interaction into a distinctly new type?"[10]

It became apparent during the decades before World War I that immigrants were not giving up the ways of their origins as the price of assimilation and were not mixing together in the great crucible to form the new American.

This frame of mind was certainly plausible, but the vision itself could not be realized. When it became apparent during the decades before World War I that immigrants were not giving up the ways of their origins as the price of assimilation and were not mixing together in the great crucible to form the new American, the melting-pot idea as a natural laissez-faire process was abandoned. At the turn of the twentieth century, the policy of coerced assimilation, known as "Americanization," was inaugurated. Public schools, patriotic societies, chambers of commerce, women's clubs, public libraries, social settlements, and even industrial plants were enlisted to divest the immigrant of his foreign heritage, suppress his native language, teach him English, make him a naturalized citizen, and inject into him a loyalty to American institutions.[11]

The Americanization movement was coercive, condescending, and suppressive; it implied that American culture was a finished product, in an Anglo-Saxon pattern, that it was superior to all others, and that immigrants should adapt to Anglo-

American culture as fast as possible. Immigrants were under no illusion; they knew that Americanization was the precondition for access to better jobs, higher education, political participation, and other opportunities. Nevertheless, the policy fell into disrepute. The most celebrated opponent of the melting pot and Americanization was the philosopher Horace Kallen, who developed the theory of cultural pluralism. The real meaning of American history, argued Kallen, was cultural pluralism, freedom, and unity through group diversity.[12]

Since the appearance of Kallen's theory, most of the major studies of American minority groups have been alternately guided by the theories of assimilation and cultural pluralism. Yet the failure of the melting-pot thesis to become policy has not prevented it from being of great ideological influence, becoming the utopian lens through which Americans view their society.

MELTING-POT THEORY

Theoretically, the melting-pot model is one of several answers to the question: What is the best way of integrating disparate peoples into a single nation? The form of this question is as old as questions posed by the founders of Western philosophy; but in modern thought it dates back to Thomas Hobbes' question: How and why is society possible? The issue, known as the Hobbesian "problem of order," was central in the thought of eighteenth- and nineteenth-century social philosophers and sociologists. It was no less the preoccupation of the framers of the American nation, whose particular concern was the creation of one nation out of thirteen colonies: Would the United States be politically one nation, or would it not? Their answer is represented in the motto on the face of the Great Seal of the United States: *E pluribus unum* (out of many, one).[13] Although *E pluribus unum* shares with the melting-pot metaphor the same species (the problem of social organization), they are of different genera. The former expresses the political ideal of fashioning one nation out of many states, and is more appropriate to today's federal system; the latter refers to the biological and cultural amalgamation of groups into a new group.

In the extreme form of cultural assimilation, the previously distinct cultural groups would lose all their distinguishable behavior and values.

Although technically the concept of the melting pot refers to the amalgamation of groups, it is also used variously to refer to two different patterns of assimilation: (1) unidimensional, one-way assimilation, or Anglo-conformity, by which immigrants relinquish their own culture in favor of the dominant culture and are remade according to the idealized Anglo-Saxon mold;[14] and (2) reciprocal assimilation or acculturation, which may involve either direct social interaction or exposure to other cultures by means of mass media. As the outcome of such contact, the dominant group adopts some traits of minorities while the cultural patterns of the dominant group are taken over by minority groups. An example of Anglo-conformity is learning the English language; acculturation can be seen in the Americanization of foreign cuisine.

Suppose the plausibility of the melting-pot model. Given a structural environment of democratic political institutions, voluntary association, and a relatively free and open economic system, exactly what attitudes and behavior would be necessary to realize the blending, melting, and fusing processes portrayed by melting-pot visionaries? Gordon has identified subprocesses of assimilation that, when linked together, could theoretically produce a culturally and biologically amalgamated people. Foremost among these processes would be "the complete mixture of the various stocks through intermarriage—in other words, *marital* assimilation, or amalgamation."[15] *Cultural* assimilation or acculturation would involve the intermixing of cultural traits (language, values, religion, everyday norms, dress, diet) of various groups to "form a blend somewhat different from the cultures of any one of the groups separately." This is the process by which Italians become Italian Americans, Poles become Polish Americans, and Haitians become Haitian Americans. In the extreme form of cultural assimilation, the previously distinct cultural groups would lose all their distinguishable behavior and values.

Large-scale intermarriage presupposes *structural* assimilation of immigrants; that they have "entered into cliques, clubs, and other primary groups, and institutions of the host society and, in addition, placed their own impress upon these social structures to some extent." Melting would most certainly require *identificational* assimilation "in the form of all groups merging their previous sense of peoplehood into a new and larger ethnic identity which, in some fashion, honors its multiple origins at the same time that it constitutes an entity distinct from them all." Individuals would no longer see themselves as distinctive and would stake their personal identities to participation and success in the mainstream institutions of the society; they may maintain what Herbert Gans calls "symbolic ethnicity," which can be taken on or off without any real social cost to the individual, but they would think of themselves as Americans.[16]

When the melting-pot vision is measured against these combined processes that are the necessary conditions of its creation, it has no basis in reality.

Since, as a consequence of amalgamation, there would not be any identifiably separate groups to be a target, attitude-receptional assimilation would be evident in the absence of prejudicial attitudes and stereotyping on the part of both dominant and minority ethnic groups. Behavioral-receptional assimilation

Black slaves on the deck of the bark *Wildfire*. Its arrival into Key West, Florida, on April 30, 1860, violated the 1809 law prohibiting the importation of slaves.

Library of Congress/Harper's Weekly, June 2, 1860

would be apparent in the absence of intentional discrimination against groups. Finally, civic assimilation would have taken place, "since disparate cultural values are assumed to have merged and power conflict between groups would be neither necessary nor possible."

An example of assimilation using these dimensions is as follows. An immigrant arrives in the United States, takes on American customs, and learns to speak flawless English (cultural assimilation). She encounters no prejudice from neighbors or employers (*attitude-receptional* assimilation), and is able to live and work where she pleases (behavioral-receptional assimilation). She observes that no political or social issues separate her group from the host society (civic assimilation). Increasingly she no longer thinks of herself as an immigrant, or as having ties to "the old country," but sees herself as an American (identificational assimilation). She marries a member of the dominant group (marital assimilation) and joins bridge clubs, professional societies, and sororities that are composed entirely of core society members (structural assimilation).[17]

Such a detailed account of the subprocesses of assimilation indicates just how difficult assimilation is for an individual, let alone an entire ethnic group, particularly racially visible groups such as Negroes, Indians, and Asians. When the melting-pot vision is measured against these combined processes that are the necessary conditions of its creation, it has no basis in reality. If all the assimilation processes that the melting pot entails were completed, says Martin Marger, the result would be a homogeneous society

in which ethnicity plays no role in the distribution of wealth, power, and prestige. This does not mean, of course, that other forms of social differentiation and stratification such as age, sex, and class would not exist; it means only that the ethnic forms would no longer be operative. In essence, a society in which all groups have perfectly assimilated is no longer a multiethnic society. However, this complete form of assimilation is rarely achieved, either for the society as a whole or for specific groups and individuals. Instead, assimilation takes different forms and is evident in different degrees.[18]

Sociologist Seymour Martin Lipset believes that the melting pot is validated by intermarriage statistics, which, as he surmises, "indicate that majorities of Catholics, Jews, Italians, Irish, and Japanese Americans marry out of their ancestral groups."[19] Indeed, demographic data also show greater tolerance for black-white intermarriages, although they are the least common form of racial intermarriage for whites.[20] However, while some degree of amalgamation occurs between groups in a pluralistic society, it is not often a total societal process in the sense meant by the melting-pot theory. As for the emergence of a distinct new national culture evolving from elements of all other cultures, Marger notes: "Ideologically, societies may advocate some kind of ethnic melting pot wherein all groups contribute in proportionate amounts to form a new social system, but such a cultural and, particularly, structural fusion is a chimera."[21]

ASSIMILATION IMPEDIMENTS

An example of the demographic and socioeconomic variability with which groups assimilate is Frances Fitzgerald's description of the impact of the movement of ethnic groups to the suburbs. When members of European ethnic communities left the cities in the wake of the flight of manufacturing, they did not "melt" into the white middle class; rather, instead of a melting pot, what they experienced was "a centrifuge that spun them around and distributed them out again across the landscape according to new principles: families with incomes of, say, thirty to sixty thousand dollars a year went to one suburb; families with incomes of, say, sixty to a hundred thousand dollars went to another; and young, single people were flung, en masse, into the recently vacated downtown neighborhoods." Ethnicity, class, and lifestyle were no longer correlated. Many of the young people came from blue-collar backgrounds but were college educated and did not think of themselves as hyphenated Americans. "By the mid-sixties the whole deck of white middle-class society had been reshuffled, and the old cards of identity—Italian-American, WASP, Russian Jewish-American—had lost much of their meaning."[22]

The situation for lower-class minorities in the central cities—where ethnicity, class, and lifestyle remain highly correlated—has been just the opposite of the suburbanization experience of the white ethnics Fitzgerald describes. Data from a study of seventy-four of the country's largest cities and metropolitan areas from 1970 to 1990 show that despite an increase in employment opportunities and a decline in formal discrimination in the wake of civil rights legislation, low wages and lack of access and opportunity continue to plague minorities concentrated in central cities. The housing patterns of minorities, particularly blacks, have not kept pace with the movement of employment to the suburbs. The percent of employment in the suburbs has been rising faster than the percent of population moving to the suburbs.[23] William Julius Wilson refers to this trend in which minorities live where the jobs aren't as "spatial mismatch."[24] The situation is exacerbated by the lack of rail and bus lines that accommodate commuting from the city to the suburbs.

Housing segregation such as this means that minorities lack the social networks and resources that are conducive to fostering entry into the mainstream. It illustrates the difficulty of achieving structural assimilation, particularly to the degree that is necessary for the realization of the other processes of assimilation. Yet, despite the assimilation problems of inner-city minorities, demographic data show modest declines in racial residential segregation in most metropolitan areas, and the growing suburbanization of blacks, Hispanics, and Asians matches the broad shift in attitudes on residential integration and openness to racial mixing in neighborhoods.

In the 1970s scholars found that although there had been considerable "melting" of ideas and cultural attributes, the ethnics themselves had proved "unmeltable" in any ultimate sense.

In the 1970s scholars found that although there had been considerable "melting" of ideas and cultural attributes, the ethnics themselves had proved "unmeltable" in any ultimate sense. Not only had ethnic belonging survived, but so had the subjective evaluations of ethnic categories in the community. A decade later, as noted above, Fitzgerald observed that for later-generation white ethnics, ethnicity was not something that influenced their lives unless they wanted it to. Mary Waters, who has studied patterns of "optional ethnicity," writes that "for an increasing number of European-origin individuals whose parents and grandparents have intermarried, the ethnicity they claim is largely a matter of personal choice as they sort through all of the possible combinations of groups in their genealogies."[25]

But the situation is quite different for visible minorities. Waters writes that the freedom to include or exclude ancestries in one's identification is not the same for those defined racially in American society. Racially defined minorities "are constrained to identify with the part of their ancestry that has been socially defined as the 'essential' part. African Americans, for example, have been highly socially constrained to identify as blacks, without other options available to them, even when they know that their forebears included many people of American Indian or European background."[26]

Being a white ethnic is not entirely unproblematic. That researchers do not include them among "racially-defined groups" does not mean that they are not racially defined by others and that there are no negative consequences for being so defined. While the ethnic components of white identity are receding with each generation's increased distance from its immigrant ancestors, the racial component of their identity is a handicap for many. As Michael Omni and Howard Winant point out, whites have been racialized in the post-civil rights movement era, and "now, the very meaning of 'white' has become a matter of anxiety and concern."[27]

In a study of racial diversity at the University of California at Berkeley, students expressed several themes and dilemmas of contemporary white identity. Lacking a sense of ethnic identity, one student said, "I think that I may be missing something that other people have, that I am not experiencing." Another identified the disadvantages of being white with respect to the distribution of resources: "Being white means that you're less likely to get financial aid.... It means that there are all sorts of tutoring groups and special programs that you can't get into, because you're not a minority." Said another: "If you want to go with stereotypes, Asians are the smart people, the blacks are great athletes, what is white? We're just here. We're the oppressors of the nation."[28]

Caribbean-American immigrants even push their children to adopt strategies, such as invoking their accents or other references to French or British colonial culture, to differentiate themselves from U.S.-born blacks and avoid the stigma of "blackness."

As the authors point out, although white Americans have not been immune to the process of racialization, unlike "people of color," they are prohibited from asserting their racial identity in political life.[29] In the aftermath of the civil rights movement, a double standard developed by which the reification of racial identity was deemed appropriate for everyone but whites. Blacks, Hispanics, and American Indians are expected to assert racial and ethnic pride, and whites are expected to concede their collective culpability for the plight of minorities, accept their

stigma without protest, and to applaud minorities for resisting their stigma.

The stereotyping of *white* to mean "oppressor" and "racist" causes identity problems for colored minorities as well—ironically, because "white" is also associated with rationality, the work ethic, and intellectual achievement. Min Zhou describes how it plays out in the generational conflict between immigrant parents and their U.S.-born children in the Asian-American and Caribbean-American communities. "Ironically, the parent generation consciously struggles to push children to become 'white' by moving their families to white neighborhoods, sending their children to white schools, and discouraging their children from playing basketball and mimicking hip-hop culture. But becoming 'white' is politically incorrect, and thus unacceptable for the U.S.-born generation."[30]

Caribbean-American immigrants even push their children to adopt strategies, such as invoking their accents or other references to French or British colonial culture, to differentiate themselves from U.S.-born blacks and avoid the stigma of "blackness."[31] A common concern among Haitians in south Florida is that their children will adopt the attitudes of the inner city's underclass. Vietnamese parents in New Orleans often try to keep their children immersed in their ethnic enclave, discouraging them from assimilating too fast.[32]

The absurdity of this kind of stereotyping extends to high-achieving native black children, especially college students, who feel they must camouflage their strivings and achievements to avoid the stigma of "whiteness."

The definition of *American* to mean "white," which can be traced to the writings of melting-pot visionaries like Crèvecoeur, also has a negative impact on the identificational assimilation of "people of color." In a study of children of Haitians, Cubans, West Indians, Mexicans, and Vietnamese in south Florida and Southern California, the researchers asked repondents how they identified themselves. Most chose categories of hyphenated Americans, few chose "American" as their identity. Asked if they believed the United States was the best country in the world, most of them answered no.[33]

On the other hand, as Min Zhou points out, U.S.-born children and grandchildren of Asian and Hispanic ancestry find that although they are already assimilated and think of themselves as American, their American identity is often questioned because they look like the contemporary influx of "colored" immigrants. "Suddenly they are confronted with the renewed image of themselves as 'foreigners'," notes Zhou. "Harassment of a Mexican American accused of being an undocumented immigrant, or comments about a third-generation Japanese American's 'good English' are frequently reported."[34]

THE PLURALIST REALITY

As the sources of tension and conflict in intergroup relations indicate, assimilation is not an inevitable outcome of immigration. Most groups in America are incompletely assimilated. Although there has been widespread cultural assimilation in American society—due, in part, to mass communications, mass transportation, and education— structural assimilation has not yet occurred on a grand scale. Gordon stresses that structural assimilation is more difficult to achieve than cultural assimilation because it involves penetration into the close interactions and associations of dominant ethnic groups. Even when members of ethnic groups penetrate secondary and formal organizational structures—schools, workplaces, and political arenas—they may still lack more primary and personal ties with members of dominant ethnic groups.

Nathan Glazer and Daniel Moynihan were among the first to emphasize that even as many of their customs are replaced with those of the dominant American society, white ethnic groups continue to reveal residential, behavioral, organizational, and cultural patterns that mark their distinctive ethnic identity, one that subtly separates them from the middle-class, American Protestant core.[35] They think of themselves as Americans sharing one national culture and as members of distinct groups with distinctive ways of life.

America has always been a pluralistic society. In its rejection of ethnic exclusivity and denial of the political recognition or formal status of ethnic groups, the American political system has made ethnic-group formation and maintenance a voluntary matter. Despite many policies of exclusivism, the history of American society has been such that the structural basis for ethnic preservation has been progressively undermined by a system of justice based on individual rights and the demands of a market economy. However, while ethnicity (as a sense of peoplehood) has been undermined by the forces of modernization and transformed by acculturation, and while social mobility has taken members of ethnic groups across boundaries of the ethnic structural network, ethnic belonging has persisted and considerable structural pluralism exists along racial and religious lines.

This reality of regional differentiation as well as national origin has been totally ignored by the U.S. Census Bureau's lumping together persons from Central America, Mexico, Puerto Rico, and Cuba into a superethnic group called "Hispanics."

Gordon attempted to capture the complexity of simultaneous assimilation and pluralism by focusing on ethnic group subcultures that are to some extent organized within subsocieties. While assimilation takes place within economic, political, and educational institutions, ethnic subsocieties are maintained in the institutional areas of religion, family, and recreation. It is in this sense that Gordon sees both assimilation and cultural pluralism occurring. Moreover, while race, religion, and nationality are important determinants of these subsocieties, these three variables are intersected by three others: social class, urban-rural residence, and regional residence. The various com-

binations of these dimensions of differentiation create what Gordon calls "ethclasses." Examples of such ethclasses include southern, lower-class, Protestant, rural blacks; northern, upper-class, white, urban Jews; northern, lower-class, white, urban, Catholics; and western, middle-class, suburban, third-generation Japanese.[36]

Viewing the assimilation process from the vantage point of the ethclass reveals that immigrants do not assimilate American culture in general; rather, they tend to adopt the folkways of the regions in which they settle. So it is, for instance, that there are Yankee Jews, Philadelphia Jews, southern Jews, and backslapping Texas Jews in cowboy boots and ten-gallon hats. Such cases of regional assimilation illustrate the fact that assimilation is itself pluralistic. This reality of regional differentiation as well as national origin has been totally ignored by the U.S. Census Bureau's lumping together persons from Central America, Mexico, Puerto Rico, and Cuba into a superethnic group called "Hispanics." The ethclass also casts light on the multidimensional nature of intergroup relations in America. For instance, the factors of social class, urban-rural residence, and regional residence enable us to understand that groups that are the object of prejudice and discrimination vary according to those differences. The experiences of blacks in the South vary from those of blacks and Puerto Ricans in the North, and their experiences differ from those of Mexican Americans in the Southwest or Vietnamese in the West.

Because of the prevalence of incomplete assimilation—of the simultaneous integration into the societal mainstream and retention of ethnic group identification—it is more accurate to apply the model of pluralism in understanding American intergroup relations. The general meaning of pluralism is the coexistence and mutual toleration of groups that retain their separate identities. There are three dimensions of the generic pluralist model of intergroup relations: cultural, structural, and political. At the cultural level, each group is free to maintain and develop its own culture, not totally separated but voluntarily segregated to a considerable degree. At the structural level, groups participate in different institutions and informal arrangements rather than in the same ones. Political pluralism is the distribution of political power among various interest groups and organizations, not equally, but with equal rights to organize or join coalitions to influence political decisions that have bearing on their perceived interests.[37]

AMERICA'S PLURALIST PARADOX

In these definitions, the concept of pluralism has a sociological connotation. Pluralism also refers to an ideological position that takes the view that the cultures and identities of different groups ought to be preserved.

In his monumental study of American race relations, Gunnar Myrdal concluded that a key characteristic of American life was the contradiction between the political ideals of the American creed, which call for just treatment of all people, regardless of race, creed, or color, and the practices of prejudice and differential treatment of people on the basis of race.[38] In the six and one-half decades since Myrdal's report, the United States has clearly moved a considerable distance toward implementing the implications of the American creed for race relations. However, in the aftermath of the civil rights and immigration legislation of the mid-1960s, America has been facing what Gordon calls a new dilemma that "is oriented toward a choice of the kinds of group pluralism which American governmental action and the attitudes of the American people will foster and encourage."[39]

The question for Gordon is "which type of pluralist society is most appropriate and most beneficial for a nation composed of many ethnic groups." America has always been a pluralistic society. What causes the current dilemma of choice, says Gordon, is "the role of government in racial and ethnic relations, together with ethical and philosophical issues revolving around just rewards and whether to treat persons as individuals or as members of a categorically defined group." Nathan Glazer characterizes the situation as follows:

> We have a complex of education, culture, law, administration, and political institutions which has deflected us onto a course in which we publicly establish ethnic and racial categories for differential treatment, and believe that by so doing we are establishing a just and good society.... But this has meant that we abandon the first principle of a liberal society, that the individual's interests and good and welfare are the test of a good society, for we now attach benefits and penalties to individuals simply on the basis of their race, color, and national origin. The implications of the new course are an increasing consciousness of the significance of group membership, increasing divisiveness on the basis of race, color, and national origin, and a spreading resentment against the favored groups.[40]

Liberal pluralism seeks equality between individuals, inequality of result, and unity out of group diversity by means of individual rights.

It is these issues that point to the competing frameworks of pluralism that he distinguishes as *liberal* pluralism and *corporate* pluralism. Liberal pluralism seeks equality between individuals, inequality of result, and unity out of group diversity by means of individual rights. Corporate pluralism seeks equality between groups, equality of result, and unity out of group diversity by means of group rights. The conflict between liberal and corporate pluralism arises in part out of what Peter Berger calls "the concurrence of modernizing and demodernizing impulses in the contemporary situation." The modernizing impulse entails an aspiration for liberation from restrictive solidarities of collective life and ideologies. The demodernizing impulse, whether it looks backward into the past or forward into the future, seeks a reversal of the modern trends that its adherents believe have alienated the individual. Their aim is to liberate the individual from what they believe are the dehumanizing excesses of individualism, capitalism, and democracy.[41]

WHERE ARE WE?

Gordon ended his essay on the conflicting models of pluralism with the prediction that "what the American people decide about this patterned complex of issues in the last twenty years of the twentieth century will have much to do with determining the nature, shape, and destiny of racial and ethnic relations in America in the twenty-first century." Lipset thinks of the future of American ethnicity in terms of an ongoing conflict between two different perspectives of equality expressed in the mass behavior of average Americans on the one hand, and in the discussions and proposals of intellectuals and the ideological Left on the other.

Lipset insists that for the masses, the melting-pot image "remains as appropriate as ever."[42] By melting pot, Lipset means American universalism, the desire to incorporate groups into one culturally unified whole, [which] is inherent in the founding ideology—the American Creed."[43] Although melting pot is not technically the term that describes what Lipset means, it is clearly a vision that is consistent with the option of liberal pluralism that Gordon identifies. (My qualification of Lipset rests on the understanding of melting pot to mean a biologically and/or culturally amalgamated whole, whereas Lipset's usage refers to a culturally unified whole, which he understands to be a democratic pluralistic society.)

The liberal pluralistic society that Gordon proposes (and that Lipset calls universalistic pluralism) is characterized by David Sears as

> a "cosmopolitan liberal" society in which diverse groups comfortably coexist, tolerating each other's modest differences but sharing a strong bond of loyalty to the superordinate nation. This universalist traditional ideal of American integration is perhaps most often captured in the idea of the 'melting pot.' To its adherents, the melting pot means the intermingling of varied cultural streams in the crucible of American life. Immigrants enrich popular culture without threatening the distinctive core of national identity, a Lockean commitment to individual rights shared by all citizens. In principle, though less fully in practice, this conception of American identity is ethnically inclusive, its adherents believing that American society could assimilate all newcomers.[44]

The second option of corporate pluralism, which Lipset asserts is promoted by intellectuals and the ideological Left, is "particularism, the preservation of subnational group loyalties," which entails the right of ethnic groups to cultural survival.[45] "The emphasis on univeralism has declined in political discourse, while particularism—described by some as multiculturalism—has become more important," says Lipset. In the vision of multiculturalism, writes David Sears, "the differences between groups are not appreciated but institutionalized, in formal power-sharing coalitions." The term *multiculturalism* was first advanced in Canada. Its guiding political principles "are the recognition of and respect for individuals' cultural identity, the primacy of ethnic identity in defining political interests, the idea of communal representation, and the importance of public policies that respond to the claims of subordinate cultural groups. In that sense, multiculturalism is a redistributive ideology that justifies the claims of subordinate groups to a greater share of society's goods. It does so by invoking the notion of group rather than individual rights."

Indeed, what might be called "identity politics" goes beyond ethnicity to include such groups as women, gays, and the disabled.

Multiculturalism, which Sears calls the "'hard' particularistic version" of pluralism, "asserts the viability and merit of multiple cultures within a society and advocates government action to maintain these equally worthy cultures. As an ideal image of society, multiculturalism rejects the assimilationist ethos of the melting pot in favor of the mosaic, which typically consists of differently colored tiles isolated from each other by impenetrable grout. It construes racial or ethnic identity as the preferred choice of self-definition." Although its roots are in the black civil rights movement, Sears notes that "multiculturalism extends the model of blacks' struggle for equality in two senses. First, it regards all the distinct cultures within the country as morally and intellectually equal, most notably including the new immigrants from Latin America and Asia. Indeed, what might be called 'identity politics' goes beyond ethnicity to include such groups as women, gays, and the disabled. Second, it advocates official action to achieve equality for all groups."[46]

Clearly, it is toward mutuality and respect for differences that we should be headed, not toward melting or politicized "diversity."

The success of the multiculturalists in promoting their vision is indicated by Aguirre and Turner's observation that "it is now politically incorrect to question pluralism or, worse, to extol the virtues of integration of ethnics into an Anglo-Saxon cultural core—at least within academia. But if there is no cultural core to which each wave of immigrants adjusts, or if ethnic populations of any size refuse or cannot adjust, then societal integration will be tenuous."[47] This is not a rejection of the reality of ethnic pluralism but recognition of the requirement of a demo-

cratic republic (and capitalism) that ethnic pluralism revolve around weak ethnic identification.

Public opinion research indicates that the vast majority of Americans believe that this is still the land of opportunity, where meritorious achievement is possible. Their opposition to government-enforced pluralism should be seen as a reflection of loyalty to an idealized and seemingly threatened civic culture in which individual equality was enshrined as a core democratic principle. Omni and Winant believe that culture, which was espoused across the political and cultural spectrum as a central ideal, seems to many Americans to be a receding ideal. Yet, they argue, "Avoiding racial polarization in our society may well depend on resuscitating and rearticulating that very vision so as to go beyond race-specific demands to a society of greater social justice for all."[48] There is some hope in the paradoxical reality, as Marger points out, that "while groups extoll the need to retain an ethnic culture and encounter declining resistance to its retention from the dominant group, societal trends continue to erode those cultural differences," compressing cultural singularities into common forms.[49] We may also hope that the erosion of cultural differences will reveal the unique "Americanness" that is a key component of our cultural core. It has the capacity to facilitate the universalism of the American creed.

Denying the existence of the melting pot leaves much to be explained. No denial has been made here of the existence of a metaphorical "pot," only that the processes occurring within amount to a universal "melting." Australian author and art critic Robert Hughes correctly argues that it is too simplistic to say that America is, or ever was, a melting pot. "But it is also too simple to say none of its contents actually melted," writes Hughes. "No single metaphor can do justice to the complexity of cultural crossing and perfusion in America."[50] To be sure, there is some melting (marital and cultural assimilation); however, as pointed out, there is also unevenly spread structural, identificational, attitude-receptional, behavior-receptional, and civic assimilation.

For utopians who dream of a unified, monoethnic, homogenous society, the lack of universal melting is a pathological situation that must be overcome. For realists, to say universal melting is not occurring is not to claim an unnecessary failure but to assert that the facts of human nature, history, and voluntary human association preclude universal melting. However, this is not to deny the possibility of cohesion and unity. Peace, harmony, prosperity, and unity do not require homogeneity, but they do require cohesion. What many Americans experience, and some resist, is not melting but mutuality—a mutuality that, as Hughes points out, "has no choice but to live in recognition of difference."[51] Whether differences persist as distinctions, or are intermingled or merged into something unlike the original form, is no threat to social order so long as mutuality is maintained and distinctions are not used as political clubs of tribal warfare. If mutuality is destroyed, however, differences become the "cultural ramparts" of the current cultural wars. Clearly, it is toward mutuality and respect for differences that we should be headed, not toward melting or politicized "diversity."

NOTES

1. Actually numerous waves of immigrants came from many nations to America, including but not confined to these.

2. William Newman, American Pluralism: *A Study of Minority Groups and Social Theory* (New York: Harper & Row, 1973), 63.

3. J. Hector St. John (Michel-Guillaume-Jean de Crèvecoeur), *Letters From an American Farmer* (New York: Fox, Duffield & Co., 1904), 54–55.

4. Vincent Parrillo, *Diversity in America* (Thousand Oaks, California: Pine Forge Press, 1996), 18.

5. *The Journals and Miscellaneous Notebooks of Ralph Waldo Emerson*, ed. Ralph Orth and Alfred Ferguson (Cambridge: Belknap, 1971), 9; 299–300.

6. Frederick Jackson Turner, *The Frontier in American History* (New York: Henry Holt, 1920), 3–4.

7. Vincent Parrillo, *Strangers to These Shores*, 5th ed. (Boston: Allyn and Bacon, 1997), 11.

8. Israel Zangwill, *The Melting Pot* (New York: Macmillan, 1909).

9. As quoted in Peter Rose, *They and We: Racial and Ethnic Relations in the United States*, 3rd ed. (New York: Random House, 1981), 64.

10. Milton Gordon, *Assimilation in American Life* (New York: Oxford University Press, 1964), 115.

11. Brewton Berry, *Race and Ethnic Relations*, 3rd ed. (Boston: Houghton Mifflin, 1965), 212–13.

12. Horace Kallen, "Democracy Versus the Melting Pot," *The Nation*, 25 Feb., 1915, 220.

13. The phrase, which can be traced back to Horace's *Epistles*, was suggested by the designer of the Great Seal, Philadelphia artist and painter Pierre Eugene Du Simitiere, who became a naturalized citizen in 1769. Du Simitiere was consultant to Benjamin Franklin, John Adams, and Thomas Jefferson, members of the first committee for the selection of the seal. The official motto of the United States is "In God We Trust," adopted on July 30, 1956.

14. The term "Anglo-conformity" was introduced by Stewart G. Cole and Mildred Wise Cole, *Minorities and the American Promise* (New York: Harper & Row, 1937).

15. This quotation and those that follow in this paragraph are from Gordon, *Assimilation in American Life*, 124–26.

16. Herbert Gans, "Symbolic Ethnicity: The Future of Ethnic Groups and Cultures in America," *Ethnic and Racial Studies* 2 (January 1979): 1–20.

17. From Richard Schaefer, *Racial and Ethnic Groups* (Boston: Little, Brown, 1979), 40–41.

18. Martin Marger, *Race and Ethnic Relations: American and Global Perspectives*, (Belmont, California: Wadsworth Publishing, 1985), 71.

19. Seymour Martin Lipset, *American Exceptionalism: A Double-Edged Sword* (New York: W.W. Norton, 1996), 249. See also Seymour Martin Lipset and Earl Raab, *Jews and the New American Scene* (Cambridge: Harvard University Press, 1995); Stanley Lieberson and Mary Waters, *From Many Strands: Ethnic and Racial Groups in Contemporary America* (New York: Russell Sage Foundation, 1989); and Mary Waters, *Ethnic Options*: Choosing Identities in America (Berkeley: University of California Press, 1990).

20. Lawrence Bobo, "Racial Attitudes and Relations," in *America Becoming: Racial Trends and Their Consequences*, vol. I, ed. Neil Smelser, William Wilson, and Faith Mitchell (Washington, D.C.: National Academy Press, 2001), 295.

21. Marger, *Race and Ethnic Relations*, 78.

22. Frances Fitzgerald, Cities on a Hill: *A Journey Through Contemporary American Cultures* (New York: Simon & Schuster, 1981), 16–17, 387.

23. Manuel Pastor Jr. "Geography and Opportunity," in *America Becoming*, 435–67. See also Douglas Massey, "Residential Segregation and Neighborhood Conditions in U.S. Metropolitan Areas," in *America Becoming*, 391–434.

24. William Julius Wilson, *The Truly Disadvantaged: The Inner City, the Underclass, and Public Policy* (Chicago: University of Chicago Press, 1987).

25. Mary Waters, "Optional Ethnicities: For Whites Only?" in *Origins and Destinies: Immigration, Race and Ethnicity in America*, ed. Silvia Pedraza and Ruben G. Rumbaut (Belmont, California: Wadsworth, 1996), 447.

26. Waters, "Optional Ethnicities."

27. Michael Omni and Howard Winant, "Contesting the Meanings of Race in the Post-Civil Rights Movement Era," in *Origins and Destinies*.

28. Omni and Winant, "Contesting the Meaning of Race."

29. Omni and Winant, "Contesting the Meaning of Race."

30. Min Zhou, "Immigration and the Dynamics of Race and Ethnicity," *America Becoming*, 222–23.

31. Alejandro Portes and A. Stepick, *City on the Edge: The Transformation of Miami* (Berkeley: University of California Press, 1993).

32. William Booth, "The Myth of the Melting Pot, Part 1: One Nation, Indivisible: Is It History?" *Washington Post*, February 22, 1998.

33. Alejandro Portes and Rubin Rumbaut, *Immigrant America: A Portrait*, 2nd ed. (Berkeley: University of California Press, 1996).

34. Zhou, "Immigration and the Dynamics of Race and Ethnicity."

35. Nathan Glazer and Daniel Moynihan, *Beyond the Melting Pot*, 2nd ed. (Cambridge: MIT Press, 1970).

36. Gordon, *Assimilation in American Life*, 18–54.

37. F. James Davis, *Minority-Dominant Relations: A Sociological Analysis* (Arlington Heights, Illinois: AHM Publishing, 1979), 152–54.

38. Gunnar Myrdal, *An American Dilemma* (New York: Harper and Brothers, 1944).

39. Milton Gordon, "Models of Pluralism: The New American Dilemma," *Annals of the American Academy of Political and Social Science*, March 1981.

40. Nathan Glazer, *Affirmative Discrimination: Ethnic Inequality and Public Policy* (New York: Basic Books, 1976), 220.

41. Peter Berger, Brigitte Berger, and Hansfried Kellner, *The Homeless Mind* (New York: Vintage, 1974), 196.

42. Lipset, *American Exceptionalism*, 249–50.

43. Seymour Martin Lipset, "Historical Traditions and National Characteristics: A Comparative Analysis of Canada and the United States," in *Patterns of Modernity, Volume I: The West*, ed. S.N. Eisenstadt, (New York: New York University Press, 1987), 77–78.

44. David Sears, Jack Citrin, Sharmaaine Cheleden, and Colette van Laar, "Cultural Diversity and Multicultural Politics: Is Ethnic Balkanization Psychologically Inevitable?" in *Cultural Divides: Understanding and Overcoming Group Conflict*, ed. Deborah Prentice and Dale Miller, (New York: Russell Sage Foundation, 1999), 35–79.

45. Lipset, "Historical Traditions and National Characteristics."

46. Sears et al., "Cultural Diversity and Multicultural Politics."

47. Adalberto Aguirre Jr. and Jonathan Turner, *American Ethnicity: The Dynamics and Consequences of Discrimination*, 2nd ed. (Boston: McGraw-Hill, 1998), 247.

48. Omni and Winant, "Contesting the Meaning of Race," 476.

49. Marger, *Race and Ethnic Relations*, 290–91.

50. Robert Hughes, *Culture of Complaint: The Fraying of America* (New York: Oxford University Press, 1993), 12–13.

51. Hughes, *Culture of Complaint*, 12–13.

Anne Wortham is associate professor of sociology at Illinois State University.

* Part II of this article [was] published in a subsequent issue.

REVERSING *The* "GENDER GAP"

By Joel Wendland

"**B**oys are becoming the second sex" proclaimed *Business Week* last May in a cover story titled "The New Gender Gap." *Business Week's* article appeared as part of a spate of articles and television news segments on the subject of increased educational opportunities for women. The basics of the story are that in the education system, teachers have become so conscious of catering to the needs of girls and young women that boys are being left behind. Boys, they say, are being punished for "boyish" behavior. They are being put more often into special education programs or disciplinary classes, and the outcome is that boys have a negative educational experience. This trend translates into poorer high school performances and perhaps college as well.

According to statistics offered by *Business Week*, 57 percent of all new bachelor's degrees and 58 percent of master's degrees are awarded to women. This "education grab," according to the article, was the source of the "new gender gap." Though, the article did hint that even with the new trend in the numbers, women still had some ways to go in order to catch up after 350 years of being almost entirely excluded from the university.

Most observers of this situation will find such an article perplexing. Certainly most women will likely be skeptical of its major argument. That this "reverse gender gap" argument exists, however, is not surprising. Like its cousins in other areas of social life (reverse discrimina-

tion or reverse class warfare), it is being generated primarily by the ultra-right. The purpose is to stifle the struggle for equality by implying (or stating directly) that the gains made by women through struggle over the last 40 years have gone too far and have detrimentally affected society.

Some in this camp go so far as to suggest that women who demand equality are out to hurt men. At worst, it demonstrates that the right wants to twist the outcome of social progress to divide us. They say that a struggle between men and women for social goods is the fundamental source of social conflict and that women are winning—a situation that, for some, means reversed gender inequality and for others goes against natural laws of male supremacy invoked by God.

Any way you look at it, however, this picture is a distortion of reality. So what does the real gender gap look like?

Barbara Gault, director of research at the Institute for Women's Policy Research, recently told *Women'sWallStreet.com* that there are several explanations for and holes in the current data on the educational experiences of men and women. First, high-paying occupations that do not require college degrees, such as skilled trades, are still male dominated. Second, women need a college degree in order to earn roughly hat men do with only high school diplomas, giving them stronger motives to make a special effort to obtain financial security. Third, among African Ameri-

cans, where the difference between women and men earning college degrees is the widest among all racial or ethnic groups, it is clear that institutional racism directed at African American men plays a large role in keeping them out of college. Fourth, in the crucial field of information technology, women continue to earn only about one-third of the degrees awarded and get only about one-third of the jobs available. Finally, men continue to outpace women in completing doctoral and professional degrees (81 women for every 100 men), resulting in continued male dominance in corporate board rooms, the seats of political power, the highest positions in universities, etc.

> The average **woman**, according to the AFL-CIO, **will lose $523,000** in her lifetime due to **unequal pay**.

The successes of the women's equality movement, progressive changes in attitudes about roles women can have and the implementation of affirmative action policies (which benefited women as a whole most) have had a tremendous positive impact on the access women have had in education. Just 30 years ago, women earned advanced or professional degrees at a rate of only 23 women per 100 men. In other arenas, such as the workforce or the political field, the gender gap, in sheer numbers, has largely narrowed. But the numbers still don't paint the whole picture.

While higher education is a major factor in gaining financial security, it is something that is only available to about one-fifth of the adult population. So for the vast majority of women, this supposed "new gender gap" means absolutely nothing. Other data on the condition of women's economic security paint another picture altogether. About eight of ten retired women are not eligible for pension benefits. When retired women do get a pension, it is typically far less than retired men get. Fifty percent of women who receive pension benefits get only about 60 cents for every dollar of male pensioners. On the average, retired women depend on Social Security for 71 percent of their income, and about 25 percent of retired women rely solely on Social Security for their income.

In the work force, women's pay averages only 76 percent of men's pay (at a cost of about $200 billion for working families annually). A report produced by the General Accounting Office last October shows that since 1983, the wage differential has actually increased. 60 percent of all women earn less than $25,000 annually. Women are one-third more likely to live below the poverty level. Black women and Latinas are between two and three times more likely to live below the poverty line than men are.

For women of color, facing the double oppression of racism and sexism, pay losses are even greater: 64 cents on the dollar at a loss of about $210 a week. The average woman, according to the AFL-CIO, will lose $523,000 in her lifetime due to unequal pay.

Even more costly to women, is the "price of motherhood," as journalist Ann Crittenden argues in her recent book of that title. In almost every case, women lose income, jobs, job experience and retirement income (while work hours increase) when they decide to have children. With some slight improvements, women remain the primary caregiver in nearly every family. For many mothers, single or married, the economic inequalities described above are exacerbated. For married women, dependence on men is heightened and the threat of economic hardship enforces interpersonal inequality and conflict. Divorced mothers and their children have among the highest rates of poverty of any demographic.

Crittenden argues that unless other sources of financial support for motherhood are made available institutionalized inequality will persist. She suggests retirement benefits for mothers, public funding for day care and health care for children and their caregivers, salaries for primary caregivers, expanded public education for pre-school children, equalized social security for spouses, increased financial contri-

butions from husbands and fathers, increased educational and support resources for parents and equalization of living standards for divorced parents.

As for the fallacy of female supremacy, the gains made by women through struggle and implementation of policies such as affirmative action point to the necessity of broader systematic change. But if female supremacy is a fallacy, does this mean that men go unhurt by gender inequalities? No. Men and boys are hurt when their families suffer because pay inequity causes their mothers, grandmothers, sisters and aunts to lose income, get fired, face hiring discrimination, are refused pensions, don't have equal Social Security benefits, lose out on promotions or have limited access to higher education. Additionally, if the average woman loses $523,000 in income in her life, does this mean that the average man is enriched by $523,000 in his lifetime? If pay inequity costs women $200 billion yearly, does this mean that men are enriched by $200 billion? The answer is no. These billions are savings in labor costs to employers. Employers enjoy the profits of male supremacy and gendered divisions among working people. So it makes sense that the right tries to portray the benefits of progressive social change toward equality as bad. It cuts into their bottom line.

From *Political Affairs*, March 2004, pp. 24-25, 43. Copyright © 2004 by Political Affairs. Reprinted by permission.

Human Rights, Sex Trafficking, and Prostitution

by Alice Leuchtag

Despite laws against slavery in practically every country, an estimated twenty-seven million people live as slaves. Kevin Bales, in his book *Disposable People: New Slavery in the Global Economy* (University of California Press, Berkeley, 1999), describes those who endure modern forms of slavery. These include indentured servants, persons held in hereditary bondage, child slaves who pick plantation crops, child soldiers, and adults and children trafficked and sold into sex slavery.

A Life Narrative

Of all forms of slavery, sex slavery is one of the most exploitative and lucrative with some 200,000 sex slaves worldwide bringing their slaveholders an annual profit of $10.5 billion. Although the great preponderance of sex slaves are women and girls, a smaller but significant number of males—both adult and children—are enslaved for homosexual prostitution.

The life narrative of a Thai girl named Siri, as told to Bales, illustrates how sex slavery happens to vulnerable girls and women. Siri is born in northeastern Thailand to a poor family that farms a small plot of land, barely eking out a living. Economic policies of structural adjustment pursued by the Thai government under the aegis of the World Bank and the International Monetary Fund have taken former government subsidies away from rice farmers, leaving them to compete against imported, subsidized rice that keeps the market price artificially depressed.

Siri attends four years of school, then is kept at home to help care for her three younger siblings. When Siri is fourteen, a well-dressed woman visits her village. She offers to find Siri a "good job," advancing her parents $2,000 against future earnings. This represents at least a year's income for the family. In a town in another province the woman, a trafficker, "sells" Siri to a brothel for $4,000. Owned by an "investment club" whose members are business and professional men—government bureaucrats and local politicians—the brothel is extremely profitable. In a typical thirty-day period it nets its investors $88,000.

To maintain the appearance that their hands are clean, members of the club's board of directors leave the management of the brothel to a pimp and a bookkeeper. Siri is initiated into prostitution by the pimp who rapes her. After being abused by her first "customer," Siri escapes, but a policeman—who gets a percentage of the brothel profits—brings her back, whereupon the pimp beats her up. As further punishment, her "debt" is doubled from $4,000 to $8,000. She must now repay this, along with her monthly rent and food, all from her earnings of $4 per customer. She will have to have sex with three hundred men a month just to pay her rent. Realizing she will never be able to get out of debt, Siri tries to build a relationship with the pimp simply in order to survive.

The pimp uses culture and religion to reinforce his control over Siri. He tells her she must have committed terrible sins in a past life to have been born a female; she must have accumulated a karmic debt to deserve the enslavement and abuse to which she must reconcile herself. Gradually Siri begins to see herself from the point of view of the slaveholder—as someone unworthy and deserving of punishment. By age fifteen she no longer protests or runs away. Her physical enslavement has become psychological as well, a common occurrence in chronic abuse.

Siri is administered regular injections of the contraceptive drug Depo-Provera for which she is charged. As the same needle is used for all the girls, there is a high risk of HIV and other sexual diseases from the injections. Siri knows that a serious illness threatens her and she prays to Buddha at the little shrine in her room, hoping to earn merit so he will protect her from dreaded disease. Once a month she and the others, at their own expense, are tested for HIV. So far Siri's tests have been negative. When Siri tries to get the male customers to wear condoms—distributed free to brothels by the Thai Ministry of Health—some resist wearing them and she can't make them do so.

As one of an estimated 35,000 women working as brothel slaves in Thailand—a country where 500,000 to one million prostituted women and girls work in conditions of degradation and exploitation short of brothel slavery—Siri faces at least a 40 percent chance of contracting the HIV virus. If she is lucky, she can look forward to live more years before she becomes too ill to work and is pushed out into the street.

Thailand's Sex Tourism

Though the Thai government denies it, the World Health Organization finds that HIV is epidemic in Thailand, with the largest segment of new cases among wives and girlfriends of men who buy prostitute sex. Viewing its women as a cash crop to be exploited, and depending on sex tourism for foreign exchange dollars to help pay interest on the foreign debt, the Thai government can't acknowledge the epidemic without contradicting the continued promotion of sex tourism and prostitution.

By encouraging investment in the sex industry, sex tourism creates a business climate conducive to the trafficking and enslavement of vulnerable girls such as Siri. In 1996 nearly five million sex tourists from the United States, Western Europe, Australia, and Japan visited Thailand. These transactions brought in about $26.2 billion—thirteen times more than Thailand earned by building and exporting computers.

In her 1999 report *Pimps and Predators on the Internet: Globalizing the Sexual Exploitation of Women and Children,* published by the Coalition Against Trafficking in Women (CATW), Donna Hughes quotes from postings on an Internet site where sex tourists share experiences and advise one another. The following is one man's description of having sex with a fourteen-year-old prostituted girl in Bangkok:

> "Even though I've had a lot of better massages… after fifteen minutes, I was much more relaxed… Then I asked for a condom and I fucked her for another thirty minutes. Her face looked like she was feeling a lot of pain…. She blocked my way when I wanted to leave the room and she asked for a tip. I gave her 600 bath. Altogether, not a good experience."

Hughes says, "To the men who buy sex, a 'bad experience' evidently means not getting their money's worth, or that the prostituted woman or girl didn't keep up the act of enjoying

what she had to do… one glimpses the humiliation and physical pain most girls and women in prostitution endure."

Nor are the men oblivious to the existence of sexual slavery. One customer states, "Girls in Bangkok virtually get sold by their families into the industry; they work against their will." His knowledge of their sexual slavery and lack of sensitivity thereof is evident in that he then names the hotels in which girls are kept and describes how much they cost!

As Hughes observes, sex tourists apparently feel they have a right to prostitute sex, perceiving prostitution only from a self-interested perspective in which they commodify and objectify women of other cultures, nationalities, and ethnic groups. Their awareness of racism, colonialism, global economic inequalities, and sexism seems limited to the way these realities benefit them as sex consumers.

Sex Traffickers Cast Their Nets

According to the *Guide to the New UN Trafficking Protocol* by Janice Raymond, published by the CATW in 2001, the United Nations estimates that sex trafficking in human beings is a $5 billion to $7 billion operation annually. Four million persons are moved illegally from one country to another and within countries each year, a large proportion of them women and girls being trafficked into prostitution. The United Nations International Children's Emergency Fund (UNICEF) estimates that some 30 percent of women being trafficked are minors, many under age thirteen. The International Organization on Migration estimates that some 500,000 women per year are trafficked into Western Europe from poorer regions of the world. According to *Sex Trafficking of Women in the United States: International and Domestic Trends,* also published by the CATW in 2001, some 50,000 women and children are trafficked into the United States each year, mainly from Asia and Latin America.

Because prostitution as a system of organized sexual exploitation depends on a continuous supply of new "recruits," trafficking is essential to its continued existence. When the pool of available women and girls dries up, new women must be procured. Traffickers cast their nets ever wide and become ever more sophisticated. The Italian Camorra, Chinese Triads, Russian Mafia, and Japanese Yakuza are powerful criminal syndicates consisting of traffickers, pimps, brothel keepers, forced labor lords, and gangs which operate globally.

After the breakdown of the Soviet Union, an estimated five thousand criminal groups formed the Russian Mafia, which operates in thirty countries. The Russian Mafia traffics women from African countries, the Ukraine, the Russian Federation, and Eastern Europe into Western Europe, the United States, and Israel. The Triads traffic women from China, Korea, Thailand, and other Southeast Asian countries into the United States and Europe. The Camorra traffics women from Latin America into Europe. The Yakuza traffics women from the Philipines, Thailand, Burma, Cambodia, Korea, Nepal, and Laos into Japan.

A Global Problem Meets a Global Response

Despite these appalling facts, until recently no generally agreed upon definition of trafficking in human beings was written into international law. In Vienna, Austria, during 1999 and 2000, 120 countries participated in debates over a definition of trafficking. A few nongovernmental organizations (NGOs) and a minority of governments—including Australia, Canada, Denmark, Germany, Ireland, Japan, the Netherlands, Spain, Switzerland, Thailand, and the United Kingdom—wanted to separate issues of trafficking from issues of prostitution. They argued that persons being trafficked should be divided into those who are forced and those who give their consent, with the burden of proof being placed on persons being trafficked. They also urged that the less explicit means of control over trafficked persons—such as abuse of a victim's vulnerability—not be included in the definition of trafficking and that the word *exploitation* not be used. Generally supporters of this position were wealthier countries where large numbers of women were being trafficked and countries in which prostitution was legalized or sex tourism encouraged.

People being trafficked shouldn't be divided into those who are forced and those who give their consent because trafficked persons are in no position to give meaningful consent.

The CATW—140 other NGOs that make up the International Human Rights Network plus many governments (including those of Algeria, Bangladesh, Belgium, China, Columbia, Cuba, Egypt, Finland, France, India, Mexico, Norway, Pakistan, the Philippines, Sweden, Syria, Venezuela, and Vietnam)—maintains that trafficking can't be separated from prostitution. Persons being trafficked shouldn't be divided into those who are forced and those who give their consent because trafficked persons are in no position to give meaningful consent. The subtler methods used by traffickers, such as abuse of a victim's vulnerability, should be included in the definition of trafficking and the word *exploitation* be an essential part of the definition. Generally supporters of this majority view were poorer countries from which large numbers of women were being trafficked or countries in which strong feminist, anti-colonialist, or socialist influences existed. The United States, though initially critical of the majority position, agreed to support a definition of trafficking that would be agreed upon by consensus.

The struggle—led by the CATW to create a definition of trafficking that would penalize traffickers while ensuring that all victims of trafficking would be protected—succeeded when a compromise proposal by Sweden was agreed to. A strongly worded and inclusive *UN Protocol to Prevent, Suppress, and Punish Trafficking in Persons*—especially women and children—was drafted by an ad hoc committee of the UN as a supplement to the Convention Against Transnational Organized Crime. The UN protocol specifically addresses the trade in human beings for purposes of prostitution and other forms of sexual exploitation, forced labor or services, slavery or practices similar to slavery, servitude, and the removal of organs. The protocol defines trafficking as:

> The recruitment, transportation, transfer, harboring or receipt of persons, by means of the threat or use of force or other forms of coercion, of abduction, of fraud, of deception, of the abuse of power or of a position of vulnerability or of the giving or receiving of payments or benefits to achieve the consent of a person having control over another person, for the purpose of exploitation.

While recognizing that the largest amount of trafficking involves women and children, the wording of the UN protocol clearly is gender and age neutral, inclusive of trafficking in both males and females, adults and children.

In 2000 the UN General Assembly adopted this convention and its supplementary protocol; 121 countries signed the convention and eighty countries signed the protocol. For the convention and protocol to become international law, forty countries must ratify them.

Highlights

Some highlights of the new convention and protocol are:

For the first time there is an accepted international definition of trafficking and an agreed-upon set of prosecution, protection, and prevention mechanisms on which countries can base their national legislation.

- The various criminal means by which trafficking takes place, including indirect and subtle forms of coercion, are covered.
- Trafficked persons, especially women in prostitution and child laborers, are no longer viewed as illegal migrants but as victims of a crime.

For the first time there is an accepted international definition of trafficking and an agreed-upon set of prosecution, protection, and prevention mechanisms on which countries can base their national legislation.

- The convention doesn't limit its scope to criminal syndicates but defines an organized criminal group as "any structured group of three or more persons which engages in criminal activities such as trafficking and pimping."

- All victims of trafficking in persons are protected, not just those who can prove that force was used against them.
- The consent of a victim of trafficking is meaningless and irrelevant.
- Victims of trafficking won't have to bear the burden of proof.
- Trafficking and sexual exploitation are intrinsically connected and not to be separated.
- Because women trafficked domestically into local sex industries suffer harmful effects similar to those experienced by women trafficked transnationally, these women also come under the protections of the protocol.
- The key element in trafficking is the exploitative purpose rather than the movement across a border.

The protocol is the first UN instrument to address the demand for prostitution sex, a demand that results in the human rights abuses of women and children being trafficked. The protocol recognizes an urgent need for governments to put the buyers of prostitution sex on their policy and legislative agendas, and it calls upon countries to take or strengthen legislative or other measures to discourage demand, which fosters all the forms of sexual exploitation of women and children.

As Raymond says in the *Guide to the New UN Trafficking Protocol*:

> "The least discussed part of the prostitution and trafficking chain has been the men who buy women for sexual exploitation in prostitution…. If we are to find a permanent path to ending these human rights abuses, then we cannot just shrug our shoulders and say, "men are like this," or "boys will be boys," or "prostitution has always been around." Or tell women and girls in prostitution that they must continue to do what they do because prostitution is inevitable. Rather, our responsibility is to make men change their behavior, by all means available—educational, cultural and legal."

Two U.S. feminist, human rights organizations—Captive Daughters and Equality Now—have been working toward that goal. Surita Sandosham of Equality Now says that when her organization asked women's groups in Thailand and the Philippines how it could assist them, the answer came back, "Do something about the demand." Since then the two organizations have legally challenged sex tours originating in the United States and have succeeded in closing down at least one operation.

Refugees, Not Illegal Aliens

In October 2000 the U.S. Congress passed a bill, the Victims of Trafficking and Violence Protection Act of 2000, introduced by New Jersey republican representative Chris Smith. Under this law penalties for traffickers are raised and protections for victims increased. Reasoning that desperate women are unable to give meaningful consent to their own sexual exploitation, the law adopts a broad definition of sex trafficking so as not to exclude so-called consensual prostitution or trafficking that occurs solely within the United States. In these respects the new federal law conforms to the UN protocol.

Two features of the law are particularly noteworthy:

- In order to pressure other countries to end sex trafficking, the U.S. State Department is to make a yearly assessment of other countries' anti-trafficking efforts and to rank them according to how well they discourage trafficking. After two years of failing to meet even minimal standards, countries are subject to sanctions, although not sanctions on humanitarian aid. "Tier 3" countries—those failing to meet even minimal standards—include Greece, Indonesia, Israel, Pakistan, Russia, Saudi Arabia, South Korea, and Thailand.
- Among persons being trafficked into the United States, special T-visas will be provided to those who meet the criteria for having suffered the most serious trafficking abuses. These visas will protect them from deportation so they can testify against their traffickers. T-non immigrant status allows eligible aliens to remain in the United States temporarily and grants specific non-immigrant benefits. Those acquiring T-1 non-immigrant status will be able to remain for a period of three years and will be eligible to receive certain kinds of public assistance—to the same extent as refugees. They will also be issued employment authorization to "assist them in finding safe, legal employment while they attempt to retake control of their lives."

A Debate Rages

A worldwide debate rages about legalization of prostitution fueled by a 1998 International Labor Organization (ILO) report entitled *The Sex Sector: The Economic and Social Bases of Prostitution in Southeast Asia.* The report follows years of lobbying by the sex industry for recognition of prostitution as "sex work." Citing the sex industry's unrecognized contribution to the gross domestic product of four countries in Southeast Asia, the ILO urges governments to officially recognize the "sex sector" and "extend taxation nets to cover many of the lucrative activities connected with it." Though the ILO report says it stops short of calling for legalization of prostitution, official recognition of the sex industry would be impossible without it.

Raymond points out that the ILO's push to redefine prostitution as sex work ignores legislation demonstrating that countries can reduce organized sexual exploitation rather than capitulate to it. For example, Sweden prohibits the purchase of sexual services with punishments of still fines or imprisonment, thus declaring that prostitution isn't a desirable economic and labor sector. The government also helps women getting out of prostitution to rebuild their lives. Venezuela's Ministry of Labor has ruled that prostitution can't be considered work because it lacks the basic elements of dignity and social justice. The Socialist Republic of Vietnam punishes pimps, traffickers, brothel owners, and buyers—sometimes publishing buyer's names in the mass media. For women in prostitution, the government finances medical, educational, and economic rehabilitation.

Instead of transforming the male buyer into a legitimate customer, the ILO should give thought to innovative programs that make the buyer accountable for his sexual exploitation.

Raymond suggests that instead of transforming the male buyer into a legitimate customer, the ILO should give thought to innovative programs that make the buyer accountable for his sexual exploitation. She cites the Sage Project, Inc. (SAGE) program in San Francisco, California, which educates men arrested for soliciting women in prostitution about the risks and impacts of their behavior.

Legalization advocates argue that the violence, exploitation, and health effects suffered by women in prostitution aren't inherent to prostitution but simply result from the random behaviors of bad pimps or buyers, and that if prostitution were regulated by the state these harms would diminish. But examples show these arguments to be false.

Prostituted women are even more marginalized and tightly locked into the system of organized sexual exploitation while the state, now an official party to the exploitation, has become the biggest pimp of all.

In the pamphlet entitled *Legalizing Prostitution Is Not the Answer: The Example of Victoria, Australia,* published by the CATW in 2001, Mary Sullivan and Sheila Jeffreys describe the way legalization in Australia has perpetuated and strengthened the culture of violence and exploitation inherent in prostitution. Under legalization, legal and illegal brothels have proliferated, and trafficking in women has accelerated to meet the increased demand. Pimps, having even more power, continue threatening and brutalizing the women they control. Buyers continue to abuse women, refuse to wear condoms, and spread the HIV virus—and other sexually transmitted diseases—to their wives and girlfriends. Stigmatized by identity cards and medial inspections, prostituted women are even more marginalized and tightly locked into the system of organized sexual exploitation while the state, now an official party to the exploitation, has become the biggest pimp of all.

The government of the Netherlands has legalized prostitution, doesn't enforce laws against pimping, and virtually lives off taxes from the earnings of prostituted women. In the book *Making the Harm Visible* (published by the CATW in 1999), Marie-Victoire Louis describes the effects on prostituted women of municipal regulation of brothels in Amsterdam and other Dutch cities. Her article entitled "Legalizing Pimping, Dutch Style" explains the way immigration policies in the Netherlands are shaped to fit the needs of the prostitution industry so that traffickers are seldom prosecuted and a continuous supply of women is guaranteed. In Amsterdam's 250 officially listed brothels, 80 percent of the prostitutes have been trafficked in from other countries and 70 percent possess no legal papers. Without money, papers, or contact with the outside world, these immigrant women live in terror instead of being protected by the regulations governing brothels, prostituted women are frequently beaten up and raped by pimps. These "prostitution managers" have practically been given a free hand by the state and by buyers who, as "consumers of prostitution," feel themselves entitled to abuse the women they buy. Sadly and ironically the "Amsterdam model" of legalization and regulation is touted by the Netherlands and Germany as "self-determination and empowerment for women." In reality it simply legitimizes the "right" to buy, sexually use, and profit from the sexual exploitation of someone else's body.

A Human Rights Approach

As part of a system of organized sexual exploitation, prostitution can be visualized along a continuum of abuse with brothel slavery at the furthest extreme. All along the continuum, fine lines divide the degrees of harm done to those caught up in the system. At the core lies a great social injustice no cosmetic reforms can right: the setting aside of a segment of people whose bodies can be purchased for sexual use by others. When this basic injustice is legitimized and regulated by the state and when the state profits from it, that injustice is compounded.

In her book *The Prostitution of Sexuality* (New York University Press, 1995), Kathleen Barry details a feminist human rights approach to prostitution that points the way to the future. Ethically it recognizes prostitution, sex trafficking, and the globalized industrialization of sex as massive violations of women's human rights. Sociologically it considers how and to what extent prostitution promotes sex discrimination against individual women, against different racial categories of women, and against women as a group. Politically it calls for decriminalizing prostitutes while penalizing pimps, traffickers, brothel owners, and buyers.

Understanding that human rights and restorative justice go hand in hand, the feminist human rights approach to prostitution addresses the harm and the need to repair the damage. As Barry says:

> "Legal proposals to criminalize customers, based on
> the recognition that prostitution violates and harms
> women, must... include social-service, health and
> counseling and job retraining programs. Where states
> would be closing down brothels if customers were
> criminalized, the economic resources poured into the

former prostitution areas could be turned toward producing gainful employment for women."

With the help of women's projects in many countries—such as Buklod in the Philippines and the Council for Prostitution Alternatives in the United States—some women have begun to confront their condition by leaving prostitution, speaking out against it, revealing their experiences, and helping other women leave the sex industry.

Ending the sexual exploitation of trafficking and prostitution will mean the beginning of a new chapter in building, a hu- manist future—a more peaceful and just future in which men and women can join together in love and respect, recognizing one another's essential dignity and humanity. Humanity's sex- uality then will no longer be hijacked and distorted.

Freelance writer Alice Leuchtag has worked as a social worker, coun- selor, college instructor, and researcher. Active in the civil rights, peace, socialist, feminist, and humanist movements, she has helped or- ganize women in Houston to oppose sex trafficking.

THE NEW GENDER GAP

From kindergarten to grad school,
boys are becoming the second sex.

BY MICHELLE CONLIN

Lawrence High is the usual fortress of manila-brick blandness and boxy 1960s architecture. At lunch, the metalheads saunter out to the smokers' park, while the AP types get pizzas at Marinara's, where they talk about—what else?—other people. The hallways are filled with lip-glossed divas in designer clothes and packs of girls in midriff-baring track tops. The guys run the gamut, too: skate punks, rich boys in Armani, and saggy-panted crews with their Eminem swaggers. In other words, they look pretty much as you'd expect.

But when the leaders of the Class of 2003 assemble in the Long Island high school's fluorescent-lit meeting rooms, most of these boys are nowhere to be seen. The senior class president? A girl. The vice-president? Girl. Head of student government? Girl. Captain of the math team, chief of the yearbook, and editor of the newspaper? Girls.

It's not that the girls of the Class of 2003 aren't willing to give the guys a chance. Last year, the juniors elected a boy as class president. But after taking office, he swiftly instructed his all-female slate that they were his cabinet and that he was going to be calling all the shots. The girls looked around and realized they had the votes, says Tufts University-bound Casey Vaughn, an Intel finalist and one of the alpha femmes of the graduating class. "So they impeached him and took over."

The female lock on power at Lawrence is emblematic of a stunning gender reversal in American education. From kindergarten to graduate school, boys are fast becoming the second sex. "Girls are on a tear through the educational system," says Thomas G. Mortenson, a senior scholar at the Pell Institute for the Study of Opportunity in Higher Education in Washington. "In the past 30 years, nearly every inch of educational progress has gone to them."

Just a century ago, the president of Harvard University, Charles W. Eliot, refused to admit women because he feared they would waste the precious resources of his school. Today, across the country, it seems as if girls have built a kind of scholastic Roman Empire alongside boys' languishing Greece. Although Lawrence High has its share of boy superstars—like this year's valedictorian—the gender takeover at some schools is nearly complete. "Every time I turn around, if something good is happening, there's a female in charge," says Terrill O. Stammler, principal of Rising Sun High School in Rising Sun, Md. Boys are missing from nearly every leadership position, academic honors slot, and student-activity post at the school. Even Rising Sun's girls' sports teams do better than the boys'. *[handwritten: meaning some other girls from class more?]*

At one exclusive private day school in the Midwest, administrators have even gone so far as to mandate that all awards and student-government positions be divvied equally between the sexes. "It's not just that boys are falling behind girls," says William S. Pollock, author of *Real Boys: Rescuing Our Sons from the Myths of Boyhood* and a professor of psychiatry at Harvard Medical School. "It's that boys themselves are falling behind their own functioning and doing worse than they did before."

It may still be a man's world. But it is no longer, in any way, a boy's. From his first days in school, an average boy is already developmentally two years behind the girls in reading and writing. Yet he's often expected to learn the same things in the same way in the same amount of time.

[handwritten: How? They don't know how to read or write yet]

While every nerve in his body tells him to run, he has to sit still and listen for almost eight hours a day. Biologically, he needs about four recesses a day, but he's lucky if he gets one, since some lawsuit-leery schools have banned them altogether. Hug a girl, and he could be labeled a "toucher" and swiftly suspended—a result of what some say is an increasingly anti-boy culture that pathologizes their behavior.

If he falls behind, he's apt to be shipped off to special ed, where he'll find that more than 70% of his classmates are also boys. Squirm, clown, or interrupt, and he is four times as likely to be diagnosed with attention deficit hyperactivity disorder. That often leads to being forced to take Ritalin or risk being expelled, sent to special ed, or having parents accused of negligence. One study of public schools in Fairfax County, Va., found that more than 20% of upper-middle-class white boys were taking Ritalin-like drugs by fifth grade.

Once a boy makes it to freshman year of high school, he's at greater risk of falling even further behind in grades, extracurricular activities, and advanced placement. Not even science and math remain his bastions. And while the girls are busy working on sweeping the honor roll at graduation, a boy is more likely to be bulking up in the weight room to enhance his steroid-fed Adonis complex, playing Grand Theft Auto: Vice City on his PlayStation2, or downloading rapper 50 Cent on his iPod. All the while, he's 30% more likely to drop out, 85% more likely to commit murder, and four to six times more likely to kill himself, with boy suicides tripling since 1970. "We get a bad rap," says Steven Covington, a sophomore at Ottumwa High School in Ottumwa, Iowa. "Society says we can't be trusted."

As for college—well, let's just say this: At least it's easier for the guys who get there to find a date. For 350 years, men outnumbered women on college campuses. Now, in every state, every income bracket, every racial and ethnic group, and most industrialized Western nations, women reign, earning an average 57% of all BAs and 58% of all master's degrees in the U.S. alone. There are 133 girls getting BAs for every 100 guys—a number that's projected to grow to 142 women per 100 men by 2010, according to the U.S. Education Dept. If current trends continue, demographers say, there will be 156 women per 100 men earning degrees by 2020.

Overall, more boys and girls are in college than a generation ago. But when adjusted for population growth, the percentage of boys entering college, master's programs, and most doctoral programs—except for PhDs in fields like engineering and computer science—has mostly stalled out, whereas for women it has continued to rise across the board. The trend is most pronounced among Hispanics, African Americans, and those from low-income families.

The female-to-male ratio is already 60–40 at the University of North Carolina, Boston University, and New York University. To keep their gender ratios 50–50, many Ivy League and other elite schools are secretly employing a kind of stealth affirmative action for boys. "Girls present better qualifications in the application process— better grades, tougher classes, and more thought in their essays," says Michael S. McPherson, president of Macalester College in St. Paul, Minn., where 57% of enrollees are women. "Boys get off to a slower start."

The trouble isn't limited to school. Once a young man is out of the house, he's more likely than his sister to boomerang back home and sponge off his mom and dad. It all adds up to the fact that before he reaches adulthood, a young man is more likely than he was 30 years ago to end up in the new and growing class of underachiever—what the British call the "sink group."

For a decade, British educators have waged successful classroom programs to ameliorate "laddism" (boys turning off to school) by focusing on teaching techniques that re-engage them. But in the U.S., boys' fall from alpha to omega status doesn't even have a name, let alone the public's attention. "No one wants to speak out on behalf of boys," says Andrew Sum, director of the Northeastern University Center for Labor Market Studies. As a social-policy or educational issue, "it's near nonexistent."

Women are rapidly closing the M.D. and PhD gap and make up almost half of law students.

On the one hand, the education grab by girls is amazing news, which could make the 21st the first female century. Already, women are rapidly closing the M.D. and PhD gap and are on the verge of making up the majority of law students, according to the American Bar Assn. MBA programs, with just 29% females, remain among the few old-boy domains.

Still, it's hardly as if the world has been equalized: Ninety percent of the world's billionaires are men. Among the super rich, only one woman, Gap Inc. co-founder Doris F. Fisher, made, rather than inherited, her wealth. Men continue to dominate in the highest-paying jobs in such leading-edge industries as engineering, investment banking, and high tech—the sectors that still power the economy and build the biggest fortunes. And women still face sizable obstacles in the pay gap, the glass ceiling, and the still-Sisyphean struggle to juggle work and child-rearing.

But attaining a decisive educational edge may finally enable females to narrow the earnings gap, punch through more of the glass ceiling, and gain an equal hand in rewriting the rules of corporations, government, and society. "Girls are better able to deliver in terms of what modern society requires of people—paying attention, abiding by rules, being verbally competent, and dealing with interpersonal relationships in offices," says James Garbarino, a professor of human development at Cornell

University and author of *Lost Boys: Why Our Sons Turn Violent and How We Can Save Them*.

Righting boys' problems needn't end up leading to reversals for girls. But some feminists say the danger in exploring what's happening to boys would be to mistakenly see any expansion of opportunities for women as inherently disadvantageous to boys. "It isn't a zero-sum game," says Susan M. Bailey, executive director of the Wellesley Centers for Women. Adds Macalester's McPherson: "It would be dangerous to even out the gender ratio by treating women worse. I don't think we've reached a point in this country where we are fully providing equal opportunities to women."

Men could become losers in a global economy that values mental powers over might.

Still, if the creeping pattern of male disengagement and economic dependency continues, more men could end up becoming losers in a global economy that values mental powers over might—not to mention the loss of their talent and potential. The growing educational and economic imbalances could also create societal upheavals, altering family finances, social policies, and work-family practices. Men are already dropping out of the labor force, walking out on fatherhood, and disconnecting from civic life in greater numbers. Since 1964, for example, the voting rate in Presidential elections among men has fallen from 72% to 53%—twice the rate of decline among women, according to Pell's Mortenson. In a turnaround from the 1960s, more women now vote than men.

Boys' slide also threatens to erode male earnings, spark labor shortages for skilled workers, and create the same kind of marriage squeeze among white women that already exists for blacks. Among African Americans, 30% of 40- to 44-year-old women have never married, owing in part to the lack of men with the same academic credentials and earning potential. Currently, the never-married rate is 9% for white women of the same age. "Women are going to pull further and further ahead of men, and at some point, when they want to form families, they are going to look around and say, 'Where are the guys?'" says Mortenson. *Amazing. Unquestioned—that marriage only works if men myth make $*

Corporations should worry, too. During the boom, the most acute labor shortages occurred among educated workers—a problem companies often solved by hiring immigrants. When the economy reenergizes, a skills shortage in the U.S. could undermine employers' productivity and growth.

Better-educated men are also, on average, a much happier lot. They are more likely to marry, stick by their children, and pay more in taxes. From the ages of 18 to 65, the average male college grad earns $2.5 million over his lifetime, 90% more than his high school counterpart. That's

A WIDENING GULF IN SCHOOL...

girls | boys

Girls Trounce Boys in Reading...
National Reading scores, 4th-graders, 2000

| 222 | 212 |

Average reading scores; on a scale of 0 to 500

...And Are Catching Up in Math
National Math Scores, 12th-graders, 2000

| 299 | 303 |

Average math scores; on a scale of 0 to 500
Data: National Center for Education Statistics

Girls Also Dominate in Extracurricular Activities...
Percent of high school seniors involved in:

Student Government

| 27% | 19% |

Music/Performing Arts

| 46% | 35% |

Yearbook/Newspaper

| 29% | 21% |

Academic Clubs

| 36% | 28% |

Athletic Teams

| 49% | 63% |

Data: Education Dept.; National Center for Education Statistics

...While Boys Make Up the Bulk of Special Ed Students...
Kids diagnosed with learning disabilities

| 27% | 73% |

Kids diagnosed as emotionally disturbed

| 24% | 76% |

Secondary students in special ed, K-12
Data: U.S. Education Dept.

...Account for Most Stimulant Prescriptions...
Kids under 20 in an HMO* on Ritalin and other stimulant drugs

| 1% | 4% |

*NORTHWEST REGION HMO WITH 131,000 YOUTHS
Data: Dr. Julie Magno Zito, University of Maryland, Psychotropic Practice Patterns for Youth

...And Are More Likely to Commit Suicide than Girls

Suicide Rates Ages 15-24
MALE
FEMALE
PER 100,000
'60 '70 '80 '90 '00

Data: Centers for Disease Control and Prevention; Thomas G. Mortenson, Pell Center for the Study of Opportunity in Higher Education

Graphics by Rob Doyle/BW

up from 40% more in 1979, the peak year for U.S. manufacturing. The average college diploma holder also contributes four times more in net taxes over his career than a high school grad, according to Northeastern's Sum. Meanwhile, the typical high school dropout will usually get $40,000 more from the government than he pays in, a net drain on society.

Certainly, many boys continue to conquer scholastic summits, especially boys from high-income families with

...LEADS MORE AND MORE TO A GIRLS' CLUB IN COLLEGE

The Gender Gap Spans Every Racial and Ethnic Group...
Bachelor's degrees awarded to students by race/ethnicity, as a percent of total

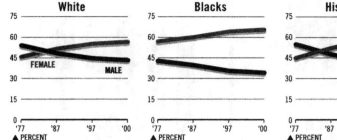

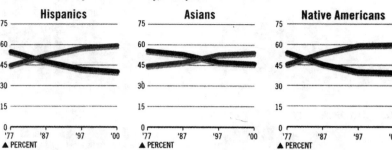

...And Most of the Industrialized World...
Ages 25 to 34, with at least a college education, plus advanced degrees

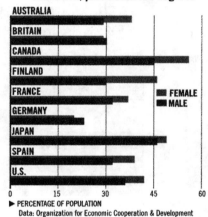

▶ PERCENTAGE OF POPULATION
Data: Organization for Economic Cooperation & Development

...And Is Projected to Get Worse...
Number of U.S. women awarded degrees per 100 men

Bachelor's Degrees

1999-2000	Est. 2009-10
133	142

Master's Degrees

1999-2000	Est. 2009-10
138	151

Data: Andrew Sum, Northeastern University Center for Labor Market Studies

...Threatening the Marriage Squeeze Among Whites That Blacks Already Face

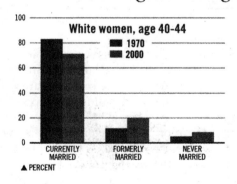

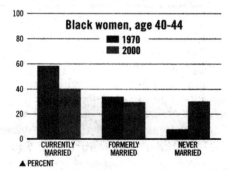

Data: *Mismatch*, by Andrew Hacker; National Center for Education Statistics; Bureau of Labor Statistics; Census Bureau

Graphics by Rob Doyle/BW

educated parents. Overall, boys continue to do better on standardized tests such as the scholastic aptitude test, though more low-income girls than low-income boys take it, thus depressing girls' scores. Many educators also believe that standardized testing's multiple-choice format favors boys because girls tend to think in broader, more complex terms. But that advantage is eroding as many colleges now weigh grades—where girls excel—more heavily than test scores.

Still, it's not as if girls don't face a slew of vexing issues, which are often harder to detect because girls are likelier to internalize low self-esteem through depression or the

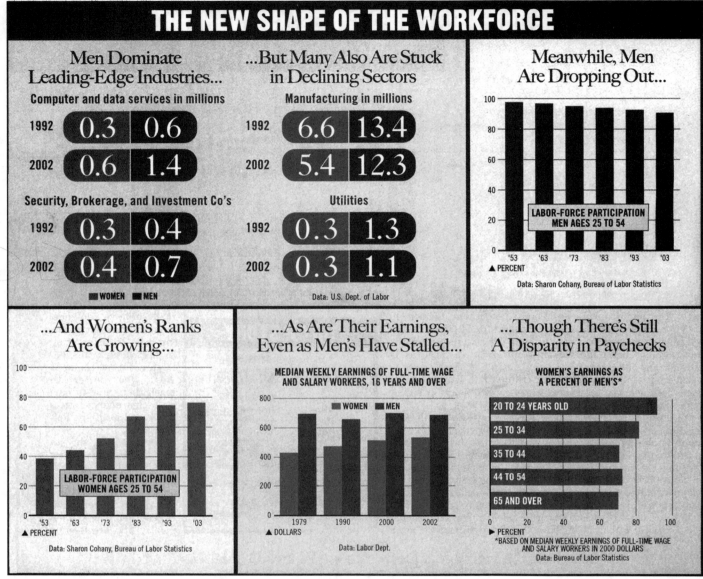

THE NEW SHAPE OF THE WORKFORCE

Men Dominate Leading-Edge Industries...

Computer and data services in millions

	WOMEN	MEN
1992	0.3	0.6
2002	0.6	1.4

Security, Brokerage, and Investment Co's

	WOMEN	MEN
1992	0.3	0.4
2002	0.4	0.7

■ WOMEN ■ MEN

...But Many Also Are Stuck in Declining Sectors

Manufacturing in millions

	WOMEN	MEN
1992	6.6	13.4
2002	5.4	12.3

Utilities

	WOMEN	MEN
1992	0.3	1.3
2002	0.3	1.1

Data: U.S. Dept. of Labor

Meanwhile, Men Are Dropping Out...

LABOR-FORCE PARTICIPATION MEN AGES 25 TO 54

▲ PERCENT

Data: Sharon Cohany, Bureau of Labor Statistics

...And Women's Ranks Are Growing...

LABOR-FORCE PARTICIPATION WOMEN AGES 25 TO 54

▲ PERCENT

Data: Sharon Cohany, Bureau of Labor Statistics

...As Are Their Earnings, Even as Men's Have Stalled...

MEDIAN WEEKLY EARNINGS OF FULL-TIME WAGE AND SALARY WORKERS, 16 YEARS AND OVER

■ WOMEN ■ MEN

▲ DOLLARS

Data: Labor Dept.

...Though There's Still A Disparity in Paychecks

WOMEN'S EARNINGS AS A PERCENT OF MEN'S*

- 20 TO 24 YEARS OLD
- 25 TO 34
- 35 TO 44
- 44 TO 54
- 65 AND OVER

▶ PERCENT
*BASED ON MEDIAN WEEKLY EARNINGS OF FULL-TIME WAGE AND SALARY WORKERS IN 2000 DOLLARS
Data: Bureau of Labor Statistics

Graphics by Rob Doyle/BW

desire to starve themselves into perfection. And while boys may act out with their fists, girls, given their superior verbal skills, often do so with their mouths in the form of vicious gossip and female bullying. "They yell and cuss," says 15-year-old Keith Gates, an Ottumwa student. "But we always get in trouble. They never do."

Before educators, corporations, and policymakers can narrow the new gender gap, they will have to understand its myriad causes. Everything from absentee parenting to the lack of male teachers to corporate takeovers of lunch rooms with sugar-and-fat-filled food, which can make kids hyperactive and distractable, plays a role. So can TV violence, which hundreds of studies—including recent ones by Stanford University and the University of Michigan—have linked to aggressive behavior in kids. Some believe boys are responding to cultural signals—downsized dads cast adrift in the New Economy, a dumb-and-

dumber dude culture that demeans academic achievement, and the glamorization of all things gangster that makes school seem so uncool. What can compare with the allure of a gun-wielding, model-dating hip hopper? Boys, who mature more slowly than girls, are also often less able to delay gratification or take a long-range view.

Schools have inadvertently played a big role, too, losing sight of boys—taking for granted that they were doing well, even though data began to show the opposite. Some educators believed it was a blip that would change or feared takebacks on girls' gains. Others were just in denial. Indeed, many administrators saw boys, rather than the way schools were treating them, as the problem.

Thirty years ago, educational experts launched what's known as the "Girl Project." The movement's noble objective was to help girls wipe out their weaknesses in math and science, build self-esteem, and give them the undisputed message: The opportunities are yours; take them. Schools focused on making the classroom more girl-friendly by including teaching styles that catered to them. Girls were also powerfully influenced by the women's movement, as well as by Title IX and the Gender & Equity Act, all of which created a legal environment in which discrimination against girls—from classrooms to the sports field—carried heavy penalties. Once the chains were off, girls soared.

For 30 years, the focus at schools has been to empower girls, in and out of the classroom.

Yet even as boys' educational development was flat-lining in the 1990s—with boys dropping out in greater numbers and failing to bridge the gap in reading and writing—the spotlight remained firmly fixed on girls. Part of the reason was that the issue had become politically charged and girls had powerful advocates. The American Association of University Women, for example, published research cementing into pedagogy the idea that girls had deep problems with self-esteem in school as a result of teachers' patterns, which included calling on girls less and lavishing attention on boys. Newspapers and TV newsmagazines lapped up the news, decrying a new confidence crisis among American girls. Universities and research centers sponsored scores of teacher symposiums centered on girls. "All the focus was on girls, all the grant monies, all the university programs—to get girls interested in science and math," says Steve Hanson, principal of Ottumwa High School in Iowa. "There wasn't a similar thing for reading and writing for boys."

Some boy champions go so far as to contend that schools have become boy-bashing laboratories. Christina Hoff Sommers, author of *The War Against Boys*, says the AAUW report, coupled with zero-tolerance sexual harassment laws, have hijacked schools by overly feminizing classrooms and attempting to engineer androgyny.

The "earliness" push, in which schools are pressured to show kids achieving the same standards by the same age or risk losing funding, is also far more damaging to boys, according to Lilian G. Katz, co-director of ERIC Clearinghouse on Elementary and Early Childhood Education. Even the nerves on boys' fingers develop later than girls', making it difficult to hold a pencil and push out perfect cursive. These developmental differences often unfairly sideline boys as slow or dumb, planting a distaste for school as early as the first grade.

Instead of catering to boys' learning styles, Pollock and others argue, many schools are force-fitting them into an unnatural mold. The reigning sit-still-and-listen paradigm isn't ideal for either sex. But it's one girls often tolerate better than boys. Girls have more intricate sensory capacities and biosocial aptitudes to decipher exactly what the teacher wants, whereas boys tend to be more

anti-authoritarian, competitive, and risk-taking. They often don't bother with such details as writing their names in the exact place instructed by the teacher.

Experts say educators also haven't done nearly enough to keep up with the recent findings in brain research about developmental differences. "Ninety-nine-point-nine percent of teachers are not trained in this," says Michael Gurian, author of *Boys and Girls Learn Differently*. "They were taught 20 years ago that gender is just a social function."

In fact, brain research over the past decade has revealed how differently boys' and girls' brains can function. Early on, boys are usually superior spatial thinkers and possess the ability to see things in three dimensions. They are often drawn to play that involves intense movement and an element of make-believe violence. Instead of straitjacketing boys by attempting to restructure this behavior out of them, it would be better to teach them how to harness this energy effectively and healthily, Pollock says.

As it stands, the result is that too many boys are diagnosed with attention-deficit disorder or its companion, attention-deficit hyperactivity disorder. The U.S.—mostly its boys—now consumes 80% of the world's supply of methylphenidate (the generic name for Ritalin). That use has increased 500% over the past decade, leading some to call it the new K–12 management tool. There are school districts where 20% to 25% of the boys are on the drug, says Paul R. Wolpe, a psychiatry professor at the University of Pennsylvania and the senior fellow at the school's Center for Bioethics: "Ritalin is a response to an artificial social context that we've created for children."

Instead of recommending medication—something four states have recently banned school administrators from doing—experts say educators should focus on helping boys feel less like misfits. Experts are designing new developmentally appropriate, child-initiated learning that concentrates on problem-solving, not just test-taking. This approach benefits both sexes but especially boys, given that they tend to learn best through action, not just talk. Activities are geared toward the child's interest level and temperament. Boys, for example, can learn math through counting pinecones, biology through mucking around in a pond. They can read *Harry Potter* instead of *Little House on the Prairie*, and write about aliens attacking a hospital rather than about how to care for people in the hospital. If they get antsy, they can leave a teacher's lecture and go to an activity center replete with computers and manipulable objects that support the lesson plan.

Paying attention to boys' emotional lives also delivers dividends. Over the course of her longitudinal research project in Washington (D.C.) schools, University of Northern Florida researcher Rebecca Marcon found that boys who attend kindergartens that focus on social and emotional skills—as opposed to only academic learning—perform better, across the board, by the time they reach junior high.

Really... How do they test this?

So it is social

Indeed, brain research shows that boys are actually more empathic, expressive, and emotive at birth than girls. But Pollock says the boy code, which bathes them in a culture of stoicism and reticence, often socializes those aptitudes out of them by the second grade. "We now have executives paying $10,000 a week to learn emotional intelligence," says Pollock. "These are actually the skills boys are born with."

The gender gap also has roots in the expectation gap. In the 1970s, boys were far more likely to anticipate getting a college degree—with girls firmly entrenched in the cheerleader role. Today, girls' expectations are ballooning, while boys' are plummeting. There's even a sense, including among the most privileged families, that today's boys are a sort of payback generation—the one that has to compensate for the advantages given to males in the past. In fact, the new equality is often perceived as a loss by many boys who expected to be on top. "My friends in high school, they just didn't see the value of college, they just didn't care enough," says New York University sophomore Joe Clabby. Only half his friends from his high school group in New Jersey went on to college.

They will face a far different world than their dads did. Without college diplomas, it will be harder for them to find good-paying jobs. And more and more, the positions available to them will be in industries long thought of as female. The services sector, where women make up 60% of employees, has ballooned by 260% since the 1970s. During the same period, manufacturing, where men hold 70% of jobs, has shrunk by 14%.

These men will also be more likely to marry women who outearn them. Even in this jobless recovery, women's wages have continued to grow, with the pay gap the smallest on record, while men's earnings haven't managed to keep up with the low rate of inflation. Given that the recession hit male-centric industries such as technology and manufacturing the hardest, native-born men experienced more than twice as much job loss as native-born women between 2000 and 2002.

Some feminists who fought hard for girl equality in schools in the early 1980s and '90s say this: So what if girls have gotten 10, 20 years of attention—does that make up for centuries of subjugation? Moreover, what's wrong with women gliding into first place, especially if they deserve it? "Just because girls aren't shooting 7-Eleven clerks doesn't mean they should be ignored," says Cornell's Garbarino. "Once you stop oppressing girls, it stands to reason they will thrive up to their potential."

Moreover, girls say much of their drive stems from parents and teachers pushing them to get a college degree because they have to be better to be equal—to make the same money and get the same respect as a guy. "Girls are more willing to take the initiative… they're not afraid to do the work," says Tara Prout, the Georgetown-bound senior class president at Lawrence High. "A lot of boys in my school are looking for credit to get into college to look good, but they don't really want to do the grunt work."

A new world has opened up for girls, but unless a symmetrical effort is made to help boys find their footing, it may turn out that it's a lonely place to be. After all, it takes more than one gender to have a gender revolution.

BOYS' STORY

For further reading:

- *Lost Boys* by James Garbarino
- *Boys and Girls Learn Differently* by Michael Gurian
- *Mismatch* by Andrew Hacker
- *Raising Cain* by Dan Kindlon and Michael Thompson
- *Real Boys* by William Pollack
- *The War Against Boys* by Christina Hoff Sommers

UNIT 5

Social Institutions: Issues, Crises, and Changes

Unit Selections

Key Points to Consider

- Discuss whether or not it is important to preserve some continuity in institutions.

- How can institutions outlive their usefulness? How can they be changed for the better?

- Why are institutions so difficult to change? Cite examples where changes are instituted from the top down and others where they are instituted from the bottom up. Do you see a similar pattern of development for these types of changes?

- Is it possible to reform the political system to greatly reduce the corrupting role of money in politics? Why or why not?

- What basic changes in the economic system are evident in the things that you observe daily?

- How would you reform the educational system in America?

- How would you change the health care system?

 **Links: www.dushkin.com/online/**
These sites are annotated in the World Wide Web pages.

Center for the Study of Group Processes
http://www.uiowa.edu/~grpproc/

International Labour Organization (ILO)
http://www.ilo.org

IRIS Center
http://www.iris.umd.edu

National Center for Policy Analysis
http://www.ncpa.org

National Institutes of Health (NIH)
http://www.nih.gov

Social institutions are the building blocks of social structure. They accomplish the important tasks of society—for example, regulation of reproduction, socialization of children, production and distribution of economic goods, law enforcement and social control, and organization of religion and other value systems.

Social institutions are not rigid arrangements; they reflect changing social conditions. Institutions generally change slowly. At the present time, however, many of the social institutions in the United States and many other parts of the world are in crisis and are undergoing rapid change. Eastern European countries are literally transforming their political and economic institutions. Economic institutions, such as stock markets, are becoming truly international, and when a major country experiences a recession, many other countries feel the effects. In the United States, major reform movements are active in political, economic, family, medical, and educational institutions.

The first subsection of unit 5 examines American political institutions. In the first article, G. William Domhoff examines the power structure of the American political system and finds it dominated by the corporate community. But how does his view account for democracy and the power that it gives the average person? What about the evident influence of workers, liberals, environmentalists, and challenge groups? Domhoff argues that these forces may get media coverage, but they cannot prevent the corporate community from controlling the federal government on basic issues of income, wealth, and economic power. Moreover, he shows how this community exercises its power. The next article is one of those uncommon accounts of successful government actions that serve the public good. Several policies dealing with the environment, health, and safety have greatly benefitted American citizens.

The following subsection deals with major issues and problems of the economy. The first issue is the big question of how "good" is the U.S. economy? W. Michael Cox and Richard Alm provide an assessment that includes and goes beyond economic statistics. They say that we are the world's wealthiest nation with the highest consumption (e.g., home ownership) but also have a balanced life. This includes more leisure, more pleasant work, greater safety, more convenience, a cleaner environment, and more variety. All this supports the authors' thesis that our type of free enterprise system is one of the best in the world.

The next two issues deal with the work-world. First, Murray Weidenbaum shows that globalization is blurring the distinctions between national and foreign companies and that national and foreign economies are blending together. Honda has more parts made in America than Pontiac and many large American companies make more money abroad than at home. Weidenbaum argues that globalization is good for America. The second work-world issue is the migration of American jobs to overseas as described by Jyoti Thottam in the next article. Blue-collar jobs have gone abroad for decades. Now increasingly white-collar jobs are

migrating overseas. The numbers are small today but increasing very rapidly.

The social sphere is also in turmoil, as illustrated by the articles in the last subsection. A key issue for many parents and children is the quality of education, and the public's perception is rather negative. But the problems of middle-class schools are small compared to the problems of some inner-city schools. Their problems are best understood through stories and the story of Joshua Kaplowitz's experience teaching at Emery Elementary School in Washington D.C. gets to the heart of the matter. One of many problems is just maintaining order in class. Another problem are fraudulent harassment lawsuits that ruined his and others' careers at Emery. The medical sphere is also in turmoil and plagued with problems. The particular problem discussed in the next article is the closing of many badly needed hospitals by for-profit hospital chains for lower than acceptable profit rates. Arthur Allen tells the story of the closing of the Medical College of Pennsylvania Hospital in Philadelphia as an example of "more that 560 hospitals [that] have closed since 1990—clobbered by stagnant reimbursement rates from government and the insurance industry, rising malpractice rates, skyrocketing prices for drugs and medical equipment, and increasing numbers of uninsured patients who can't pay their bills." In the final article, Samuel Huntington examines the role of religion in our national life. "American have been extremely religious and overwhelmingly Christian throughout their history." Many early settlers came here for religious reasons and the founding fathers were guided by religious observances in their deliberations. Religion has been important to this nation ever since.

Who Rules America?

G. William Domhoff

Power and Class in the United States

Power and *class* are terms that make Americans a little uneasy, and concepts like *power elite* and *dominant class* immediately put people on guard. The idea that a relatively fixed group of privileged people might shape the economy and government for their own benefit goes against the American grain. Nevertheless,... the owners and top-level managers in large income-producing properties are far and away the dominant power figures in the United States. Their corporations, banks, and agribusinesses come together as a *corporate community* that dominates the federal government in Washington. Their real estate, construction, and land development companies form *growth coalitions* that dominate most local governments. Granted, there is competition within both the corporate community and the local growth coalitions for profits and investment opportunities, and there are sometimes tensions between national corporations and local growth coalitions, but both are cohesive on policy issues affecting their general welfare, and in the face of demands by organized workers, liberals, environmentalists, and neighborhoods.

As a result of their ability to organize and defend their interests, the owners and managers of large income-producing properties have a very great share of all income and wealth in the United States, greater than in any other industrial democracy. Making up at best 1 percent of the total population, by the early 1990s they earned 15.7 percent of the nation's yearly income and owned 37.2 percent of all privately held wealth, including 49.6 percent of all corporate stocks and 62.4 percent of all bonds. Due to their wealth and the lifestyle it makes possible, these owners and managers draw closer as a common social group. They belong to the same exclusive social clubs, frequent the same summer and winter resorts, and send their children to a relative handful of private schools. Members of the corporate community thereby become a *corporate rich* who create a nationwide *social upper class* through their social interaction.... Members of the growth coalitions, on the other hand, are *place entrepreneurs,* people who sell locations and buildings. They come together as local upper classes in their respective cities and sometimes mingle with the corporate rich in educational or resort settings.

The corporate rich and the growth entrepreneurs supplement their small numbers by developing and directing a wide variety of nonprofit organizations, the most important of which are a set of tax-free charitable foundations, think tanks, and policy-discussion groups. These specialized nonprofit groups constitute a *policy-formation network* at the national level. Chambers of commerce and policy groups affiliated with them form similar policy-formation networks at the local level, aided by a few national-level city development organizations that are available for local consulting.

Those corporate owners who have the interest and ability to take part in general governance join with top-level executives in the corporate community and the policy-formation network to form the *power elite,* which is the leadership group for the corporate rich as a whole. The concept of a power elite makes clear that not all members of the upper class are involved in governance; some of them simply enjoy the lifestyle that their great wealth affords them. At the same time, the focus on a leadership group allows for the fact that not all those in the power elite are members of the upper class; many of them are high-level employees in profit and nonprofit organizations controlled by the corporate rich....

The power elite is not united on all issues because it includes both moderate conservatives and ultraconservatives. Although both factions favor minimal reliance on government on all domestic issues, the moderate conservatives sometimes agree to legislation advocated by liberal elements of the society, especially in times of social upheaval like the Great Depression of the 1930s and the Civil Rights Movement of the early 1960s. Except on defense spending, ultraconservatives are characterized by a complete distaste for any kind of government programs under any circumstances—even to the point of opposing government support for corporations on some issues. Moderate conservatives often favor foreign aid, working through the United Nations, and making attempts to win over foreign enemies through patient diplomacy, treaties, and trade agreements. Historically, ultraconservatives have opposed most forms of foreign involvement, although they have become more tolerant of foreign trade agreements over the past thirty or forty years. At the same time, their hostility to the United Nations continues unabated.

Members of the power elite enter into the electoral arena as the leaders within a *corporate-conservative coalition,* where they are aided by a wide variety of patriotic, antitax, and other single-issue organizations. These conservative advocacy organizations are funded in varying degrees by the corporate rich, direct-mail appeals, and middle-class conservatives. This coalition has played a large role in both political parties at the presidential level and usually succeeds in electing a conservative majority to both houses of Congress. Historically, the conservative majority in Congress was made up of most Northern Republicans and most Southern Democrats, but that arrangement has been changing gradually since the 1960s as the conservative Democrats of the South are replaced by even more conservative Southern Republicans. The corporate-conservative coalition also has access to the federal government in Washington through lobbying and the appointment of its members to top positions in the executive branch....

Despite their preponderant power within the federal government and the many useful policies it carries out for them, members of the power elite are constantly critical of government as an alleged enemy of freedom and economic growth. Although their wariness toward government is expressed in terms of a dislike for taxes and government regulations, I believe their underlying concern is that government could change the power relations in the private sphere by aiding average Americans through a number of different avenues: (1) creating government jobs for the unemployed; (2) making health, unemployment, and welfare benefits more generous; (3) helping employees gain greater workplace rights and protections; and (4) helping workers organize unions. All of these initiatives are opposed by members of the power elite because they would increase wages and taxes, but the deepest opposition is toward any government support for unions because unions are a potential organizational base for advocating the whole range of issues opposed by the corporate rich....

Where Does Democracy Fit In?

...[T]o claim that the corporate rich have enough power to be considered a dominant class does not imply that lower social classes are totally powerless. *Domination* means the power to set the terms under which other groups and classes must operate, not total control. Highly trained professionals with an interest in environmental and consumer issues have been able to couple their technical information and their understanding of the legislative and judicial processes with well-timed publicity, lobbying, and lawsuits to win governmental restrictions on some corporate practices. Wage and salary employees, when they are organized into unions and have the right to strike, have been able to gain pay increases, shorter hours, better working conditions, and social benefits such as health insurance. Even the most powerless of people—the very poor and those discrim-

inated against—sometimes develop the capacity to influence the power structure through sit-ins, demonstrations, social movements, and other forms of social disruption, and there is evidence that such activities do bring about some redress of grievances, at least for a short time.

More generally, the various challengers to the power elite sometimes work together on policy issues as a *liberal-labor coalition* that is based in unions, local environmental organizations, some minority group communities, university and arts communities, liberal churches, and small newspapers and magazines. Despite a decline in membership over the past twenty years, unions are the largest and best-financed part of the coalition, and the largest organized social force in the country (aside from churches). They also cut across racial and ethnic lines more than any other institutionalized sector of American society....

The policy conflicts between the corporate-conservative and liberal-labor coalitions are best described as *class conflicts* because they primarily concern the distribution of profits and wages, the rate and progressivity of taxation, the usefulness of labor unions, and the degree to which business should be regulated by government. The liberal-labor coalition wants corporations to pay higher wages to employees and higher taxes to government. It wants government to regulate a wide range of business practices, including many that are related to the environment, and help employees to organize unions. The corporate-conservative coalition resists all these policy objectives to a greater or lesser degree, claiming they endanger the freedom of individuals and the efficient workings of the economic marketplace. The conflicts these disagreements generate can manifest themselves in many different ways: workplace protests, industrywide boycotts, massive demonstrations in cities, pressure on Congress, and the outcome of elections.

Neither the corporate-conservative nor the liberal-labor coalition includes a very large percentage of the American population, although each has the regular support of about 25–30 percent of the voters. Both coalitions are made up primarily of financial donors, policy experts, political consultants, and party activists....

Pluralism. The main alternative theory [I] address.... claims that power is more widely dispersed among groups and classes than a class-dominance theory allows. This general perspective is usually called *pluralism,* meaning there is no one dominant power group. It is the theory most favored by social scientists. In its strongest version, pluralism holds that power is held by the general public through the pressure that public opinion and voting put on elected officials. According to this version, citizens form voluntary groups and pressure groups that shape public opinion, lobby elected officials, and back sympathetic political candidates in the electoral process....

The second version of pluralism sees power as rooted in a wide range of well-organized "interest groups" that are often based in economic interests (e.g., industrialists, bankers, labor unions), but also in other interests as well (e.g., environmental, consumer, and civil rights groups). These interest groups join together in different coalitions depending on the specific issues. Proponents of this version of pluralism sometimes concede that public opinion and voting have only a minimal or indirect influence, but they see business groups as too fragmented and antagonistic to form a cohesive dominant class. They also claim that some business interest groups occasionally join coalitions with liberal or labor groups on specific issues, and that business-dominated coalitions sometimes lose. Furthermore, some proponents of this version of pluralism believe that the Democratic Party is responsive to the wishes of liberal and labor interest groups.

In contrast, I argue that the business interest groups are part of a tightly knit corporate community that is able to develop classwide cohesion on the issues of greatest concern to it: opposition to unions, high taxes, and government regulation. When a business group loses on a specific issue, it is often because other business groups have been opposed; in other words, there are arguments within the corporate community, and these arguments are usually settled within the governmental arena. I also claim that liberal and labor groups are rarely part of coalitions with business groups and that for most of its history the Democratic Party has been dominated by corporate and agribusiness interests in the Southern states, in partnership with the growth coalitions in large urban areas outside the South. Finally, I show that business interests rarely lose on labor and regulatory issues except in times of extreme social disruption like the 1930s and 1960s, when differences of opinion between Northern and Southern corporate leaders made victories for the liberal-labor coalition possible....

How the Power Elite Dominates Government

This [section] shows how the power elite builds on the ideas developed in the policy-formation process and its success in the electoral arena to dominate the federal government. Lobbyists from corporations, law firms, and trade associations play a key role in shaping government on narrow issues of concern to specific corporations or business sectors, but their importance should not be overestimated because a majority of those elected to Congress are predisposed to agree with them. The corporate community and the policy-formation network supply top-level governmental appointees and new policy directions on major issues.

Once again, as seen in the battles for public opinion and electoral success, the power elite faces opposition from a minority of elected officials and their supporters in labor unions and liberal advocacy groups. These opponents are sometimes successful in blocking ultra-conservative initiatives, but most of the victories for the liberal-labor coalition are the result of support from moderate conservatives....

Appointees to Government

The first way to test a class-dominance view of the federal government is to study the social and occupational backgrounds of the people who are appointed to manage the major departments of the executive branch, such as state, treasury, defense, and justice. If pluralists are correct, these appointees should come from a wide range of interest groups. If the state autonomy theorists are correct, they should be disproportionately former elected officials or longtime government employees. If the class-dominance view is correct, they should come disproportionately from the upper class, the corporate community, and the policy-formation network.

There have been numerous studies over the years of major governmental appointees under both Republican and Democratic administrations, usually focusing on the top appointees in the departments that are represented in the president's cabinet. These studies are unanimous in their conclusion that most top appointees in both Republican and Democratic administrations are corporate executives and corporate lawyers—and hence members of the power elite....

Conclusion

This [section] has demonstrated the power elite's wide-ranging access to government through the interest-group and policy-formation processes, as well as through its ability to influence appointments to major government positions. When coupled with the several different kinds of power discussed in earlier [sections] this access and involvement add up to power elite domination of the federal government.

By *domination,* as stated in the first [section], social scientists mean the ability of a class or group to set the terms under which other classes or groups within a social system must operate. By this definition, domination does not mean control on each and every issue, and it does not rest solely on involvement in government. Influence over government is only the final and most visible aspect of power elite domination, which has its roots in the class structure, the corporate control of the investment function, and the operation of the policy-formation network. If government officials did not have to wait for corporate leaders to decide where and when they will invest, and if government officials were not further limited by the general public's acceptance of policy recommendations from the policy-formation network, then power elite involvement in elections and government would count for a lot less than they do under present conditions.

Domination by the power elite does not negate the reality of continuing conflict over government policies, but few conflicts, it has been shown, involve challenges to the rules that create privileges for the upper class and domination by the power elite. Most of the numerous battles within the interest-group process, for example, are only over specific spoils and favors; they often involve disagreements among competing business interests.

Similarly, conflicts within the policy-making process of government often involve differences between the moderate conservative and ultraconservative segments of the dominant class. At other times they involve issues in which the needs of the corporate community as a whole come into conflict with the needs of specific industries, which is what happens to some extent on tariff policies and also on some environmental legislation. In neither case does the nature of the conflict call into question the domination of government by the power elite.

...Contrary to what pluralists claim, there is not a single case study on any issue of any significance that shows a liberal-labor victory over a united corporate-conservative coalition, which is strong evidence for a class-domination theory on the "Who wins?" power indicator. The classic case studies frequently cited by pluralists have been shown to be gravely deficient as evidence for their views. Most of these studies reveal either conflicts among rival groups within the power elite or situations in which the moderate conservatives have decided for their own reasons to side with the liberal-labor coalition....

More generally, it now can be concluded that all four indicators of power introduced in [the first section] point to the corporate rich and their power elite as the dominant organizational structure in American society. First, the wealth and income distributions are skewed in their favor more than in any other industrialized democracy. They are clearly the most powerful group in American society in terms of "Who benefits?" Second, the appointees to government come overwhelmingly from the corporate community and its associated policy-formation network. Thus, the power elite is clearly the most powerful in terms of "Who sits?"

Third, the power elite wins far more often than it loses on policy issues resolved in the federal government. Thus, it is the most powerful in terms of "Who wins?" Finally, as shown in reputational studies in the 1950s and 1970s,... corporate leaders are the most powerful group in terms of "Who shines?" By the usual rules of evidence in a social science investigation using multiple indicators, the owners and managers of large income-producing properties are the dominant class in the United States.

Still, as noted at the end of the first [section], power structures are not immutable. Societies change and power structures evolve or crumble from time to unpredictable time, especially in the face of challenge. When it is added that the liberal-labor coalition persists in the face of its numerous defeats, and that free speech and free elections are not at risk, there remains the possibility that class domination could be replaced by a greater sharing of power in the future.

Excerpted from G. William Domhoff, *Who Rules America? Power and Politics in the Year 2000,* 3rd ed, pp. 241, 246–249, 286–289. Copyright © 1997 by The McGraw-Hill Companies/Mayfield Publishing Company. Reprinted by permission. Notes omitted.

Where the Public Good prevailed

Lessons from Success Stories in Health

BY STEPHEN L. ISAACS AND STEVEN A. SCHROEDER

Many Americans know, all too well, what is wrong with health care. Ask the single mother who waits half a day in a crowded clinic for a five-minute visit with a harried physician, or the unemployed worker who has been down-sized out of his job and his health insurance. Their experience tells a devastating tale about our system's shortcomings.

But there is another, equally important story that concerns the problems we don't see anymore—at least not in the numbers of the past young victims of polio, mumps, and measles; preschoolers with neurological problems caused by lead poisoning; people in the prime of life dying prematurely from tuberculosis and influenza; hordes of patients with rotting teeth. While we need to address persistent inequities, we also need to understand the basis of victories in public health—not just to keep up our hopes, but to learn how research, advocacy, public discussion, and policy fit together in successful campaigns for change.

GETTING THE LEAD OUT

Children in America today carry far less lead in their blood than they did just 20 years ago. The origins of that change go back nearly a century to 1904, when Australian pediatrician J. Lockhart Gibson found that lead paint caused lead poisoning of children in Queensland. A decade later, reports linking neurological damage in American children to lead began to appear. Mounting evidence of the metal's harmful effects led to sporadic local efforts to prevent poisoning caused by lead paint.

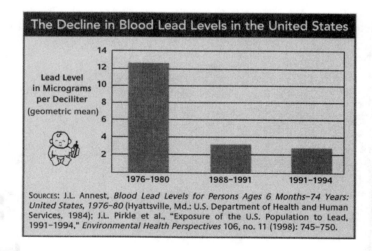

The Decline in Blood Lead Levels in the United States

SOURCES: J.L. Annest, *Blood Lead Levels for Persons Ages 6 Months–74 Years: United States, 1976–80* (Hyattsville, Md.: U.S. Department of Health and Human Services, 1984); J.L. Pirkle et al., "Exposure of the U.S. Population to Lead, 1991–1994," *Environmental Health Perspectives* 106, no. 11 (1998): 745–750.

The single greatest source of lead, however, came from automobile engines. Leaded gasoline was introduced in the American market in 1923, less than a year after Thomas Midgely and his co-workers at the General Motors Research Corporation in Dayton, Ohio, discovered that adding tetraethyl lead to gasoline as an antiknock agent gave cars more zip and allowed them to go farther on a tank of gas. The potential health effects of tetraethyl lead became known shortly after its discovery. In 1924 a fire in Standard Oil's lead processing plant in Bayway, New Jersey, led to five deaths and caused severe tremors, psychosis, hallucinations, and other symptoms of serious lead poisoning in 35 injured workers.

The next year, the U.S. surgeon general convened a conference on the safety of lead in gasoline. Although public-health advocates testified in opposition to the release of a poison—lead—into the air, the lead, automotive, and chemical industries dominated the conference. Representing Standard Oil of New Jersey, Frank Howard said, "We have an apparent gift of God—tetraethyl lead" and accused opponents of standing in the way of progress. The surgeon general concluded that there were no good grounds for prohibiting the use of leaded gasoline as a motor fuel.

So matters stood until the 1960s, when a new generation of scientists began challenging the assertion that lead was harmless. Dr. Herbert Needleman, who became an advocate for efforts to lower lead levels, revealed that extremely low amounts could damage a child's nervous system. At hearings on air pollution chaired by Senator Edmund Muskie in 1966, Clair Patterson, a highly respected California Institute of Technology geochemist, testified that the amount of lead in the air was 100 times what it had been in the 1930s. The Muskie hearings led, ultimately, to passage of the Clean Air Act of 1970, which required automakers to reduce hazardous emissions drastically.

In fulfilling the mandate of the Clean Air Act, the newly formed Environmental Protection Agency began issuing standards for the maximum level of lead in gasoline. These regulations were consistently challenged by the lead and petroleum-refining industries. For example, in 1973 the EPA issued its initial lead standard—one that was to be phased in over five years beginning in 1975. The Ethyl Corporation promptly went to court. The lawsuit, ultimately resolved in the EPA's favor by the U.S. Court of Appeals, delayed implementation of the standard for two years.

Next came a challenge from another direction. In the anti-regulation climate of the 1980s, Vice President George Bush's Task Force on Regulatory Relief pressured the EPA to roll back its lead standard. Activists from the Natural Resources Defense Council, the Environmental Defense Fund, Consumers Union, and other organizations fought back, and the press jumped on the story. "Incredibly, the Reagan administration appears willing to risk the health of hundreds of thousands of anonymous preschoolers, just so the oil companies can make a few bucks" wrote influential columnist Jack Anderson. At congressional hearings, witnesses presented new evidence demonstrating the effects of even very low levels of lead on the nervous systems of children.

At about this time, the U.S. Centers for Disease Control analyzed the results of the second National Health and Nutrition Examination Survey (NHANES). The survey showed that levels of lead in Americans' blood had dropped 37 percent between 1976 and 1980, largely because of reduced lead in gasoline. In the face of these data, plus all the negative publicity it was receiving, the EPA backed down. Instead of weakening the lead standard, it toughened it.

By the early 1990s, Congress was again involved. The 1990 amendments to the Clean Air Act banned the manufacture, sale, or introduction after 1992 of any engine requiring leaded gasoline. Congress also prohibited the use of all leaded gasoline for highway use after 1995. Since 1996, an outright ban on leaded gasoline has been in effect. These actions complemented laws that ban lead in paint, food containers, and solder joints. While lead-based paint continues to be a serious health hazard in inner-city buildings, legal restrictions have eliminated most new sources of lead poisoning. The results have been impressive. The third NHANES found that the average blood lead level in the United States had dropped by 78 percent between 1976 and 1994, largely because lead had virtually disappeared from gasoline—and because researchers and policy makers had overcome entrenched industry opposition in order to improve the public's health.

GETTING THE FLUORIDE IN

Sometimes the obstacle to better health isn't an economic interest but public hysteria. Fluoridation has proved to be one of the cheapest, most effective public-health measures of the past century. Yet during the Red Scare of the 1950s, it faced strenuous opposition from groups who feared that it was part of a communist plot to poison Americans.

The origins of fluoridation also go back a century, to 1901, when Frederick McKay opened a dental practice in Colorado Springs, Colorado, and noticed that many of his patients had chocolate-like stains on their teeth. Even stranger, few of these patients had cavities. Dr. McKay spent the next 40 years investigating why some people developed what came to be known as Colorado Brown Stain. By 1931 scientists had established a link between fluorine and mottled teeth, and attention turned to whether fluorine protected against tooth decay.

Enter the U.S. government. H. Trendley Dean, director of dental research at the National Institutes of Health, collected water samples and examined children's teeth throughout the country; and in 1943, he concluded that children exposed to minuscule amounts of fluorine in water developed few or no cavities and avoided brown teeth. The next step for the Public Health Service was to test this conclusion. In January 1945, Grand Rapids, Michigan, became the first community to add fluoride, a compound of the element fluorine, to its drinking water, while residents of neighboring Muskegon, who continued to drink unfluoridated water, served as the comparison group. Three other communities began testing fluoride in the water shortly thereafter. The results were dramatic. In the four demonstration communities, cavities fell by 40 percent to 60 percent. Even as results were coming in, activists were campaigning to have fluoride added to the water supply. Wisconsin was the hotbed of dental activism; 50 communities in the state fluoridated their water by 1950. That year, under intense pressure from pro-fluoridation advocates, the Public Health Service and the American Dental Association endorsed fluoridation.

Then came Joe McCarthy and the backlash. In 1949, Stevens Point, Wisconsin, became the first community to

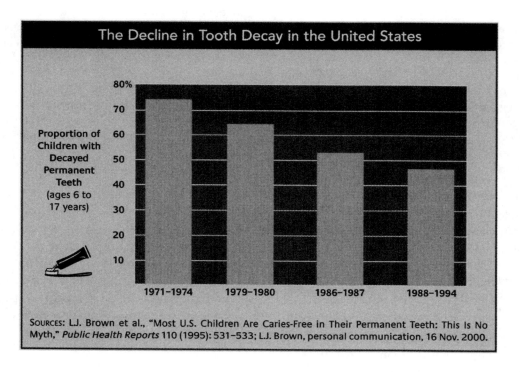

The Decline in Tooth Decay in the United States

Proportion of Children with Decayed Permanent Teeth (ages 6 to 17 years)

80%
70
60
50
40
30
20
10

1971–1974   1979–1980   1986–1987   1988–1994

SOURCES: L.J. Brown et al., "Most U.S. Children Are Caries-Free in Their Permanent Teeth: This Is No Myth," *Public Health Reports* 110 (1995): 531–533; L.J. Brown, personal communication, 16 Nov. 2000.

reject fluoridation of the community's water supply. Opposition in other communities followed. At the height of the Cold War, opponents linked fluoridation to a perceived communist threat and spread tales of dead fish washing up on the shores of fluoridated reservoirs.

Those in favor of fluoridation struck back. The endorsements of major dental and medical organizations, supported by ongoing research, provided persuasive support for the safety of water fluoridation. When opponents went to court, they invariably lost as judges upheld local decisions to fluoridate water as a legitimate exercise of governmental authority. Of the 50 largest cities in the United States, 43 presently have fluoridated water systems. Some 62 percent of Americans live in communities with fluoridated water supplies. Cavities in children have dropped significantly (although the oral health of poor children is worse than that of well-to-do children). In the years 1971–1974, 74 percent of children six to 17 years old had one or more cavities in their permanent teeth. By the period 1988–1994, the percentage had dropped to 46 percent.

THE AUTO-SAFETY CRUSADE

Public-health progress has often had to overcome the belief that nothing can be done about a problem until individuals improve their behavior. From the time of the nation's first automobile fatality, conventional wisdom had it that traffic accidents were the fault of bad drivers, not of the automobile itself. This viewpoint was articulated pithily by Harry Barr, Chevrolet's chief engineer: "We feel our cars are quite safe and reliable.... If drivers did everything they should, there wouldn't be any accidents."

By the 1950s, however, a respectable body of thought began to challenge the conventional wisdom. The medical profession—most particularly physicians who treated crash victims—weighed in early. By the mid-1950s, both the American Medical Association and the American College of Surgeons were recommending that automobile manufacturers design their cars for better passenger safety and equip them with safety belts. Triggered by concerns about the mounting toll of highway deaths, Senator Abraham Ribicoff of New York convened hearings that began in 1965 and continued into 1966. A 32-year-old lawyer named Ralph Nader was the star witness. Nader's book *Unsafe at Any Speed*, published in 1965, lambasted the automobile industry for its lack of concern about safety, singling out General Motors for selling the Chevrolet Corvair, an automobile produced with a defective and dangerous gas tank. The rest is the stuff of legend: GM hired private detectives to tail Nader and come up with dirt about his personal life, which they failed to do. When the attempted smear campaign came to light in March 1966, Nader became an instant national hero and used his new celebrity as a platform to promote auto safety.

The publicity galvanized public opinion and provided the impetus for Congress to pass the National Traffic and Motor Vehicle Safety Act and the Highway Safety Act in 1966. These laws established the National Highway Safety Bureau, the precursor of today's National Highway Traffic Safety Administration, and gave it the authority to set automobile safety standards.

As in the case of lead, new legislation precipitated legal and regulatory battles about how the law should be interpreted and carried out. Proposed federal regulations required that cars come equipped with padded instrument

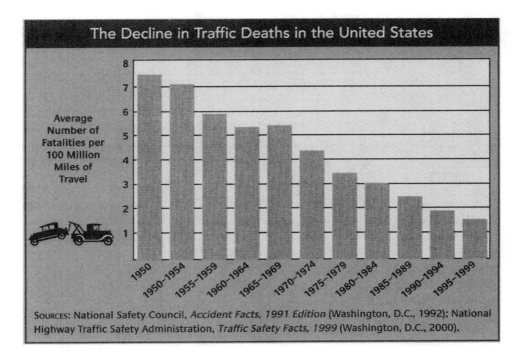

The Decline in Traffic Deaths in the United States

Average Number of Fatalities per 100 Million Miles of Travel

SOURCES: National Safety Council, *Accident Facts, 1991 Edition* (Washington, D.C., 1992); National Highway Traffic Safety Administration, *Traffic Safety Facts, 1999* (Washington, D.C., 2000).

panels and seat belts, among other safety features. These rules were challenged by automobile manufacturers as unrealistic and by consumer safety advocates as weak and ineffectual. The battle over seat belts and, later, air bags lasted nearly a decade. Now, of course, they are both standard equipment.

During the late 1970s and early 1980s, an extraordinary grass-roots movement took shape across the nation. Doris Aiken founded Remove Intoxicated Drivers (RID) in 1978 after a drunk driver ran over and killed a teenager in her hometown of Schenectady, New York. Candy Lightner organized Mothers Against Drunk Driving (MADD) in 1980 after her daughter was run over and killed by a man who had been drinking. Aiken and Lightner cultivated the media, who responded by regularly featuring the speeches and activities of the anti-drunk-driving activists, particularly those of the charismatic Lightner. Hundreds of newspapers and magazine articles reported on the victims of drunk driving and their families. Drunk driving was the subject of television specials and dramatizations. Activists formed chapters of RID, MADD, and SADD (Students Against Driving Drunk) in communities around the country and began telling their stories though the media, providing victims' services, lobbying government officials, and monitoring the courts.

The effect of this grass-roots movement on public policy was stunning. Between 1981 and 1985 alone, state legislatures passed 478 laws to deter drunk driving. In 1982 Congress passed the Alcohol Traffic Safety Act, which provided extra funds to states that enacted stricter drunk-driving laws. To be eligible, a state had to require that a blood alcohol level of .10 percent was conclusive evidence of drunkenness. (The permissible alcohol level was lowered to .08 in 2000.) Two years later, in 1984, Congress stepped

in again and passed a law requiring states to enact a minimum drinking age of 21 or lose some of their federal highway funds. All states eventually complied.

Since the 1970s, public attitudes have changed remarkably. Drunk driving is no longer tolerated in a way it once was; even the liquor and beer industry recommends that drinkers give their car keys to a "designated driver" (a term that would not have been understood two decades ago). Behavior has changed, too. Between 1982 and 1999, deaths from alcohol-related crashes dropped by 37 percent. Safer cars, improved highways, better emergency medical services, and a decline in drunk driving have sent the nation's traffic fatality rate tumbling. On average in 1950, 7.6 individuals were killed for every 100 million vehicle miles traveled. By 1999 that statistic had plummeted to 1.6 persons—a decrease of more than 75 percent.

AN UNFINISHED CRUSADE

Not very long ago, a movie star drawing slowly on a cigarette was considered the height of sophistication; medical-society meetings took place in rooms clouded with tobacco smoke; R.J. Reynolds and Philip Morris were considered so powerful that few dared to challenge them.

How things have changed! Planes are now smoke-free, as are many restaurants and offices; Joe Camel has been put out to pasture; and the $246-billion settlement between the tobacco companies and the states made front-page headlines. Americans have given up smoking in record numbers, and many of those who continue are trying to kick the habit. The percentage of adult male smokers in the United States dropped from a high of more than 50 percent in 1965 to about 26 percent in 1998. The percentage of adult fe-

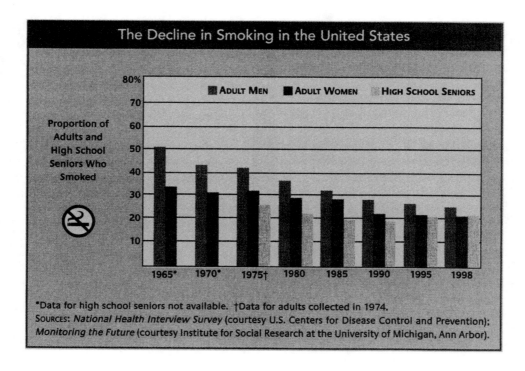

The Decline in Smoking in the United States

Proportion of Adults and High School Seniors Who Smoked

*Data for high school seniors not available. †Data for adults collected in 1974.
SOURCES: *National Health Interview Survey* (courtesy U.S. Centers for Disease Control and Prevention); *Monitoring the Future* (courtesy Institute for Social Research at the University of Michigan, Ann Arbor).

male smokers fell from its high of 34 percent in 1965 to 22 percent in 1998. Teenagers present more of a mixed picture. Although the percentage of American high school seniors who smoke daily decreased from a high of 29 percent in 1976 to a low of 17 percent in 1990, it then rose to 22 percent in 1998, before dropping slightly, to 21 percent, in 2000. Research, advocacy, media coverage, public education, politics, and government contributed to this unexpected transformation.

While the dangers of tobacco have long been recognized (in 1604 King James I branded the tobacco habit as "a loathsome custom to the Eye, Harmfull to the Braine, and dangerous to the lungs"), the scientific community ignored smoking until the last half of the twentieth century. As late as 1948, the *Journal of the American Medical Association (JAMA)* wrote, "More can be said on behalf of smoking as a form of escape from tension than against it."

Only two years later, in May 1950, *JAMA* published two articles linking smoking and lung cancer. In one of them, Ernst Wynder (who remained an anti-tobacco activist until his death in 1999) and Evarts Graham reported that of the more than 600 lung cancer patients they interviewed, 97 percent were moderately heavy to very heavy smokers. From there, the evidence mushroomed. By the late 1980s, some 60,000 studies had made it abundantly clear that tobacco causes cancers, stroke, and heart disease.

From published research to public awareness, however, there is often a long journey. In the case of smoking, the federal government played a critical role in narrowing the distance. In 1964 Surgeon General Luther Terry's widely publicized report woke up the nation to the dangers of tobacco. And in 1986, C. Everett Koop, surgeon general during the Reagan administration, reported that secondhand smoke caused cancers and other life-threatening illnesses—a finding that legitimized local, state, and federal efforts to limit smoking in public places.

Public-health advocates challenged the tobacco industry and kept the issues alive. Among the leaders were John Banzhaf, a Georgetown University law professor, whose organization ASH (Action on Smoking and Health) brought lawsuits and petitioned regulatory agencies, and Stanton Glantz, a University of California professor, whose advocacy groups Californians for Nonsmokers' Rights and, later, Americans for Nonsmokers' Rights, fought for the enactment of local and state anti-tobacco measures. Long-established organizations also joined the fray. The American Cancer Society, the American Lung Association, and the American Heart Association were relatively early participants. In 1982 these three organizations formed the Coalition on Smoking and Health, directed by Matt Myers, another longtime antismoking activist. The American Medical Association was the last to come to the table. Long ambivalent about smoking, the AMA ultimately proved to be an influential ally through its *Journal* articles and its work to organize antismoking coalitions.

Although some media organizations were slow to publicize the dangers of smoking (tobacco ads are a significant source of advertising revenues), others played an important early role. In December of 1952, *Reader's Digest* ran an article entitled "Cancer by the Carton." In it the most widely read magazine of its day reported, in plain English, the link between smoking and lung cancer and accused the tobacco industry of a cover-up. From then on, despite the best efforts of the tobacco industry, the danger of tobacco has become increasingly well known.

Laws and regulations have long been the backbone of antismoking efforts. A week after the release of the surgeon general's report in 1964, the Federal Trade Commission proposed that cigarette packages and advertising carry a strong warning label. In response the tobacco industry cried foul and tried to sabotage the legislation, a scenario that was to be replayed many times in the succeeding years. Ultimately, in 1965, over the fierce opposition of the tobacco industry, Congress passed a law requiring that cigarette packs and ads carry a watered-down warning. This was the first of many federal laws and regulations aimed at reducing smoking. Equally if not more important were local ordinances and state laws banning smoking in public places and making the sale of cigarettes to minors illegal. As Victor Crawford, a former Tobacco Institute lobbyist who became an anti-tobacco advocate after developing lung cancer, recalled, "We [the tobacco lobby] could never win at the local level. The reason is that all the health advocates are local activists who run the little political organizations. On the local level, I couldn't compete with them."

While Americans' attitudes toward smoking have changed, the tobacco industry remains a formidable force. Cigarettes and spit tobacco are still attractive to young people, and the commitment of the Bush administration to tobacco-control measures is, at best, uncertain. While the victories won so far in the national effort against tobacco are a cause for cheering, it is too early to celebrate them as permanent.

INGREDIENTS OF SUCCESS

Cavities, lead poisoning, traffic fatalities, smoking—although serious health concerns remain, each of these examples involves a success story. These experiences are not triumphs of medical technology; rather—and this may explain why they are unappreciated—they are the result of social and behavioral change. Four elements shared by these quiet victories offer lessons for shaping public policy.

1. Highly credible scientific evidence can persuade policy makers and withstand attack from those whose interests are threatened. Tobacco is the clearest example. The evidence linking smoking with cancer and other deadly illnesses was so strong and so consistent that—over the legal and scientific objections of the tobacco companies—it provided a scientific basis for legislation, regulations, and judicial decisions; ultimately, it was persuasive enough to move public opinion. Similarly, well-structured comparative trials provided convincing evidence that moderate amounts of fluoride added to the water supply reduced tooth decay. The federal government's National Health and Nutrition Examination Surveys gave the EPA the foundation on which to base regulations—strongly challenged by the gasoline and lead lobbies—that eventually eliminated lead from the nation's gasoline supply.

2. Public-health campaigns need advocates who are passionately committed to their cause, who have the inner resources to withstand the tremendous pressure applied by the industries whose practices they are criticizing, and who continue to fight even at the risk of their professional reputations. Ralph Nader, Candy Lightnet, Herbert Needleman, and other crusaders have had a tremendous effect on social policy. But advocacy from outside the system is rarely enough. When government agencies and their leaders speak out, new ideas about public health become more acceptable to the mainstream media and the populace. Similarly, campaigns for change gain legitimacy from the backing of authoritative groups outside government, notably professional societies—such as the American Medical Association on seat belts, the American Dental Association on fluoridated water, and the American Cancer Society on tobacco.

3. Public awareness and discussion depend on a partnership with the media. Advocates need the media to reach the public, and the media, looking for good stories, also need the advocates. "Behind virtually every public-health-and-safety measure enacted in this half-century has been a media advocacy campaign to dramatize both the risks and the public-policy solution" says the Advocacy Institute's Michael Pertschuk. As a result of the media, few now doubt that smoking is bad for health, that drinking and driving is a lethal combination, that seat belts save lives, and that fluoridated water prevents cavities.

> For all our country's achievements, the United States still ranks 24th in measures of national health, according to the World Health Organization

---

4. Law and regulation, often at the federal level, have been critical elements in focusing Americans' attention on health concerns, providing policy direction, and setting standards that have led to improvement in the public's health. Despite all the criticism they have received, federal laws and regulations have vastly improved people's health. They have been—and continue to be—the underpinning that protects the health of the American public.

Because of the Clean Air Act, the Lead-Based Paint Act, and federal regulations that reduced or eliminated other sources of lead contamination, lead poisoning has been significantly reduced as a health concern. Because of highway safety laws and federal regulations mandating the use of seat belts and other safety features, drivers and their passengers are now much safer. Because of congressionally mandated warning labels on cigarette packs, bans on cigarette advertising, and similar legislation, plus lawsuits by state attorneys general and local ordinances banning smoking in public places, the nation is moving toward kicking the nicotine habit. Even at a time when many people are disillusioned with government, its role in protecting the health of the public cannot be underestimated.

As impressive as these victories appear, the United States still has a long way to go even to catch up with the rest of the developed world. For all our achievements, we still rank 24th in measures of national health, according to the World Health Organization. Imagine what we could do if we had social movements against homicide, HIV infection, unhealthy foods, and physical inactivity that could match what public-health initiatives have achieved in such areas as lead and tobacco. Without the energy of such social movements, the United States will be doomed to suffer from inferior health, no matter how much we invest in basic biomedical research or cutting-edge medical technologies. Yet if we put that research to positive use in the public arena, combine it with committed advocacy, and follow up with intelligent policy-making, we can do much to improve America's health—not with miracles but with just hard work.

For more on success stories in public health, see the links to this article at www.prospect.prg.

STEPHEN L. ISAACS is the president of Health Policy Associates in San Francisco. STEVEN A. SCHROEDER is the president of the Robert Wood Johnson Foundation.

Off the Books

The benefits of free enterprise that economic statistics miss

W. Michael Cox and Richard Alm

AMERICA'S CONSUMER CULTURE is all around us. It's along our highways, studded with shopping malls, fast food joints, and flashy neon signs. It's in our homes, filled with gadgets, furnishings, toys, and closets of clothes. It permeates the media, where ads tell us happiness and sex appeal are as close as the nearest store. It's even within us, at least to the extent that we tie status and identity to the cars we drive, the clothes we wear, and the food we eat.

That's our reputation: a consumer-driven, somewhat crass, shop-'til-you-drop society. As the world's wealthiest nation, we *should* consume a lot, but the portrait of Americans as consumption crazed misses as much as it captures. We're not working just to acquire more goods and services. Most of us strive for something broader: a balanced life.

Consumption is part of that, of course. We buy myriad things: Chevrolet cars, Sony TV sets, Levi's jeans, Nike sneakers, McDonald's hamburgers, Dell computers. But our wish list doesn't stop there. We also want leisure time, a respite to enjoy life. We want pleasant working conditions and good jobs, so earning a living isn't too arduous. We want safety and Security, so we don't live in fear. We want variety, the spice of life. We want convenience, which makes everyday life a little easier. We want a cleaner environment, which enhances health and recreation.

A full description of a balanced life would entail much more, with considerations for family and friends, perhaps even spirituality. Here we want to focus on the components of happiness that clearly depend on the market but are not reflected in the gross domestic product (GDP). Our free enterprise system provides much more than the goods and services we consume; it furnishes ingredients of a balanced life that are often overlooked in discussions of economic performance.

Capitalism creates wealth. During the last two centuries, the United States became the world's richest nation as it embraced an economic system that promotes growth, efficiency, and innovation. Real GDP per capita tripled from 1900 to 1950; then it tripled again from 1950 to 2000, reaching $35,970.

The wealth didn't benefit just a few. It spread throughout society. For many people, owning a home defines the American Dream, and 68 percent of families now do—the highest percentage on record. Three-quarters of Americans drive their own cars. The vast majority of households possess color televisions (98 percent), videocassette recorders (94 percent), microwave ovens (90 percent), frost-free refrigerators (87 percent), washing machines (83 percent), and clothes dryers (75 percent). In the past decade or so, computers and cell phones have become commonplace.

As people become wealthier, they continue to consume more, but they also look to take care of other needs and wants. They typically choose to forgo at least some additional goods and services, taking a portion of their new wealth in other forms.

Compared to previous generations, today's Americans are starting work later in life, spending less time on chores at home, and living longer after retirement. All told, 70 percent of a typical American's waking life-time hours are available for leisure, up from 55 percent in 1950.

Consider a nation that rapidly increases its productive capacity with each passing generation. Workers could toil the same number of hours, taking all of the gains as consumption. They may choose to do so for a while, but eventually they will give up some potential material gains for better working conditions or additional leisure. Hours of work shrink. Workplaces become more comfortable. In the same way, we give up consumption in favor of safety, security, variety, convenience, and a cleaner environment.

Less Work, More Play

In the early years of the Industrial Revolution, most Americans were poor, and they wanted, above all, more goods and services. These factory workers sharply improved their lives as consumers, even though for most of them it meant long hours of toil in surroundings we'd consider abominable today. As America grew richer, what workers wanted began to change, and leisure became a higher priority.

Few of us want to dedicate every waking hour to earning money. Free time allows us to relax and enjoy ourselves, spend time with family and friends. Higher pay means that each hour of work yields more consumption—in essence, the price for an hour of leisure is going up—but we're still choosing to work less than ever before. According to economists' estimates and Department of Labor figures, the average workweek shrank from 59 hours in 1890 to 40 hours in 1950. Although today we hear stories about harried, overworked Americans who never seem to have enough time, the proportion of time spent on the job has continued to fall. Average weekly hours for production workers dropped from 39 in 1960 to 34 in 2001.

Since 1950 time off for holidays has doubled, to an average of 12 days a year. We've added an average of four vacation days a year. Compared to previous generations, today's Americans are starting work later in life, spending less time on chores at home, and living longer after retirement. All told, 70 percent of a typical American's waking lifetime hours are available for leisure, up from 55 percent in 1950.

Even at work, Americans aren't always doing the boss's bidding. According to University of Michigan time diary studies, the average worker spends more than an hour a day engaged in something other than assigned work while on the job. Employees run errands, socialize with colleagues, make personal telephone calls, send e-mail, and surf the Internet. More than a third of American workers, a total of 42 million, access the Internet during working hours. The peak hours for submitting bids on eBay, the popular online auction site, come between noon and 6 p.m., when most Americans are supposedly hard at work.

With added leisure, the United States has turned arts, entertainment, and recreation into a huge industry. Since 1970, attendance per 100,000 people has risen for symphonies, operas, and theaters as well as for national parks and big-league sporting events. The annual *Communications Industry Forecast*, compiled by New York-based Veronis, Suhler & Associates, indicates that we watch an average of 58 hours of movies at home each year. Yet Americans go out to an average of 5.4 movies a year, up from 4.5 three decades ago.

Adjusted for inflation, per capita spending on recreation nearly quadrupled in the last three decades. Leisure and recreation are even important enough to have become an academic subject: 350 colleges and universities offer degree programs in it.

The number of amusement parks has increased from 362 in 1970 to 1,164 today. The number of health and fitness facilities has more than doubled, to 11,241. Adjusted for inflation, per capita spending on recreation nearly quadrupled in the last three decades. Leisure and recreation are even important enough to

have become an academic subject: 350 colleges and universities offer degree programs in it.

The explosion of leisure spending and activities confirms the addition of more free time to our lives. If we hadn't reduced our hours of work, we couldn't spend as much time and money as we do on entertainment and recreation. Americans may find themselves pressed for time, but it's not because we're working harder than we used to. We're busy having fun.

Better Work Too

As the Industrial Revolution arrived in the 19th century, workers migrated from family farms to factories, from the Old World to the New World. They saw their paychecks rise but became, like Charlie Chaplin's character in *Modern Times*, mere cogs in a vast engine of mass production. Work was often brutal. Early factories were noisy, smelly, and dirty; they were cold in the winter and hot in the summer. The labor itself was repetitive, physically exhausting, and often dangerous. It was a time of mind-numbing repetition, standing on assembly lines, nose to the conveyor belt. To eke out a meager living, employees toiled an average of 10 hours a day, Monday through Friday, plus another half-day on the weekend. Breaks were few and far between. Work rules were draconian: no talking, no eating or drinking, not a minute late punching the time clock.

We've come a long way since then. For the most part, modern work takes place in a clean, well-lit, and air conditioned environment. A growing number of modern workplaces offer on-the-job amenities previous generations didn't even contemplate, such as on-site day care for children, exercise facilities, and concierge services. More and more employees are getting paternity leave, stock options, personal days off, and paid sabbaticals.

Jeans, sport shirts, and slacks are in. Ties and pantyhose are out. A July 2000 survey by the catalog retailer Land's End found that dress had become more casual in the previous five years at more than 80 percent of *Fortune* 500 firms.

More Americans than ever are free to choose the time and place for work, as long as the job gets done. In 1997, 28 percent of American workers were on flexible schedules, double the percentage in 1985. With laptop computers, cell phones, fax machines, electronic mail, and the Internet, fewer employees are tethered to the office. Telecommuting began with a handful of workers three decades ago. By 2001, 29 million Americans worked at least part of the time away from their companies' places of business.

Work isn't just more pleasant. It's also safer. Occupational injuries and illnesses, as tallied by the National Safety Council, are at an all-time low of 63 per 1,000 workers. The number of Americans killed on the job has fallen to a record low of 38 per million workers, down from 87 in 1990 and 214 in 1960.

Safer workplaces come in part from fewer accidents in such dangerous occupations as construction and manufacturing. At the same time, our economic base is shifting toward services, where jobs are less risky. The nature of the work we do is changing too. For most Americans in past generations, long days on the job involved tasks that were repetitive, physically exhausting, and often dangerous. Modern work is more likely to require analytical and interpersonal skills. Fewer employees make their livings with their backs and hands.

Jobs Rated Almanac 2001 provides a handy database of 300 occupations, ranked from best to worst. To focus on working conditions rather than pay, wages are taken out of the equation. Once that's done, it's clear our employment base is shifting in a positive direction. Since 1970 the 30 best jobs—including computer scientist, legal assistant, and engineer—have risen from 9 percent to 13 percent of total employment. At the same time, the 30 worst occupations—from logger to textile mill worker—have declined from 13 percent to 9 percent of all jobs. The trend toward better jobs is likely to continue. The Bureau of Labor Statistics estimates that the 10 best jobs will grow by 27 percent through 2008, while the 30 worst jobs will expand by just 7 percent.

Making workplaces more pleasant takes money. The added expense figures, along with wages, into the overall bill for labor. Companies pay it to attract new workers and retain those already on board. Employers shouldn't care whether the money goes for wages, time off, or working conditions. By their decisions on where to work, employees reveal their preferences.

Safer Lives

Although concerns about security have come to the fore since September 11, we shouldn't forget how far the United States has already come in making life safer. The toll of death and disease has been steadily reduced. Annual deaths per 1 million people are at an all-time low. The age-adjusted death rate has fallen by two-thirds since 1900. Fatalities from nearly all major diseases, tracked by the U.S. Centers for Disease Control and Prevention, have declined sharply from their peak rates. The rate of fatalities per 100,000 due to natural causes has fallen from 767 in 1950 to 422 in 1998, the most recent year for which data are available. The incidence of accidental deaths, both at home and on the job, is declining. So are fatalities associated with floods, tornadoes, and hurricanes.

Gains in transportation safety have been dramatic. In the five-year period ending in 2000, according to the Federal Highway Administration, annual deaths on American roads averaged 16 per billion miles driven, compared with 53 in the five years ending in 1970 and 83 for the post-World War II years. The Air Transportation Association reports that deaths per billion passenger miles flown fell from 16.7 a year in 1946–50 to 1.3 in 1966–70 to 0.14 in 1996–2000.

As a wealthy nation, we can afford to spend time and money to reduce life's risks. We can buy alarms for our homes and cars. We can buy insurance on our property and our lives. We can reduce the financial risks of illness and old age by taking part of our pay in health benefits and retirement savings.

We can also shift resources to the military to create an even more fearsome fighting force. During World War 11, defense spending per capita averaged $3,475 a year in today's dollars,

or 29 percent of total output. Today, each American's share of the defense budget comes to $1,079, just 3 percent of GDP.

Making America a safer place owes much to advances in engineering and technology. Divided highways, better roads, antilock brakes, radial tires, and air bags are reducing the highway death toll. More-sophisticated weather forecasting gear provides warnings of severe weather, so we can take refuge in time.

New medicines and treatments have reduced the incidence of fatal diseases. More are probably on the way. The stock market values the nation's 10 largest pharmaceutical companies at more than $1 trillion, an indication that we expect their sales to grow from future advances in health.

Greater safety and security didn't come about by accident. It's what we, as a people, wanted. We put a high value on our lives and physical well-being, and we're willing to pay the costs of protecting ourselves against the sometimes unpleasant facts of life.

Life is inherently risky, and protecting ourselves must be weighed against the considerations of cost and convenience. We'll never achieve a perfect safety record. In an uncertain world, we possess the wealth to afford more safety and security and the know-how to provide it, if that's what we decide we want.

A Safer, Healthier Life

	1970	The Latest *
Age-adjusted death rate per 100,000 people	1,222.6	872.4
Deaths per 100,000 people from 15 leading diseases	**731.6**	**605.3**
Accidental deaths in the home per 1 million people	132.0	107.0
Work-related deaths per 1 million workers	**178.0**	**38.0**
Deaths per billion miles driven	53.3	15.9
Deaths per billion miles flown	**1.3**	**0.14**
Homicide deaths per 1 million people	79.0	57.0
Deaths per 100 tornadoes per 100,000 people	**6.8**	**1.8**
Deaths per hurricane per 100,000 people	10.1	3.3
Life expectancy at birth	**70.8**	**77.1**
Median age of the population	28.1	35.3
Injuries per 100 full- time workers in manufacturing	**15.2**	**7.8**
Incidence per 100,000 people of 14 reportable diseases	659.0	184.0

* Years range from 1999 to 2000 depending on the original source.
Source: Federal Reserve Bank of Dallas

Convenience and Variety

By introducing industrial efficiency to his factories, Henry Ford brought the automobile within the reach of an emerging middle class. The miracle of mass production delivered the goods but didn't adapt easily, so all Model T's looked alike. Ford's attitude can be summed up in what he reputedly said about the car's paint: "The consumer can have any color he wants, as long as it's black." Ford's company still makes black cars for drivers who want them, but it now offers a rainbow of colors: red, green, aquamarine, white, silver, purple.

The U.S. marketplace teems with variety. Just since the early 1970s, there's been an explosion of choice: The number of car models is up from 140 to 239, soft drinks from 50 to more than 450, toothpaste brands from four to 35, over-the-counter pain relievers from two to 41.

The market offers 7,563 prescription drugs, 3,000 beers, 340 kinds of breakfast cereal, 50 brands of bottled water. Plain milk sits on the supermarket shelf beside skim milk, 0.5-percent-fat milk, 1-percent-fat milk, 2-percent-fat milk, lactose-reduced milk, hormone-free milk, chocolate milk, buttermilk, and milk with a shelf life of six months. Not long ago, the typical TV viewer had access to little more than NBC, CBS, ABC, and PBS. Today, more than 400 channels target virtually every consumer interest—science, history, women's issues, Congress, travel, animals, foreign news, and more.

Like variety, convenience has emerged as a hallmark of our times. Companies compete for business by putting their products and services within easy reach of their customers.

In 1970 the nation's lone automated teller machine was at the main office of the Chemical Bank in New York. Now ATMs are ubiquitous—not just at banks but at supermarkets, service stations, workplaces, sports facilities, and airports. All told, 273,000 machines offer access to cash 24 hours a day.

Remote controls are proliferating, the newest models incorporating voice-activated technology. Computers and digital devices go with us everywhere. A cell phone is no longer a pricey luxury: The average bill fell from $150 a month in 1988 to $45 in 2001 in constant dollars. No wonder 135 million Americans now own mobile telephones. The number will continue to rise as prices continue to decline and more of us seek the peace of mind and convenience that come with communications in the pocket or purse.

Convenience stores are in nearly every neighborhood. Just one firm, industry leader 7-Eleven, has increased its locations from 3,734, in 1970 to 21,142 today. The Internet may be the ultimate convenience store, bringing shopping into the home. We're buying music, clothing, software, shoes, toys, flowers, and other products with a click of the mouse. Last year, a third of all computers and a fifth of all peripherals were sold online. Thirty-three million buyers ordered books on the Internet, accounting for $1 of every $8 spent in that category.

Convenience and variety aren't trivial extravagances. They're a wealthy, sophisticated society's way of improving consumers' lot. The more choices, the easier access to goods and services, the better. A wide selection of goods and services increases the chance that each of us will find, somewhere among all the shelves, showrooms, and Web sites, products that meet our requirements. Convenience allows us to economize on the valuable commodity of time, getting what we want more quickly and easily.

A Cleaner Environment

The environment presents a textbook case for tradeoffs between consumption and other aspects of life. Traditionally, economists teach that markets undervalue clean air, fresh water, pristine vistas, and endangered species because they aren't owned, like factories, houses, or other private property. Without clear title and market prices, there's little economic incentive to reduce pollution or husband resources. The nation's natural assets end up underpriced and overexploited.

GDP may be accurate as a tally of how much our farms, factories, and offices produce, but it's increasingly inadequate as a measure of how well the economy provides us with what we want. Our ability to choose a balanced life is one of the market's most important success stories.

Our desire for a balanced life mitigates the classic dilemma of market failure and the environment. A wealthier nation possesses the time, money, and inclination to shift the balance from exploiting the environment to preserving it. We want clean air and water for reasons of health, recreation, and aesthetics. We've developed a sense of moral obligation toward lesser species. We find unspoiled nature pleasant—although we tend to want clean linens and good food along with it.

Our desires have had a dramatic effect in recent decades. Levels of such major air pollutants as particulate matter, sulfur oxides, volatile organic compounds, carbon monoxide, and lead were at their peaks in 1970 or earlier. Levels of nitrogen oxides peaked in 1980. Water quality has improved since the 1960s, when authorities banned fishing in Lake Erie. Through government and private foundations, we're spending billions of dollars every year to preserve natural areas from development and save threatened species from extinction.

Capitalism's penchant for innovation is helping us act on our concern for the environment. We've developed less polluting gases for air conditioning systems, so we can stay cool at a lower cost to air quality. Fish farms are creating another compromise, providing salmon for our dinner tables while reducing fishing for wild species.

Taking better care of the environment is a natural extension of economic progress. At one time, the air in Pittsburgh was very dirty. It was the price we were willing to pay for all those consumer goods the industrial age offered. It wasn't that we liked pollution; it was just that the price of cleaner air was too high. Today, having grown richer, we can afford the pollution controls that have made Pittsburgh's air sweeter than an ocean breeze. Exploitation of the environment is worst in poor countries, where the economic imperative lies in producing the food, goods, and services needed for daily life. Wealthier countries possess the means and motive for a balanced life, and they do a better job of taking care of their surroundings.

Beyond Statistics

The statistics that measure our economy are reasonably good at counting the value of the cars, clothing, food, sports gear, jewelry, and other goods and services we buy. When we choose an additional hour off over additional income, though, GDP shrinks with the loss of the hour's income and output. We don't count leisure as an economic benefit because we haven't assigned a dollar value to it, even though we opt for time off because it improves our lives.

When it comes to many aspects of a balanced life, our economic barometers come up short. Safety and security are all about preventing bad things from happening. Increased spending on highway safety registers in GDP, but we don't track how much better off we are because of the accidents, injuries, and deaths we avoid. If investing in prevention works, it can actually reduce total output, at least the way we measure it, because less money is spent treating the sick and injured, repairing damage, and replacing lost property.

Variety makes products more valuable by giving us the designs, colors, and features that fit our preferences, but the statistics count everything as plain vanilla. How conveniently our wants and needs are fulfilled doesn't matter to GDP. A cleaner environment makes for a better country, but it may come at the cost of economic growth.

Inflation-adjusted GDP figures indicate economic growth at an annual average of 3 percent during the last two decades. GDP may be entirely accurate as a tally of how much our farms, factories, and offices produce, but it's increasingly inadequate as a measure of how well the economy provides us with what we want. Our ability to choose a balanced life is one of the market's most important success stories.

Some may argue that it isn't the market that makes a balanced life possible. They might concede that our economy produces abundant goods and services, but they credit government agencies, with their regulations, and unions and pressure groups, with their advocacy, for everything else. History tells us government and advocates play their roles, but they aren't the ultimate source of progress. They don't foot the bill for the choices we make to gain a balanced life. Whatever we want must be paid for, and money ultimately comes from the economy.

Companies improve working conditions because they can afford to, not simply because workers, unions, or government agencies demand it. The dismal work environments in now-defunct socialist nations—all supposedly designed to benefit the worker and eradicate the capitalist—provide a powerful testament to the fact that good intentions are hollow without the ability to pay.

The main role of collective action has been to act as a voice for what we want. Environmental groups formed as the result of our desire for cleaner air and water. When we take our preferences for leisure and better working conditions to unions or elected officials, they help create consensus among employees and lower the cost of communicating these desires to employers.

In the long run, we cannot afford any component of a balanced life—be it consumption, leisure, easier workdays, safety and security, variety and convenience, or environmental cleanup—that we don't earn by becoming more productive. When counting our blessings, we should first thank the economic system. Not federal agencies, not advocacy groups, not unions.

Our quest for a balanced life will never end. The U.S. economy, now recovering from its first recession in a decade, will make our society wealthier in the years ahead. We'll take some of our gains in goods and services, but we will also continue to satisfy our desires for the less tangible aspects of life.

W. Michael Cox (wm.cox@dal.frb.org), senior vice president and chief economist at the Federal Reserve Bank of Dallas, and Richard Alm (rgalm@aol.com), a business writer for The Dallas Morning News, are the authors of Myths of Rich and Poor: Why We're Better Off Than We Think (Basic Books).

Reprinted with permission from the August 2002 issue of *Reason* Magazine, pp. 47–53. © 2002 by the Reason Foundation, 3415 S. Sepulveda Blvd., Suite 400, Los Angeles, CA 90034.

Surveying the Global Marketplace

"Half of Xerox's employees work on foreign soil and less than half of Sony's employees are Japanese. More than 50% of IBM's revenues originate overseas; the same is true for Citigroup, ExxonMobil, DuPont, Procter & Gamble, and many other corporate giants."

By Murray Weidenbaum

A FEW YEARS AGO, an overnight frost occurred in Brazil. What followed may remind us of the lyrics to the old song: "The ankle bone is connected to the leg bone. The leg bone is connected to the knee bone...." The global economy truly is interconnected. An official in Brasilia that morning announced an expected decline in coffee production. The news instantly reached the Chicago Options Exchange. The price of coffee futures began to rise. Traders in other agricultural products responded by bidding up their futures prices. Forecasts of commodity prices jumped around the world, triggering concern over rising inflation—and tightening by central banks. Traders started selling off bonds, driving yields and interest rates higher. Finally, stock prices fell. Just another day in the global economy.

The global marketplace has been around since ancient times. The Greeks and the Phoenicians traded all over their known world and invested abroad heavily. They called the results colonies. What is different today is more advanced technology and more open economies. It took explorer Marco Polo years to travel to China and back. Today, one can fly the round trip in a couple of days. Information can flow in a fraction of a second. In 1980, 3,000,000,000 minutes of international phone calls were made into and out of the U.S. Currently, the annual total is over 30,000,000,000.

Globalization—the increased movement of goods, services, people, information, and ideas across national borders and around the world—no longer is just a buzzword; it has arrived. There is substantial evidence for an increasingly global marketplace. World trade is expanding much faster than world production and crossborder investments are growing at a more rapid rate than trade. People in one country are more likely to be affected by economic actions in other nations in many capacities: as customers, entrepreneurs and investors, managers and workers, taxpayers, and citizens.

An example of the global economy is illustrated in a cartoon of an auto show. The customer asks, "Is this car made in the United States?" The dealer responds, "Which part?" The Pontiac with a General Motors nameplate was sold through the Pontiac dealer network. However, the car was assembled in Korea using components made mainly in Asia. In contrast, Honda models, produced in Marysville, Ohio, have many more U.S.-made parts—but they have a Japanese brand nameplate and are sold through the Honda dealer network. Which is the American car? Another example of globalization is furnished by the shipping label used by a U.S. firm: "Made in one or more of the following countries: Korea, Hong Kong, Malaysia, Singapore, Taiwan, Mauritius, Thailand, Indonesia, Mexico, Philippines." The label continues, "Exact country of origin is unknown."

Yet another way of looking at the international marketplace is to examine the flow of imports and exports, not just in and out of the U.S., but in and out of the European Union and Japan. Almost half of what we call foreign trade actually involves transactions between different parts of the same company—between a domestic firm and its overseas subsidiaries or between a foreign firm and its domestic subsidiaries. In a geopolitical sense, this is foreign commerce. To the company, however, these international flows of goods and services are internal transfers.

Globalization, though, does not mean a unified global economy. Not every product is "tradable" internationally. Cement and haircuts are produced and consumed locally. Even most international trade stays in the region where it originates. Three vast regions are now economically dominant and are likely to remain so far into the 21st century: North America, Europe, and East Asia. In North America, Canada is the U.S.'s number-one customer and Mexico is number two. The integration of other national economies is a continuing process. In the case of the European Union (EU), economic integration seems quite secure. Nevertheless, the EU's most important accomplishment is not economic. Rather, for the first time since the days of the Frankish king Charlemagne, war between France and Germany is unthinkable. The EU is reducing restrictions on business, trade, and labor. People as well as goods, services, and investments increasingly are able to move freely from one EU nation to another. This trend makes European businesses more efficient as they achieve greater economies of scale.

For countries outside the EU, however, serious disadvantages result. The EU has reduced the internal trade barriers, but it has common external trade restrictions against nonmembers. In 1960, before the European Common Market gained momentum, more than 60% of the foreign trade of the 15 member nations was outside the EU. At present, about 70-80% stays in the EU. This is not particularly good news for American companies that are trying to export to Europe.

Nevertheless, the EU is not a static concept. Originally, it comprised six countries: Germany, France, Italy, Belgium, the Netherlands, and Luxembourg. Gradually, it expanded to 15 nations to include the United Kingdom, Ireland, Denmark, Greece, Spain, Portugal, Austria, Sweden, and Finland. Who is missing? Norway, Switzerland, and Eastern Europe. Ten Eastern European countries are scheduled to join May 1, 2004—subject to national vote: Hungary, the Czech Republic, Slovakia, Poland, Slovenia, Latvia, Lithuania, Estonia, Malta, and Cyprus. Poland, Slovenia, and Slovakia already have voted yes. Add up all those gross domestic products and Europe becomes the world's largest marketplace. Yet, there are limits to economic unification. Each member nation retains its own tax system, language, and culture. Different national growth rates place stress on the European Monetary System and not all EU countries have adopted the euro as their currency.

East Asian growth has come in three waves. First was Japan. Although its dominance over Asia is weakening, it still is a world powerhouse. The second wave—albeit slowed by the 1997-98 financial crisis—included Taiwan, South Korea, Hong Kong, Singapore, Thailand, and Malaysia. The new tier of rapidly developing nations—composed of low-cost industrial suppliers—is dominated by China. However, most of East Asia's "foreign" trade is with other Asian countries, as is most of the foreign investment in the region.

Impact on business

Globalization is producing fundamental changes in business. The consequences for many firms are profound. Half of Xerox's employees work on foreign soil and less than half of Sony's employees are Japanese. More than 50% of IBM's revenues originate overseas; the same is true for Citigroup, Exxon-Mobil, DuPont, Procter & Gamble, and many other corporate giants. Joint ventures no longer are merely a domestic decision. Coming obtains one-half of its profits from foreign joint ventures with Samsung in Korea, Asahi Glass in Japan, and Ciba-Geigy in Switzerland. Strategic alliances increasingly have shifted overseas. They now involve previously competitive companies on different continents.

The automotive and electronics industries provide numerous examples. Boeing and British Aerospace have teamed up for military projects. Volkswagen produces cars with Ford for the Brazilian market, while General Motors and Toyota operate a major joint venture in the U.S. In today's global marketplace, the same companies often are suppliers, customers, and competitors for and to each other. Whatever approach is used, becoming an internationally oriented company usually pays off. Sales by American firms with no foreign activities grow at half the rate of those with international operations. Companies with international business grow faster in every industry and their profits are higher.

While private enterprise increasingly is global, government policy often is extremely parochial. Voters care about their jobs and locality, and politicians readily exploit those concerns. Consider Pres. Bush's steel protection plan. It benefits steel producing industries in a few states—but it hurts steel-using industries far more. However, the effects are spread out over all 50 states. Remember, consumers, who think more about price and quality than country of origin, vote every day—in dollars, yen, euros, and pounds. They buy products and services made anywhere in the world. I recently saw a bumper sticker that proclaimed, "Save whales, boycott Japanese products." It was on a Toyota.

The extremists on both sides of the debate should be ignored. Many proglobalization proponents are true believers, urging government to get out of the way entirely, thus allowing the marketplace to work its magic. At the same time, antiglobalization critics also are dedicated to their beliefs. They want to eliminate the entire capitalistic system. Let us try to develop a high middle ground. The serious views on globalization can be divided into a bright side and a dark side. As to the former, international cooperation increases economic growth and living standards—but not uniformly. It offers consumers greater variety of products and lower prices while raising the number of jobs and wage levels. Improvements in overall working conditions, however, do not occur for every worker.

Globalization keeps business on its toes, although firms unable to compete wind up on their backs. A global economy encourages a greater exchange of information and use of technology. Yet, terrorists take advantage of that. Global economic development provides wealth for environmental cleanup, but there is no guarantee that the resources will be used for that purpose. The record shows it helps developing nations and lifts millions of people out of poverty by creating a new middle class, although not every poor country develops. For example, globalization has bypassed central Africa. International economic development extends business and political freedom, yet corruption can be rampant. Finally, the result of a more global economy is longer life expectancy, improved health standards, and higher literacy rates.

On the dark side, widespread poverty occurs in the midst of global prosperity. The critics assert that is caused by globalization. International income disparity tends to increase, but fewer people remain in poverty. On balance, the rich are getting richer faster than the poor. In terms of geographical differences, eastern and southern Asia are developing much faster than Africa and western Asia.

Critics contend that globalization moves jobs to low-wage factories that abuse workers' rights. True,

many children work in sweatshops, but few of them are employed by the large multinational corporations. Overwhelmingly, the poor working conditions are found in indigenous firms, producing goods for local markets. When we ask why children work, the response is troublesome—because their families are in poverty. In many cases, the entire region has been left behind by globalization, which is why low-income countries welcome foreign investment, a process that exerts an upward force on wages, production, and national income. A basic economic principle is at work here: raise the demand for labor and wages will rise.

The puppet-parading protesters at the World Trade Organization meetings in Seattle and Mexico were wrong. On balance, globalization—warts and all—is working. Those "terrible" multinational enterprises are creating widespread wealth. In recent years, the poorer countries have been growing at a 50% faster rate than the more developed nations. More people have moved out of poverty in the last two decades than ever before. Economic development is far from complete, though. Many societies are not participating in the world economy, especially in Africa. They need the opportunity to reap the benefits achieved by other hitherto undeveloped economies, such as South Korea.

Finally, we should not ignore the challenges that arise in a dynamic global economy, notably, the development of China as an industrial power and the rise of India as a major service center. Their growing economic strength is generating

problems as well as opportunities for business firms, workers, and consumers everywhere. History provides examples of such basic changes. In the 19th century, Europe dominated the world economy. That monopoly ended with the rise of the U.S. as a major industrial power. Europe's share of world commerce declined, but the absolute results were very positive. Total world trade rose. So did living standards in each nation. A similar situation is developing in Asia. Japan emerged as a major economic power in the 20th century—and the pace of economic development accelerated. A comparable result occurred in the 19th century. The American economy in effect was the new boy on the block. In the 21st century, we can expect China and India to fill that role.

Much will depend on the policies they pursue. History demonstrates that six factors are key to global economic success: an economy open to foreign trade and investment; minimal government controls over business, but the effective supervising of financial institutions; an uncorrupt judicial system; economic information that is transparent and readily available; high labor mobility; and easy entry into the marketplace by new businesses. These six points underscore an even more basic notion: Vigorous competition is the key to long-term international economic success.

Murray Weidenbaum, Ecology Editor of *USA Today,* is Mallinckrodt Distinguished University Professor, Washington University, St. Louis, Mo.

WHERE THE GOOD JOBS ARE GOING

Forget sweatshops. U.S. companies are now shifting high-wage work overseas, especially to India

By **JYOTI THOTTAM**

LITTLE BY LITTLE, SAB MAGLIONE could feel his job slipping away. He worked for a large insurance firm in northern New Jersey, developing the software it uses to keep track of its agents. But in mid-2001, his employer introduced him to Tata Consultancy Services, India's largest software company. About 120 Tata employees were brought in to help on a platform-conversion project. Maglione, 44, trained and managed a five-person Tata team. When one of them was named manager, he started to worry. By the end of last year, 70% of the project had been shifted to India and nearly all 20 U.S. workers, including Maglione, were laid off.

Since then, Maglione has been able to find only temporary work in his field, taking a pay cut of nearly 30% from his former salary of $77,000. For a family and mortgage, he says, "that doesn't pay the bills." Worried about utility costs, he runs after his two children, 11 and 7, to turn off the lights. And he has considered a new career as a house painter. "It doesn't require that much skill, and I don't have to go to school for it," Maglione says. And houses, at least, can't be painted from overseas.

Jobs that stay put are becoming a lot harder to find these days. U.S. companies are expected to send 3.3 million jobs overseas in the next 12 years, primarily to India, according to a study by Forrester Research. If you've ever called Dell about a sick PC or American Express about an error on your bill, you have already bumped the tip of this "offshore outsourcing" iceberg. The friendly voice that answered your questions was probably a customer-service rep

in Bangalore or New Delhi. Those relatively low-skilled jobs were the first to go, starting in 1997.

But more and more of the jobs that are moving abroad today are highly skilled and highly paid—the type that U.S. workers assumed would always remain at home. Instead Maglione is one of thousands of Americans adjusting to the unsettling new reality of work. "If I can get another three years in this industry, I'll be fortunate," he says. Businesses are embracing offshore outsourcing in their drive to stay competitive, and almost any company, whether in manufacturing or services, can find some part of its work that can be done off site. By taking advantage of lower wages overseas, U.S. managers believe they can cut their overall costs 25% to 40% while building a more secure, more focused work force in the U.S. Labor leaders—and nonunion workers, who make up most of those being displaced—aren't buying that rationale. "How can America be competitive in the long run sending over the very best jobs?" asks Marcus Courtney, president of the Seattle-based Washington Alliance of Technology Workers. "I don't see how that helps the middle class."

On the other side of the world, though, educated Indian workers are quickly adjusting to their new status as the world's most sought-after employees. They have never been more confident and optimistic—as Americans usually like to think of themselves. For now, at least, in ways both tangible and

emotional, educated Americans and Indians are trading places.

INCOMING
Uma Satheesh
Bangalore, India

Satheesh, 32, manages 38 Wipro employees who work on networking software for Hewlett-Packard in Bangalore—in jobs that were once done mainly in the U.S.

Uma Satheesh, 32, an employee of Wipro, one of India's leading outsourcing companies, is among her country's new elite. She manages 38 people who work for Hewlett-Packard's enterprise-servers group doing maintenance, fixing defects and enhancing the networking software developed by HP for its clients. Her unit includes more than 300 people who work for HP, about 90 of whom were added last November when HP went through a round of cost-cutting.

"We've been associated with HP for a long time, so it was an emotional thing," Satheesh says. "It was kind of a mixed feeling. But that is happening at all the companies, and it's going to continue." Satheesh says that five years ago, computer-science graduates had one career option in India: routine, mind-numbing computer programming. Anything more rewarding required emigrating. "Until three years ago, the first preference was to go overseas," she says. Nowadays her colleagues are interested only in business trips to the U.S. "People are pretty comfortable with the

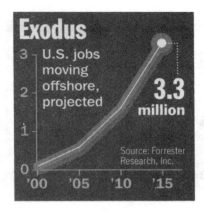

Exodus
U.S. jobs moving offshore, projected
3.3 million
Source: Forrester Research, Inc.

jobs here and the pay here"—not to mention the cars and houses that once seemed out of reach. Employees in her group earn from $5,200 a year to $36,000 for the most experienced managers.

And as American companies have grown more familiar with their Indian outsourcing partners, they have steadily increased the complexity of work they are willing to hand over. Rajeshwari Rangarajan, 28, leads a team of seven Wipro workers enhancing the intranet site on which Lehman Brothers employees manage personal benefits like their 401(k) accounts. "I see myself growing with every project that I do here," Rangarajan says. "I really don't have any doubts about the growth of my career."

Her experience with a leading brokerage will probably help. Financial-services companies in the U.S. are expected to move more than 500,000 jobs overseas in the next five years, according to a survey by management consultant A.T. Kearney, and India is by far the top destination. U.S. banks, insurance firms and mortgage companies have been using outsourcing to handle tech support for years. Now these firms are using Indian workers to handle the business operations—say, assessing loan applications and credit checks—that the technology supports. Kumar Mahadeva, CEO of the thriving outsourcing firm Cognizant, explains the appeal: "It becomes logical for them to say, 'Hey, you know everything about the way we do claims processing. Why not take a piece of it?'"

The next logical step, says Andrea Bierce, a co-author of the A.T. Kearney study, is jobs that require more complex financial skills such as equity research

and analysis or market research for developing new business. Evalueserve, a niche outsourcing company in Delhi, already performs research for patent attorneys and consulting firms in the U.S. In April, J.P. Morgan Chase said it would hire about 40 stock-research analysts in Bombay—about 5% of its total research staff. Novartis employs 40 statisticians in Bombay who process data from the drug company's clinical research.

OUTSOURCED
Bernie Lantz
Logan, Utah

Lantz, 58, says offshore hirings made his troubleshooting job with a Texas software firm obsolete. He left the tech business to teach computer science at Utah State University

But as educated workers in India are finding new opportunities, those in the U.S. feel the doors closing. Last week Bernie Lantz drove 1,400 miles from his home in Plano, Texas, to begin a new life in Utah. He is 58 years old, a bachelor, and had lived in the Dallas area for 24 years. "I'm leaving all my friends," he says with a sigh. "It's quite an upheaval." Lantz used to earn $80,000 a year as a troubleshooter for Sabre, a company based in Southlake, Texas, whose software powers airline-reservations systems. But over the past two years, Sabre has gradually standardized and has centralized its software service. As Sabre began to outsource its internal IT services, Lantz says, he became convinced that jobs like his were becoming endangered. He was laid off in December. (A company spokesman denies that Lantz's firing was related to outsourcing.)

Discouraged by a depressed job market in Dallas, Lantz realized he would have to do something else. In the fall he will begin teaching computer science at Utah State University in Logan, and in the meantime he has learned a lesson of his own: "Find a job that requires direct hands-on work on site," Lantz advises. "Anything that can be sent overseas is going to be sent overseas."

Pat Fluno, 53, of Orlando, Fla., says she, like Maglione, had to train her replacement—a common practice in the

Playing the Savings Game
As these average-salary figures show, outsourcing lowers costs
SOFTWARE PROGRAMMER U.S. $66,100 INDIA $10,000
MECHANICAL ENGINEER U.S. $55,600 INDIA $5,900
IT MANAGER U.S. $55,000 INDIA $8,500
ACCOUNTANT U.S. $41,000 INDIA $5,000
FINANCIAL OPERATIONS U.S. $37,625 INDIA $5,500
Sources: PayScale Inc; the Paàras Group

domestic outsourcing industry—when her data-processing unit at Germany-based Siemens was outsourced to India's Tata last year. "It's extremely insulting," she says. "The guy's sitting there doing my old job." After 10 months of looking, she is working again, but she had to take a $10,000 pay cut.

BYPASSED
Pat Fluno
Orlando, Fla.

Fluno's 12-person data-processing unit at the local Siemens operation was replaced by a team from Tata Consultancy Services in India. It took her 10 months—and a $10,000 cut in pay—to find a new job.

To protect domestic jobs, U.S. labor activists are pushing to limit the number of H-1B and L-1 visas granted to foreign workers. That would make it harder for offshore companies to have their employees working on site in the U.S. "Those programs were designed for a booming high-tech economy, not a busting high-tech economy," says Courtney of the Washington Alliance of Technology Workers. Courtney and his allies are starting to get the attention of lawmakers. Several congressional committees have held hearings on the impact of offshore outsourcing on the U.S. economy, and lawmakers in five states have introduced bills that would limit or forbid filling government contracts through offshore outsourcing.

Stephanie Moore, a vice president of Forrester Research, says companies are concerned about the backlash but mainly because of the negative publicity. "The retail industry is very hush-hush about its offshoring," she says. But within the boardroom, such outsourcing enjoys wide support. In a June survey of 1,000 firms by Gartner Research, 80% said the backlash would have no effect on their plans.

The advantages, businesses say, are just too great to ignore. They begin with cost but don't end there. Jennifer Cotteleer, vice president of Phase Forward, a Waltham, Mass., company that designs software for measuring clinical-trials data for drug companies, has for the past two years used offshore employees from Cognizant to customize the application for specific drug trials. Lately she has been relying on their expertise to develop even more-tailored programming. "I certainly couldn't have grown this fast without them," Cotteleer says. Her company is growing 30% annually, on track to reach $65 million in revenue this year. "What I've been able to do in very tough economic times is manage very directly to my margins," she says. "I'm providing job security for the workers I do have."

Creative use of offshore outsourcing, says Debashish Sinha of Gartner Research, offers benefits that outweigh the direct loss of jobs. In an economy that has shed 2 million jobs over two years, he contends, the 200,000 that have moved overseas are less significant than the potential for cost savings and strategic growth. But he concedes that "when you're a laid-off employee who can't find a job, that's hard to understand."

Perhaps some will follow the example of Dick Taggart, 41, of Old Greenwich, Conn. After 18 years in financial services, most recently at J.P. Morgan Chase, he now works for Progeon, an affiliate of the Indian outsourcing giant Infosys, as its man on Wall Street. One week out of every six or seven, he takes securities firms to India to show them the savings that are possible. He knows the transition is painful for the workers left behind, but he has seen it before. "It was the same thing when we moved from Wall Street to New Jersey and then to Dallas," he says. "Guess what? This is next."

—With reporting by Sean Gregory/ New York City

How I Joined Teach for America— and Got Sued for $20 Million

Joshua Kaplowitz

It was May 2000, and the guy at Al Gore's polling firm seemed baffled. A Yale political-science major, I'd already walked away from a high-paying consulting job a few weeks earlier, and now I was walking away from a job working on a presidential campaign to do … *what*?

Well, when push came to shove, I didn't want to devote my life to helping the rich get richer or crunching numbers to see what views were most popular for the vice president to adopt. This wasn't what my 17 years of education were for.

My doctor parents had drummed into me that education was the key to every door, the one thing they couldn't take away from my ancestors during pogroms and persecutions. They had also filled me with a strong sense of social justice. I couldn't help feeling guilty dismay when I thought of the millions of kids who'd never even tasted the great teaching—not to mention the supportive family—I'd enjoyed for my entire life.

I told the Al Gore guy, "Thanks, but no thanks." Weird as he might have thought it, I had decided to teach in an inner-city school.

Five weeks later, I found myself steering my parents' old Volvo off R Street and into a one-block cul-de-sac. There it was: Emery Elementary School, a 1950s-ugly building tucked behind a dead-end street—an apt metaphor, I thought, for the lives of many of the children in this almost all-black neighborhood a mile north of the U.S. Capitol in Washington. I had seen signs of inner-city blight all over the neighborhood, from the grown men who skulked in the afternoon streets to the bulletproof glass that sealed off the cashier at the local Kentucky Fried Chicken. This was the "other half" of Washington, the part of the city I had missed during my grade-school field trips to the Smithsonian and my two summers as a Capitol Hill intern.

I parked the car and bounded into the main office to say hi to Mr. Bledsoe, the interim principal who had hired

me a few weeks before. As he showed me around the clean but bare halls, my head filled with visions of my students happily painting imaginative murals under my artistic direction. I peered through windows into classrooms, where students were bent over their desks, quietly filling out worksheets. I smiled to myself as I imagined the creative lessons I would give to these children, who had never had a dynamic young teacher to get them excited about scholarship the way I knew I could. Their minds were like kindling, I reflected; all they needed was a spark to ignite a love of learning that would lift them above the drugs, violence, and poverty. The spark, I hoped, would be me.

As the tour ended and I was about to leave, Mr. Bledsoe pulled me aside. "The one thing you need to do above all else is to have your children under control. Once you have done that, you'll be fine."

Fine. But as I learned to my great cost, that was easier said than done.

I was supposed to pick up that skill over the summer from Teach for America (TFA), an organization, affiliated with AmeriCorps, that places young people with no ed-school background, and usually just out of college, in disadvantaged school districts suffering from teacher shortages. Applicants request placement in one of over a dozen rural and urban school districts around the country that contract with TFA, and I got my first choice, in the city I hoped to live in for the rest of my life.

Teach for America conducts an intensive five-week training program for its inductees during the summer before they start teaching. My year, this "teacher boot camp" took place in Houston. It was there that I quickly figured out that enthusiasm and creativity alone wouldn't suffice in an inner-city classroom. I was part of a tag team of four recruits teaching a summer-school class of low-income fourth-graders. Even in one- to two-hour blocks of teaching, I quickly realized that my best-planned, most imaginative lessons fell apart if I didn't have control of my students.

In the seminars we attended when we weren't teaching, I learned the basics of lesson planning and teaching theory. I also internalized the TFA philosophy of high expectations, the idea that if you set a rigorous academic course, all students will rise to meet the challenge.

But the training program skimped on actual teaching and classroom-management techniques, instead overwhelming us with sensitivity training. My group spent hours on an activity where everyone stood in a line and then took steps forward or backward based on whether we were the oppressor or the oppressed in the categories of race, income, and religion. The program had a college bull session, rather than professional, atmosphere. And it had a college-style party line: I heard of two or three trainees being threatened with expulsion for expressing in their discussion groups politically incorrect views about inner-city poverty—for example, that families and culture, not economics, may be the root cause of the achievement gap.

Nothing in the program simulated what I soon learned to be the life of a teacher. Though I didn't know it, I was completely ill equipped when I stepped into my own fifth-grade classroom at Emery Elementary in September 2000.

The year before I taught, a popular veteran principal had been dismissed without explanation. Mr. Bledsoe finished out the rest of the year on an interim basis, hired me and four other Teach for America teachers, and then turned over the reins to a woman named V. Lisa Savoy. Ms. Savoy had been an assistant principal at the District's infamous Anacostia High School, in Washington's equivalent of the South Bronx. Before the start of school, she met with her four first-year TFA teachers to assure us that we would be well supported, and that if we needed anything we should just ask. Most of my veteran colleagues, 90 percent of them black, also seemed helpful, though a few showed flickers of disdain for us eager, young white teachers. By the time school opened, I was thrilled to start molding the brains of my children.

My optimism and naiveté evaporated within hours. I tried my best to be strict and set limits with my new students; but I wore my inexperience on my sleeve, and several of the kids jumped at the opportunity to misbehave. I could see clearly enough that the vast majority of my fifth-graders genuinely wanted to learn—but all it took to subvert the whole enterprise were a few cutups.

On a typical day, DeAngelo (a pseudonym, as are the other children's names in this and the next paragraph) would throw a wad of paper in the middle of a lesson. Whether I disciplined him or ignored him, his actions would cause Kanisha to scream like an air-raid siren. In response, Lamond would get up, walk across the room, and try to slap Kanisha. Within one minute, the whole class was lost in a sea of noise and fists. I felt profoundly sorry for the majority of my students, whose education was being hijacked. Their plaintive cries punctuated the din: "Quiet everyone! Mr. Kaplowitz is trying to teach!"

Ayisha was my most gifted student. The daughter of Senegalese immigrants, she would tolerantly roll her eyes as Darnetta cut up for the ninth time in one hour, patiently waiting for the day when my class would settle down. Joseph was a brilliant writer who struggled mightily in math. When he needed help with a division problem, I tried to give him as much attention as I could, before three students wandering around the room inevitably distracted me. Eventually, I settled on tutoring him after school. Twenty more students' educations were sabotaged, each kid with specific needs that I couldn't attend to, because I was too busy putting out fires. Though I poured my heart into inventive lessons and activities throughout the entire year, they almost always fell apart in the face of my students' disrespect and indifference.

To gain control, I tried imposing the kinds of consequences that the classroom-management handbooks recommend. None worked. My classroom was too small to give my students "time out." I tried to take away their recess, but depriving them of their one sanctioned time to blow off steam just increased their penchant to use my classroom as a playground. When I called parents, they were often mistrustful and tended to question or even disbelieve outright what I told them about their children. It was sometimes worse when they believed me, though; the tenth time I heard a mother swear that her child was going to "get a beating for this one," I almost decided not to call parents. By contrast, I saw immediate behavioral and academic improvement in students whose parents had come to trust me.

I quickly learned from such experiences how essential parental support is in determining whether a school succeeds in educating a child. And of course, parental support not just of the teachers but of the kids: as I came to know my students better, I saw that those who had seen violence, neglect, or drug abuse at home were usually the uncontrollable ones, while my best-behaved, hardest-working kids were typically those with the most nurturing home environments.

Being a white teacher in a mostly black school unquestionably hindered my ability to teach. Certain students hurled racial slurs with impunity; several of their parents intimated to my colleagues that they didn't think a white teacher had any business teaching their children—and a number of my colleagues agreed. One parent who was also a teacher's aide threatened to "kick my white ass" in front of my class and received no punishment from the principal, beyond being told to stay out of my classroom. The failure of the principal, parents, and teachers to react more decisively to racist disrespect emboldened students to behave worse. Such poisonous bigotry directed at a black teacher at a mostly white school would of course have created a federal case.

Still, other colleagues, friendly and supportive, helped me with my discipline problems. They let me send unruly students to their classrooms for brief periods of time to cool off, allowing me to teach the rest of my class effectively. But when I turned to my school administration for similar help, I was much less fortunate.

I had read that successful schools have chief executives who immerse themselves in the everyday operations of the institution, set clear expectations for the student body, recognize and support energetic and creative teachers, and foster constructive relationships with parents. Successful principals usually are mavericks, too, who skirt stupid bureaucracy to do what is best for the children. Emery's Principal Savoy sure didn't fit this model.

To start with, from all that I could see, she seemed mostly to stay in her office, instead of mingling with students and observing classes, most of which were up at least one flight of stairs, perhaps a disincentive for so heavy a woman. Furthermore, I saw from the first month that she generally gave delinquents no more than a stern talking-to, followed by a pat on the back, rather than suspensions, detentions, or any other meaningful punishment. The threat of sending a student to the office was thus rendered toothless.

Worse, Ms. Savoy effectively undermined my classroom-management efforts. She forbade me from sending students to other teachers—the one tactic that had any noticeable effect. Exiling my four worst students had produced a vast improvement in the conduct of the remainder of my class. But Ms. Savoy was adamant, insisting that the school district required me to teach all my children, all the time, in the "least restrictive" environment. This was just the first instance of Ms. Savoy blocking me with a litany of D.C. Public Schools regulations, as she regularly frustrated my colleagues on disciplinary issues.

Some of Ms. Savoy's actions defied explanation. She more than once called me to her office in the middle of my lessons to lecture me on how bad a teacher I was—well before her single visit to observe me in my classroom. She filled my personnel file with lengthy memos articulating her criticisms. I eventually concluded that Ms. Savoy tended similarly to trouble any teacher, experienced or novice, who rocked the boat.

And in November I really rocked it. By then, despite mounting tension with Ms. Savoy, and despite the pandemonium that continued to ravage my teaching efforts, I had managed—painstakingly—to build a rapport with my fifth-graders. I felt I was turning a corner. I thought that my students (and their parents) would completely shape up once they saw their abysmal first report cards. D.C. Public Schools grade kids on a highly subjective 1 to 4 scale, 4 being the highest. Most of my students entered fifth grade with grave academic deficiencies, yet their cumulative records revealed fair to excellent grades, making clear that social promotion was standard practice at Emery. I wasn't playing along. I had given regular tests and quizzes that first semester, and most of my students had earned straight 1s by any rational measure. True to the credo of high expectations, I would give them the grades they earned.

I submitted my report cards to Ms. Savoy, who insisted that my grades were "too low" and demanded that I raise them immediately. I offered to show her all of my students' work portfolios; but she demurred, informing me that the law obliged me to pass a certain percentage of my students. I paid no attention, gave my students the grades they deserved, and patiently explained to every parent that their child's grades would improve once he or she started behaving in class and doing the assigned lessons. For this, Ms. Savoy cited me for insubordination.

Just after the New Year, Ms. Savoy informed me that she was switching me from fifth grade to second grade; the veteran second-grade teacher would then take over my fifth-graders. Her justification was that I would be able to control younger students more effectively—though I assumed she thought that I could wreak less disruption with the younger kids, who were relatively flunk-proof.

From the start, I tried my best to combat understandable parental resentment that their experienced teacher was being yanked out and replaced by me, a first-year teacher with notoriously poor classroom-management skills. I wrote letters home describing my ambitious plans, called parents with enthusiastic words about their children, and walked my students home after school to increase my visibility in the neighborhood.

Unfortunately, I never got a chance to show that I was in control. Unbelievable as it sounds, my second-graders were even wilder than my fifth-graders. Just as before, a majority of kids genuinely wanted to learn, but the antics of a few spun my entire class into chaos. This time, though, my troublemakers were even more immature and disruptive, ranging from a boy who roamed around the room punching his classmates and threatening to kill himself to a borderline-mentally retarded student, who would throw crumpled wads of paper all day. I was so busy trying to quell anarchy that I never had the chance to get to know my new students, let alone teach them anything.

Ms. Savoy had abandoned all pretense of administrative support by this point. Nearly every student I sent to the office returned within minutes.

This lack of consequences encouraged a level of violence I never could have imagined among any students, let alone second-graders. Fights broke out daily—not just during recess or bathroom breaks but also in the middle of lessons. And this wasn't just playful shoving: we're talking fists flying, hair yanked, heads slammed against lockers.

When I asked other teachers to come help me stop a fight, they shook their heads and reminded me that D.C. Public Schools banned teachers from laying hands on students for any reason, even to protect other children. When a fight brewed, I was faced with a Catch-22. I could call the office and wait ten minutes for the security guard to arrive, by which point blood could have been shed and students injured. Or I could intervene physically, in violation of school policy.

Believe me, you have to be made of iron, or something other than flesh and blood, to stand by passively while some enraged child is trying to inflict real harm on another eight-year-old. I couldn't do it. And each time I let normal human instinct get the best of me and broke up a fight, one of the combatants would go home and fabricate a story about how I had hurt him or her. The parent, already suspicious of me, would report this accusation to Ms. Savoy, who would in turn call in a private investigative firm employed by D.C. Public Schools. Investigators would come to Emery and interview me, as well as several students whom the security guard thought might tell the truth about the alleged incident of corporal punishment.

I had previously heard of three other teachers at Emery that year who were being investigated for corporal punishment. When I talked to them—they were all experienced male teachers—they heatedly protested their innocence and bitterly complained about Ms. Savoy's handling of the situation. Now that I had joined the club, I began to understand their fears and frustrations.

To define as "corporal punishment" the mere physical separation of two combatants not only puts students at risk but also gives children unconscionable power over teachers who choose to intervene. False allegations against me and other teachers snowballed, as certain students realized that they had the perfect tool for getting their teacher in deep trouble. As I began to be investigated on almost a weekly basis, parents came to school to berate and threaten me—naturally, without reprisals from the administration. One day, a rather large father came up to me after school and told me he was going to "get me" if he heard that I put my hands on his daughter one more time. Forget the fact that I had pulled her off of a boy whom she was clobbering at the time.

With such a weak disciplinary tone set by the administration, by late February the whole school atmosphere had devolved into chaos. Gangs of students roamed the halls at will. You could hear screaming from every classroom—from students and teachers alike. Including me, four teachers (or 20 percent of the faculty) were under investigation on bogus corporal-punishment charges, including a fourth-grade instructor whose skills I greatly respected. The veteran teachers constantly lamented that things were better the previous year, when the principal ran a tight disciplinary ship, and the many good instructors were able to do their job.

It was nearly March, and the Stanford-9 standardized tests, the results of which determine a principal's success in D.C. Public Schools, were imminent. Ms. Savoy unexpectedly instituted a policy allowing teachers to ship their two or three most disruptive students to the computer lab to be warehoused and supervised by teachers' aides. My classroom's behavior and attentiveness improved dramatically for two weeks. Unfortunately, Ms. Savoy abandoned this plan the instant the standardized tests had passed.

After that, my classroom became more of a gladiatorial venue than a place of learning. Fights erupted hourly; no student was immune. The last three months were a blur of violence, but several incidents particularly stand out. One week, two of my emotionally disturbed boys went on a binge of sexual harassment, making lewd gestures and grabbing girls' buttocks—yes, *seven-* and *eight-year-olds*. On another occasion, three students piled on top of one of their peers and were punching him with their fists before I intervened. My students were not even afraid to try to hurt me: two boys spent a month throwing pencils at me in the middle of lessons; another child slugged me in the gut.

But for Ms. Savoy, apparently I was the problem. It seemed to me that she was readier to launch investigations when a student or parent made an accusation against me than to help me out when my students were acting up.

Faced with a series of corporal-punishment charges, no administrative support, and no hope of controlling my second-grade class in the foreseeable future, I should have packed up and left midyear. Surely there were other schools, even inner-city ones, where I could have developed and succeeded as a teacher.

Why did I stay on? Part of the answer lay in my own desperate desire not to fail. I felt that if I just worked harder, I could turn my children around and get them to learn. Another part of the answer was Teach for America's having instilled in each corps member the idea that you have made a commitment to the children and that you must stick with them at all costs, no matter how much your school is falling apart. Because of this mentality, my TFA friends and I put up with nonsense from our schools and our students that few regular teachers would have tolerated.

The three-person TFA-D.C. staff was stretched too thin to support any of us. When I told them about the debacle at Emery, the D.C. program directors told me to keep my chin up and work harder. They wouldn't transfer me to another TFA-affiliated elementary school, and pooh-poohed the idea that I had it worse than anyone else in the program. So I was stuck at Emery, unwilling to incur the disgrace that came with quitting.

Fate made the decision for me.

Four days before the end of my first year, I was still planning to return to Emery in the fall. The rumor was that Ms. Savoy would be replaced. With her gone, I thought, I could start fresh and use my hard-won battlefield experience to make a positive difference in underprivileged children's lives.

The afternoon of June 13 started with the usual mixture of disorder and disrespect. This time, a boy named Raynard, a particularly difficult child, whom I had seen punch other students and throw things in the past, was repeating over and over, "I got to go to the bathroom. I need some water." The rest of the class tittered as I told him in my sternest teacher voice that we would be having a class bathroom break once everyone was quiet and in his seat.

"I got to go to the bathroom. I need some water."

Frustrated, I led him to the classroom door with my hand on the small of his back. I nudged him into the hall and closed the door. He would probably spend the remainder of the day roaming the halls with the rest of the troublemakers at Emery, but at least he would be out of sight, so I could get the rest of my class under control. I had given up on teaching for the rest of the day; my class was slated to watch a movie with Ms. Perkins's first-graders across the hall.

Once Raynard left, I guided my students through a characteristically raucous bathroom break and filed them into Ms. Perkins's room, where they lapsed into a rare TV-induced calm.

After 15 minutes, the school security guard appeared at the door and beckoned for me. My stomach hit the floor, as I guessed what this meant: yet another corporal-punishment charge. But this time was different. Chaos reigned in the main entranceway as police officers swarmed into the building. Raynard's mother, I was told, had been in school for a meeting to place her son in a class for emotionally disturbed children. Raynard had told her that I had violently shoved him in the chest out the door of my classroom, injuring his head and back. His mother had dialed 911 and summoned the cops and the fire department. The police hustled me into the principal's office, where I sat in bewilderment and desperately denied I had hurt Raynard in any way.

In the blink of an afternoon, my search for the perfect lesson plan gave way to my search for the perfect lawyer. I was lucky that my parents could afford Hank Asbill, a highly regarded Washington defense attorney.

Two months later, Raynard's mother filed a $20 million lawsuit against the school district, Ms. Savoy, and myself—and the D.C. police charged me with a misdemeanor count of simple assault against my former student. Thus ended my first and last year as a public school teacher.

After I was charged, Hank Asbill chose a day in early September for me to turn myself in at the District 5 police station near Emery and receive a trial date. The whole ordeal was supposed to take about six hours—but five minutes after I was admitted into custody, the two planes hit the World Trade Center. After the third plane crashed into the Pentagon, the D.C. courts shut down. It was only after 33 hours in jail that I saw daylight again, on September 12.

My criminal trial spanned six days in early March of 2002. It was agonizing watching several former students testifying against me, not to mention facing the very real prospect of spending time in the D.C. jail. The children's stories as to what happened on June 13 were wildly inconsistent—not surprising, considering that the layout of my classroom precluded them from witnessing anything Raynard had alleged. Hank Asbill countered with a string of character witnesses, friends who attested to my peaceful nature and law-abiding ways, as well as other teachers at Emery who reported on the brutal atmosphere of the school. Hank then brought me to the stand to explain what had actually happened, and he also brought to light Raynard's medical records from June 13, which showed that the emergency-room doctors had found no evidence of any injury. Fortunately, we drew a rational, deliberative judge, unswayed by the case's racially charged nature: a poor black kid against a rich white Ivy Leaguer. He found me not guilty, touching off an outpouring of relief from my friends and former colleagues and—not least—me.

My elation was short-lived. As I had surmised, this whole case finally came down to money. Even after my acquittal, even after the accuracy of Raynard's story had been seriously undermined, his mother and her big-firm lawyers aggressively pursued multi-million-dollar damage claims on the civil side. Yet even as the lawsuit dragged on and the legal cloud over me caused me to lose a job opportunity I really wanted, I refused to entertain Raynard's mother's offers to settle the case by my paying her $200,000—a demand that ultimately diminished to $40,000. The school system had no such scruples; it settled the mother's tort claim in October 2002 for $75,000 (plus $15,000 from the teachers' union's insurance company—chump change compared with the cost of defending the litigation). It wasn't $20 million, but it was still more money than I imagine this woman had seen in her life—a pretty good payout and hardly deterrence to other parents in the neighborhood who felt entitled to shanghai the system.

I stayed in touch with several of my more supportive colleagues and parents, who have told me that Emery, although it has a new principal, is just as out of control two years after I taught there. Veteran teachers with nowhere else to go, they say, are giving up all pretense of teaching; their goal is to make it through the end of each year. Young teachers like my TFA colleagues are staying for a year or two and moving on to private, charter, or suburban schools, or to new careers.

In all the reading and talking I've done to try to make sense out of what happened to me, I've learned that Emery is hardly unique. Numerous new friends and acquaintances who have taught in D.C.'s inner-city schools—some from Teach for America, some not—report the same outrageous discipline problems that turned them from educators into U.N. peacekeepers.

I've learned that an epidemic of violence is raging in elementary schools nationwide, not just in D.C. A recent *Philadelphia Inquirer* article details a familiar pattern—kindergartners punching pregnant teachers, third-graders hitting their instructors with rulers. Pennsylvania and New Jersey have reported nearly 30 percent increases in elementary school violence since 1999, and many school districts have established special disciplinary K-6 schools. In New York City, according to the *New York Post*, some 60 teachers recently demonstrated against out-of-control pupil mayhem, chanting, "Hey, hey, ho, ho; violent students must go." Kids who stab each other, use teachers as shields in fights, bang on doors to disrupt classes, and threaten to "kick out that baby" from a pregnant teacher have created a "climate of terror," the *Post* reports.

Several of my new acquaintances in the Washington schools told me of facing completely fabricated corporal-punishment allegations, as I did. Some even faced criminal charges. Washington teachers' union officials won't give me hard numbers, but they intimate that each year they are flooded with corporal-punishment or related charges against teachers, most of which get settled without the media ever learning of this disturbing new trend. It is a state of affairs that Philip K. Howard vividly describes in his recent *The Collapse of the Common Good*: parents sue teachers and principals for suspending their children, for allegedly meting out corporal punishment,

and for giving failing marks. As a result, educators are afraid to penalize misbehaving students or give students grades that reflect the work they do. The real victims are the majority of children whose education is being commandeered by their out-of-control classmates.

I've come to believe that the most unruly and violent children should go to alternative schools designed to handle students with chronic behavior problems. A school with a more military structure can do no worse for those children than a permissive mainstream school, and it spares the majority of kids the injustice of having their education fall victim to the chaos wreaked by a small minority.

I know for sure that inner-city schools don't have to be hellholes like Emery and its District of Columbia brethren, with their poor administration and lack of parental support, their misguided focus on children's rights, their anti-white racism, and their lawsuit-crazed culture. Some of my closest TFA friends, thrilled to be liberated from the D.C. system, went on to teach at D.C. charter schools, where they really can make a difference in underprivileged children's lives. For example, at Paul Junior High School, which serves students with the same economic and cultural background as those at Emery, the principal's tough approach to discipline fosters a serious atmosphere of scholarship, and parents are held accountable, because the principal can kick their children back to the public school system if they refuse to cooperate. A friend who works at the Hyde School, which emphasizes character education (and sits directly across a field from Emery), tells me that this charter school is quiet and orderly, the teachers are happy, and the children are achieving at a much higher level—so much higher that several of the best students at Emery who transferred to Hyde nearly flunked out of their new school.

It should come as no surprise that students are leaving Emery in droves, in hopes of enrolling in this and other alternative schools. Enrollment, 411 when I was there, now is about 350. If things don't change, it will soon be—and should be—zero.

---

whose hospital is it?

MCP Hospital didn't have any celebrity doctors or slick ad campaigns All it had was a 150-year history serving its Philadelphia neighborhood—and in today's cutthroat health care industry that's no longer enough.

By Arthur Allen

GREGORY GAY WAS BORN 21 years ago at the Medical College of Pennsylvania Hospital (MCP), a venerable community hospital in Philadelphia's East Falls neighborhood. He was shot six blocks away on January 24, not long after Tenet Healthcare Corp. decided to close the hospital. Tenet, the second-largest for-profit hospital chain in the United States, was in the process of shuttering or selling a quarter of its more than 100 hospitals nationwide. As it waited for a judge's permission to shut down MCP, the company was slowly withdrawing services, closing floors, and letting the staff fade away through attrition.

When police and paramedics arrived moments after four bullets pierced Gay's body that icy Friday night, he was fighting for his life and lucid enough to give the names of two men who had shot him. But instead of zipping up Henry Avenue to MCP, the ambulance raced to Temple University Hospital, some 20 minutes away. MCP'S struggling emergency room was on "diversion"—temporarily closed to new patients—that night, as it had been for much of that month. Gay died less than an hour later.

Gay's death, one of many in the violent North Philadelphia streets whose sick and wounded feed the hospital, has become part of a lawsuit seeking to keep MCP open while charging that Tenet neglected its obligations to the city. (Tenet management refused to comment for this story.) Of course, it is uncertain whether Gay would have survived even had the hospital been fully operational. But the closing of MCP, a community hospital in every sense of the word, would clearly mean more hardship for thousands of its neighbors. Symbolically, in the minds of the hospital's defenders, Gay's death has come to stand for the deaths to come—not only the gunshot wounds, but the asthma attacks, the strokes and embolisms and diabetic comas that are likely to be aggravated by new delays and complications.

Not that MCP's fate is unusual. Tenet has closed three hospitals during its five years in Philadelphia; over the past decade,

four other North Philadelphia hospitals have shut down their inpatient units. Nationwide, according to data compiled by the federal government and *Modern Healthcare* magazine, more than 560 hospitals have closed since 1990—clobbered by stagnant reimbursement rates from government and the insurance industry, rising malpractice rates, skyrocketing prices for drugs and medical equipment, and increasing numbers of uninsured patients who can't pay their bills.

Still, when Tenet tried to shut MCP, it hit a particular nerve. The hospital, whose 70,000 potential clients ranged from homeless crack addicts to the governor of Pennsylvania, has become a local cause célèbre. This is partly because Tenet has blossomed into the Enron of the hospital business, notorious for creative accounting and out-size payouts to its executives. It is a corporate behemoth whose entry into Philadelphia in the late 1990s was subsidized with generous tax breaks because of the city's desperate need to save hospitals then on the verge of bankruptcy. The struggle to keep MCP open, in other words, embodies a frightening larger story about the decline of health care in the United States.

BY A STRANGE PARADOX, we live in a time in which scientific breakthroughs are revolutionizing American medicine, while the system for caring for the majority of the population seems to be breaking down. "As a microdelivery system, medicine provides increasingly exquisite molecular elegance," says Eliot Sorel, a professor of psychiatry at George Washington University School of Medicine and the former president of the D.C. Medical Society. "As a macrodelivery system, it is falling apart."

All across the nation, doctors and other health care providers are battling thick layers of bureaucracy and crushing financial burdens to deliver care. "We're watching the meltdown of the medical system," says Dr. Donald Palmisano, the president of the American Medical Association. "We have a broken medical liability system, price-fixing on Medicare and Medicaid, and managed care has such monopoly power in many states that the physician has no power to negotiate a contract." Nurses have also been leaving their field, creating serious shortages that imperil care. "I advise all my patients before they go into the hospital," Palmisano's predecessor at the AMA, Dr. Yank Coble, recently told *Medical Economics*, "to take somebody with them. A friend or relative will increase safety more than anything else, especially in these days of nursing shortage." According to a 1999 Institute of Medicine report, as many as 98,000 people die in hospitals each year as the result of medical mistakes, making such errors—often caused by staff shortages and overwork—the eighth leading cause of death in this country.

A growing number of hospitals are facing an even more fundamental crisis: They simply cannot make ends meet. The price of a pint of blood went up 30 percent in just one year; a CAT scan machine costs $1 million. Malpractice insurance rates have been rising at vertiginous rates—20 to 30 percent nationally, and 40 to 50 percent in some areas, including Pennsylvania. The MCP emergency room has seen its malpractice rates increase from $18,000 to $40,000 for each doctor in five years.

And even as the cost of caring for patients has increased, a decade of payment cuts from insurers as well as the government—especially Medicare and Medicaid, the public programs designed to provide coverage for the elderly and the poor—has pushed hospital finances into the red. In Philadelphia, Medicaid now pays only 75 percent of the cost of patient care, leaving hospitals and doctors to absorb the rest. In his fiscal year 2005 budget, President Bush has proposed another $2 billion cut in federal funding for Medicaid, and Medicare reimbursements are failing to keep up with costs. "Hospitals," concluded a recent report by the American Hospital Association, "are bearing the cumulative impact of a series of forces that are beginning to erode the foundation of the essential public service they provide."

Nowhere are those forces more apparent than in the community hospitals that serve as the nation's health care system of last resort. A shortage of primary care doctors in urban neighborhoods is driving more and more patients to crowded hospital emergency rooms: ER visits in community hospitals rose from 92 million in 1990 to 106 million in 2001, according to the American Hospital Association. The ERs at 3 out of 4 urban hospitals are "at" or "over" capacity, and more than half of all urban hospitals sometimes turn ambulances away. Last year, 25,000 MCP patients—60 percent of the hospital's total—came in through the ER.

Many of those patients can't pay their bills. Nationally, the number of uninsured people is on the rise after declining through the 1990s; in 2003 it stood at 42.3 million, 3.6 million more than in 1999, according to the National Center for Health Statistics. In Philadelphia, surveys by the Philadelphia Health Management Corp. show that the number of uninsured people in the city of 1.4 million has increased by nearly one-third, rising from 94,000 to 136,000 in only two years; that's 42,000 people who lost health benefits. And given that a single intensive-care visit can cost hundreds of thousands of dollars—and that hospitals by law cannot turn away patients who need treatment—any increase in the number of uninsured people is disastrous for a hospital's bottom line. In 2003, according to Richard Centafont of the Delaware Valley Healthcare Council, a hospital trade group, Philadelphia hospitals saw 22 percent more uninsured patients than they did the previous year, resulting in half a billion dollars' worth of uncompensated care.

Traditionally, hospitals subsidized their "charity" care for uninsured patients by collecting a substantial margin on private insurance reimbursements. But insurers, under pressure from employers, have pushed hard to trim those payments over the past decade. In the Philadelphia area, where a single private insurer—Independent Blue Cross and its health management organization, Keystone—dominates the market, this squeeze has become painful. Nationally, insurance payments cover 115 percent of hospitals' actual costs for patient care; in Philadelphia they cover an average of 104 percent. "It used to be that the rich subsidized health care for the poor," says Dr. Philip S. Mead, medical director of MCP's Emergency Department. "It ain't that way in Pennsylvania anymore."

Not that MCP is a poverty hospital. Though it never attracted the jet-set clientele you'd find at the best university medical centers, its patient base has always been diverse. The hospital traces its roots to the Female Medical College of Pennsylvania, founded in 1850 as the first school in the world established to provide full medical training to women. It outlasted other women-only institutions, admitting men for the first time in 1969. By 1990, at least 10 African American women had been trained at the school, including Dr. Eliza Grier, who was born a slave. Today, MCP retains an almost old-fashioned aura of collegiality. Most of its doctors, as one physician notes, are "not major egos or out to make money," but rather salaried academic medicine types in the traditional mold.

While many of MCP's patients have been the impoverished and working-class people of neighborhoods like Strawberry Mansion, to its north the hospital borders East Falls, a well-to-do district where Governor Ed Rendell, U.S. Senator Arlen Specter, and Rep. Chaka Fattah live. These high-profile neighbors have proved crucial in the fight to keep MCP open. But as patients, East Falls residents increasingly patronize upscale Center City hospitals.

More than 560 hospitals have closed in the past 14 years—

clobbered by stagnant reimbursement rates, high

malpractice costs, rising drug prices, and increasing numbers of

uninsured patients who can't pay their bills.

Partly, this is due to the failure of MCP Hospital's academic overseers, most recently Drexel University College of Medicine, to cultivate relationships with private physicians that could bring in well-insured clients. To be a moneymaking hospital in today's market, it helps to do the sort of complex procedures well reimbursed by insurers or the federal government. For example, a wrinkle in the Medicare system explains why so many companies have opened "heart centers" in the past few years—surgery on the heart is among the most lavishly reimbursed by Medicare. Unless a community hospital like MCP can attract the well insured, it's at risk.

As more such hospitals close, cities like Philadelphia are moving to a two-tiered health system. "If you have good insurance and want a hip replacement, there are plenty of nice hospitals that will schedule you at your convenience," says Dr. Steven Peitzman, a longtime MCP physician who has written a history of the Woman's Medical College and its successor. "Whereas if you're wheezing with the worst asthma attack of your life, there isn't likely to be a hospital nearby."

AROUND THE TIME Tenet was negotiating to run MCP, Thomas Morgan, a community activist who has lived his entire life on the same quiet block in the Germantown neighborhood where Grace Kelly's family lived, was diagnosed with a thyroid disorder and kidney failure. On September 4, 1999—his 44th birthday—Morgan, who has four children and works nights as a toll collector, went on dialysis for the first time. The procedure required at least 15 hours in the hospital each week, but there was a silver lining. It turns out that universal health care already exists for one kind of patient in America—the dialysis patient.

Under a 1972 law, passed after an end-stage kidney disease patient testified before the House Ways and Means Committee while undergoing dialysis in the committee room, Congress expanded Medicare to fully fund the medical costs of kidney patients, whether or not they have private insurance. When it comes to dialysis, the American health care system actually lives up to its promise, says Dr. Walter Tsou, a former Philadelphia health commissioner. "The solution to the crisis at MCP and every health care facility in Philadelphia and the nation," he says, "is a properly financed, single-payer, national health-insurance program like this."

For reasons that are not entirely clear, blacks are four times more likely than whites to suffer kidney failure in America, and nearly all of the 130 or so dialysis patients at MCP are African Americans. Dialysis is an exhausting, at times painful, procedure, but for Morgan, who is dialyzed from 6:00 a.m. to 10:30 a.m. three times a week after he gets off work, it's almost something to look forward to. "It's my community," he says of the 25 or so patients who share his shift. "We talk for a while—politics, sports, whatever—then you drift off to sleep. And you care for the other patients. We look out for each other. We have a Christmas party. We've had bus trips to Atlantic City." The dialysis unit is attached to the hospital, which means that emergency or inpatient care is available for kidney patients when they need it.

Morgan's life's rhythms—work, sleep, taking his six-year-old daughter to school—are all linked to the dialysis center. If it closes, he will find another dialysis center, but many such centers are not located at hospitals. Morgan may have to wait months to find a rotation in a dialysis center with the care available at MCP. A warm, soft-spoken man with closely cropped salt-and-pepper hair and beard, Morgan, a Democratic Party committeeman for the city's 12th Ward, says his political activism has always come from a sense of duty to others in his neighborhood. But MCP's struggle, to him, is also profoundly personal. "If the hospital closes," he says, "it throws my whole life into turmoil."

FOR A WHILE IT SEEMED as though Tenet Healthcare had figured out a way around the hospital-financing conundrum, a way to game the system; gaming the system, in fact, turns out to have been one of the company's principal assets. The Santa Barbara, California-based company arose from the ashes of Santa Monica-based National Medical Enterprises, a firm that flamed out in the early 1990s after being targeted by the federal government for confining psychiatric patients over long periods to collect more money from their insurers. In 1993, Jeffrey Barbakow, a financial wizard who had been an investment banker and chairman of MGM, was brought in to remake the company.

For several years in the late 1990s, Tenet seemed to produce miraculous results in Philadelphia. MCP and Hahnemann hospitals, which had been losing millions, were suddenly in the black. At MCP, Tenet says it spent more than $43 million for capital improvements; it spruced up hallways, bed units, and operating rooms, and purchased a high-tech Gamma Knife to perform brain surgery.

The first inkling of trouble for MCP filtered east from California in 2002. Dr. Chae Hyun Moon, the chief cardiologist at Tenet's Redding Medical Center, and Dr. Fidel Realyvasquez, a cardiac surgeon, were accused that year of running a macabre for-profit fraud upon Medicare—conducting hundreds of unnecessary heart catheterizations and bypass surgeries for which they billed the federal government. Tenet later agreed to pay the government $54 million to resolve federal fraud charges, although civil suits against the hospital and the doctors are still pending.

"If you have good insurance and want a hip replacement,

there are plenty of nice hospitals that will schedule you," says one
longtime MCP doctor. "Whereas if you're wheezing with the worst asthma
attack of your life, there isn't likely to be a hospital nearby."

As it turns out, there was more to the scam than a couple of zealous cardiologists. In the 12 months ending in December 2002, Redding Medical Center reported $92 million in pretax income. Its similarly sized neighbor down the street in Redding, Mercy Medical Center, brought in only $4 million. There wasn't $88 million worth of difference in the services they offered. Moon's procedures were part of the explanation, but the hospital was also using a more general practice to squeeze millions out of Medicare. This involved a complex billing category known as "outlier payments." Intending to support the care of particularly sick, or "outlier," patients, Medicare essentially allowed hospitals with very high patient costs—which were determined by whatever amounts the hospital chose to put in its bills—to charge the government—higher fees.

It boiled down to a remarkably simple scheme: To qualify for more outlier payments, Tenet hiked its prices. By 2002, when Medicare began to crack down on the practice, the company was earning more than $800 million a year on outlier payments. That year, Barbakow cashed in a whopping $111 million in stock options, a few months before resigning from his position as chairman and CEO.

At the MCP emergency room, Dr. Mead remembers one moment that tipped him off to the outlier system. An uninsured college student had come to the ER with a bad cut that required 27 stitches. About a month later, the student appeared in Mead's office, crying, in her hand a bill for $600 for the removal of the sutures, a procedure that had taken Mead all of 20 seconds using a pair of cheap scissors. Mead called administrators to complain but was told that was how things were done. What had happened, Mead would later realize, was that he had stumbled upon the iceberg of Tenet's inflated billings. "If Blue Cross had gotten the bill they would have said, 'Yeah, right,' and paid $30," he explains. "But since this was an uninsured person, they were charged the full price." Tenet had to charge someone the full price to demonstrate its high costs to Medicare.

"It turns out they don't know how to run hospitals," says Mead, who has a degree from Wharton Business School and was a Pepsico executive before going to medical school. "They know financial tricks."

WITH THE OUTLIER PAYMENTS yanked out from under Tenet, MCP suddenly fell deep into the red—the hospital lost more than $30 million in 2003, according to Tenet—and the full consequences of some of the company's management decisions began to hit home. Many of MCP's potentially money-earning fixtures, including its orthopedics department and pathology labs, had been allowed to wither away as doctors left in droves. "Most people who used those services were insured," notes Ginny Holzworth, an intensive-care nurse. "They removed these services, leaving basically services for the poor, which brought in no money. They stabbed MCP and let it bleed to death."

A consultant's report delivered in December concluded that MCP could be turned around, "if given a new clinical direction and a reasonable period of time." Tenet, losing massive amounts of money and heavily exposed to lawsuits and multiple federal and state investigations, couldn't be bothered. Management advised Drexel's medical school of the closing on December 17, 2003, the evening before the news release was faxed out. More than 150 years of history would essentially be erased without so much as a sniff.

In public statements, Tenet officials have said that the company did the best it could under difficult conditions, but that MCP was simply no longer viable. "This hospital was run by competent people and by a competent hospital management company," Philip Schaengold, Tenet's vice president for Pennsylvania, told a testy meeting of the Philadelphia City Council.

After much protest, and an intervention by Governor Rendell, Tenet and the state agreed to keep the hospital open until at least June 30 to give it time to seek a buyer. Temple and Einstein, two large Philadelphia hospital systems, were said to be interested, but as of this writing, neither had made a commitment to either buy MCP or keep its doors open long-term.

Whether or not MCP can survive with a different owner, the critical condition of hospitals around the country shows that it is not an isolated case. One-third of the nation's hospitals are now losing money every year, according to a 2002 report from the American Hospital Association, and many are in such precarious condition, they can't even get loans for badly needed improvements: Only 30 percent of hospitals seeking credit to fix their buildings or buy new equipment, the association reported, were able to get commercial bank financing. "As Wall Street experts have recognized," the report noted, "many of America's hospitals are on the edge of financial viability."

Dragged before the City Council repeatedly to explain their decision, Tenet officials sometimes sounded like Howard Dean. "We need universal health insurance in this country," Thomas Leonard, a Tenet attorney, said at a February 12 hearing. "It's a national problem. You can't solve it. Tenet can't solve it. And beating up Tenet isn't going to solve it."

At the same hearing, Morgan, the activist and dialysis patient, told his story while Tenet's Schaengold sat a few feet away. Morgan described the high-tension juggle of a working life with severe illness—the dozens of pills, the disturbed sleep and odd hours, the effort to be a normal father for his children. He told of his anxiety about finding another dialysis center. Then he began to weep. "I feel like you're playing with my life," he said, looking angrily at Schaengold. "I've got a family just like you. I've got a home, I live right."

Schaengold, a mustachioed man in his 50s, maintained an icy, composure. A week later, Tenet sacked him too.

ARE WE A NATION "UNDER GOD"?

BY SAMUEL HUNTINGTON

As this issue of *The American Enterprise* goes to press in June, the U.S. Supreme Court is considering whether the words "under God" in the Pledge of Allegiance are a violation of the separation of church and state. In 2002, a three-judge panel of the Ninth Circuit Court of Appeals in San Francisco decided by a two-to-one vote that the phrase represented an un-Constitutional "endorsement of religion" and "a profession of religious belief ... in monotheism."

President Bush termed this decision "ridiculous." Senate minority leader Tom Daschle (D-SD) called it "nuts"; Governor George Pataki of New York said it was "junk justice." The Senate passed a resolution, 99 to zero, urging that the decision be reversed, and members of the House of Representatives gathered on the steps of the Capitol to recite the Pledge and sing "God Bless America." A *Newsweek* poll found that 87 percent of the public supported inclusion of the words, while 9 percent were opposed. Eighty-four percent also said they approved of references to God in public settings, including schools and government buildings, so long as no "specific religion" was mentioned.

This battle over the Pledge has stimulated vigorous controversy on an issue central to America's identity. Opponents of "under God" (which was added to the pledge in 1954) argue that the United States is a secular country, that the First Amendment prohibits rhetorical or material state support for religion, and that people should be able to pledge allegiance to their country without implicitly also affirming a belief in God. Supporters point out that the phrase is perfectly consonant with the views of the framers of the Constitution, that Lincoln had used these words in the Gettysburg Address, and that the Supreme Court has long held that no one could be compelled to say the Pledge.

The man who brought this court challenge, Michael Newdow, aims "to ferret out all insidious uses of religion in daily life," according to the *New York Times*. "Why should I be made to feel like an outsider?" he asked. The Court of Appeals in San Francisco agreed that the words "under God" sent "a message to unbelievers that they are outsiders, not full members of the political community."

Newdow and the court majority got it right: Atheists are "outsiders" in the American community. Americans are one of the most religious people in the world, particularly compared to the peoples of other highly industrialized democracies. But they nonetheless tolerate and respect the rights of atheists and nonbelievers. Unbelievers do not have to recite the Pledge, or engage in any religiously tainted practice of which they disapprove. They also, however, do not have the right to impose their atheism on all those Americans whose beliefs now and historically have defined America as a religious nation.

Statistics say America is not only a religious nation but also a Christian one. Up to 85 percent of Americans identify themselves as Christians. Brian Cronin, who litigated against a cross on public land in Boise, Idaho, complained, "For Buddhists, Jews, Muslims, and other non-Christians in Boise, the cross only drives home the point that they are strangers in a strange land." Like Newdow and the Ninth Circuit judges, Cronin was on target. America is a predominantly Christian nation with a secular government. Non-Christians may legitimately see themselves as strangers because they or their ancestors moved to this "strange land" founded and peopled by Christians—even as Christians become strangers by moving to Israel, India, Thailand, or Morocco.

Americans have been extremely religious and overwhelmingly Christian throughout their history. The seventeenth-century settlers founded their communities in America in large part for religious reasons. Eighteenth-century Americans and their leaders saw their Revolution in religious and largely biblical terms. The Revolution reflected their "covenant with God" and was a war between "God's elect" and the British "Antichrist." Jefferson, Paine, and other Deists and nonbelievers felt it necessary to invoke religion to justify the Revolution. The Continental Congress declared days of fasting to implore the forgiveness and help of God, and days of thanksgiving for what He had done to promote their cause. Well into the nineteenth century, Sunday church services were held in the chambers of the Supreme Court and the House of Representatives. The Declaration of Independence appealed to "Nature's God," the "Creator," "the Supreme Judge of the World," and "divine Providence" for approval, legitimacy, and protection.

The Constitution includes no such references. Yet its framers firmly believed that the republican government they were creating could only last if it was deeply rooted in morality and religion. "A Republic can only be supported by pure religion or austere morals," John Adams said. The Bible offers "the only system that ever did or ever will preserve a republic in the world." Washington agreed: "Reason and experience both forbid us to expect that national morality can prevail in exclusion of religious principles." The happiness of the people, good order, and civil government, declared the Massachusetts constitution of 1780, "essentially depend on piety, religion, and morality." Fifty years after the Constitution was adopted, Tocqueville reported that all Americans held religion "to be indispensable to the maintenance of republican institutions."

The words "separation of church and state" do not appear in the Constitution, and, as the historian Sidney Mead has pointed out, Madison spoke not of "church" and "state," European concepts with little relevance to America, but of "sects" and "Civil authority," and the "line" not the "wall" between them. Religion and society were coterminous.

Some people cite the absence of religious language in the Constitution and the provisions of the First Amendment as evidence that America is fundamentally a secular country. Nothing could be further from the truth. At the end of the eighteenth century, religious establishments existed throughout Europe and in several American states. Control of the church was a key element of state power, and the established church, in turn, provided legitimacy to the state. The framers of the American Constitution prohibited an established national church in order to limit the power of government and to protect and strengthen religion. The purpose of "separation of church and state," as William McLoughlin has said, was not to establish freedom *from* religion but establish freedom *for* religion. It was spectacularly successful. In the absence of a state religion, Americans were not only free to believe as they wished but also free to create whatever religious communities and organizations they desired. As a result, Americans have been unique among peoples in the diversity of sects, denominations, and religious movements to which they have given birth, almost all embodying some form of Protestantism. When substantial numbers of Catholic immigrants arrived, it was eventually possible to accept Catholicism as one more denomination within the broad framework of Christianity. The proportion of the population who were "religious adherents," that is church members, percent of Americans said they America's religious commitment increased fairly steadily through prayed one or more times a day, most of American history.

America's religious commitment is the primary source of our exceptional history.

European observers repeatedly commented on the high levels of religious commitment of Americans compared to that of their own peoples. As usual, Tocqueville said it most eloquently: "On my arrival in the United States the religious aspect of the country was the first thing that struck my attention, and the longer I stayed there, the more I perceived the great political consequences resulting from this new state of things." In France religion and liberty opposed each other. The Americans, in contrast, "have succeeded [in] combining admirably … the spirit of religion and the spirit of liberty." Religion in America "must be regarded as the first of their political institutions."

A half century after Tocqueville, English historian and statesman James Bryce came to a similar conclusion. The Americans are "a religious people"; religion "influences conduct … probably more than it does in any other modern country, and far more than it did in the so-called ages of faith." And again, "the influence of Christianity seems to be … greater and more widespread in the United States than in any part of western Continental Europe, and I think greater than in England." A half century after Bryce, the eminent Swedish observer Gunnar Myrdal judged that "America probably is still the most religious country in the Western world." And a half century after him, the English historian Paul Johnson described America as "a God-fearing country, with all it implies." America's religious commitment "is a primary source—*the* primary source, I think—of American exceptionalism."

Today, overwhelming majorities of Americans affirm religious beliefs. When asked in 1999 whether they believed in God, or a universal spirit, or neither, 86 percent of those polled said they believed in God, 8 percent in a universal spirit, and 5 percent in neither. When asked in 2003 simply whether they believed in God or not, 92 percent said yes. In a series of 2002–03 polls, 57 to 65 percent of Americans said religion was very important in their lives, 23 to 27 percent said fairly important, and 12 to 18 percent said not very important. In 1996, 39 percent of Americans said they believed the Bible is the actual word of God and should be taken literally; 46 percent said they believed the Bible is the word of God but not everything in it should be taken literally word for word; 13 percent said it is not the word of God.

Large proportions of Americans also appear to be active in the practice of their religion. In 2002 and 2003, an average of 65 percent of Americans claimed membership in a church or synagogue. About 40 percent said they had attended church or synagogue in the last seven days. Roughly 33 percent said they went to church at least once a week, 10 percent almost every week, 15 percent about once a month, 27 percent seldom or a few times a year, and 15 percent never. In the same time period, about 60 percent of Americans said they prayed one or more times a day, more than 20 percent once or more a week, about 10 percent less than once a week, and 10 percent never. Given human nature, these claims of religious practice may be overstated, but even accounting for this factor, the level of religious activity was still high; and the extent to which Americans believe the right response is to affirm their religiosity is itself evidence for the centrality of religious norms in American society.

Reflecting on the depth of American religiosity, the Swedish theologian Krister Stendhal remarked, "Even the atheists in America speak in a religious key." Only about 10 percent of Americans, however, espouse atheism, and most Americans do not approve of it. A 1973 poll asked: "Should a socialist or an atheist be allowed to teach in a college or university?" The community leaders surveyed approved of both teaching. The American public as a whole agreed that socialists could teach (52 percent yes, 39 percent no), but decisively rejected the idea of atheists on college or university faculties (38 percent yes, 57 percent no). Since the 1930s, the willingness of Americans to vote for a Presidential candidate from a minority group has increased dramatically, with over 90 percent of those polled in 1999 saying they would vote for a black, Jewish, or female Presidential candidate, while 59 percent were willing to vote for a homosexual. Only 49 percent, however, were willing to vote for an atheist. Americans seem to agree with the Founding Fathers that their republican government requires a religious base, and hence they find it difficult to accept the explicit rejection of God and religion.

These high levels of religiosity would be less significant if they were the norm for other countries. Americans differ dramatically, however, in their religiosity from the people of other economically developed countries. This religiosity is conclusively revealed in three cross-national surveys. First, in general, the level of religious commitment of countries varies inversely with their level of economic development: People in poor countries are highly religious, those in rich countries are not. America is the glaring exception. If America were like most other countries at her level of economic development, only 5 percent of Americans would think religion very important.

Second, an International Social Survey Program questionnaire in 1991 asked people in 17 countries seven questions concerning their belief in God, life after death, heaven, and other religious concepts. Reporting the results, George Bishop ranked the countries according to the percentage of their population that affirmed these religious beliefs. The United States was far ahead in its overall level of religiosity, ranking first on four questions, second on one, and third on two, for an average ranking of 1.7. It was followed by Northern Ireland (2.4), where religion is obviously of crucial importance to both Protestants and Catholics, and then by four Catholic countries. After them came New Zealand, Israel, five Western European countries, and four former communist countries, with East Germany last, the least religious on six of the seven questions. According to this poll, Americans are more deeply religious than even the people of countries like Ireland and Poland, where religion has been the core of national identity differentiating them from their traditional British, German, and Russian antagonists.

Third, the 1990–93 World Values Survey asked nine questions concerning religiosity in 41 countries. Overall these data show the United States to be one of the most religious countries in the world. Most striking is the high religiosity of America in comparison to other Protestant countries. The top 15 religious countries include Nigeria, India, and Turkey (the only African and predominantly Hindu and Muslim countries in the sample), eight predominantly Catholic countries, one Orthodox country (Romania), sharply divided Northern Ireland, and two predominantly Protestant countries, the United States in fifth place and Canada in fifteenth place. Except for Iceland, all the other predominantly Protestant countries fall well into the lower half of those surveyed. America is thus by a large margin the most religious Protestant country.

A long with their general religiosity, the Christianity of Americans has also impressed foreign observers. "There is no country in the world," Tocqueville said, "where the Christian religion retains a greater influence over the souls of men than in America." Christianity, Bryce similarly observed, is "the national religion" of Americans. Americans have also affirmed their Christian identity. "We are a Christian people," the Supreme Court declared in 1811. The Senate Judiciary Committee echoed these words exactly in 1853, adding that "almost our entire population belong to or sympathize with some one of the Christian denominations." In the midst of the Civil War, Lincoln also described Americans as "a Christian people." In 1892 the Supreme Court again declared, "This is a Christian nation." In 1908, a House of Representatives committee said that "the best and only reliance for the perpetuation of the republican institution is upon a Christian patriotism." In 1917 Congress passed legislation declaring a day of prayer in support of the war effort and invoking America's status as a Christian nation. In 1931 the Supreme Court reaffirmed its earlier view: "We are a Christian people, according to one another the equal right of religious freedom, and acknowledging with reverence the duty of obedience to the will of God."

While the balance between Protestants and Catholics shifted over the years, the proportion of Americans identifying themselves as Christian has remained relatively constant. In three surveys between 1989 and 1996, between 84 and 88 percent of Americans said they were Christians. The proportion of Christians in America rivals or exceeds the proportion of Jews in Israel, of Muslims in Egypt, of Hindus in India, and of Orthodox believers in Russia.

America's Christian identity has, nonetheless, been questioned on two grounds. First, it is argued that America is losing that identity because non-Christian religions are expanding in numbers, and Americans are thus becoming a multireligious and not simply a multidenominational people. Second, it is argued that Americans are losing their religious identity and are becoming secular, atheistic, materialistic, and indifferent to their religious heritage. Neither of these propositions comes close to the truth.

The argument that America is losing its Christian identity due to the spread of non-Christian religions was advanced by several scholars in the 1980s and 1990s. They pointed to the growing numbers of Muslims, Sikhs, Hindus, and Buddhists in American society. Hindus in America increased from 70,000 in 1977 to 800,000 in 1997. Muslims amounted to at least 3.5 million in 1997, while Buddhists numbered somewhere between 750,000 and 2 million. From these developments, the proponents of de-Christianization argue, in the words of Professor Diana Eck, that "religious diversity" has "shattered the paradigm of America" as an overwhelmingly Christian country with a small Jewish minority. Another scholar suggested that public holidays should be adjusted to accommodate this increasing religious diversity and that, for a start, it would be desirable to "have one Christian holiday (say, Christmas), but replace Easter and Thanksgiving with a Muslim and Jewish holiday." In some measure, however, the holiday trend was in the opposite direction. Hanukkah, "traditionally a minor Jewish holiday," has, according to Professor Jeff Spinner, been elevated into the "Jewish Christmas" and displaced Purim as a holiday, so as "to fit in better with the dominant culture."

The increases in the membership of some non-Christian religions have not, to put it mildly, had any significant effect on America's Christian identity. As a result of assimilation, low birth rates, and intermarriage, the proportion of Jews dropped from 4 percent in the 1920s to 3 percent in the 1950s to slightly over 2 percent in 1997. If the absolute numbers claimed by their spokesmen are correct, by 1997 about 1.5 percent of Americans were Muslim, while Hindus and Buddhists were each less than one percent. The numbers of non-Christian, non-Jewish believers undoubtedly will continue to grow, but for years to come they will remain extremely small. Some increases in the membership of non-Christian religions come from conversions, but the largest share is from immigration and high birth rates. The immigrants of these religions, however, are far outnumbered by the huge numbers of immigrants from Latin America and the Philippines, almost all of whom are Catholic and also have high birth rates. Latin American immigrants are also converting to evangelical Protestantism. In addition, Christians in Asia and the Middle East have been more likely than non-Christians to migrate to America. As of 1990, a majority of Asian Americans were Christian rather than Buddhist or Hindu. Among Korean Americans, Christians outnumber Buddhists by at least ten to one. Roughly one third of Vietnamese immigrants are Catholic. About two thirds of Arab Americans have been Christian rather than Muslim, although the number of Muslims was growing rapidly before September 11. While a precise judgment is impossible, at the start of the twenty-first century the United States was probably becoming more rather than less Christian in its religious composition.

Americans tend to have a certain catholicity toward religion: All deserve respect. Given this general tolerance of religious diversity, non-Christian faiths have little alternative but to recognize and accept America as a Christian society. "Americans have always thought of themselves as a Christian nation," argues Jewish neoconservative Irving Kristol, "equally tolerant of all religions so long as they were congruent with traditional Judeo-Christian morality. But equal toleration … never meant perfect equality of status in fact." Christianity is not legally established, "but it is established informally, nevertheless." And, Kristol warns his fellow Jews, that is a fact they must accept.

But if increases in non-Christian membership haven't diluted Christianity in America, hasn't it been diluted, dissolved, and supplanted over time by a culture that is pervasively secular and irreligious, if not anti-religious? These terms describe segments of American intellectual, academic, and media elites, but not the bulk of the American people. American religiosity could still be high by absolute measures and high relative to that of comparable societies, yet the secularization thesis would still be valid if the commitment of Americans to religion declined over time. Little or no evidence exists of such a decline. The one significant shift that does appear to have occurred is a drop in the 1960s and 1970s in the religious commitment of Catholics. An overall falloff in church attendance in the 1960s was due to a decline in the proportion of Catholics attending mass every Sunday. In 1952, 83 percent of Catholics said that religion was very important in their lives; in 1987, 54 percent of Catholics said this. This shift brought Catholic attitudes on religion more into congruence with those of Protestants.

Over the course of American history, fluctuations did occur in levels of American religious commitment and religious involvement. There has not, however, been an overall downward trend in American religiosity. At the start of the twenty-first century, Americans are no less committed, and are quite possibly more committed, to their Christian identity than at any time in their history.

Samuel Huntington is Albert J. Weatherhead III University Professor at Harvard, and a member of AEI's Council of Academic Advisers. This is adapted from his latest book Who Are We? The Challenges to America's National Identity.

UNIT 6

Social Change and The Future

Unit Selections

Key Points to Consider

- How can the aging of the world's population cause problems?

- What dangers does humankind's overexploitation of the environment create?

- What are some of the major problems that technology is creating?

- How bright is America's future? What are the main threats to it? What are some of its main challenges?

- How should America handle the terrorist threat?

- Would you say that both democracy and capitalism are triumphant today? Explain your answer. What kind of problems can democracy and capitalism cause?

 **Links: www.dushkin.com/online/**
These sites are annotated in the World Wide Web pages.

Human Rights and Humanitarian Assistance
http://www.etown.edu/vl/humrts.html

The Hunger Project
http://www.thp.org

Terrorism Research Center
http://www.terrorism.com/index.shtml

United Nations Environment Program (UNEP)
http://www.unep.ch

William Davidson Institute
http://www.wdi.bus.umich.edu

Fascination with the future is an enduring theme in literature, art, poetry, and religion. Human beings are anxious to know if tomorrow will be different from today and in what ways it might differ. Coping with change has become a top priority in the lives of many. One result of change is stress. When the future is uncertain and the individual appears to have little control over what happens, stress can be a serious problem. On the other hand, stress can have positive effects on people's lives if they can perceive changes as challenges and opportunities.

Any discussion of the future must begin with a look at issues of population and the environment. In the first unit article, the authors discuss a problem of world population that has gone largely unnoticed—which is its aging. We celebrate the wonderful decline in mortality that has occurred this century, but it does eventually present societies with the problem of caring for swelling ranks of the elderly. Costs will be considerable and raises the question of how those costs will be paid. In Japan the elderly population is already 71 percent as large as the working age population and a burden upon them. In the next article Lester R. Brown reviews the ways that the environment is declining and portrays the planet as a global bubble economy that is based on the overconsumption of the Earth's natural capital assets. Unless world consumption and the resulting environmental depletion and damage are reduced, the global bubble will burst with severe economic, political, and social consequences. He also provides much advice on how to solve the problems. The last article that focuses on the environment reports on the Pentagon study of the potential severe impacts of global warming that may include economic and political instability and even war. Extreme impacts of global warming may be unlikely but they must not be ignored.

The next subsection in unit 6 addresses the linkage between technological change and society. Both articles in this section raise concerns about the possible negative effects of supposedly beneficial technologies. The first article, by Eduardo Goncalves, evaluates another sophisticated technology—nuclear power. It can win wars and supply useful electrical energy, but it may have already killed 175 million people. Furthermore, the way scientists and governments have acted regarding nuclear energy shows that they cannot always be trusted to pursue the public good in their decisions regarding new technologies. One big technology story concerns genetic engineering, and one of its important areas of application is agriculture. The crucial question is whether it produces great agricultural advances or ecological nightmares. Graham T.T. Molitor evaluates the potential of genetic engineering in agriculture. The benefits are numerous and large and growing populations will make them absolutely necessary. Not only will it increase agricultural productivity but also it will make foods much more nutritious.

The next subsection focuses on the new crisis of terrorism. It begins with an article by Steven Simon that discusses how terrorism has changed from limited violence as a tactic in political struggles to religiously motivated indiscriminate mass killings to inflict maximum harm on a hated people. How can the U.S. protect itself from such a foe? Not being land based, it is very hard

to combat militarily. Its attacks will be surprises and defense is nearly impossible with so many potential targets to protect. The next article by Shmuel Bar examines the religious sources of Islamic Terrorism. His thesis is that "Modern international Islamist terrorism is a natural offshoot of twentieth-century Islamic fundamentalism." Jihad against infidels who rule over Muslim lands is a traditional belief that modern radical Muslims use to mobilize Islamist terrorists. Bar explains the way these ideas are operating today.

The final subsection looks at the future in terms of some of the most important trends and how to create a good future out of them. William Van Dusen Wishard, president of a firm that does research on trends, has authored the first of these articles. Armed with many interesting statistics on trends he argues that the world is undergoing a great transition that is based on globalization, rapid technological development, and "a long-term spiritual and psychological reorientation that's increasingly generating uncertainty and instability." As a result, "the soul of America—indeed, of the world—is in a giant search for some deeper and greater expression of life." The last article by Fareed Zakaria provides a hopeful picture of world progress in the twentieth century in political development toward democracy and in economic development toward competitive capitalism. However, these processes can also be destructive and challenging to old orders that make it difficult to speculate about what these trends will bring about in the twenty first century.

COPING WITH METHUSELAH

Public Policy Implications of a Lengthening Human Life Span

Henry J. Aaron; William B. Schwartz

The capacity to manipulate the genetic templates that shape all living beings was long the plaything of science fiction. In the final decades of the 20th century, however, intellectual advance transmuted genetic tinkering from alchemy into science. In 1953 two young scientists identified the double helix comprising four nucleotides entwined in the code of all life, thereby opening the first chapter in the saga of molecular biology. Then in 2001 two competing scientific teams produced a draft of the human genome, introducing a new therapeutic era in which medical professionals may be able to slow human aging and make celebrating 100th birthdays almost routine.

No one can predict the precise extent or timing of advances in molecular biology. No one can know exactly when particular diseases will be prevented or cured. No one can foresee when, or even if, human aging will be slowed or stopped. No one yet knows for sure whether humans' genetic makeup limits life span or, if it does, what those limits might be. Some families include more nonagenarians and centenarians than any roll of nature's dice could explain, a fact that suggests genes' powerful influence on longevity. Even if life span is now limited, molecular biology may reveal that these limits are not fixed and may provide ways to slow aging and prevent or cure illnesses that cause physical decline and death.

Scientific advance has revolutionized man's centuries-old assault on human illness. Physicians have long understood, in some sense, the basis of successful medical treatments, without being able to penetrate the underlying processes by which their interventions worked. The fundamental reasons wiry antibiotics killed pathogens, for example, remained for years as mysterious to the discoverers of those drugs and to the physicians who used them as they were to the patients whose lives they saved.

As the 21st century begins, scientists are increasingly working from a fundamental understanding of cells, proteins, and genes to design interventions that reverse, block, or otherwise forestall illnesses. In the words of Nobel Prize winner Alfred Gilman, scientists are now "able to complete [their] understanding of the wiring diagram of" the signaling switchboard in each type of cell." With that knowledge in hand, they now have—or soon will—the means to design drugs or to directly change how cells operate to correct the genetic defects each person inherits or acquires during life from mutations or other sources.

In the coming century, human mortality rates may begin falling rapidly. Eventually molecular biology may lengthen human life almost unimaginably. Is the Age of Methuselah at hand? And if so, what will it mean for public policy in the United States—and the world?

Our Uncertain Demographic Future

Advances in public health, nutrition, and medical treatment over the past century first set in motion an increase in human life expectancy. With mortality rates now declining roughly 0.6

percent a year, demographers project that longevity will continue to increase and that the elderly will constitute a growing share of the U.S. population. A biomedical revolution causing mortality rates to fall more rapidly could intensify these trends and have important demographic implications.

Many scientists have long believed that the human life span has a natural limit. The finding by 19th-century scientist August Wiseman that cells stopped reproducing after a certain number of divisions seems consistent with this hypothesis. But even if a natural limit exists, the practical question is how far that limit exceeds current average life span and what can be done to push today's life span closer to that limit. One theory of aging draws an analogy between a person and a machine consisting of many systems, each essential for its operation. Each system within the machine remains functional until too many of its constituent parts fail, leading the machine itself to fail over time in patterns that closely resemble human mortality rates. The implication is that medical progress comes through interventions that prevent or postpone the failure of the constituent parts of each of the biological "systems" essential for life.

Rapidly falling mortality rates would affect longevity relatively quickly but would take many years to alter the age distribution of the population. The U.S. Social Security Administration, which assumes that mortality rates will continue to decline at the current annual rate, about 0.6 percent, projects that people born in 2030 will have a life expectancy at birth of just over 84 years; those born in 2075, just over 86. If mortality rates decline 2 percent a year, babies born in 2030 could expect to live 104 years; those born in 2075, more than 115 years. But even this rapid rate of decline would have little effect on the U.S. population distribution until past mid-century.

How would rapidly declining mortality affect the U.S. workplace and public programs to support the elderly? Much would depend on the onset of physical decline in the longer-lived Americans. Would greatly increased longevity mean longer periods of dependency? Or would older Americans stay healthy longer? If workers were able to keep working for a greater portion of their lives than they do now, the cost of supporting the elderly might increase only slightly because the ratio of retirees to active workers might increase only a little. If current retirement age patterns persisted, however, the cost of increased longevity would rise sharply as people spent ever more years outside the labor force.

Little in economic theory or empirical evidence suggests that sharply increased longevity would directly affect retirement behavior. But if workers extended their years in retirement, it would boost pension costs, which, in turn, would probably force changes in public policy to encourage workers to extend their working lives. Higher pension costs would necessitate sharply increased pension contributions by workers or their employers, or higher taxes on workers and employers to support public pensions, or cuts in benefits and increases in the age at which pensions are first paid. These changes would likely cause Americans to work more years than they now do.

Rapidly falling mortality would certainly affect government revenues and spending. If longer-living Americans extended their working lives, they would earn and produce more, swelling tax revenues. But increased longevity would also boost government spending on Social Security, Medicare, and Medicaid, all of which are already projected to grove rapidly as baby boomers begin retiring. And a major new decline in mortality rates would drive spending above these already steeply rising trends.

Social Security costs are officially projected to increase between now and 2080, from just under 11 percent to just over 20 percent of earnings subject to the Social Security payroll tax. If mortality rates were to fall 2 percent annually while the duration of working lives remained the same, Social Security costs would reach more than 25 percent of payroll. Raising the age at which full Social Security benefits are paid by one month a year starting in 2018 would eliminate most of the additional longevity-related cost. The message is simple and clear: as longevity increased, so too would Social Security costs.

Projecting the effects of longevity on Medicare and Medicaid costs is much trickier because spending depends not only on the number of beneficiaries, but also on trends in the cost of medical care. Regardless of trends in mortality rates, Medicare and Medicaid costs will soar because per capita medical costs for everyone will increase. Medical spending also rises with age as people's bodies gradually wear out or become subject to disease. Some observers see decline as an immutable consequence of a person's age since birth—an 80-year-old whose life expectancy is 85 will be in the same state of decline as an 80-year-old whose life expectancy is 110. But Stanford University economist John Shoven thinks it more plausible that medical spending depends on years until death. And the fact that disability rates have fallen as mortality rates have improved supports that view. If mortality declines at historical rates, projections based on the years-since-birth assumption show Medicare costing about 2 percent of gross domestic product more in 2070 than if costs art: projected on the years-until-death assumption. The difference jumps to roughly 5 percent of GDP if mortality rates fall 2 percent a year. In the case of Medicaid, the cost difference in 2070 between projections is a bit over 1 percent of GDP if mortality declines at officially assumed rates, but nearly 6 percent if it declines 2 percent a year.

The story is straightforward. Costs of Social Security, Medicare, and Medicaid will rise during the early part of the 21st century, primarily because of the aging of the baby-boom generation and—in the case of the health programs—increases in medical costs. Accelerated increases in longevity would affect costs primarily in the second half of the century and beyond. If, in the best scenario, physical decline were delayed as lives were lengthened, the added health care costs would be modest. If, in addition, working lives increased, the added revenues from a bigger labor force would help defray these costs.

A Global Perspective

The effects of a sharp increase in longevity would not be confined to one nation. The swelling ranks of the elderly already threaten pension systems in many countries and may have important effects on international capital flows. Dramatically increased longevity would require most developed nations to reform their retirement systems to keep them sustainable. Increased public spending on retirement would lower saving rates in developed nations, which could prevent many developing nations from borrowing to finance growth.

Over the past 150 years, both birth and mortality rates have fallen nearly everywhere. From the standpoint of economic development, the ideal pattern is a drop in birth rates followed years later by declining mortality. That pattern keeps the ratio of the working-age population to the total population quite high for a time, enabling domestic saving to support high rates of investment. Eventually, however, the aged population increases. If birth rates remain low, overall population, excluding immigration, will fall.

Only wealthy nations would be able to afford the costly medical interventions that would sharply increase longevity. Because mortality rates in those nations are already low among younger citizens, declining mortality rates primarily would increase the number of those over age 50. The ratio of the elderly to the working-age population would therefore increase most in wealthy nations. The most extreme effects would show up in nations such as Japan, where the elderly population is already 71 percent as large as the working-age population. The effect in the United States would be much smaller because above-average birth and immigration rates are projected to keep the working-age population growing at least slowly.

Current population aging is already likely to lower both saving and investment in high-income countries and to increase saving in middle-income and poor nations, pushing foreign trade balances of rich nations into deficit and those of the rest of the world into surplus. A 2-percent-a-year reduction in mortality rates would intensify these effects. Saving would decline sharply, investment somewhat less. With mortality falling fastest in nations that can afford medical innovation, trade deficits are especially likely for rich nations.

These projections are tentative and depend heavily on how increasing longevity affects the world of work. If people's working lives lengthen, investment will be higher, the cost of private and public pensions lower. Technological change will also influence investment opportunities and the call on saving to finance that investment. Nevertheless, extending longevity is likely to be quite expensive, and rich nations are far more likely than poor nations to incur those costs.

The Ethical Dilemmas of Increasing Longevity

Throughout the 20th century, public health advances, rising income, and medical discoveries added decades to life expectancy at birth. These advances raised practical questions, such as how to pay for pension and health costs for the elderly, but relatively few ethical problems. Some painful moral problems did arise: whether it is ever right—and, if so, under what circumstances and after what steps—to curtail care for extremely ill patients or to allow severely damaged newborns to die. But few observers questioned whether clean water, the reduction of poverty, or effective antibiotics were ethically desirable.

The prospect of an engineered extension of human life, however, has created a major stir among ethicists. As Alexander Morgan Capron, University Professor of Law and Medicine at the University of Southern California, notes, past developments in longevity took opportunities once available to the few and extended them to the many. But some interventions now in prospect would change the fundamental character of humans—for example, by changing their genes.

The ethical issues raised by life extension depend in part on its consequences. Most problematic would be increasing the average age of death primarily by increasing a person's years of physical and mental decline. But, as Capron points out, no one can foresee whether the coming scientific advances will add decades of mental and physical vigor or decades of senility and debility.

The ethical issues will also be shaped by the means used to increase longevity. Irreversible interventions, such as altering human genes, raise more questions than do interventions that can be stopped, such as a hormone that a patient can stop taking. And many innovations that promise to extend life will require risky experimentation and must be attended by stringent procedural safeguards.

Another issue is access to life-extending interventions. Capron dismisses the views of some ethicists that once a person has reached a "normal" life span, access to life-extending care is not ethically required. Both the duration of "normal" lives and the content of "normal" interventions, he notes, are inescapably elastic. Both depend on expectations that are themselves influenced by technological possibilities.

Finally, Capron notes that questions about suicide and passive euthanasia are likely to become increasingly prominent. If the capacity to extend life is available, is it euthanasia if caregivers do not use it—or suicide if patients actively reject it?

Leon Kass, Francis Fukayama, and others have posited that life extension is not a legitimate goal of science and that success in such an endeavor threatens to deprive people of essential attributes of their humanity. Finitude, they argue, lends life savor, sweetness, and value. A quest for superhuman intelligence, looks, or longevity is quite literally inhuman. Gradually, step by step, like the person immersed in a bath slowly warming from comfortable to lethal, humans would surrender what it means to be human by a series of steps each seemingly reasonable, but cumulatively dehumanizing. Capron is more concerned that successful life extension could produce a dystopia with ever-larger parts of life spent in dependence.

When Imagined Futures Become Real

A flowering of biomedical science holds the promise, though not the certainty, that human beings will soon live routinely to ages almost unthinkable today. Although such a development still has an air of science fiction for most Americans, its implications must be considered seriously. Authors of fiction tend to place utopias and dystopias in an imagined future. Readers may be revulsed by the nightmares of *Brave New World* or *1984*, chilled by the cold impersonality of *The Rise of the Meritocracy*, or swept by the romantic notions of *Looking Backward*.

The authors of these imagined futures had a free hand to paint with their chosen palettes. Social scientists, having no such license, must contemplate with academic detachment the problems, challenges, and opportunities to be faced if living to 90, 100, or beyond becomes common. Utopias do not adorn the pages of honest analysis.

Henry J. Aaron is Bruce and Virginia MacLaury Senior Fellow in the Brookings Economic Studies program. William B. Schwartz is a professor of medicine at the Keck School of Medicine at the University of Southern California. They are the editors of Coping with Methuselah: The Impact of Molecular Biology on Medicine and Society *(Brookings, 2003), from which this article is drawn.*

Rescuing a planet under stress

Lester R. Brown

Understanding the Problem

As world population has doubled and as the global economy has expanded sevenfold over the last half-century, our claims on the Earth have become excessive. We are asking more of the Earth than it can give on an ongoing basis.

We are harvesting trees faster than they can regenerate, overgrazing rangelands and converting them into deserts, overpumping aquifers, and draining rivers dry. On our cropland, soil erosion exceeds new soil formation, slowly depriving the soil of its inherent fertility. We are taking fish from the ocean faster than they can reproduce.

We are releasing carbon dioxide into the atmosphere faster than nature can absorb it, creating a greenhouse effect. As atmospheric carbon dioxide levels rise, so does the earth's temperature. Habitat destruction and climate change are destroying plant and animal species far faster than new species can evolve, launching the first mass extinction since the one that eradicated the dinosaurs sixty-five million years ago.

Throughout history, humans have lived on the Earth's sustainable yield—the interest from its natural endowment. But now we are consuming the endowment itself. In ecology, as in economics, we can consume principal along with interest in the short run but in the long run it leads to bankruptcy.

In 2002 a team of scientists led by Mathis Wackernagel, an analyst at Redefining Progress, concluded that humanity's collective demands first surpassed the Earth's regenerative capacity around 1980. Their study, published by the U.S. National Academy of Sciences, estimated that our demands in 1999 exceeded that capacity by 20 percent. We are satisfying our excessive demands by consuming the Earth's natural assets, in effect creating a global bubble economy.

Bubble economies aren't new. U.S. investors got an up-close view of this when the bubble in high-tech stocks burst in 2000 and the NASDAQ, an indicator of the value of these stocks, declined by some 75 percent. According to the *Washington Post*, Japan had a similar experience in 1989 when the real estate bubble burst, depreciating stock and real estate assets by 60 percent. The bad-debt fallout and other effects of this collapse have left the once-dynamic Japanese economy dead in the water ever since.

The bursting of these two bubbles affected primarily people living in the United States and Japan but the global bubble economy that is based on the overconsumption of the Earth's natural capital assets will affect the entire world. When the food bubble economy, inflated by the overpumping of aquifers, bursts, it will raise food prices worldwide. The challenge for our generation is to deflate the economic bubble before it bursts.

Unfortunately, since September 11, 2001, political leaders, diplomats, and the media worldwide have been preoccupied with terrorism and, more recently, the occupation of Iraq. Terrorism is certainly a matter of concern, but if it diverts us from the environmental trends that are undermining our future until it is too late to reverse them, Osama bin Laden and his followers will have achieved their goal in a way they couldn't have imagined.

In February 2003, United Nations demographers made an announcement that was in some ways more shocking than the 9/11 attack: the worldwide rise in life expectancy has been dramatically reversed for a large segment of humanity—the seven hundred million people living in sub-Saharan Africa. The HIV epidemic has reduced life expectancy among this region's people from sixty-two to forty-seven years. The epidemic may soon claim more lives than all the wars of the twentieth century. If this teaches us anything, it is the high cost of neglecting newly emerging threats.

The HIV epidemic isn't the only emerging mega-threat. Numerous nations are feeding their growing populations by overpumping their aquifers—a measure that virtually guarantees a future drop in food production when the aquifers are depleted. In effect, these nations are creating a food bubble economy—one where food production is artificially inflated by the unsustainable use of groundwater.

Another mega-threat—climate change—isn't getting the attention it deserves from most governments, particularly that of the United States, the nation responsible for one-fourth of all carbon emissions. Washington, D.C., wants to wait until all the evidence on climate change is in, by which time it will be too late to prevent a wholesale warming of the planet. Just as governments in Africa watched HIV infection rates rise and did little about it, the United States is watching atmospheric carbon dioxide levels rise and doing little to check the increase.

Other mega-threats being neglected include eroding soils and expanding deserts, which jeopardize the livelihood and food supply of hundreds of millions of the world's people. These issues don't even appear on the radar screen of many national governments.

Thus far, most of the environmental damage has been local: the death of the Aral Sea, the burning rainforests of Indonesia, the collapse of the Canadian cod fishery, the melting of the glaciers that supply Andean cities with water, the dust bowl forming in northwestern China, and the depletion of the U.S. great plains aquifer. But as these local environmental events expand and multiply, they will progressively weaken the global economy, bringing closer the day when the economic bubble will burst.

Humanity's demands on the Earth have multiplied over the last half-century as our numbers have increased and our incomes have risen. World population grew from 2.5 billion in 1950 to 6.1 billion in 2000. The growth during those fifty years exceeded that during the four million years since our ancestors first emerged from Africa.

Incomes have risen even faster than population. According to Erik Assadourian's *Vital Signs* 2003 article, "Economic Growth Inches Up," income per person worldwide nearly tripled from 1950 to 2000. Growth in population and the rise in incomes together expanded global economic output from just under $7 trillion (in 2001 dollars) of goods and services in 1950 to $46 trillion in 2000—a gain of nearly sevenfold.

Population growth and rising incomes together have tripled world grain demand over the last half-century, pushing it from 640 million tons in 1950 to 1,855 million tons in 2000, according to the U.S. Department of Agriculture (USDA). To satisfy this swelling demand, farmers have plowed land that was highly erodible—land that was too dry or too steeply sloping to sustain cultivation. Each year billions of tons of topsoil are being blown away in dust storms or washed away in rainstorms, leaving farmers to try to feed some seventy million additional people but with less topsoil than the year before.

Demand for water also tripled as agricultural, industrial, and residential uses increased, outstripping the sustainable supply in many nations. As a result, water tables are falling and wells are going dry. Rivers are also being drained dry, to the detriment of wildlife and ecosystems.

Fossil fuel use quadrupled, setting in motion a rise in carbon emissions that is overwhelming nature's capacity to fix carbon dioxide. As a result of this carbon-fixing deficit, atmospheric carbon dioxide concentrations climbed from 316 parts per million (ppm) in 1959, when official measurement began, to 369 ppm in 2000, according to a report issued by the Scripps Institution of Oceanography at the University of California.

The sector of the economy that seems likely to unravel first is food. Eroding soils, deteriorating rangelands, collapsing fisheries, falling water tables, and rising temperatures are converging to make it more difficult to expand food production fast enough to keep up with demand. According to the USDA, in 2002 the world grain harvest of 1,807 million tons fell short of world grain consumption by 100 million tons, or 5 percent. This shortfall, the largest on record, marked the third consecutive year of grain deficits, dropping stocks to the lowest level in a generation.

Now the question is: can the world's farmers bounce back and expand production enough to fill the hundred-million-ton shortfall, provide for the more than seventy million people added each year, and rebuild stocks to a more secure level? In the past, farmers responded to short supplies and higher grain prices by planting more land and using more irrigation water and fertilizer. Now it is doubtful that farmers can fill this gap without further depleting aquifers and jeopardizing future harvests.

At the 1996 World Food Summit in Rome, Italy, hosted by the UN Food and Agriculture Organization (FAO), 185 nations plus the European community agreed to reduce hunger by half by 2015. Using 1990–1992 as a base, governments set the goal of cutting the number of people who were hungry—860 million—by roughly 20 million per year. It was an exciting and worthy goal, one that later became one of the UN Millennium Development Goals.

But in its late 2002 review of food security, the UN issued a discouraging report:

> This year we must report that progress has virtually ground to a halt. Our latest estimates, based on data from the years 1998-2000, put the number of undernourished people in the world at 840 million.... a decrease of barely 2.5 million per year over the eight years since 1990–92.

Since 1998–2000, world grain production per person has fallen 5 percent, suggesting that the ranks of the hungry are now expanding. As noted earlier, life expectancy is plummeting in sub-Saharan Africa. If the number of hungry people worldwide is also increasing, then two key social indicators are showing widespread deterioration in the human condition.

The ecological deficits just described are converging on the farm sector, making it more difficult to sustain rapid growth in world food output. No one knows when the growth in food production will fall behind that of demand, driving up prices, but it may be much sooner than we think. The triggering events that will precipitate future food shortages are likely to be spreading water shortages interacting with crop-withering heat waves in key food-producing regions. The economic indicator most likely to signal serious trouble in the deteriorating relationship between the global economy and the Earth's ecosystem is grain prices.

Food is fast becoming a national security issue as growth in the world harvest slows and as falling water tables and rising temperatures hint at future shortages. According to the USDA more than one hundred nations import part of the wheat they consume. Some forty import rice. While some nations are only marginally dependent on imports, others couldn't survive without them. Egypt and Iran, for example, rely on imports for 40 percent of their grain supply. For Algeria, Japan, South Korea, and Taiwan, among others, it is 70 percent or more. For Israel and Yemen, over 90 percent. Just six nations—Argentina,

Australia, Canada, France, Thailand, and the United States—supply 90 percent of grain exports. The United States alone controls close to half of world grain exports, a larger share than Saudi Arabia does of oil.

Thus far the nations that import heavily are small and middle-sized ones. But now China, the world's most populous nation, is soon likely to turn to world markets in a major way. As reported by the International Monetary Fund, when the former Soviet Union unexpectedly turned to the world market in 1972 for roughly a tenth of its grain supply following a weather-reduced harvest, world wheat prices climbed from $1.90 to $4.89 a bushel. Bread prices soon rose, too.

If China depletes its grain reserves and turns to the world grain market to cover its shortfall—now forty million tons per year—it could destabilize world grain markets overnight. Turning to the world market means turning to the United States, presenting a potentially delicate geopolitical situation in which 1.3 billion Chinese consumers with a $100-billion trade surplus with the United States will be competing with U.S. consumers for U.S. grain. If this leads to rising food prices in the United States, how will the government respond? In times past, it could have restricted exports, even imposing an export embargo, as it did with soybeans to Japan in 1974. But today the United States has a stake in a politically stable China. With an economy growing at 7 to 8 percent a year, China is the engine that is powering not only the Asian economy but, to some degree, the world economy.

For China, becoming dependent on other nations for food would end its history of food self-sufficiency, leaving it vulnerable to world market uncertainties. For Americans, rising food prices would be the first indication that the world has changed fundamentally and that they are being directly affected by the growing grain deficit in China. If it seems likely that rising food prices are being driven in part by crop-withering temperature rises, pressure will mount for the United States to reduce oil and coal use.

For the world's poor—the millions living in cities on $1 per day or less and already spending 70 percent of their income on food—rising grain prices would be life threatening. A doubling of world grain prices today could impoverish more people in a shorter period of time than any event in history. With desperate people holding their governments responsible, such a price rise could also destabilize governments of low-income, grain-importing nations.

Food security has changed in other ways. Traditionally it was largely an agricultural matter. But now it is something that our entire society is responsible for. National population and energy policies may have a greater effect on food security than agricultural policies do. With most of the three billion people to be added to world population by 2050 (as estimated by the UN) being born in nations already facing water shortages, child-bearing decisions may have a greater effect on food security than crop planting decisions. Achieving an acceptable balance between food and people today depends on family planners and farmers working together.

Climate change is the wild card in the food security deck. The effect of population and energy policies on food security differ from climate in one important respect: population stability can be achieved by a nation acting unilaterally. Climate stability cannot.

Instituting the Solution

Business as usual—Plan A—clearly isn't working. The stakes are high, and time isn't on our side. The good news is that there are solutions to the problems we are facing. The bad news is that if we continue to rely on timid, incremental responses our bubble economy will continue to grow until eventually it bursts. A new approach is necessary—a Plan B—an urgent reordering of priorities and a restructuring of the global economy in order to prevent that from happening.

Plan B is a massive mobilization to deflate the global economic bubble before it reaches the bursting point. Keeping the bubble from bursting will require an unprecedented degree of international cooperation to stabilize population, climate, water tables, and soils—and at wartime speed. Indeed, in both scale and urgency the effort required is comparable to the U.S. mobilization during World War II.

Our only hope now is rapid systemic change—change based on market signals that tell the ecological truth. This means restructuring the tax system by lowering income taxes and raising taxes on environmentally destructive activities, such as fossil fuel burning, to incorporate the ecological costs. Unless we can get the market to send signals that reflect reality, we will continue making faulty decisions as consumers, corporate planners, and government policymakers. Ill-informed economic decisions and the economic distortions they create can lead to economic decline.

Stabilizing the world population at 7.5 billion or so is central to avoiding economic breakdown in nations with large projected population increases that are already overconsuming their natural capital assets. According to the Population Reference Bureau, some thirty-six nations, all in Europe except Japan, have essentially stabilized their populations. The challenge now is to create the economic and social conditions and to adopt the priorities that will lead to population stability in all remaining nations. The keys here are extending primary education to all children, providing vaccinations and basic health care, and offering reproductive health care and family planning services in all nations.

Shifting from a carbon-based to a hydrogen-based energy economy to stabilize climate is now technologically possible. Advances in wind turbine design and in solar cell manufacturing, the availability of hydrogen generators, and the evolution of fuel cells provide the technologies needed to build a climate-benign hydrogen economy. Moving quickly from a carbon-based to a hydrogen-based energy economy depends on getting the price right, on incorporating the indirect costs of burning fossil fuels into the market price.

On the energy front, Iceland is the first nation to adopt a national plan to convert its carbon-based energy economy to one based on hydrogen. Denmark and Germany are leading the world into the age of wind. Japan has emerged as the world's leading manufacturer and user of solar cells. With its commercialization of a solar roofing material, it leads the world in electricity generation from solar cells and is well positioned to assist in the electrification of villages in the developing world. The Netherlands leads the industrial world in exploiting the bicycle as an alternative to the automobile. And the Canadian province of Ontario is emerging as a leader in phasing out coal. It plans to replace its five coal-fired power plants with gas-fired plants, wind farms, and efficiency gains.

Stabilizing water tables is particularly difficult because the forces triggering the fall have their own momentum, which must be reversed. Arresting the fall depends on quickly raising water productivity. In pioneering drip irrigation technology, Israel has become the world leader in the efficient use of agricultural water. This unusually labor-intensive irrigation practice, now being used to produce high-value crops in many nations, is ideally suited where water is scarce and labor is abundant.

In stabilizing soils, South Korea and the United States stand out. South Korea, with once denuded mountainsides and hills now covered with trees, has achieved a level of flood control, water storage, and hydrological stability that is a model for other nations. Beginning in the late 1980s, U.S. farmers systematically retired roughly 10 percent of the most erodible cropland, planting the bulk of it to grass, according to the USDA. In addition, they lead the world in adopting minimum-till, no-till, and other soil-conserving practices. With this combination of programs and practices, the United States has reduced soil erosion by nearly 40 percent in less than two decades.

Thus all the things we need to do to keep the bubble from bursting are now being done in at least a few nations. If these highly successful initiatives are adopted worldwide, and quickly, we can deflate the bubble before it bursts.

Yet adopting Plan B is unlikely unless the United States assumes a leadership position, much as it belatedly did in World War II. The nation responded to the aggression of Germany and Japan only after it was directly attacked at Pearl Harbor on December 7, 1941. But respond it did. After an all-out mobilization, the U.S. engagement helped turn the tide, leading the Allied Forces to victory within three and a half years.

This mobilization of resources within a matter of months demonstrates that a nation and, indeed, the world can restructure its economy quickly if it is convinced of the need to do so. Many people—although not yet the majority—are already convinced of the need for a wholesale restructuring of the economy. The issue isn't whether most people will eventually be won over but whether they will be convinced before the bubble economy collapses.

History judges political leaders by whether they respond to the great issues of their time. For today's leaders, that issue is how to deflate the world's bubble economy before it bursts. This bubble threatens the future of everyone, rich and poor alike. It challenges us to restructure the global economy, to build an eco-economy.

We now have some idea of what needs to be done and how to do it. The UN has set social goals for education, health, and the reduction of hunger and poverty in its Millennium Development Goals. My latest book, *Plan B*, offers a sketch for the re-

structuring of the energy economy to stabilize atmospheric carbon dioxide levels, a plan to stabilize population, a strategy for raising land productivity and restoring the earth's vegetation, and a plan to raise water productivity worldwide. The goals are essential and the technologies are available.

We have the wealth to achieve these goals. What we don't yet have is the leadership. And if the past is any guide to the future, that leadership can only come from the United States. By far the wealthiest society that has ever existed, the United States has the resources to lead this effort.

Yet the additional external funding needed to achieve universal primary education in the eighty-eight developing nations that require help is conservatively estimated by the World Bank at $15 billion per year. Funding for an adult literacy program based largely on volunteers is estimated at $4 billion. Providing for the most basic health care is estimated at $21 billion by the World Health Organization. The additional funding needed to provide reproductive health and family planning services to all women in developing nations is $10 billion a year.

Closing the condom gap and providing the additional nine billion condoms needed to control the spread of HIV in the developing world and Eastern Europe requires $2.2 billion—$270 million for condoms and $1.9 billion for AIDS prevention education and condom distribution. The cost per year of extending school lunch programs to the forty-four poorest nations is $6 billion per year. An additional $4 billion per year would cover the cost of assistance to preschool children and pregnant women in these nations.

In total, this comes to $62 billion. If the United States offered to cover one-third of this additional funding, the other industrial nations would almost certainly be willing to provide the remainder, and the worldwide effort to eradicate hunger, illiteracy, disease, and poverty would be under way.

The challenge isn't just to alleviate poverty, but in doing so to build an economy that is compatible with the Earth's natural systems—an eco-economy, an economy that can sustain progress. This means a fundamental restructuring of the energy economy and a substantial modification of the food economy. It also means raising the productivity of energy and shifting from fossil fuels to renewables. It means raising water productivity over the next half-century, much as we did land productivity over the last one.

It is easy to spend hundreds of billions in response to terrorist threats but the reality is that the resources needed to disrupt a modern economy are small, and a Department of Homeland Security, however heavily funded, provides only minimal protection from suicidal terrorists. The challenge isn't just to provide a high-tech military response to terrorism but to build a global society that is environmentally sustainable, socially equitable, and democratically based—one where there is hope for everyone. Such an effort would more effectively undermine the spread of terrorism than a doubling of military expenditures.

We can build an economy that doesn't destroy its natural support systems, a global community where the basic needs of all the Earth's people are satisfied, and a world that will allow us to think of ourselves as civilized. This is entirely doable. To paraphrase former President Franklin Roosevelt at another of those hinge points in history, let no one say it cannot be done.

The choice is ours—yours and mine. We can stay with business as usual and preside over a global bubble economy that keeps expanding until it bursts, leading to economic decline. Or we can adopt Plan B and be the generation that stabilizes population, eradicates poverty, and stbilizes climate. Historians will record the choice—but it is ours to make.

Lester R. Brown is president of the Earth Policy Institute. This article is adapted from his recently released book *Plan B: Rescuing a Planet Under Stress and a Civilization in Trouble*, which is available for free downloading at www.earth-policy.org

The Pentagon and Climate Change

THE EDITORS

Climate Collapse: The Pentagon's Weather Nightmare
—*Fortune*, February 9, 2004

Now the Pentagon Tells Bush: Climate Change Will Destroy Us

—*Observer* (London), February 22, 2004

Pentagon-Sponsored Climate Report Sparks Hullabaloo in Europe

—*San Francisco Chronicle*, February 25, 2004

The Sky is Falling! Say Hollywood and, Yes, the Pentagon

—*New York Times*, February 29, 2004

Abrupt climate change has been a growing topic of concern for about a decade for climate scientists, who fear that global warming could shut down the ocean conveyer that warms the North Atlantic, plunging Europe and parts of North America into Siberian-like conditions within a few decades or even years. But it was only with the recent appearance of a Pentagon report on the possible social effects—in terms of instability and war—of abrupt climate change that it riveted public attention. As the *Observer* (February 22) put it, "Climate change over the next 20 years could result in global catastrophe costing millions of lives in wars and natural disasters."

Indeed, widespread public alarm, particularly in Europe, was the predictable response to the Pentagon's October 2003 report, *An Abrupt Climate Change Scenario and its Implications for United States National Security*, once it became available early this year.[1] In an attempt to quiet these fears Defense Department officials and the authors of the report quickly came forward to say that the entire exercise was speculative and "intentionally extreme"; that the whole thing had been misconstrued and overblown in certain press accounts.

Was this then simply a "hullabaloo" about nothing, as the *San Francisco Chronicle* suggested, or are there dangers associated with global warming that have not been sufficiently appreciated thus far? To answer this question it is necessary to approach the issue in stages, by first addressing global warming, then abrupt climate change and its inherent social dangers, and finally how the present system of production constitutes a barrier to any ready solution.

Global Warming: How Bad Is It?

A natural greenhouse effect is crucial to the earth's atmosphere. As carbon dioxide, methane, and other greenhouse gases accumulate in the atmosphere they trap heat that would otherwise radiate off into space. This natural greenhouse effect along with proximity to the sun serves to warm the earth making it habitable to diverse species. But now, as a result of enhanced greenhouse gas emissions from human production, most notably the burning of fossil fuels, this same life-supporting greenhouse effect is pushing average global temperatures higher and higher. Carbon dioxide concentration in the atmosphere is now at its highest point in the last 420,000 years and likely in the last 20 million years. Rising sea levels, heat waves, crop failures, worsening floods and droughts, and more extreme weather conditions in general are all to be expected as a result of such increases in average global temperature.

Some of the warming to be experienced in coming decades is already locked-in. Greenhouse gases have atmospheric lifetimes of decades to centuries. Even if societies were to cease fossil fuel use and end all other forms of greenhouse gas emissions today the accumulation of such gases in the atmosphere would likely generate further warming on the order of 0.5°C (0.9°F) during this century. While if we do nothing to limit such emissions global average surface temperature could conceivably rise as much as 5.8°C (10.4°F) between 1990 and 2100, exceeding the change in average temperature separating us from the last ice age. Few informed analysts now expect the increase in average global temperature from 1990–2100 to be kept below a 2°C (3.6°F) increase, even with the most concerted social action over the next couple of decades. The main fear at present is that the rise in global temperature will be two or three times as large if human society is unable to act decisively.[2]

Global warming is expected to be a growing factor in coming decades in species extinction, the rate of which at present is higher than at any time since the disappearance of the dinosaurs 65 million years ago. In mountainous regions all around the earth plant and animal species are ascending higher and higher as warming occurs. But mountains only reach so far. Consequently, the species occupying the topmost ecological niches are now in the process of ascending "to heaven."[3] We do not know how many other species will share this fate during this century. But we do know that the earth's species in general will be massively affected, that biological diversity will continue to decrease, and that if we do nothing and average global temperatures rise to the upper levels that leading climate scientists think possible by the year 2100 it could prove catastrophic, seriously threatening ecosystems and destabilizing human society.

Still, the ruling economic and political interests and their attendant elites tell us not to be worried. Never mind the threats to other species. Human society, we are frequently told, is different. It can evolve rapidly by economic and technological means and thus adapt to global warming, which from its standpoint can be viewed as slow, "gradual" change. What is often projected for global society then is increased discomfort rather than massive social upheaval and dislocation. Orthodox economists generally caution that we should do nothing that might limit economic growth. Instead they see the only answer as lying in a bigger economy, which will give us more means of addressing future contingencies.

Abrupt Climate Change

Nevertheless, there is every reason to believe that placing so much faith in economic growth and technological change as answers to global warming is short-sighted and naive. Considerable uncertainty exists as to how far human society can actually support such "gradual" climate change—since human beings are themselves part of nature and dependent on the world around them in manifold ways. But the problem does not stop there. Scientists are now raising the even more alarming question of abrupt climate change, i.e., climate change of a scale and suddenness—shifting dramatically in years rather than decades or centuries—that would definitely have catastrophic effects for human society.

Abrupt climate change is usually seen as change arising from gradual causes that lead to the crossing of a threshold, triggering a sudden shift to a new state—with the shift determined by the climate system itself and oc-

curring at a rate much faster than the initial cause.[4] Such shifts have occurred numerous times in history, one of the clearest being the abrupt cooling of the Younger Dryas (named after an arctic wildflower that thrived in the climate of the time), which began 12,700 years ago and lasted 1,300 years, interrupting the warming associated with the end of the last ice age. A lesser instance of abrupt climate change occurred 8,200 years ago and lasted around a century. In the worst of all current, plausible scenarios, such "abrupt climate change" could occur sometime over the next couple of decades—though this is still seen by scientists as highly unlikely.

Abrupt climate change is believed to result from disruption of the thermohaline circulation, a global ocean conveyor that moves warm, saline tropical waters northward in the Atlantic with the Gulf Stream as its northern arm, and then loops south. ("Thermohaline" comes from the Greek words for heat "thermos" and for salt "halos.") The heat from this warmer water, when it reaches the North Atlantic, is released into the atmosphere, creating milder winters than would otherwise exist at those latitudes, and allowing the dense surface waters to cool and sink. This draws additional warmer, saline water from the south, helping to keep the conveyor going. Differences in the density of ocean waters associated with the saline content thus drive this ocean conveyor. Abrupt climate change arises from a lessening or collapse of the thermohaline circulation due to increased river runoff, melting ice, and changes in precipitation—all of which serve to increase the amount of freshwater supplied to the North Atlantic. As the salinity of the ocean waters decreases a dramatic lessening or complete collapse of the North Atlantic conveyor circulation can occur. The current global warming is seen as potentially triggering this effect. According to the UN Intergovernmental Panel on Climate Change (IPCC), in *Climate Change 2001*,"beyond 2100, the thermohaline circulation could completely, and possibly irreversibly, shut-down in either hemisphere" if global warming is "large enough and applied long enough" (p. 16).

Two basic scenarios are worth considering. (1) If the ocean conveyor slows down or collapses during the next two decades it could cool the North Atlantic region by as much as 5°C (9°F), creating winters of much greater severity. (2) If, however, the conveyor slows down in a century the drop in temperature in the North Atlantic could temporarily compensate for the rise in surface temperature associated with the enhanced greenhouse effect—though once the thermohaline circulation recovered the "deferred" warming could be delivered within a decade. The second of these two scenarios is viewed as much more likely. Yet, recent scientific studies, including a major report in 2002 by the National Academy of Sciences, have stressed that the thermohaline circulation could possibly "decrease . . . very fast,"—resulting in a sudden switch of climate early this century that although still thought unlikely cannot be ruled out altogether. Seeming to confirm these fears, a report in *Nature* in 2002 concluded that the North Atlantic has been freshening dramatically for 40 years; while a report a year earlier suggested that the ocean conveyor may already be slowing down.[5]

Faced with the uncertain hazards of such a "low probability, high impact" event, scientists associated with the National Academy of Sciences study recommended that society take what steps it could, if not too costly, to protect itself against such an extreme outcome. "If a shutdown were to happen soon," Richard Alley, who chaired the scientific team releasing the National Academy of Sciences study, observed in *The Two-Mile Time Machine*, "it could produce a large event, perhaps almost as large as the Younger Dryas, dropping northern temperatures and spreading droughts far larger than the changes that have affected humans through recorded history, and perhaps speeding warming in the far south. The end of humanity? No. An uncomfortable time for humanity? Yes."[6]

These assessments and recommendations on abrupt climate change were offered with so much caution by climate scientists that they might easily have been ignored altogether by a society that in its upper echelons is devoted to the accumulation of capital and little else. That this did not happen is due to the fact that the issue was taken up and dramatized in the Pentagon report.

The Pentagon Elevates the Threat

The story behind the Pentagon report on abrupt climate change is almost as remarkable as the contents of the report itself. The National Academy study of this issue crossed the desk of Andrew Marshall, director of the Pentagon's Office of Net Assessment. Marshall, who has worked for every secretary of defense since James Schlesinger in the 1970s, is a legendary "wise man," known as "Yoda," at the Pentagon. When they need someone to think about big things, the Department of Defense turns to Marshall. His most famous achievement was the promotion of missile defense. It was Marshall who authorized the $100,000 grant for Peter Schwartz and Doug Randall of the Global Business Network to analyze abrupt climate change for the Pentagon. The intent was obviously to have economic futurologists visualize the possible effects of such abrupt climate change, since they would be in the best position to speculate on the economic and social fallout of such a catastrophic development, and thus upgrade it to a major Pentagon concern.

Schwartz was a surprising choice for such a task since he was best known previously for his book *The Long Boom* (1999). In the 1990s he was a contributing writer to *Wired* magazine. Together with Peter Leyden, a senior editor of the magazine, and Joe Hyatt of the Stanford University Business School he got caught up in the idea that the New Economy, rooted in today's digital high technology, pointed to a long economic boom stretching from 1980 to at least 2020. During this time the economy would, they argued in the book, simply "grow more" based on the

New Economy model pioneered by the United States, with global growth of "possibly even 6 percent" (p. 266). Their first version of this thesis in their *Wired* article on the long boom came out in July 1997 and created a stir. The article together with the book that followed two years later, constituted the most extreme version of the great millennial celebration. According to Schwartz and his co-authors, who grossly misunderstood the main economic tendencies of the time, the U.S. economy was rocketing throughout the 1990s and was likely to accelerate further in the 2000s. All such New Economy mythology was put to an end, however, by the bursting of the speculative bubble and the dramatic stock market decline of 2000, followed by recession in 2001 and slow growth and employment stagnation ever since. Nevertheless, it was to Schwartz, the failed prophet of a long New Economy boom, to whom Marshall turned to dramatize the consequences of abrupt climate change.[7]

An Abrupt Climate Change Scenario and its Implications for United States National Security by Peter Schwartz and Doug Randall begins by challenging the way in which climate change is usually approached:

> When most people think about climate change, they imagine gradual increases in temperature and only marginal changes in other climatic conditions, continuing indefinitely or even leveling off at some time in the future. The conventional wisdom is that modern civilization will either adapt to whatever weather conditions we face and that the pace of climate change will not overwhelm the adaptive capacity of society, or that our efforts such as those embodied in the Kyoto protocol will be sufficient to mitigate the impacts. The IPCC documents the threat of gradual climate change and its impact to food supplies and other resources of importance to humans will not be so severe as to create security threats. Optimists assert that the benefits from technological innovation will be able to outpace the negative effects of climate change.
>
> Climatically, the gradual view of the future assumes that agriculture will continue to thrive and growing seasons will lengthen. Northern Europe, Russia, and North America will prosper agriculturally while southern Europe, Africa, and Central and South America will suffer from increased dryness, heat, water shortages, and reduced production. Overall, global food production under many typical climate scenarios increases (p. 4).

Schwartz and Randall argue against such complacent views of global warming, insisting that they do not take sufficient account of the discontinuities that may arise as warming causes various thresholds to be crossed. More frequent droughts, for example, could have disastrous and cumulative effects. Still, the worst effects from such gradual warming are seen as applying mainly to the poorer countries of the global South rather than the richer countries of the global North—the main source of carbon dioxide emissions. All of this encourages a do-nothing or do-little attitude in the northern centers of world power.

Abrupt climate change alters this picture dramatically. Such change would create catastrophic conditions for human society; and rather than falling first and foremost on the global South the direct effects of a shutdown of the thermohaline conveyor would bear down on the global North—specifically those countries bordering the North Atlantic. Schwartz and Randall are clear that they are not actually predicting such abrupt climate change in the near future (though it is certain to occur in the long-term future). Rather, they offer a "plausible" if unlikely scenario "for which there is reasonable evidence" so as to "explore potential implications for United States national security" (p. 5). They model their scenario on the event of 8,200 years ago rather than on the much worse Younger Dryas. In their scenario a "thermohaline circulation collapse" causes a drop in average surface temperature in northern Europe of up to 3.3°C (6°F) along with severe temperature drops throughout the North Atlantic, lasting about a century. Colder temperatures, wind and dryness in the global North are accompanied by increased warmth and drought in much of the rest of the world.

The picture they paint is one of agricultural decline and extreme weather conditions, stretching energy resources, throughout the globe. Relatively well-off populations with ample natural resources and food producing capabilities, such as the United States and Australia, are seen as building "defensive fortresses" around themselves to keep massive waves of would-be immigrants out, while much of the world gyrates toward war. "Violence and disruption stemming from the stresses created by abrupt changes in the climate pose a different type of threat to national security than we are accustomed to today. Military confrontation may be triggered by a desperate need for natural resources such as energy, food and water rather than by conflicts over ideology, religion, or national honor. The shifting motivation for confrontation would alter which countries are most vulnerable and the existing warning signs for security threats" (p. 14). As the world's carrying capacity declines under harsh climatic conditions, warfare becomes widespread—producing increased dangers of thermonuclear war.

For Schwartz and Randall the lesson is clear. Human society must "prepare for the inevitable effects of abrupt climate change—which will likely come [the only question is when] regardless of human activity" (p. 21). If the scenario that they depict is actually in the cards, it is already too late to do anything to stop it. What can be done under these circumstances is to make sure that the necessary security measures are in place to stave off the most disastrous consequences resulting from social instability. Since this is a report commissioned by the Pentagon, the emphasis is on how to "create vulnerability metrics" to determine which countries are likely to be hit the hardest ecologically, economically, and socially and thus will be propelled in the direction of war. Such information will make it possible for the United States to act in its own security interest. The narrow objective is thus to safeguard fortress America at all cost.

Although the ecological repercussions are supposed to hit the global North the hardest, the scenario provided by the Pentagon report with respect to instability and war follows conventional ideological paths, focusing mostly on the global South. The possibility that the United States itself might in such circumstances attempt to seize world oil supplies and other natural resources is not raised by the report. The U.S. response is depicted as entirely defensive, mainly concerned with holding off unwelcome waves of would-be immigrants, and trying to create an atmosphere of peace and stability in the world under much harsher global conditions.

Given the contents of this report it is not surprising that it initially generated dismay and widespread fears when it was made public in February. At that point the Pentagon quickly stepped in to quiet the alarm that the report had set off. Marshall himself released a statement that the Pentagon study "reflects the limits of scientific models and information when it comes to predicting the effects of abrupt global warming." Although backed up by "significant scientific evidence … much of what this study predicts," Marshall indicated, "is still speculation." Pentagon officials meanwhile declared that the abrupt climate change report, although commissioned by their legendary "Yoda," had not been passed on to Marshall's superiors in the Defense Department and the Bush administration (*San Francisco Chronicle*, February 25, 2004; *New York Times*, February 29, 2004).

Yet the real importance of *An Abrupt Climate Change Scenario* does not lie in its impact on the top brass in the Pentagon much less their envionmentally-challenged superiors in the White House. Instead, its historical significance derives from the more general contention made at the beginning of the report that "because of the potentially dire consequences, the risk of abrupt climate change, although uncertain and quite possibly small, should be elevated beyond a scientific debate to a U.S. national security concern" (p. 3). It is a small step from this view to one that insists that the nature of the threat demands that we begin to consider other, radical social alternatives to business as usual, which must be elevated to the forefront of public discussions.

Accelerated Climate Change

Here it is crucial to recognize that abrupt climate change as currently modeled by scientists, though the most dramatic, is not the only nongradual outcome possible as a result of global warming. Scientists are even more concerned at present about the potential for positive feedbacks that will greatly amplify global warming, increasing the rate of its advance and the speed with which it crosses various ecological thresholds. According to the IPCC in *Climate Change 2001*, "As the CO_2 concentration of the atmosphere increases, ocean and land will take up a decreasing fraction of anthropogenic CO_2 emissions. The net effect of land and ocean climate feedbacks as indicated by models is to further increase projected atmospheric CO_2 concentrations, by reducing both the ocean and land uptake of CO_2" (p. 12). The hydrological cycle (evaporation, precipitation, and runoff) could accelerate as a result of global warming, driving temperatures higher faster. Water vapor, the most potent natural greenhouse gas, could trap additional heat increasing the rate at which average surface temperatures rise. The melting of highly reflective ice and snow could result in further absorbtion of sunlight, leading to additional global warming. The capacity of both forests and oceans to absorb carbon dioxide could decrease, creating a positive feedback loop that accelerates climate change. All of this is taken into account to some extent in the IPCC reports. But given the level of uncertainty the possibility of surprising developments under these circumstances is very great.

The grim reality is that the more threatening scenarios with respect to global warming are becoming increasingly plausible as the data keeps coming in. Carbon dioxide levels in the atmosphere increased at an accelerated level over the past year. The increase of 3 parts per million was well above the 1.8 parts per million annual increase on average over the past decade, and three times the year-to-year increase experienced half a century ago. Although it is too soon to be sure if this means anything or not (it may reflect mere annual variance), this kind of evidence is leading scientists to worry that positive feedbacks may already be at work, serving to accelerate the whole problem (*New York Times*, March 21, 2004).

Capitalism and Carbon Dioxide

Both the capitalist economy and the world climate represent complex, dynamic systems. The uncertainty with respect to climate change and its economic effects has to do with the interaction of these two complex systems. To make matters worse, both the climate system and the human economy are subsets of the biosphere and are inseparably interconnected in extremely complex ways with innumerable other biogeochemical processes. Many of these other biospheric processes are also being transformed by human action.

It is not uncommon for analyses of climate change to assume that the world economy is essentially healthy except for disturbances that could result from the climate. This, however, is in error and underestimates the economic vulnerability of populations and whole societies. As indicated only a few months ago in this space, at present "half the world's population lives on less than two dollars per day, with most of those either chronically malnourished or continually concerned with where their next meal will come from. Many have no access to clean water (1 billion), electricity (2 billion), or sanitation (2.5 billion)" (Fred Magdoff, "A Precarious Existence," *Monthly Review*, February 2004). Economic growth is slowing in ways that have deepened the economic crisis for human populations. At the same time, "nature's economy" is also in trouble, viewed in terms of the diversity of life on the planet. Economic and ecological vulnerabilities are everywhere.

For the Pentagon, the answer to all of these dangers would seem to be straightforward: arm to the teeth, prepare for greater threats than ever from thermonuclear war, and build an impregnable wall around the United States, closing the global masses out. All of this is depicted by Schwartz and Randall. Yet a more rational response to potential highimpact climate events would be to seek to reorganize society, and to move away from imperatives of accumulation, exploitation, and degradation of the natural environment—the "after me the deluge" philosophy—that lies at the base of most of our global problems.

The truth is that addressing the global warming threat to any appreciable degree would require at the very least a chipping away at the base of the system. The scientific consensus on global warming suggests that what is needed is a 60–80 percent reduction in greenhouse gas emissions below 1990 levels in the next few decades in order to avoid catastrophic environmental effects by the end of this century—if not sooner. The threatening nature of such reductions for capitalist economies is apparent in the rather hopeless state at present of the Kyoto Protocol, which required the rich industrial countries to reduce their greenhouse gas emissions by an average of 5.2 percent below 1990 levels by 2008–2012. The United States, which had steadily increased its carbon dioxide emissions since 1990 despite its repeated promises to limit its emissions, pulled out of the Kyoto Protocol in 2001 on the grounds that it was too costly. Yet, the Kyoto Protocol was never meant to be anything but the first, small, in itself totally inadequate step to curtail emissions. The really big cuts were to follow.

Even if the Kyoto Protocol were to be enacted (its future right now is uncertain and depends largely on whether Russia decides to go along with the climate treaty) this would only open the door to bigger questions: Will the rich countries of the global North agree to cut their carbon emissions to the extent required? How can the poorer countries of the global South be brought into the climate accord? There would be little opportunity for most of these poor countries—still the victims of imperialism—to develop economically if they were forced to cut back sharply in their average level of per capita greenhouse gas emissions at this point. Since the atmosphere cannot support increasing levels of carbon dioxide and most of its capacity to do so without high levels of global warming has already been taken up by the rich countries of the center, countries in the periphery are likely to be severely constrained in their use of fossil fuels unless the countries in the center drastically reduce their levels of emissions—on the order of 80–90 percent.

Third world countries insist that the North has an ecological debt to the South, arising from a history of ecological imperialism, and that the only way to redress this and to create a just and sustainable climate regime is to base any solution on per capita emissions. Such a position is rooted in the recognition that the United States, to take the most notorious example, emits 5.6 metric tons of carbon dioxide per person per year,[8] while the whole rest of the world outside of the G-7 countries (the United States, Canada, Germany, Britain, Japan, Italy and France) releases only 0.7 tons of carbon dioxide per person annually on average.[9] Inequality of this kind is a major barrier to a smooth climate transition and means that the necessary change must be revolutionary in nature. The only just and sustainable climate regime will be one in which there is a contraction of per capita carbon dioxide emissions to levels that are globally sustainable, together with a convergence of rich and poor countries around these low, globally sustainable emissions levels. Such safe per capita emissions levels would be less than a tenth of what the North currently emits per capita. One estimate claims that "based on the 1990 target for climate stabilization, everyone in the world would have a per capita allowance of carbon of around 0.4 tonnes, per year."[10]

Obviously, equalization of per capita emissions at low levels for all countries is not something that the United States and the other nations at the center of the system will readily accept. Yet third world countries that desperately need development cannot be expected to give up the right to equality in per capita emissions. Any attempt to impose the main burdens for global warming on underdeveloped countries in accordance with past imperialistic practices will thus inevitably fail. To the extent that the United States and other advanced capitalist nations promote such a strategy they will only push the world into a state of barbarism, while catastrophically undermining the human relation to the biosphere.

Easter Island and the Earth

For environmentalists the destruction of the ecology and civilization of Easter Island around 1400–1600 A.D. has long been both a mystery and metaphor for our times. We now know that the giant stone statues, the erection of which resulted in the destruction of the island's forests and with them a whole ecology and civilization, were the main symbols of the power and prestige of competing chiefs and their clans. As Jared Diamond explains: "A chief's status depended on his statues: any chief who failed to cut trees to transport and erect statues would have found himself out of a job."[11] Due to such a narrow acquisitive logic—an early treadmill of production analogous to our own—the Easter Islanders drove their ecology and society to the point of extinction.

Are we headed for a similar disaster today—only on a planetary scale? To quote Diamond again:

Thanks to globalization, international trade, jet planes, and the Internet, all countries on Earth today share resources and affect each other, just as did Easter's eleven clans. Polynesian Easter Island was as isolated in the Pacific Ocean as the Earth is today in space. When the Easter Islanders got into difficulties, there was nowhere to which they could flee, or to which they could turn for help; nor shall we modern Earthlings have recourse elsewhere if our troubles increase. Those are the reasons why people see the collapse of Easter Island society as a metaphor, a worst-case scenario, for what may lie ahead in our own future.

Easter Island society got into trouble because of a class system. With its island world increasingly under ecological strain, the chiefs and priests were overthrown by military leaders and the society descended into the barbarism of civil war and then declined completely. Here too is a lesson for our time: we need to confront the class system and reorganize society in line with the needs of all of its inhabitants before barbarism descends upon us.

The Pentagon report itself takes on a different meaning here. It depicted abrupt climate change and a descent into internecine war. It was "intentionally extreme." But as the fate of Easter Island suggests, it may not have been extreme enough.

Notes

1. Available at **www.ems.org**.
2. Thomas R. Karl & Kevin E. Trenberth, "Modern Global Climate Change," *Science* 302, p. 1721; Intergovernmental Panel on Climate Change, *Climate Change 2001* (Cambridge: Cambridge University Press, 2001), pp. 7, 13; Tom Athanasiou & Paul Baer, *Dead Heat* (New York: Seven Stories, 2002), pp. 43–47.
3. "All Downhill from Here?," *Science* 303 (March 12, 2004).
4. National Research Council, *Abrupt Climate Change: Inevitable Surprises* (Washington, D.C.: National Academy Press, 2002) p. 14.
5. Robert B. Gagosian, "Abrupt Climate Change: Should We Be Worried?," World Economic Forum, Davos, Switzerland, January 27, 2003, http://www.whoi.edu; National Research Council, *Abrupt Climate Change*, pp. 115–16B. Dickson, et. al., "Rapid Freshening in the Deep Atlantic Ocean Over the Past Four Decades," *Nature*, 416 (April 25, 2002); B. Hansen, et. al., "Decreasing Overflow from the Nordic Seas into the Atlantic Ocean Through the Faroe Bank Channel Since 1950," *Nature*, 411 (June 21, 2001).
6. Richard B. Alley, *The Two-Mile Time Machine* (Princeton: Princeton University Press, 2000), p. 184.
7. There were no doubt rational motives to assigning the task of writing such a report to Schwartz, who had shown that he had all the necessary dramatic skills of the professional futurologist. Given his past history, and his absolute faith in the system, he could not be viewed as a prophet of doom and gloom or as an enemy of business. Further, a paragraph of *The Long Boom* (p. 153) had actually pointed to the possibility of a shutdown of the thermohaline circulation and the coming of a "another Ice Age"—though this was introduced in a generally pollyan-

naish view of the ecological crisis in which the "long boom" itself provided all the answers.

8. Measured in carbon units.

9. John Bellamy Foster, *Ecology Against Capitalism* (New York: Monthly Review Press, 2002), p. 18; John Bellamy Foster and Brett Clark, "Ecological Imperialism: The Curse of Capitalism," in Leo Panitch and Colin Leys, ed., *The Socialist Register* 2004 (New York: Monthly Review Press, 2004), pp. 186–201.

10. Andrew Sims, Aubrey Meyer, and Nick Robbins, *Who Owes Who?: Climate Change, Debt, Equity and Survival*, http://www.jubilee2000uk.; Athanasiou and Baer, Dead Heat, pp. 63–97.

11. Jared Diamond, "Twilight at Easter," *New York Review* of Books, March 25, 2004, pp. 6–10.

The secret nuclear war

The equivalent of a nuclear war has already happened. Over the last half-century, millions have died as a result of accidents, experiments, lies and cover-ups by the nuclear industry. **Eduardo Goncalves** pulls together a number of examples, and counts the fearful total cost.

Hugo Paulino was proud to be a fusilier. He was even prouder to be serving as a UN peacekeeper in Kosovo. It was his chance to help the innocent casualties of war. His parents did not expect him to become one.

Hugo, says his father Luis, died of leukaemia caused by radiation from depleted uranium (DU) shells fired by NATO during the Kosovo war. He was one of hundreds of Portuguese peacekeepers sent to Klina, an area heavily bombed with these munitions. Their patrol detail included the local lorry park, bombed because it had served as a Serb tank reserve, and the Valujak mines, which sheltered Serbian troops.

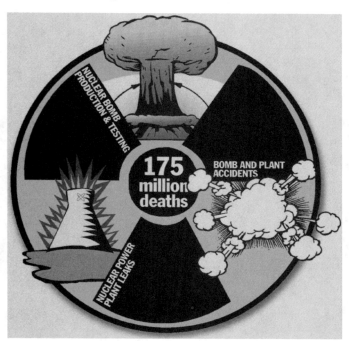

In their time off, the soldiers bathed in the river and gratefully supplemented their tasteless rations with local fruit and cheeses given to them by thankful nuns from the convent they guarded. Out of curiosity, they would climb inside the destroyed Serbian tanks littering the area.

Hugo arrived back in Portugal from his tour of duty on 12 February 2000, complaining of headaches, nausea and 'flu-like symptoms'. Ten days later, on 22 February, he suffered a major seizure. He was rushed to Lisbon's military hospital, where his condition rapidly deteriorated. On 9 March, he died. He was 21.

The military autopsy, which was kept secret for 10 months, claimed his death was due to septicaemia and 'herpes of the brain'. Not so, says Luis Paulino. 'When he was undergoing tests, a doctor called me over and said he thought it could be from radiation.'

It was only then that Luis learnt about the uranium shells—something his son had never been warned about or given protective clothing against. He contacted doctors and relatives of Belgian and Italian soldiers suspected of having succumbed to radiation poisoning.

'The similarities were extraordinary', he said. 'My son had died from leukaemia. That is why the military classified the autopsy report and wanted me to sign over all rights to its release.'

Today, Kosovo is littered with destroyed tanks, and pieces of radioactive shrapnel. NATO forces fired 31,000 depleted uranium shells during the Kosovo campaign, and 10,800 into neighbouring Bosnia. The people NATO set out to protect—and the soldiers it sent out to protect them—are now dying. According to Bosnia's health minister, Boza Ljubic, cancer deaths among civilians have risen to 230 cases per 100,000 last year, up from 152 in 1999. Leukaemia cases, he added, had doubled.

Scientists predict that the use of DU in Serbia will lead to more than 10,000 deaths from cancer among local residents, aid workers, and peacekeepers. Belated confessions that plutonium was also used may prompt these estimates to be revised. But while NATO struggles to stave off accusations of a cover-up, the Balkans are merely the newest battlefield in a silent world war that has claimed millions of lives. Most of its victims have died not in war-zones, but in ordinary communities scattered across the globe.

The hidden deaths of Newbury

Far away from the war-torn Balkans is Newbury, a prosperous white-collar industrial town in London's commuter belt. On its outskirts is Greenham Common, the former US Air Force station that was one of America's most important strategic bases during the Cold War. The base was closed down after the signing of the INF (Intermediate Nuclear Forces) Treaty by Ronald Reagan and Mikhail Gorbachev. The nuclear threat was over. Or so people thought.

In August 1993, Ann Capewell—who lived just one mile away from the base's former runway—died of acute myeloid leukaemia. She was 16 when she passed away, just 40 days after diagnosis. As they were coming to terms with their sudden loss, her parents—Richard and Elizabeth—were surprised to find a number of other cases of leukaemia in their locality.

The more they looked, the more cases they found. 'Many were just a stone's throw from our front door,' says Richard, 'mainly cases of myeloid leukaemia in young people.' What none of them knew was that they were the victims of a nuclear accident at Greenham Common that had been carefully covered up by successive British and American administrations.

> **'It is believed that the estimated 1,900 nuclear tests conducted during the Cold War released fallout equivalent to 40,000 Hiroshimas in every corner of the globe.'**

On February 28 1958, a laden B-47 nuclear bomber was awaiting clearance for take-off when it was suddenly engulfed in a huge fireball. Another bomber flying overhead had dropped a full fuel tank just 65 feet away. The plane exploded and burnt uncontrollably for days. As did its deadly payload.

A secret study by scientists at Britain's nearby nuclear bomb laboratory at Aldermaston documented the fallout, but the findings were never disclosed. The report showed how radioactive particles had been 'glued' to the runway surface by fire-fighters attempting to extinguish the blazing bomber—and that these were now being slowly blown into Newbury and over other local communities by aircraft jet blast.

'Virtually all the cases of leukaemias and lymphomas are in a band stretching from Greenham Common into south Newbury,' says Elizabeth. However, the British government continues to deny the cluster's existence, whilst the Americans still insist there was no accident.

Yet this was just one of countless disasters, experiments and officially-sanctioned activities which the nuclear powers have kept a closely-guarded secret. Between them, they have caused a global human death toll which is utterly unprecedented and profoundly shocking.

Broken Arrows

In 1981, the Pentagon publicly released a list of 32 'Broken Arrows—official military terminology for an accident involving a nuclear weapon. The report gave few details and did not divulge the location of some accidents. It was prepared in response to mounting media pressure about possible accident cover-ups.

But another US government document, this time secret, indicates that the official report may be seriously misleading. It states that 'a total of 1,250 nuclear weapons have been involved in accidents during handling, storage and transportation', a number of which 'resulted in, or had high potential for, plutonium dispersal.'[1]

Washington has never acknowledged the human consequences of even those few accidents it admits to, such as the Thule disaster in Greenland in 1968. When a B-52 bomber crashed at this secret nuclear base, all four bombs detonated, and a cloud of plutonium rose 800 metres in the air, blowing deadly radioactive particles hundreds of miles. The authorities downplayed the possibility of any health risks. But today, many local Eskimos, and their huskies, suffer from cancer, and over 300 people involved in the clean-up operation alone have since died of cancer and mysterious illnesses.

We may never know the true toll from all the bomb accidents, as the nuclear powers classify these disasters not as matters of public interest but of 'national security' instead. Indeed, it is only now that details are beginning to emerge of some accidents at bomb factories and nuclear plants that took place several decades ago.

Soviet sins

In 1991, Polish film-maker Slawomir Grunberg was invited to a little-known town in Russia's Ural mountains that was once part of a top-secret Soviet nuclear bomb-making complex. What he found was a tragedy of extraordinary dimensions, largely unknown to the outside world, and ignored by post-Cold War leaders.

His film—*Chelyabinsk: The Most Contaminated Spot on the Planet*—tells the story of the disasters at the Soviet Union's first plutonium factory, and the poisoning of hundreds of thousands of people. For years, the complex dumped its nuclear waste—totalling 76 million cubic metres—into the Techa River, the sole water source for scores of local communities that line its banks. According to a local doctor, people received an average radiation dose 57 times higher than that of Chernobyl's inhabitants.

In 1957, there was an explosion at a waste storage facility that blew 2 million curies of radiation into the atmosphere. The kilometre-high cloud drifted over three

The cancer epidemic

Scientists at St Andrew's University recently found that cells exposed to a dose of just two alpha particles of radiation produced as many cancers as much higher doses of radiation. They concluded that a single alpha particle of radiation could be carcinogenic.

Herman Muller, who has received a Nobel Prize for his work, has shown how the human race's continuous exposure to so-called 'low-level' radiation is causing a gradual reduction in its ability to survive, as successive generations are genetically damaged. The spreading and accumulation of even tiny genetic mutations pass through family lines, provoking allergies, asthma, juvenile diabetes, hypertension, arthritis, high blood cholesterol conditions, and muscular and bone defects.

Dr Chris Busby, who has extensively researched the low-level radiation threat, has made a link between everyday radiation exposure and a range of modern ailments: 'There have been tremendous increases in diseases resulting from the breakdown of the immune system in the last 20 years: diabetes, asthma, AIDS and others which may have an immune-system link, such as MS and ME. A whole spectrum of neurological conditions of unknown origin has developed'.[10]

Around the world, a pattern is emerging. For the first time in modern history, mortality rates among adults between the ages of 15 and 54 are actually increasing, and have been since 1982. In July 1983, the US Center for Birth Defects in Atlanta, Georgia, reported that physical and mental disabilities in the under-17s had doubled—despite a reduction in diseases such as polio, and improved vaccines and medical care.

Defects in new-born babies doubled between the 1950s and 1980s, as did long-term debilitating diseases. The US Environmental Protection Agency adds that 23 per cent of US males were sterile in 1980, compared to 0.5 per cent in 1938.

Above all, cancer is now an epidemic. In 1900, cancer accounted for only 4 per cent of deaths in the US. Now it is the second leading cause of premature mortality. Worldwide, the World Health Organisation (WHO) estimates the number of cancers will double in most countries over the next 25 years.

Within a few years, the chances of getting cancer in Britain will be as high as 40 per cent—virtually the toss of a coin.

Soviet provinces, contaminating over 250,000 people living in 217 towns and villages. Only a handful of local inhabitants were ever evacuated.

10 years later, Lake Karachay, also used as a waste dump, began to dry up. The sediment around its shores blew 5 million curies of radioactive dust over 25,000 square kilometres, irradiating 500,000 people. Even today, the lake is so 'hot' that standing on its shore will kill a person within one hour.

Grunberg's film tells of the terrible toll of these disasters on local families, such as that of Idris Sunrasin, whose grandmother, parents and three siblings have died of cancer. Leukaemia cases increased by 41 per cent after the plant began operations, and the average life span for women in 1993 was 47, compared to 72 nationally. For men it was just 45.

The secret nuclear war

Russia's nuclear industry is commonly regarded as cavalier in regard to health and safety. But the fact is that the nuclear military-industrial complex everywhere has been quite willing to deliberately endanger and sacrifice the lives of innocent civilians to further its ambitions.

The US government, for example, recently admitted its nuclear scientists carried out over 4,000 experiments on live humans between 1944 and 1974. They included feeding radioactive food to disabled children, irradiating prisoners' testicles, and trials on new-born babies and pregnant mothers. Scientists involved with the Manhat-

tan Project injected people with plutonium without telling them. An autopsy of one of the victims reportedly showed that his bones 'looked like Swiss cheese'. At the University of Cincinnati, 88 mainly low-income, black women were subjected to huge doses of radiation in an experiment funded by the military. They suffered acute radiation sickness. Nineteen of them died.

'Scientists predict that millions will die in centuries to come from nuclear tests that happened in the 1950s and 1960s.'

Details of many experiments still remain shrouded in secrecy, whilst little is known of the more shocking ones to come to light—such as one when a man was injected with what a report described as 'about a lethal dose' of strontium-89.[2]

In Britain too, scientists have experimented with plutonium on new-born babies, ethnic minorities and the disabled. When American colleagues reviewed a British proposal for a joint experiment, they concluded: 'What is the worst thing that can happen to a human being as a result of being a subject? Death.'[3]

They also conducted experiments similar to America's 'Green Run' programme, in which 'dirty' radiation was released over populated areas in the western states of Washington and Oregon contaminating farmland, crops and water. The 'scrubber' filters in Hanford's nuclear stacks were deliberately switched off first. Scientists, posing as agriculture department officials, found radiation contamination levels on farms hundreds of times above 'safety' levels.

But America's farmers and consumers were not told this, and the British public has never been officially told about experiments on its own soil.

Forty thousand Hiroshimas

It is believed that the estimated 1,900 nuclear tests conducted during the Cold War released fallout equivalent to 40,000 Hiroshimas in every corner of the globe. Fission products from the Nevada Test site can be detected in the ecosystems of countries as far apart as South Africa, Brazil, and Malaysia. Here, too, ordinary people were guinea pigs in a global nuclear experiment. The public health hazards were known right from the beginning, but concealed from the public. A 1957 US government study predicted that recent American tests had produced an extra 2,000 'genetically defective' babies in the US each year, and up to 35,000 every year around the globe. They continued regardless.

Ernest Sternglass's research shows how, in 1964, between 10,000 and 15,000 children were lost by miscarriage and stillbirth in New York state alone—and that there were some 10 to 15 times this number of foetal deaths across America.[4]

'Over the years, the Harwell, Aldermaston and Amersham plants have pumped millions of gallons of liquid contaminated with radioactive waste into the River Thames.'

Those who lived closest to the test sites have seen their families decimated. Such as the 100,000 people who were directly downwind of Nevada's fallout. They included the Mormon community of St George in Utah, 100 miles away from 'Ground Zero'—the spot where the bombs were detonated. Cancer used to be virtually unheard of among its population. Mormons do not smoke or drink alcohol or coffee, and live largely off their own home-grown produce.

Mormons are also highly patriotic. They believe government to be 'God-given', and do not protest. The military could afford to wait until the wind was blowing from the test site towards St George before detonating a device. After all, President Eisenhower had said: 'We can afford to sacrifice a few thousand people out there in defence of national security.'[5]

When the leukaemia cases suddenly appeared, doctors—unused to the disease—literally had no idea what it was. A nine-year-old boy, misdiagnosed with diabetes, died after a single shot of insulin. Women who complained of radiation sickness symptoms were told they had 'housewife syndrome'. Many gave birth to terribly deformed babies that became known as 'the sacrifice babies'. Elmer Pickett, the local mortician, had to learn new embalming techniques for the small bodies of wasted children killed by leukaemia. He himself was to lose no fewer than 16 members of his immediate family to cancer.

By the mid-1950s, just a few years after the tests began, St George had a leukaemia rate 2.5 times the national average, whereas before it was virtually non-existent. The total number of radiation deaths are said to have totalled 1,600—in a town with a population of just 5,000.

The military simply lied about the radiation doses people were getting. Former army medic Van Brandon later revealed how his unit kept two sets of radiation readings for test fallout in the area. 'One set was to show that no one received an [elevated] exposure' whilst 'the other set of books showed the actual reading. That set was brought in a locked briefcase every morning.'[6]

Continuous fallout

The world's population is still being subjected to the continuous fallout of the 170 megatons of long-lived nuclear fission products blasted into the atmosphere and returned daily to earth by wind and rain—slowly poisoning our bodies via the air we breathe, the food we eat, and the water we drink. Scientists predict that millions will die in centuries to come from tests that happened in the 1950s and 1960s.

But whilst atmospheric testing is now banned, over 400 nuclear bomb factories and power plants around the world make 'routine discharges' of nuclear waste into the environment. Thousands of nuclear waste dumping grounds, many of them leaking, are contaminating soil and water every day. The production of America's nuclear weapons arsenal alone has produced 100 million cubic metres of long-lived radioactive waste.

The notorious Hanford plutonium factory—which produced the fissile materials for the Trinity test and Nagasaki bomb—has discharged over 440 billion gallons of contaminated liquid into the surrounding area, contaminating 200 square miles of groundwater, but concealed the dangers from the public. Officials knew as early as the late 1940s that the nearby Columbia River was becoming seriously contaminated and a hazard to local fishermen. They chose to keep information about discharges secret and not to issue warnings.

In Britain, there are 7,000 sites licensed to use nuclear materials, 1,000 of which are allowed to discharge wastes. Three of them, closely involved in Britain's nuclear bomb programme, are located near the River Thames. Over the years, the Harwell, Aldermaston and Amersham plants have pumped millions of gallons of liquid contaminated with radioactive waste into the river.

They did so in the face of opposition from government ministers and officials who said 'the 6 million inhabitants of London derive their drinking water from this source. Any increase in [radio-]activity of the water supply would increase the genetic load on this comparatively large group.'[7] One government minister even wrote of his fears that the dumping 'would produce between 10 and 300 severely abnormal individuals per generation'.

Public relations officers at Harwell themselves added: 'the potential sufferers are 8 million in number, including both Houses of Parliament, Fleet Street and Whitehall'. These discharges continue to this day.

Study after study has uncovered 'clusters' of cancers and high rates of other unusual illnesses near nuclear plants, including deformities and Down Syndrome. Exposure to radiation among Sellafield's workers, in north-west England, has been linked to a greater risk of fathering a stillborn child and leukaemia among off-spring. Reports also suggest a higher risk of babies developing spina bifida in the womb.

Although the plant denies any link, even official MAFF studies have shown high levels of contamination in locally-grown fruit and vegetables, as well as wild animals. The pollution from Sellafield alone is such that it has coated the shores of the whole of Britain—from Wales to Scotland, and even Hartlepool in north-eastern England. A nationwide study organised by Harwell found that Sellafield 'is a source of plutonium contamination in the wider population of the British Isles'.[8]

> **'Study after study has uncovered 'clusters' of cancers and high rates of other illnesses near nuclear plants, including deformities and Down Syndrome. Exposure to radiation among Sellafield's workers, in NW England, has been linked to a greater risk of fathering a stillborn child and leukaemia among off-spring.'**

Those who live nearest the plant face the greatest threat. A study of autopsy tissue by the National Radiological Protection Board (NRPB) found high plutonium levels in the lungs of local Cumbrians—350 per cent higher than people in other parts of the country. 'Cancer clusters' have been found around nuclear plants across the globe—from France to Taiwan, Germany to Canada. A joint White House/US Department of Energy investigation recently found a high incidence of 22 different kinds of cancer at 14 different US nuclear weapons facilities around the country.

Meanwhile, a Greenpeace USA study of the toxicity of the Mississippi river showed that from 1968-83 there were 66,000 radiation deaths in the counties lining its banks—more than the number of Americans who died during the Vietnam war.

Don't blame us

Despite the growing catalogue of tragedy, the nuclear establishment has consistently tried to deny responsibility. It claims that only high doses of radiation—such as those experienced by the victims of the Hiroshima and Nagasaki bombs—are dangerous, though even here they have misrepresented the data. They say that the everyday doses from nuclear plant discharges, bomb factories and transportation of radioactive materials are 'insignificant', and that accidents are virtually impossible.

The truth, however, is that the real number and seriousness of accidents has never been disclosed, and that the damage from fallout has been covered up. The nuclear establishment now grudgingly (and belatedly) accepts that there is no such thing as a safe dose of radiation, however 'low', yet the poisonous discharges continue. When those within the nuclear establishment try to speak out, they are harassed, intimidated—and even threatened.

John Gofman, former head of Lawrence Livermore's biomedical unit, who helped produce the world's first plutonium for the bomb, was for years at the heart of the nuclear complex. He recalls painfully the time he was called to give evidence before a Congressional inquiry set up to defuse mounting concern over radiation's dangers.

'Chet Holifield and Craig Hosmer of the Joint Committee (on Atomic Energy) came in and turned to me and said: "Just what the hell do you think you two are doing, getting all those little old ladies in tennis shoes up in arms about our atomic energy program? There are people like you who have tried to hurt the Atomic Energy Commission program before. We got them, and we'll get you."'[9]

Gofman was eventually forced out of his job. But the facts of his research—and that of many other scientists—speak for themselves.

The final reckoning

But could radiation really be to blame for these deaths? Are the health costs really that great? The latest research suggests they are.

It is only very recently that clues have surfaced as to the massive destructive power of radiation in terms of human health. The accident at Chernobyl will kill an estimated half a million people worldwide from cancer, and perhaps more. 90 per cent of children in the neighbouring former Soviet republic of Belarus are contaminated for life—the poisoning of an entire country's gene pool.

Ernest Sternglass calculates that, at the height of nuclear testing, there were as many as 3 million foetal deaths, spontaneous abortions and stillbirths in the US alone. In addition, 375,000 babies died in their first year of life from radiation-linked diseases.[11]

The final reckoning

How many deaths is the nuclear industry responsible for? The following calculations of numbers of cancers caused by radiation are the latest and most accurate:[*]

from nuclear bomb production and testing: 385 million

from bomb and plant accidents: 9.7 million

from the 'routine discharges' of nuclear power plants
(5 million of them among populations living nearby):   6.6 million

likely number of total cancer fatalities worldwide: 175 million

[Added to this number are 235 million genetically damaged and diseased people, and 588 million children born with diseases such as brain damage, mental disabilities, spina bifida, genital deformities, and childhood cancers.]

[*]*Calculated by Rosalie Bertell, using the official 'radiation risk' estimates published in 1991 by the International Commission on Radiological Protection (ICRP), and the total radiation exposure data to the global population calculated by the UN Scientific Committee on the Effects of Atomic Radiation (UNSCEAR) in 1993.*

Rosalie Bertell, author of the classic book *No Immediate Danger*, now revised and re-released, has attempted to piece together a global casualty list from the nuclear establishment's own data. The figures she has come up with are chilling—but entirely plausible.

Using the official 'radiation risk' estimates published in 1991 by the International Commission on Radiological Protection (ICRP), and the total radiation exposure data to the global population calculated by the UN Scientific Committee on the Effects of Atomic Radiation (UNSCEAR) in 1993, she has come up with a terrifying tally:

- 358 million cancers from nuclear bomb production and testing
- 9.7 million cancers from bomb and plant accidents
- 6.6 million cancers from the 'routine discharges' of nuclear power plants (5 million of them among populations living nearby).
- As many as 175 million of these cancers could be fatal.

Added to this number are no fewer than 235 million genetically damaged and diseased people, and a staggering 588 million children born with what are called 'teratogenic effects'—diseases such as brain damage, mental disabilities, spina bifida, genital deformities, and childhood cancers.

Furthermore, says Bertell, we should include the problem of nonfatal cancers and of other damage which is debilitating but not counted for insurance and liability purposes'[12]—such as the 500 million babies lost as stillbirths because they were exposed to radiation whilst still in the womb, but are not counted as 'official' radiation victims.

It is what the nuclear holocaust peace campaigners always warned of if war between the old superpowers broke out, yet it has already happened and with barely a shot being fired. Its toll is greater than that of all the wars in history put together, yet no-one is counted as among the war dead.

'It is the nuclear holocaust that peace campaigners always warned of if war between the old superpowers broke out, yet it has already happened and with barely a shot being fired.'

Its virtually infinite killing and maiming power leads Rosalie Bertell to demand that we learn a new language to express a terrifying possibility: 'The concept of species annihilation means a relatively swift, deliberately induced end to history, culture, science, biological reproduction and memory. It is the ultimate human rejection of the gift of life, an act which requires a new word to describe it: omnicide'.[13]

*Eduardo Goncalves is a freelance journalist and environmental researcher. He is author of tile reports **Broken Arrow—Greenham Common's Secret Nuclear Accident** and **Nuclear Guinea Pigs—British Human Radiation Experiments**, published by CND (UK), and was researcher to the film **The Dragon that Slew St George**. He is currently writing a book about the hidden history of the nuclear age.*

Notes

1. 'Report of the safety criteria for plutonium-bearing weapons—summary', US Department of Energy, February 14, 1973, document RS5640/1035.

2. Strontium metabolism meeting, Atomic Energy Division–Division of Biology and Medicine, January 17,1954.

3. memorandum to Bart Gledhill, chairman, Human Subjects Committee. LLNL, from Larry Anderson, LLNL, February 21,1989.

4. see 'Secret Fallout, Low-Level Radiation from Hiroshima to Three-Mile Island'. Ernest Sternglass, McGraw-Hill, New York, 1981.

5. see 'American Ground Zero; The Secret Nuclear War', Carole Gallagher, MIT Press. Boston, 1993.

6. Washington Post, February 24, 1994.

7. see PRO files AB 6/1379 and AB 6/2453 and 3584.

8. 'Variations in the concentration of plutonium, strontium-90 and total alpha-emitters in human teeth', RG. O'Donnell et al, Sd. Tot. Env, 201 (1997) 235–243.

9. interview with Gofman, DOE/OHRE Oral History Project, December 1994, pp 49-50 of official transcripts.

10. 'Wings of Death—nuclear pollution and human health', Dr. Chris Busby, Green Audit, Wales, 1995

11. see 'Secret Fallout, Low-Level Radiation from Hiroshima to Three-Mile Island', Ernest Sternglass, McGraw-Hill, New York, 1981.

12. from 'No Immediate Danger— Prognosis for a Radioactive Earth', Dr Rosalie Bertell. Women's Press. London 1985 (revised 2001)

13. pers. Comm. 4 February 2001

Further reading:

'No Immediate Danger—Prognosis for a Radioactive Earth', Dr Rosalie Bertell, Women's Press, London (revised 2001)

'Deadly Deceit—low-level radiation, high-level cover-up', Dr. Jay Gould and Benjamin A. Goldman, Four Walls Eight Windows, New York, 1991

'Wings of Death—nuclear pollution and human health', Dr. Chris Busby, Green Audit, Wales, 1995

'American Ground Zero: The Secret Nuclear War', Carole Gallagher, MIT Press, Boston, 1993

'Radioactive Heaven and Earth—the health effects of nuclear weapons testing in, on, and above the earth', a report of the IPPNW International Commission, Zed Books, 1991

'Secret Fallout. Low-Level Radiation from Hiroshima to Three-Mile Island', Ernest Sternglass, McGraw-Hill, New York, 1981

'Clouds of Deceit—the deadly legacy of Britain's bomb tests', Joan Smith, Faber and Faber, London, 1985

'Nuclear Wastelands', Arjun Makhijani et al (eds), MIT Press, Boston, 1995 'Radiation and Human Health', Dr. John W. Gofman, Sierra Book Club, San Francisco, 1981

'The Greenpeace Book of the Nuclear Age—The Hidden History, the Human Cost', John May, Victor Gollancz, 1989

'The Unsinkable Aircraft Carrier—American military power in Britain', Duncan Campbell, Michael Joseph, London 1984

Food and Agriculture in the 21st Century

Rethinking Our Paradigms

By Graham T. T. Molitor

Squabbles over genetically modified food and pork-barrel subsidies for farmers
are just the tip of the iceberg for policy makers grappling with increasingly
complex agricultural problems.

Rarely do truly giant jumps in the applied sciences occur. When they do, they drastically alter the entire foundation—the paradigm—on which society and leaders must base their choices for the future. We are at a point in history where breakthroughs in life sciences are throwing our old paradigms into chaos.

Beginning in the 1940s, the Green Revolution dramatically boosted agricultural productivity and changed the fate and survival of untold billions of lives. Far surpassing that extraordinary advance in agricultural productivity is the New Green Revolution based on the surging momentum of biotechnologies enabling humans to control all forms of life, including plants and animals. Agricultural biotechnologies—*agbiotech*—will boost productivity increases to the point that food output will sate rapidly growing population needs worldwide.

By tracking economic development over millions of years, we can see clearly the trend toward doing more with less. Tens of thousands of

years of agricultural pursuits reveal a litany of evolutionary improvements that increase productivity by enormous measure. Over the millennia, selective breeding, hybridization, and now genetic modification (GM) changed the cornucopian farmland output. Ancient ears of corn were diminutive, measuring about the size of the little finger. Wild tomatoes were once the size of a grape. Heads of early wild wheat hefted a mere two rows of kernels, compared with today's varieties boasting six rows.

Genetic engineers are on the verge of converting annual (single growing season) plants into perennials, which thrive all year long, year after year. This development would drastically reduce planting regimens and delays, lower seed costs, and enable farm operators to cull and concentrate production on plants proven to be the most productive. Biotech already has altered citrus trees that normally require six years to reach maturity to yield fruit in a single year.

But even these advances will pale before the overwhelming changes that agbiotech promises to deliver. Synthetic citrus, for instance, would eliminate the need for citrus orchards, freeing thousands of acres of land but at the loss of fragrant orchards of citrus blossoms. Sterile bioreactors in factories could be directed to produce nothing but the substance that customers want, without any waste. End products might be engineered to yield only the most useful and valuable component, such as orange juice sacs that eliminate the need for roots, trunk, branches, leaves, rinds, or seeds.

Foods produced in sterile bioreactors may not be aesthetically appealing, but this scenario is not far removed from current reality: Witness the giant tankers shipping citrus juices or concentrate for reconstitution and repackaging at destination points. From the standpoint of actual human consumption, food production will become increasingly far removed from billowing fields and blossoming orchards.

The new paradigm—nudged by steadily increasing numbers of people to feed worldwide—must, sooner or later, take account of these changes.

Agricultural potentials inherent in the biotech revolution are truly extraordinary. Former U.S. Secretary of Agriculture John R. Block asserted in 1999 that agricultural output in developing nations could be boosted by 25% simply by resorting to agbiotech. Yet that may be an overly conservative estimate: Technological optimists believe that productivity for some modified crops could be higher by orders of magnitude in the tens of thousands compared with the traditional crops they replace. Biosynthesized sweeteners, although they may not supplant crop-based ones, possess hundreds to thousands of times the sweetness. A massive switchover to sweeteners would free up millions of acres and alter millions of jobs worldwide.

Genetically engineered crops will reach a turning point by 2020 when more acres will be devoted to GM crops than to "natural" commercial crops. By the end of this century, some commentators predict, genetically engineered plants could account for 100% of all crops. That may be overly optimistic, but over the very long term—certainly long before the year 3000 and perhaps as early as 2300—I anticipate biotech-enhanced agricultural production may be so prodigious that "utopian plenty" prevails. Providing basic essentials—food foremost among them—will become so much a part of affluent societies that hardly a second thought will be given to assuring that all people everywhere get enough of the right kinds of foods to sustain themselves in good health. Government will no longer need to confer special bounties, subsidies, or financial benefit on food providers at any level of production along the chain to consumers.

A major obstacle to this utopian scenario is the current lack of public acceptance of GM foods. Genetic engineering is unlikely to gain widespread acceptance worldwide until sometime around 2030—an awfully long time to wait for the benefits it could bring. Acceptance could be accelerated by public-policy encouragement, however. Go-slow attitudes toward many new things waylay their rapid introduction.

Farm Workforce Decline

Agribusiness generally includes food, fiber, fisheries, and forestry. These pursuits occupied 90% of the entire U.S. workforce during Colonial times, but a mere 2%-3% today. That enormous shift in workforce allocation was the result of innumerable advances, for despite this enormous reduction of labor, U.S. agriculture produces more food with less land. So prodigious is current productivity that overall output far exceeds domestic needs. Farming no longer is a dominant way of life in the United States or in other postindustrial countries.

By 2010, a minuscule 1% of workers will be directly engaged in agricultural operations. Despite the small number of workers, productivity has become so prodigious that as much as 50%-60% of some key U.S. crops are exported.

Measures of the workforce and economic productivity are somewhat arbitrary because they depend on how and what is counted. True, workers directly engaged as farmers constitute a radically shrunken proportion of overall U.S. employment. Counts limited to farm workers, however, represent only a fraction of the industry picture. Within the agribusiness sector overall, downstream workers involved in getting food to consumers are a huge number.

Farm employment in 1960 accounted for 6.3 million jobs, dwarfing all of the combined downstream sectors of agribusiness. Among downstream activities, **food manufacturers** dominated, employing 1.8 million workers, followed by food services (1.7 million), retailers (1.4 million), and wholesalers (0.8 million).

But the dominance of farm operators waned as the chain of goods and services provided beyond the farm gate began to grow by leaps and bounds. By 1980, **grocery retail** jobs in the United States surpassed those for manufacturers, and **food service providers** (an economic sector comprising leisure, hospitality, recreation, entertainment, and similar undertakings) employed far more workers than food manufacturers and grocery retailers combined: 4.5 million for food services, compared with 3.8 million for food manufacturers and grocery retailers. By 2000, this relative dominance of job distribution became more pronounced, with 8.1 million workers in the hospitality sector (eating and drinking places) compared with 1.8 million growing food on farms, 1.5 million in food manufacturing, and 3.0 million in grocery retailing and wholesaling. Obviously, jobs have shifted away from and far beyond farm gates.

How Big Is Agribusiness?

Most people think of "agribusiness" as just growing and selling crops, but there is a broader view. Agribusiness embraces a far greater and more significant part of the U.S. economy than one might expect. Included with the obvious food processing and manufacturing, wholesaling and retailing, and food services are things like the manufacturing equipment used for food processing, printing, and so on. There's also leather products (gloves, luggage, footwear); textiles, fabrics, and furs; and even household appliances such as refrigerators, stoves, and microwave ovens, all embraced in the economic measures of agribusiness. Add in related consumer goods such as silverware and cooking utensils; fertilizers and a huge range of agricultural chemicals; household and office furnishings made from forestry products; upholstery and carpeting made with natural fibers (jute, cotton, wool, lambskin, furs); alcoholic beverages and tobacco products (and even illegal drugs); resources such as water and energy supplies for cooking; and garbage collection and recycling activities.

Trends in Food and Agriculture

Demography

- World population is expected to approach 9 billion by mid-century, requiring more food and other resources generally, but most particularly in developing countries, where the largest population increases are expected.

- Developed countries are expected to experience declining birthrates but also longer life spans, suggesting that their population growth will also exert rising pressure on food supplies.

- Overconsumption in developed countries has led to obesity. As the lesser-developed countries make economic gains, people may follow the consumption and lifestyle patterns set by the affluent. For instance, they may eat more meat, which is more resource-intensive than vegetarian diets.

Economics

- Agriculture has grown increasingly efficient throughout history, as new technologies and techniques enable higher food production with fewer workers and less land.

- "Agribusiness," broadly defined to include all related economic activities—from glove making to garbage collection—represents some 30%-35% of the U.S. GDP.

- Agriculture and food production are big business, but most of the economic activity related to agribusiness happens far from farms. There are at present about 1.8 million workers growing food on U.S. farms, but more than 8 million working in eating and drinking establishments.

- Americans spend about half of their food budgets eating away from home.

Environment

- Less land is now needed to produce the same amount of food, thanks to technological advances. As populations in urban areas spread out further into the hinterlands, zoning and other land-use policies will need to be rethought.

- More land could be freed from food production and dedicated to meeting other important needs, such as energy production. Sugar cane and corn, for example, could be used as feedstocks for fuel.

- Water is likely to increase in importance as an environmental and political issue. Battles over water rights may lead to full-fledged wars. Technologies such as genetic modification to improve drought resistance, plus water-conservation techniques such as drip irrigation, may help alleviate water problems.

Government

- Governments are largely responsible for choosing which economic, research, and development activities to support, weighing the needs and desires of sometimes competing constituencies. High food prices to support family farmers may hurt many consumers, for instance. Taxpayers and voters may revolt against any policy they oppose, such as genetic engineering research, foreign aid, or subsidies on specific crops.

- International trading partners often disagree on regulations (such as the labeling of genetically modified foods), creating restrictions that can be perceived as unfair and antithetical to free trade.

- Terrorism by groups opposed to agbiotech is a growing threat. Fields of crops have been decimated. Laboratories have been raided, ransacked, and destroyed. Governments have enhanced activities to detect and discourage possible terrorist assaults on food supplies.

Society

- Food consumption comprises a major portion of leisure time activities, which will gain importance in an increasingly leisure-based economy: By 2015, Americans may devote half their lifetimes engaging in leisure activities.

- Values come into conflict in many food-related areas, such as the consumption of meat: Vegetarians oppose meat on health, environmental, and moral grounds, and animal-rights activists oppose the killing or mistreatment of animals destined for food production. Similarly, many people oppose the use of genetically modified or chemically enhanced foods, creating a demand for organic production, labeling, and compliance.

Technology

- Agricultural biotechnology (agbiotech) promises to boost crop yields without depleting other precious resources. For example, the useful components of oranges could be grown in bioreactors and eliminate the need for land-intensive orchards.

- Genetic engineering can enhance the health and safety of foods, such as increasing their shelf life by delaying decay. Improved sensors and testing devices can also quickly identify pathogens and other food impurities.

- One possible use of biotech that may gain acceptance among those opposed to it for health reasons is as a substitute for animal testing in food and drug safety research. Quite possibly, geneticists may be able to come up with alternative testing methods that sidestep the issue altogether.

*—Graham T.T. Molitor
and FUTURIST staff*

The grand total of what could be embraced as "agribusiness" is about 30%-35% of GDP. Agriculture is and will be very big business. Yet, agriculture and manufacturing, which once constituted dominant shares of jobs and livelihoods, are waning in relative importance in the Knowledge Age.

Food Services Dominate The Leisure Era

The leisure sector will begin to acquire economic dominance in the United States in 2015, when every American will spend half of his or her lifetime directly or indirectly engaged in leisure-time pursuits.

By about 2000, American consumers began spending more than 50% of their food budgets away from home.

That proportion will continue to grow. As it does, the question of controlling commodity prices and farm-level cost of foodstuffs will be nearly totally eclipsed by the host of value-added services required to get food to consumers. New governmental controls might never go so far as to regulate menu prices to lower costs to consumers. Food policy is likely to focus more on "food chits" and food stamps, which almost certainly will become a larger and more important component of social welfare programs. Domestic food assistance programs will continue to be important until the essential economic needs of every citizen are met.

Life Science Era: Farmland Importance Wanes

The movement toward a biotech-dominated agricultural sector will likely follow several stages. Early forays into agbiotech emphasized enhancing the agronomic capabilities and potentials of crops, such as the development of herbicide-resistant crop varieties. Work in this area also focused on protecting crops against the full array of pathogens and predators. The next stage was to improve quality, such as extending the shelf life, improving taste and texture, increasing sweetness, and so on. Then came a new rash of GM foods that honed in on adding new attributes to certain dietary staples. Developed nations got "nutraceuticals," foods that delivered much higher levels of desired nutrients. Poorer nations focused more on "pharmfoods" that provided vaccines and other life-enhancing drugs and nutrients. One result of this latest move has been the melding of farming with drug manufacturing, two business sectors that previously were separate and distinct. Food producers (from farm gate to final consumption), pharmaceutical companies, and purveyors of natural remedies increasingly occupy much the same business terrain.

Extending this trend line further yet into the future, we can speculate that the food sector may be shaped increasingly by developments in materials research as well as automation. In the coming **Meta-Materials Age** (around 2100-2300), there will be synthesized foods that are customized to meet the unique food and fiber needs of particular individuals. Food will not be grown but rather replicated using robotic nanotechnologies that assemble foodstuffs on demand.

Far into the distant future, a **New Space Age** (around 2500-3000) may see agribusiness drawing its needs from extraterrestrial materials and resources produced on orbiting space stations or on other planets. Around-the-clock solar radiation, shorter crop-maturation cycles, and continuous multiple cropping will increase yield potentials at a cost. These speculations are mentioned here merely to hint at how changing waves of economic activity will sweep across and alter the character of agriculture as we know it.

Too Much Food?

American agriculture suffers from a surfeit of riches. The United States achieved "food security" long ago—taking the term to mean domestic self-sufficiency, not global sufficiency. The nub of the farm problem is no longer income-assurance and shoring up a weak economic sector. U.S. agriculture is an overachiever, creating a land of cornucopian plenty from fewer and fewer farm operators.

> *"If population doubles and more people move up the food ladder, crop output may have to do much more than merely double."*

U.S. agricultural exports are big business, totaling $55 billion in 2001. A majority of the country's largest-volume crops are exported, including wheat, corn, and soybeans. The United States supplies approximately 50% of world corn and soybean exports. Overall, about 20% of all U.S. agricultural commodities were exported in 1999. If the United States continues sending huge proportions of its output abroad, export markets must figure prominently in any agricultural paradigm for the future.

The key question for U.S. policy makers is whether taxpayers should assume this responsibility for sharing agricultural abundance with the less fortunate, at home and globally. Government handouts will constitute a part of this global income redistribution effort, but the private sector could also develop commercially viable means to fulfill these humanitarian goals. If world starvation and hunger are ever to be solved, economic development policies and programs in the less-developed nations are imperative. Economic wherewithal, not continuing handouts, provide the long range and permanent solutions to world hunger.

Demographic Issues: Population Growth, Development

Population assumptions exert an enormous influence upon estimates of future food-supply needs. Currently, demographers assume population growth will level off (zero growth) or even experience negative rates (population declines) in developed nations. Theoretically, this would relieve the pressure to meet continuously escalating food needs. On the other hand, we could see dramatic and continuing population growth aided by life-science advances that increase longevity. This would continue to exert pressure on food supply, some analysts fear. Offsetting the pessimists are cornucopians, the prophets of plenty, who count on agbiotech to boost food output to previously unimaginable levels.

Another demographic issue to weigh is that increasing affluence tends to encourage diet upgrading—that is, eating more animal proteins. This choice has economic, environmental, and health implications that all must be considered by policy makers. Meat production requires high inputs of grain; for example, eight to 20 pounds of grain may be required for every pound of beef produced. Even one gallon of milk requires 2.8 pounds of grain feed. Growing populations of people gaining more affluence and demanding these grain-intensive foods will mean a need for ever-higher levels of grain production. If population doubles and more people move up the food ladder, crop output may have to do much more than merely double.

Resource Issues: Water and Land

As an environmental, nutritional, agricultural, and political issue, water will dominate policy makers' agendas for decades to come. Some doomsayers anticipate that full-fledged wars will be fought over water rights in the near future. Tax breaks or other incentives could encourage water-conserving innovations, such as drip irrigation, as well as R&D for genetic modification to produce more drought-resistant plants.

Conflicts between sprawling urban areas and their adjacent hinterlands have led to policies such as the creation of agricultural preserves of various sorts, in which governments purchase land or create zoning arrangements to reduce land-development density. As high-speed transport systems enable longer commutes, populations will spread out even more geographically. Land dedicated to farm use will wane. But land-based policy may become an anachronism as technological advances continue to allow farmers to grow more with less land and labor. Land-use policies—including favorable tax treatment, subsidized loans, and so on—will become less and less important.

Farming Off the Land: Fisheries and the Blue Revolution

The Blue Revolution of mariculture—farming of marine crops and animals—also must be included in the new policy paradigm for food and agriculture. Mariculture could become bigger than open-water commercial fisheries by 2020, according to one forecast. Already, as much as 20% of fish in the United States comes from fish-farming operations.

Biotechnologies hold enormous promise for reversing depletion of world fish stocks, though critics deride genetically altered species as "Frankenfish." Recently, breakthroughs in cloning have enabled researchers to replicate fish flesh in bioreactors. Policy makers need to consider whether supporting such promising but controversial developments is in the public interest.

Farms without Food

Agricultural advances into non-food areas include GM corn, wheat, and tree stocks that can be used to create plastics. Bacterial fermentation of corn stocks produces lactic acid that can be fashioned into biodegradable plastics. Burgeoning energy demands also may be met by agbiotech. Sugar cane and corn are among the crops that can all be used as feed stocks for fuels for internal-combustion engines. These efforts, though, have required hefty government subsidies.

Pharmaceutical production could also occupy a significant part of farming operations. Genetic engineering of animals to create compatible organs for humans (xenotransplantation) will also become common and widely available. Genetically modified animals have also been transformed into biofactories for producing chemicals, pharmaceuticals, manufactured goods, energy, and so on. Such developments must be considered in any comprehensive new agricultural paradigm.

Agbiotech ushers in the time when actually vanquishing age-old scourges may become a reality. Bioengineered crops not only will boost yields, but they will also create new varieties that thrive in hostile environments, survive without irrigation, resist drought and heat, flourish in brackish/arid soils, withstand frost, tolerate herbicides, boost nutritional content, fend off viruses, rebuff parasites, minimize fertilizer, reduce pesticide use, cut agri-chemical needs, heft plant stems (enabling crops to better withstand ravaging weather conditions), tolerate ultraviolet radiation, and diminish energy inputs and land requirements overall. Benefits bestowed simply will become too great to be ignored or discouraged.

Short-term solutions over the next 10 years will continue to be largely based on humanitarian aid and assistance. Intermediate solutions of the next 10 to 90 years will be based on technological advances, capital investments aimed at increasing productivity, lowering food costs, enhancing economic development in lesser-developed areas, and raising income levels. Long-range solutions—beyond 100 years from now—will come about by cornucopian advances in food output, including GM crops that endure and thrive in harsh conditions. Perspectives in the very long range—beyond 1,000 years—are utopian: abundant and cheap food for everyone.

Consumers may not take fondly to biotech foods—at least at first. Over time, however, they will become well accepted. Former President Carter put it aptly: "Responsible biotechnology is not the enemy; starvation is."

Graham T.T. Molitor is vice president and legal counsel for the World Future Society and president of Public Policy Forecasting, 9208 Wooden Bridge Road, Potomac, Maryland 20854. Telephone and fax 1-301-762-5174; e-mail gttmolitor@aol.com.

His last article for THE FUTURIST, "Five Forces Transforming Communications," appeared in September-October 2001.

The New Terrorism

Securing the Nation against a Messianic Foe

By Steven Simon

In the minds of the men who carried them out, the attacks of September 11 were acts of religious devotion—a form of worship, conducted in God's name and in accordance with his wishes. The enemy was the infidel; the opposing ideology, "Western culture." That religious motivation, colored by a messianism and in some cases an apocalyptic vision of the future, distinguishes al-Qaida and its affiliates from conventional terrorists groups such as the Irish Republican Army, the Red Brigades, or even the Palestine Liberation Organization. Although secular political interests help drive al-Qaida's struggle for power, these interests are understood and expressed in religious terms. Al-Qaida wants to purge the Middle East of American political, military, and economic influence, but only as part of a far more sweeping religious agenda: a "defensive jihad" to defeat a rival system portrayed as an existential threat to Islam.

The explicitly religious character of the "New Terrorism" poses a profound security challenge for the United States. The social, economic, and political conditions in the Arab and broader Islamic world that have helped give rise to al-Qaida will not be easily changed. The maximalist demands of the new terrorists obviate dialogue or negotiation. Traditional strategies of deterrence by retaliation are unlikely to work, because the jihadists have no territory to hold at risk, seek sacrifice, and court Western attacks that will validate their claims about Western hostility to Islam. The United States will instead need to pursue a strategy of containment, while seeking ways to redress, over the long run, underlying causes.

The Fabric of New Terrorism

Religiously motivated terrorism, as Bruce Hoffman of the RAND Corporation first noted in 1997, is inextricably linked to pursuit of mass casualties. The connection is rooted in the sociology of biblical religion. Monotheistic faiths are characterized by exclusive claims to valid identity and access to salvation. The violent imagery embedded in their sacred texts and the cen-

trality of sacrifice in their liturgical traditions establish the legitimacy of killing as an act of worship with redemptive qualities. In these narratives, the enemy must be eradicated, not merely suppressed.

In periods of deep cultural despair, eschatology—speculation in the form of apocalyptic stories about the end of history and dawn of the kingdom of God—can capture the thinking of a religious group. History is replete with instances in which religious communities—Jewish, Christian, Islamic—immolated themselves and perpetrated acts of intense violence to try to spur the onset of a messianic era. Each community believed it had reached the nadir of degradation and was on the brink of a resurgence that would lead to its final triumph over its enemies—a prospect that warranted and required violence on a massive scale.

Such episodes of messianic zeal are not restricted to the distant past. In the mid-1980s, a group of Israeli settlers plotted to destroy the Dome of the Rock, the 8th-century mosque atop the Haram al Sharif in Jerusalem. The settlers appeared to believe that destroying the mosque would spark an Arab invasion, which would trigger an Israeli nuclear response—the Armageddon said by the Bible to precede the kingdom of God. The plot was never carried out, because the conspirators could not get a rabbinical blessing. Analogous attempts have characterized Christian apocalypticists and even a Buddhist community whose doctrine was strongly influenced by Christian eschatology—Aum Shinrikyo.

The Doctrinal Potency of al-Qaida

Similar thinking can be detected in narrative trends that inform al-Qaida's ideology and actions. Apocalyptic tales circulating on the Web and within the Middle East in hard copy tell of cataclysmic battles between Islam and the United States, Israel, and sometimes Europe. Global battles seesaw between infidel and Muslim victory until some devastating act, often the destruction of New York by nuclear weapons, brings Armageddon to an end and leads the world's survivors to convert to Islam.

The theological roots of al-Qaida's leaders hark back to a medieval Muslim jurisconsult, Taqi al Din Ibn Taymiyya, two of whose teachings have greatly influenced Islamic revolutionary movements. The first was his elevation of jihad—not the spiritual struggle that many modern Muslims take it to be, but physical combat against unbelievers—to the rank of the canonical five pillars of Islam (declaration of faith, prayer, almsgiving, Ramadan fast, and pilgrimage to Mecca). The second was his legitimization of rebellion against Muslim rulers who do not enforce *sharia*, or Islamic law, in their domains.

Ibn Taymiyya's ideas were revived in the 1960s in Egypt, where they underpinned 25 years of violence, including the assassination of Anwar Sadat in 1981. When the Egyptian government vanquished the militants, survivors fled abroad, taking advantage of European laws regarding asylum or of the lawlessness of Yemen, Afghanistan, and Kashmir.

Ibn Taymiyya's teachings have even deeper roots in Saudi Arabia. They became part of the founding ideology of the Saudi state when Muhammad Ibn Abd al Wahhab formed an alliance with Ibn Saud in 1744.

Al-Qaida embodies both the Egyptian and the Saudi sides of the jihad movement, which came together in the 1960s when some Egyptian militants sought shelter in Saudi Arabia, which was locked in conflict with Nasserist Egypt. Osama bin Laden himself is a Saudi, and his second-in-command, Ayman al Zawahiri, is an Egyptian who served three years in prison for his role in Sadat's assassination.

The jihadist themes in Ibn Taymiyya's teachings are striking an increasingly popular chord in parts of the Muslim world.

Al-Qaida's Geopolitical Reach

Religiously motivated militants have now dispersed widely to multiple "fields of jihad." The social and economic problems that have fueled their discontent are well known—low economic growth, falling wages and increasing joblessness, poor schooling, relentless but unsustainable urban growth, and diminishing environmental resources, especially water. Political alienation and resentment over the plight of the Palestinians and the intrusion into traditional societies of offensive images and ideas compound these problems and help account for the religious voice given to these primarily secular grievances. The mobilization of religious imagery and terminology further transforms secular issues into substantively religious ones, putting otherwise negotiable political issues beyond the realm of bargaining and making violent outcomes more likely.

The political power of religious symbols has led some pivotal states—in particular, Egypt and Saudi Arabia—to use them to buttress their own legitimacy. In so doing they perversely confer authority on the very clerical opposition that threatens state power and impedes the modernization programs that might, over the long haul, materially improve quality of life. Although the jihadists are unable to challenge these states, Islamists nevertheless dominate public discourse and shape the

debate on foreign and domestic policy. For the jihadists, the "near enemy" at home once took precedence over the "far enemy," which now includes the United States and the West. Thanks to bin Laden's doctrinal creativity, in Egypt and Saudi Arabia, Islamists have inextricably intertwined the near and far enemies. The governments' need to cater to the sentiments aroused within mosques and on the Islamist airwaves to keep their regimes secure dictates their tolerance or even endorsement of anti-American views. At the same time, strategic circumstances compel both states to provide diplomatic or other practical support for U.S. policies that offend public sensitivities. It is small wonder that Egyptians and Saudis are the backbone of al-Qaida and that Saudi Arabia spawned most of the September 11 attackers.

The fields of jihad stretch far and wide. In the Middle East, al-Qaida developed ties in Lebanon and Jordan. In Southeast Asia, Indonesians, Malaysians, and Singaporeans trained in Afghanistan, or conspired with those who had, to engage in terror, most horrifically the bombing in Bali. In Central Asia, the Islamic Movement of Uzbekistan became a full-fledged jihadist group. In Pakistan, jihadists with apocalyptic instincts nearly provoked a nuclear exchange between India and Pakistan. East Africa remains a field of jihad four years after the bombings of U.S. embassies in Kenya and Tanzania. Videotapes of atrocities of the Algerian Armed Islamic Group circulate in Europe as recruitment propaganda for the global jihad.

Given its role as a springboard for the September 11 attacks, Europe may be the most crucial field of jihad. Lack of political representation and unequal access to education, jobs, housing, and social services have turned European Muslim youth against the states in which they live. In the United Kingdom, the Muslim prison population, a source of recruits for the radical cause, has doubled in the past decade. Close to a majority of young Muslims in Britain have told pollsters that they feel no obligation to bear arms for England but would fight for bin Laden.

The United States remains al-Qaida's prime target. Suleiman Abu Ghaith, the al-Qaida spokesman, has said that there can be no truce until the group has killed four million Americans, whereupon the rest can convert to Islam.

The Recalcitrance of the Jihadists

How should the United States respond to the jihadist threat? To the extent one can speak of the root causes of the new terrorism, they defy direct and immediate remedial action. Population in the Middle East is growing rapidly, and the median age is dropping. The correlation between youth and political instability highlights the potential for unrest and radicalization. In cities, social welfare programs, sanitation, transportation, housing, power, and the water supply are deteriorating. In much of the Muslim world, the only refuge from filth, noise, heat, and, occasionally, surveillance is the mosque. Economists agree that the way out of the morass is to develop institutions that facilitate the distribution of capital and create opportunity; how to do that, they are unsure. The West can offer aid but cannot as yet correct structural problems.

Improving public opinion toward the United States is also deeply problematic. Decades of official lies and controlled press have engendered an understandable skepticism toward the assertions of any government, especially one presumed hostile to Muslim interests. Trust is based on confidence in a chain of transmission whose individual links are known to be reliable. Official news outlets or government spokespersons do not qualify as such links. Nor, certainly, do Western news media.

Moreover, highly respected critics of the United States in Saudi Arabia demonstrate an ostensibly profound understanding of U.S. policies and society, while offering a powerful and internally consistent explanation for their country's descent from the all-powerful, rich supplier of oil to the West to a debt-ridden, faltering economy protected by Christian troops and kowtowing to Israel. These are difficult narratives to counter, especially in a society where few know much about the West.

The prominent role of clerics in shaping public opinion offers yet more obstacles. The people who represent the greatest threat of terrorist action against the United States follow the preaching and guidance of Salafi clerics—the Muslim equivalent of Christian "fundamentalists." Although some Salafi preachers have forbidden waging jihad as harmful to Muslim interests, their underlying assumptions are that jihad qua holy war against non-Muslims is fundamentally valid and that Islamic governments that do not enforce *sharia* must be opposed. No authoritative clerical voice offers a sympathetic view of the United States.

The prognosis regarding root causes, then, is poor. The world is becoming more religious; Islam is the fastest-growing faith; religious expression is generally becoming more assertive and apocalyptic thinking more prominent. Weapons of mass destruction, spectacularly suited to cosmic war, will become more widely available. Democratization is at a standstill. Governments in Egypt, Saudi Arabia, Pakistan, and Indonesia are unwilling or unable to oppose anti-Western religiously based popular feeling. Immigration, conversion, and inept social policies will intensify parallel trends in Europe.

At least for now, dialogue does not appear to be an option. Meanwhile, global market forces beyond the control of Western governments hasten Western cultural penetration and generate ever-greater resentment. Jihadists could conceivably argue that they have a negotiable program: cessation of U.S. support for Israel, withdrawal from Saudi Arabia, broader American disengagement from the Islamic world. But U.S. and allied conceptions of international security and strategic imperatives will make such demands difficult, if not impossible, to accommodate.

Reducing Vulnerability to New Terrorism

Facing a global adversary with maximal goals and lacking a bargaining option or means to redress severe conditions that may or may not motivate attackers, the United States is confined primarily to a strategy of defense, deterrence by denial, and, where possible and prudent, pre-emption. Deterrence through the promise of retaliation is impossible with an adversary that controls little or no territory and invites attack.

> **The United States remains al-Qaida's prime target. Suleiman Abu Ghaith, the al-Qaida spokesman, has said that there can be no truce until the group has killed four million Americans.**

Adjusting to the new threat entails disturbing conceptual twists for U.S. policymakers. After generations of effort to reduce the risk of surprise attack through technical means and negotiated transparency measures, surprise will be the natural order of things. The problem of warning will be further intensified by the creativity of this adversary, its recruitment of Europeans and Americans, and its ability to stage attacks from within the United States. Thinking carefully about the unlikely—"institutionalizing imaginativeness," as Dennis Gormley has put it—is by definition a paradox, but nonetheless essential for American planners.

With warning scarce and inevitably ambiguous, it will be necessary to probe the enemy both to put him off balance and to learn of his intentions. The United States has done so clandestinely against hostile intelligence agencies. Against al-Qaida, a more difficult target, the approach will take time to cohere. Probes could also take the form of military action against al-Qaida–affiliated cantonments, where they still exist. The greater the movement's virtuality, however, the fewer the targets available for U.S. action. Preemptive strikes could target sites that develop, produce, or harbor weapons of mass destruction.

A decade of al-Qaida activity within the United States has erased the customary distinction between the domestic and the foreign in intelligence and law enforcement. The relationship between the Central Intelligence Agency and the Federal Bureau of Investigation must change. Only a more integrated organization can adapt to the seamlessness of the transnational arenas in which the terrorists operate.

Civil liberties and security must be rebalanced. How sweeping the process turns out to be will depend largely on whether the nation suffers another attack or at least a convincing attempt. Americans will have to be convinced that curtailing civil liberties is unavoidable and limited to the need to deal with proximate threats. They will need to see bipartisan consensus in Congress and between Congress and the White House and be sure that politicians are committed to keeping the rebalancing to a minimum.

The distinction between public and private sector has also been blurred. Al-Qaida has targeted the American population and used our infrastructure against us. A perpetual state of heightened readiness would impose unacceptable opportunity costs on the civilian world, so vulnerabilities must be reduced. Civilian ownership of the infrastructure is a complication. What the U.S. government does not own, it cannot completely defend. Private owners do not necessarily share the government's perception of the terrorist threat and are often able to resist regulation. Where they accept the threat, they view it as a national security issue for which the federal government should bear the cost. The idea of public-private partnership is only now finding acceptance in the cybersecurity realm as concerns over litigation have brought about a focus on due diligence. The pursuit of public-private partnership will have to be extended to all potentially vulnerable critical infrastructures by a government that does not yet understand perfectly which infrastructures are truly critical and which apparently dispensable infrastructures interact to become critical.

> ## Governments in Egypt, Saudi Arabia, Pakistan, and Indonesia are unwilling or unable to oppose anti-Western religiously based popular feeling.

Defending these infrastructures will also present unprecedented challenges. The U.S. government is not on the lookout for military formations, but for a lone, unknown person in a visa line. Technology—biometrics, data mining, super-fast data processing, and ubiquitous video surveillance—will move this needle-in-the-haystack problem into the just-possible category by providing the means to collect and store detailed and unique characteristics of huge numbers of people and match them to the person in the visa line. The cost will be the need to archive personal information on a great mass of individuals.

The United States must also devise ways to block or intercept vehicles that deliver weapons of mass destruction. It cannot do that alone. The cruise missile threat, for instance, requires the cooperation of suppliers, which means an active American role in expanding the remit of the Missile Technology Control Regime (MTCR). Weapons components themselves must be kept out of terrorists' hands. The recent adoption of MTCR controls on cheap technologies for transforming small aircraft into cruise missiles shows what can be accomplished. Washington has been buying surplus fissile materials from Russia's large stock and helping Russians render them useless for weapons; it will be vital to continue generous funding for that effort.

Remote detection of weapons, especially nuclear ones, that have reached the United States is crucial. Emergency response teams will need to be able to pinpoint the location of a device, identify its type, and know in advance how to render it safe once it has been seized. Local authorities will have to detect and identify biological and chemical agents that have been released. Genetically engineered vaccines must be rapidly developed and produced to stop local attacks from becoming national, and ultimately global, epidemics. Special medical units must be on standby to relieve local health care personnel who become exhausted or die.

Offensive opportunities will be limited but not impossible. They do, however, require impeccable intelligence, which has been hard to come by. The Afghan nexus in which jihadis initially came together and the cohesion of the groups that constitute the al-Qaida movement have made penetration forbiddingly complicated. But as al-Qaida picks up converts to Islam and Muslims who have long resided in Western countries,

penetration may become easier. The more they look like us, the more we look like them.

Another source of potentially vital information is the jihadis picked up by local authorities abroad on the basis of U.S. intelligence and then shipped to their countries of origin for interrogation. Transfers of this sort were carried out frequently during the 1990s and sometimes produced life-saving intelligence on imminent terrorist attacks. In some cases, the authorities where a suspect resides will not wish to make an arrest, fearing terrorist retaliation, political problems, or diplomatic friction. The United States has asserted the authority to conduct these operations without the consent of the host government but has generally refrained from acting. In the wake of September 11, Washington may want to reassess the risks and benefits of these actions.

Without revoking the long-standing executive order prohibiting assassination, the United States should also consider targeted killing, to use the Israeli phrase, of jihadists known to be central to an evolving conspiracy to attack the United States or to obtain weapons of mass destruction. As a practical matter, the intelligence value of such a person alive would generally outweigh the disruptive benefits of his death, assuming that U.S. or friendly intelligence services could be relied on to keep him under surveillance. But this will not always be so. When it is not, from a legal standpoint, targeted killing falls reasonably under the right to self-defense. Such a policy departure is unsavory. But in a new strategic context, with jihadis intent on mass casualties, unsavory may not be a sensible threshold. The killing of al-Qaida operatives in Yemen by missiles fired from a CIA-controlled aerial drone suggests that this threshold may already have been crossed.

Allied Cooperation

As the al-Qaida movement dissolves into virtuality in 60 countries worldwide, international cooperation becomes ever more indispensable to countering the threat.

Many countries that host al-Qaida will cooperate with the United States out of self-interest; they do not want jihadis on their soil any more than Americans do on theirs. A durable and effective counterterrorism campaign, however, requires not just bare-bones cooperation, but political collaboration at a level that tells the bureaucracies that cooperation with their American counterparts is expected. Such a robust, wholesale working relationship is what produces vital large-scale initiatives—a common diplomatic approach toward problem states; a sustainable program of economic development for the Middle East; domestic policy reforms that lessen the appeal of jihadism to Muslim diaspora communities; improved border controls; and tightened bonds among the justice ministries, law enforcement, customs, and intelligence agencies, and special operations forces on the front lines.

Whether this level of burden sharing emerges, let alone endures, depends on the give-and-take among the players. Since September 11, the United States has fostered allied perceptions that Washington is indifferent to their priorities. The United

States has not yet paid a serious penalty in terms of allied cooperation. The scale of the attacks and the administration's blend of resolve and restraint in the war on terrorism have offset allies' disappointment in its go-it-alone posture. But as the war grinds on, good will is certain to wear thin. The United States would be wise to adopt a more flexible posture to ensure allied support in the crises that will inevitably come. Washington's willingness to seek a new Security Council resolution on Iraq was a good start.

Washington's interests would also be well served by modifying what appears at times to be a monolithic view of terrorist networks that equates the Arafats and Saddams of the world with bin Laden (or his successors). Several European partners regard Arafat and his ilk as considerably more controllable through diplomacy than bin Laden. Greater American flexibility may prove essential for ensuring European capitals' military, law-enforcement, and intelligence cooperation. And the fact remains that al-Qaida has killed more Americans than have Iraq, Iran, or Palestinian groups and would use weapons of mass destruction against the United States as soon as it acquired them. A good case can be made for a preventive war against Iraq to stave off the prospect of a nuclear-armed Saddam regime. We should recognize, though, that dealing with this strategic challenge may galvanize the equally dangerous threat of mass casualty attacks by Sunni terrorists.

Israel and the Palestinians

Since the heyday of the Middle East peace process under Ehud Barak's Labor government, jihadists have exploited the Israeli-Palestinian conflict to boost their popularity. The strategem has worked: jihadists are seen as sticking up for Palestinian rights, while Arab governments do nothing. Direct, energetic U.S. diplomatic intervention in the conflict would lessen the appeal of jihadi claims and make it marginally easier for regional governments to cooperate in the war on terrorism by demonstrating American commitment to resolving the Israeli-Palestinian conflict.

The Bush administration, for good reason, fears becoming entangled in a drawn-out, venomous negotiation between irreconcilable parties. They see it distracting them from higher priorities and embroiling them in domestic political disputes over whether Washington should pressure Israel. Still, the administration has been drawn in by degrees and has announced its support for creating a Palestinian state. If the war on terrorism is now the highest U.S. priority, then more vigorous—and admittedly risky—involvement in the Israeli-Palestinian conflict is required. The jihadi argument that the United States supports the murder of Palestinian Muslims must be countered.

Democratization in the Middle East

As it continues to engage with the authoritarian regimes in Cairo and Riyadh, Washington should try to renegotiate the im-

plicit bargain that underpins its relations with both. The current bargain is structured something like this: Egypt sustains its commitment to peace with Israel, Saudi Arabia stabilizes oil prices, and both proffer varying degrees of diplomatic support for American objectives in the region, especially toward Iraq. In return, Washington defers to their domestic policies, even if these fuel the growth and export of Islamic militancy and deflect public discontent onto the United States and Israel. With jihadis now pursuing nuclear weapons, that bargain no longer looks sensible.

Under a new bargain, Cairo and Riyadh would begin to take measured risks to lead their publics gradually toward greater political participation by encouraging opposition parties of a more secular cast and allowing greater freedom of expression. Saudi Arabia would throttle back on its wahhabiization of the Islamic world by cutting its production and export of unemployable graduates in religious studies and reducing subsidies for foreign mosques and madrasahs that propagate a confrontational and intolerant form of Islam while crowding out alternative practices. Both countries would be pushed to reform their school curricula—and enforce standards—to ensure a better understanding of the non-Islamic world and encourage respect for other cultures. With increased financial and technical assistance from the West, regimes governing societies beset by economic problems that spur radicalism would focus more consistently on the welfare of their people. In this somewhat utopian conception, leaders in both countries would use their new legitimacy to challenge Islamist myths about America and Western hostility toward Islam. In sum, Cairo and Riyadh would challenge the culture of demonization across the board, with an eye toward laying the groundwork for liberal democracy.

In the framework of this new bargain, the United States would move more boldly to establish contacts with moderate opposition figures in Egypt, Saudi Arabia, and perhaps other countries. The benefit would be twofold. Washington would get a better sense of events on the ground and would also gain credibility and perhaps even understanding on the part of critics. For this effort to bear fruit, however, the United States would have to use regional media efficiently—something for which it has as yet no well-developed strategy. Washington would also have to engage in a measure of self-scrutiny, examining how its policies contribute—in avoidable ways—to Muslim anti-Americanism. "Re-branding" is not enough.

Change will be slow. The regimes in Cairo and Riyadh face largely self-inflicted problems they cannot readily surmount without serious risks to stability. Nor is the United States entirely free to insist on the new bargain: it will need Saudi cooperation on Iraq as long as Saddam Hussein is in power, if not longer, given the uncertainties surrounding Iraq's future after Saddam leaves the stage. Egyptian support for a broader Arab-Israeli peace will also remain essential. But change has to start sometime, somewhere. It will take steady U.S. pressure and persistent attempts to convince both regimes that a new bargain will serve their countries' long-term interests. The sooner the new deals are struck, the better.

Hazardous but Not Hopeless

Western democracies face a serious, possibly transgenerational terrorist threat whose causes are multidimensional and difficult to address. The situation is hazardous, but not hopeless. The United States possesses enormous wealth, has capable allies, and stands on the leading edge of technological development that will be key to survival. A strategy that takes into account the military, intelligence, law-enforcement, diplomatic, and economic pieces of the puzzle will see America through. For the next few years, the objective will be to contain the threat, in much the same way that the United States contained Soviet power throughout the Cold War. The adversary must be prevented from doing his worst, while Washington and its allies wear down its capabilities and undermine its appeal to fellow Muslims. Success will require broad domestic support and a strong coalition abroad.

Prospects are, in many respects, bleak. But the dangers are not disproportionate to those the nation faced in the 20th century. America's initial reaction to September 11 was and indeed had to be its own self-defense: bolstering homeland security, denying al-Qaida access to weapons of mass destruction, dismantling its networks, and developing a law-enforcement and intelligence capacity to cope with the new adversary. Not all vulnerabilities can be identified and even fewer remedied, and al-Qaida need launch only one attack with a weapon of mass destruction to throw the United States into a profound crisis. Washington and its partners must convince Muslim populations that they can prosper without either destroying the West or abandoning their own traditions to the West's alien culture. That is a long-term project. American and allied determination in a war against apocalyptic—and genocidal—religious fanatics must be coupled with a generous vision about postwar possibilities. Militant Islam cannot be expected to embrace the West in the foreseeable future. But the United States can lay the foundation for a lasting accommodation by deploying its considerable economic and political advantages. It is not too late to begin.

Steven Simon is a senior fellow at the International Institute for Strategic Studies and coauthor, with Daniel Benjamin, of The Age of Sacred Terror *(Random House, October 2002).*

From the *Brookings Review*, Winter 2003, pp. 18–24. © 2003 by the Brookings Institution Press, Washington, DC. Reprinted by permission.

The Religious Sources of Islamic Terrorism

By Shmuel Bar

WHILE TERRORISM—even in the form of suicide attacks—is not an Islamic phenomenon by definition, it cannot be ignored that the lion's share of terrorist acts and the most devastating of them in recent years have been perpetrated in the name of Islam. This fact has sparked a fundamental debate both in the West and within the Muslim world regarding the link between these acts and the teachings of Islam. Most Western analysts are hesitant to identify such acts with the bona fide teachings of one of the world's great religions and prefer to view them as a perversion of a religion that is essentially peace-loving and tolerant. Western leaders such as George W. Bush and Tony Blair have reiterated time and again that the war against terrorism has nothing to do with Islam. It is a war against evil.

The non-Islamic etiologies of this phenomenon include political causes (the Israeli-Arab conflict); cultural causes (rebellion against Western cultural colonialism); and social causes (alienation, poverty). While no public figure in the West would deny the imperative of fighting the war against terrorism, it is equally politically correct to add the codicil that, for the war to be won, these (justified) grievances pertaining to the root causes of terrorism should be addressed. A skeptic may note that many societies can put claim to similar grievances but have not given birth to religious-based ideologies that justify no-holds-barred terrorism. Nevertheless an interpretation which places the blame for terrorism on religious and cultural traits runs the risk of being branded as bigoted and Islamophobic.

The political motivation of the leaders of Islamist jihadist-type movements is not in doubt. A glance at the theatres where such movements flourished shows that most fed off their political—and usually military—encounter with the West. This was the case in India and in the Sudan in the nineteenth century and in Egypt and Palestine in the twentieth. The moral justification and levers of power for these movements, however, were for the most part not couched in political terms, but based on Islamic religious sources of authority and religious principles. By using these levers and appealing to deeply ingrained religious beliefs, the radical leaders succeed in motivating the Islamist terrorist, creating for him a social environment that provides approbation and a religious environment that provides moral and legal sanction for his actions. The success of radical Islamic organizations in the recruitment, posting, and ideological maintenance of sleeper activists (the 9-11 terrorists are a prime example) without their defecting or succumbing to the lure of Western civilization proves the deep ideological nature of the phenomenon.

Therefore, to treat Islamic terrorism as the consequence of political and socioeconomic factors alone would not do justice to the significance of the religious culture in which this phenomenon is rooted and nurtured. In order to comprehend the motivation for these acts and to draw up an effective strategy for a war against terrorism, it is necessary to understand the religious-ideological factors—which are deeply embedded in Islam.

The Weltanschauung of radical Islam

MODERN INTERNATIONAL Islamist terrorism is a natural offshoot of twentieth-century Islamic fundamentalism. The "Islamic Movement" emerged in the Arab world and British-ruled India as a response to the dismal state of Muslim society in those countries: social injustice, rejection of traditional mores, acceptance of foreign domination and culture. It perceives the malaise of modern Muslim societies as having strayed from the "straight path" (*as-sirat al-mustaqim*) and the solution to all ills in a return to the original mores of Islam. The problems addressed may be social or political: inequality, corruption, and oppression. But in traditional Islam—and certainly in the worldview of the Islamic fundamentalist—there is no separation between the political and the religious. Islam is, in essence, both religion and regime (*din wa-dawla*) and no area of human activity is outside its remit. Be the nature of the problem as it may, "Islam is the solution."

The underlying element in the radical Islamist worldview is ahistoric and dichotomist: Perfection lies in the ways of the Prophet and the events of his time; therefore, religious innovations, philosophical relativism, and intellectual or political pluralism are anathema. In such a worldview, there can exist only two camps—*Dar al-Islam* ("The House of Islam"—i.e., the Muslim countries) and *Dar al-Harb* ("The House of War"—i.e., countries ruled by any regime but Islam)—which are pitted against each other until the final victory of Islam. These concepts are carried to their extreme conclusion by the radicals; however, they have deep roots in mainstream Islam.

While the trigger for "Islamic awakening" was frequently the meeting with the West, Islamic-motivated rebellions against colonial powers rarely involved individuals from other Muslim countries or broke out of the confines of the territories over which they were fighting. Until the 1980s, most fundamentalist movements such as the Muslim Brotherhood (*Ikhwan Muslimun*) were inward-looking; Western superiority was viewed as the result of Muslims having forsaken the teachings of the Prophet. Therefore, the remedy was, first, "re-Islamization" of Muslim society and restoration of an Islamic government, based on Islamic law (*shari'ah*). In this context, jihad was aimed mainly against "apostate" Muslim governments and societies, while the historic offensive jihad of the Muslim world against the infidels was put in abeyance (at least until the restoration of the caliphate).

Until the 1980s, attempts to mobilize Muslims all over the world for a jihad in one area of the world (Palestine, Kashmir) were unsuccessful. The Soviet invasion of Afghanistan was a watershed event, as it revived the concept of participation in jihad to evict an "infidel" occupier from a Muslim country as a "personal duty" (*fard 'ein*) for every capable Muslim. The basis of this duty derives from the "irreversibility" of Islamic identity both for individual Muslims (thus, capital punishment for "apostates"—e.g., Salman Rushdie) and for Muslim territories. Therefore, any land (Afghanistan, Palestine, Kashmir, Chechnya, Spain) that had once been under the sway of Islamic law may not revert to control by any other law. In such a case, it becomes the "personal duty" of all Muslims in the land to fight a jihad to liberate it.[1] If they do not succeed, it becomes incumbent on any Muslim in a certain perimeter from that land to join the jihad and so forth. Accordingly, given the number of Muslim lands under "infidel occupation" and the length of time of those occupations, it is argued that it has become a personal duty for all Muslims to join the jihad. This duty—if taken seriously—is no less a religious imperative than the other five pillars of Islam (the statement of belief or *shahadah*, prayer, fasting, charity, and *haj*). It becomes a de facto (and in the eyes of some a de jure) sixth pillar; a Muslim who does not perform it will inherit hell.

Such a philosophy attributing centrality to the duty of jihad is not an innovation of modern radical Islam. The seventh-century Kharijite sect, infamous in Islamic history as a cause of Muslim civil war, took this position and implemented it. But the Kharijite doctrine was rejected as a heresy by medieval Islam. The novelty is the tacit acceptance by mainstream Islam of the basic building blocks of this "neo-Kharijite" school.

The centrality of the duty of jihad is not an innovation of modern radical Islam.

The Soviet defeat in Afghanistan and the subsequent fall of the Soviet Union were perceived as an eschatological sign, adumbrating the renewal of the jihad against the infidel world at large and the apocalyptical war between Islam and heresy which will result in the rule of Islam in the world. Along with the renewal of the jihad, the Islamist Weltanschauung, which emerged from the Afghani crucible, developed a Thanatophile ideology[2] in which death is idealized as a desired goal and not a necessary evil in war.

An offshoot of this philosophy poses a dilemma for theories of deterrence. The Islamic traditions of war allow the Muslim forces to retreat if their numerical strength is less than half that of the enemy. Other traditions go further and allow retreat only in the face of a tenfold superiority of the enemy. The reasoning is that the act of jihad is, by definition, an act of faith in Allah. By fighting a weaker or equal enemy, the Muslim is relying on his own strength and not on Allah; by entering the fray against all odds, the *mujahed* is proving his utter faith in Allah and will be rewarded accordingly.

The politics of Islamist radicalism has also bred a mentality of *bello ergo sum* (I fight, therefore I exist)—Islamic leaders are in constant need of popular jihads to boost their leadership status. Nothing succeeds like success: The attacks in the United States gave birth to a second wave of mujahidin who want to emulate their heroes. The perception of resolve on the part of the West is a critical factor in shaping the mood of the Muslim population toward radical ideas. Therefore, the manner by which the United States deals with the present crisis in Iraq is not unconnected to the future of the radical Islamic movement. In these circles, the American occupation of Iraq is likened to the Soviet invasion of Afghanistan; a sense of American failure would feed the apocalyptical ideology of jihad.

The legality of jihad

THESE BELIEFS ARE commonly viewed as typical of radical Islamic ideology, but few orthodox Islamic scholars would deny that they are deeply rooted in orthodox Islam or would dismiss the very ideology of jihad as a military struggle as foreign to the basic tenets of Islam.

Hence, much of the debate between radicals and nonradicals is not over the religious principles themselves, but over their implication for actual behavior as based on the detailed legal interpretation of those principles. This legal interpretation is the soul of the debate. Even among moderate Islamic scholars who condemn acts of terrorism (albeit with reservation so as not to include acts perpetrated against Israel in such a category), there is no agreement on *why* they should be condemned: Many modernists acknowledge the existence of a duty of jihad in Islam but call for an "Islamic Protestantism" that would divest Islam of vestiges of anachronistic beliefs; conservative moderates find in traditional Islamic jurisprudence (*shari'ah*) legal justification to put the imperative of jihad in abeyance; others use linguistic analysis to point out that the etymology of the word jihad (*jahada*) actually means "to strive," does not mean "holy war," and does not necessarily have a military connotation.[3]

The legalistic approach is not a barren preoccupation of scholars. The ideal Islamic regime is a nomocracy: The law is given and immutable, and it remains for the leaders of the ummah (the Islamic nation) to apply it on a day-to-day basis. Islam is not indifferent to any facet of human behavior; all possible acts potentially have a religious standing, ranging between "duty" (*fard*, pl. *fara'id*); "recommended" (*mandub*); "optional" (*jaiz*); "permitted" (*mubah*); "reprehensible" (*makruh*); and "forbidden" (*haram*). This taxonomy of human behavior has far-reaching importance for the believer: By performing all his religious duties, he will inherit paradise; by failing to do so ("sins of omission") or doing that which is forbidden ("sins of commission"), he will be condemned to hell. Therefore, such issues as the legitimacy of jihad—ostensibly deriving from the roots of Islam—cannot be decided by abstract morality[4] or by politics, but by meticulous legal analysis and ruling (*fatwa*) according to the shari'ah, performed by an authoritative Islamic scholar ('*alem*, pl. '*ulama*).

The use of fatwas to call for violent action first became known in the West as a result of Ayatollah Khomeini's *fatwa* against Salman Rushdie, and again after Osama bin Laden's 1998 *fatwa* against the United States and Israel. But as a genuine instrument of religious deliberation, it has not received the attention it deserves. Analysts have frequently interpreted *fatwas* as no more than the cynical use of religious terminology in political propaganda. This interpretation does not do justice to the painstaking process of legal reasoning invested in these documents and the importance that their authors and their target audience genuinely accord to the religious truthfulness of their rulings.

The political strength of these *fatwas* has been time-tested in Muslim political society by rebels and insurgents from the Arabian peninsula to Sudan, India, and Indonesia. At the same time, they have been used by Muslim regimes to bolster their Islamic credentials against external and domestic enemies and to legitimize their policies. This was done by the Sudanese mahdi in his rebellion against the British (1881-85); by the Ottoman caliphate (December 1914) in World War I; by the Syrian regime against the rebellion in northern Syria (1981); and, mutatis mutandis, by Egyptian President Anwar Sadat to legitimize his peace policies toward Israel.

The *fatwas* promulgated by sheikhs and '*ULAMA* who stipulate that jihad is a "personal duty" play, therefore, a pivotal role in encouraging radicalism and in building the support infrastructure for radicals within the traditional Islamic community. While one may find many *fatwas* which advocate various manifestations of terrorism, *fatwas* which rule that those who perform these acts do not go to paradise but inherit hell are few and far between.

The questions relating to jihad which are referred to the religious scholars[5] relate to a number of issues:

The very definition, current existence, and area of application of the state of jihad. Is jihad one of the "pillars" (*arkan*) or "roots" (*usul*) of Islam? Does it necessarily imply military war, or can it be perceived as a duty to spread Islam through preaching or even the moral struggle between one's soul and Satan?[6] If the former, then what are the *necessary conditions for jihad*? Does a state of jihad currently exist between *Dar al-Islam* and *Dar al-Harb*? And how can one define *Dar al-Islam* today, in the absence of a caliphate? Is the rest of the world automatically defined as *Dar al-Harb* with which a state of jihad exists, or do the treaties and diplomatic relations which exist between Muslim countries and "infidel" countries (including the charter of the United Nations) change this?[7]

Who must participate in jihad, and how? Is jihad a personal duty (*fard 'ein*) for each and every Muslim under all circumstances or a collective duty (*fard kiffaya*) that can be performed only under the leadership of a leader of all Muslims (*imam, khalifa, amir al-mu'aminin*)? Is it incumbent on women? On minors? (According to Islamic law, in the case of a defensive jihad for the liberation of Islamic territory from infidel occupation, "a woman need not ask permission of her husband nor a child of his parents nor a slave of his master.") May a Muslim refrain from supporting his attacked brethren or obey a non-Muslim secular law which prohibits him from supporting other Muslims in their struggle?

How should the jihad be fought (jus in bellum)? The questions in this area relate, inter alia, to: (A) Is jihad by definition an act of conflict against the actual "infidels" or can it be defined as a spiritual struggle against the "evil inclination"? If it is the former, must it take the form of war (*jihad fi-sabil Allah*) or can it be performed by way of preaching and proselytization (*da'awah*)? (B) Who is a legitimate target? Is it permissible to kill noncombatant civilians—women, children, elderly, and clerics; "protected" non-Muslims in Muslim countries—local non-Muslims or tourists whose visas may be interpreted as Islamic guarantees of passage (*aman*); Muslim bystanders? (C) The legitimacy of suicide attacks (*istishhad*) as a form of jihad in the light of the severe prohibition on a Muslim taking his own life, on one hand, and the promise of rewards in the afterlife for the *shahid* who falls in a jihad on the other hand.[8] (D) The weapons which may be used. For example, may a hijacked plane be used as a weapon as in the attacks of September 11 in the light of Islamic prohibitions on killing prisoners? (E) The status of a Muslim who aids the "infidels" against other Muslims. (F) The authority to implement capital punishment in the absence of a caliph.

How should jihad be funded? "Pocketbook jihad" is deeply entrenched in Islamic tradition. It is based on the injunction that one must fight jihad with his soul or with his tongue (*jihad al-lissan* or *da'awah*) or with his money (*jihad fi-mal*). Therefore, financial support of jihad is politically correct and even good for business for the wealthy supporter. The transfer of *zakat* (almsgiving) raised in a community for *jihad fi-sabil Allah* (i.e., jihad on Allah's path or military jihad) has wide religious and social legitimacy.[9] The precepts of "war booty" (*ghaneema* or *fay'*) call for a fifth (*khoms*) to be rendered to the mujahidin. Acts that would otherwise be considered religiously prohibited are thus legitimized by the payment of such a "tax" for the sake of jihad. While there have been attempts to bring Muslim clerics to denounce acts of terrorism, none, to date, have condemned the donation of money for jihad.

The dilemma of the moderate Muslim

*I*T CAN BE safely assumed that the great majority of Muslims in the world have no desire to join a jihad or to politicize their religion. However, it is also true that insofar as religious establishments in most of the Arabian peninsula, in Iran, and in much of Egypt and North Africa are concerned, the radical ideology does not represent a marginal and extremist perversion of Islam but rather a genuine and increasingly mainstream interpretation. Even after 9-11, the sermons broadcast from Mecca cannot be easily distinguished from those of al Qaeda.

Facing the radical Weltanschauung, the moderate but orthodox Muslim has to grapple with two main dilemmas: the difficulty of refuting the legal-religious arguments of the radical interpretation and the aversion to—or even prohibition of—inciting an Islamic Kulturkampf which would split the ranks of the *ummah*.

The first dilemma is not uniquely Islamic. It is characteristic of revelation-based religions that the less observant or less orthodox will hesitate to challenge fundamental dogmas out of fear of being branded slack or lapsed in their faith. They will prefer to pay their dues to the religious establishment, hoping that by doing so they are also buying their own freedom from coercion. On a deeper level, many believers who are not strict in observance may see their own lifestyle as a matter of convenience and not principle, while the extreme orthodox is the true believer to whom they defer.

This phenomenon is compounded in Islam by the fact that "Arab" Sunni Islam never went though a reform.[10] Since the tenth century, Islam has lacked an accepted mechanism for relegating a tenet or text to ideological obsolescence. Until that time, such a mechanism—*ijtihad*—

existed; *ijtihad* is the authorization of scholars to reach conclusions not only from existing interpretations and legal precedents, but from their own perusal of the texts. In the tenth century, the "gates of *ijtihad*" were closed for most of the Sunni world. It is still practiced in Shiite Islam and in Southeast Asia. Reformist traditions did appear in non-Arab Middle Eastern Muslim societies (Turkey, Iran) and in Southeast Asian Islam. Many Sufi (mystical) schools also have traditions of syncretism, reformism, and moderation. These traditions, however, have always suffered from a lack of wide legitimacy due to their non-Arab origins and have never been able to offer themselves as an acceptable alternative to ideologies born in the heartland of Islam and expressed in the tongue of the Prophet. In recent years, these societies have undergone a transformation and have adopted much of the Middle Eastern brand of Islamic orthodoxy and have become, therefore, more susceptible to radical ideologies under the influence of Wahhabi missionaries, Iranian export of Islam, and the cross-pollination resulting from the globalization of ideas in the information age.

The second dilemma—the disinclination of moderates to confront the radicals—has frequently been attributed to violent intimidation (which, no doubt, exists), but it has an additional religious dimension. While the radicals are not averse to branding their adversaries as apostates, orthodox and moderate Muslims rarely resort to this weapon. Such an act (*takfir*—accusing another Muslim of heresy [*kufr*] by falsifying the roots of Islam, allowing that which is prohibited or forbidding that which is allowed) is not to be taken lightly; it contradicts the deep-rooted value that Islam places on unity among the believers and its aversion to *fitna* (communal discord). It is ironic that a religious mechanism which seems to have been created as a tool to preserve pluralism and prevent internal debates from deteriorating into civil war and mutual accusations of heresy (as occurred in Christian Europe) has become a tool in the hands of the radicals to drown out any criticism of them.

Consequently, even when pressure is put on Muslim communities, there exists a political asymmetry in favor of the radicals. Moderates are reluctant to come forward and to risk being accused of apostasy. For this very reason, many Muslim regimes in the Middle East and Asia are reluctant to crack down on the religious aspects of radical Islam and satisfy themselves with dealing with the political violence alone. By way of appeasement politics, they trade tolerance of jihad elsewhere for local calm. Thus, they lose ground to radicals in their societies.

The Western dilemma

*I*T IS A TENDENCY in politically oriented Western society to assume that there is a rational pragmatic cause for acts of terrorism and that if the political grievance is addressed properly, the phenomenon will fade. However, when the roots are not political, it is naïve to expect political gestures to change the hearts of radicals. Attempts to deal with the terrorist threat as if it were divorced from its intellectual, cultural, and religious fountainheads are doomed to failure. Counterterrorism begins on the religious-ideological level and must adopt appropriate methods. The cultural and religious sources of radical Islamic ideology must be addressed in order to develop a long-range strategy for coping with the terrorist threat to which they give birth.

However, in addressing this phenomenon, the West is at a severe disadvantage. Western concepts of civil rights along with legal, political, and cultural constraints preclude government intervention in the internal matters of organized religions; they make it difficult to prohibit or punish inflammatory sermons of imams in mosques (as Muslim regimes used to do on a regular basis) or to punish clerics for *fatwa*s justifying terrorism. Furthermore, the legacy of colonialism deters Western governments from taking steps that may be construed as anti-Muslim or as signs of lingering colonialist ideology. This exposes the Western country combating the terrorist threat to criticism from within. Even most of the new and stringent terrorism prevention legislation that has been enacted in some counties leans mainly on investigatory powers (such as allowing for unlimited administrative arrests, etc.) and does not deal with prohibition of religion-based "ideological crimes" (as opposed to anti-Nazi and anti-racism laws, which are in force in many countries in Europe).

The regimes of the Middle East have proven their mettle in coercing religious establishments and even radical sheikhs to rule in a way commensurate with their interests. However, most of them show no inclination to join a global (i.e., "infidel") war against radical Islamic ideology. Hence, the prospect of enlisting Middle Eastern allies in the struggle against Islamic radicalism is bleak. Under these conditions, it will be difficult to curb the conversion of young Muslims in the West to the ideas of radicalism emanating from the safe houses of the Middle East. Even those who are not in direct contact with Middle Eastern sources of inspiration may absorb the ideology secondhand through interaction of Muslims from various origins in schools and on the internet.

Fighting hellfire with hellfire

TAKING INTO ACCOUNT the above, is it possible—within the bounds of Western democratic values—to implement a comprehensive strategy to combat Islamic terrorism at its ideological roots? First, such a strategy must be based on an acceptance of the fact that for the first time since the Crusades, Western civilization finds itself involved in a religious war; the conflict has been defined by the attacking side as such with the eschatological goal of the destruction of Western civilization. The goal of the West cannot be defense alone or military offense or democratization of the Middle East as a panacea. It must include a religious-ideological dimension: active pressure

How could that happen?

for religious reform in the Muslim world and pressure on the orthodox Islamic establishment in the West and the Middle East not only to disengage itself clearly from any justification of violence, but also to pit itself against the radical camp in a clear demarcation of boundaries.

Such disengagement cannot be accomplished by Western-style declarations of condemnation. It must include clear and binding legal rulings by religious authorities which contradict the axioms of the radical worldview and virtually "excommunicate" the radicals. In essence, the radical narrative, which promises paradise to those who perpetrate acts of terrorism, must be met by an equally legitimate religious force which guarantees hellfire for the same acts. Some elements of such rulings should be, inter alia:

- A call for renewal of *ijtihad* as the basis to reform Islamic dogmas and to relegate old dogmas to historic contexts.

- That there exists no state of jihad between Islam and the rest of the world (hence, jihad is not a personal duty).

- That the violation of the physical safety of a non-Muslim in a Muslim country is prohibited (*haram*).

- That suicide bombings are clear acts of suicide, and therefore, their perpetrators are condemned to eternal hellfire.

- That moral or financial support of acts of terrorism is also *haram*.

- That a legal ruling claiming jihad is a duty derived from the roots of Islam is a falsification of the roots of Islam, and therefore, those who make such statements have performed acts of heresy.

Only by setting up a clear demarcation between orthodox and radical Islam can the radical elements be exorcized. The priority of solidarity within the Islamic world plays into the hands of the radicals. Only an Islamic Kulturkampf can redraw the boundaries between radical and moderate in favor of the latter. Such a struggle must be based on an in-depth understanding of the religious sources for justification of Islamist terrorism and a plan for the creation of a legitimate moderate counterbalance to the radical narrative in Islam. Such an alternative narrative should have a sound base in Islamic teachings, and its proponents should be Islamic scholars and leaders with wide legitimacy and accepted credentials.[11] The "Middle-Easternization" of Asian Muslim communities should also be checked.

A strategy to cope with radical Islamic ideology cannot take shape without a reinterpretation of Western concepts of the boundaries of the freedoms of religion and speech, definitions of religious incitement, and criminal culpability of religious leaders for the acts of their flock as a result of their spiritual influence. Such a reinterpretation impinges on basic principles of Western civilization and law. Under the circumstances, it is the lesser evil.

Notes

1. "If the disbelievers occupy a territory belonging to the Muslims, it is incumbent upon the Muslims to drive them out, and to restore the land back to themselves; Spain had been a Muslim territory for more than eight hundred years, before it was captured by the Christians. They [i.e., the Christians] literally, and practically wiped out the whole Muslim population. And now, it is our duty to restore Muslim rule to this land of ours. The whole of India, including Kashmir, Hyderabad, Assam, Nepal, Burma, Behar, and Junagadh was once a Muslim territory. But we lost this vast territory, and it fell into the hands of the disbelievers simply because we abandoned Jihad. And Palestine, as is well-known, is currently under the occupation of the Jews. Even our First Qibla, Bait-ul-Muqaddas is under their illegal possession."—*Jihaad ul-Kuffaari wal-Munaafiqeen.*

2. This is characterized by the emphasis on verses in the Koran and stories extolling martyrdom ("Why do you cling to this world when the next world is better?") and praising the virtues of paradise as a real and even sensual existence.

3. This is a rather specious argument. In all occurrences of the concept in traditional Islamic texts—and more significantly in the accepted meaning for the great majority of modern Muslims—the term means a divinely ordained war.

4. A frequently quoted verse "proving" the inadequacy of human conscience in regard to matters of jihad is Koran 2:216: "Fighting is ordered for you even though you dislike it and it may be that you dislike a thing that is good for you and like a thing that is bad for you. Allah knows but you do not know."

5. The following list of questions has been gleaned from a large corpus of *fatwas* collected by the author over recent years. The *fatwas* represent the questions of lay Muslims and responses of scholars from different countries. Some of the *fatwas* were written and published in mosques, others in the open press, and others in dedicated sites on the internet.

6. This claim, a favorite of modernists and moderates, comes from a unique and unconfirmed hadith which states: "The Prophet returned from one of his battles, and thereupon

told us, "You have arrived with an excellent arrival, you have come from the Lesser Jihad to the Greater Jihad—the striving of a servant [of Allah] against his desires."

7. Some Islamic judicial schools add to the *Dar al-Islam/Dar al-Harb* dichotomy a third category: *Dar al-'Ahad*, countries which have peace treaties with Muslims and therefore are not to be attacked. The basis for discerning whether or not a country belongs to *Dar al-Islam* is not agreed upon. Some scholars claim that as long as a Muslim can practice his faith openly, the country is not *Dar al-Harb.*

8. It should be noted that in the historic paradigms of "suicide" terror, which are used as authority for justification of such attacks, the martyr did not kill himself but rather placed himself in a situation in which he would most likely be killed. Technically, therefore, he did not violate the Koranic prohibition on a Muslim taking his own life. The targets of the suicide terrorist of ancient times were also quite different—officials of the ruling class and armed (Muslim) enemies. The modern paradigm of suicide bombing called for renewed consideration of this aspect.

9. The prominent fundamentalist Sheikh Yusuf al-Qaradawi, for example, gave a *fatwa* obliging Muslims to fund jihad out of money collected for charity (*zakat*). (*Fatwa* from April 11, 2002 in Islamonline.)

10. True, religions are naturally conservative and slow to change. Religious reforms are born and legitimized through the authority of a supreme spiritual leader (a pope or imam), an accepted mechanism of scholarly consensus (Talmud, the *ijma'* of the schools of jurisprudence in early Islam), internal revolution (Protestantism), or external force (the destruction of the Second Temple in Judaism). Islam canonized itself in the tenth century and therefore did not go through any of these "reforms."

11. Here the pessimist may inject that, today, all the leading Islamic scholars in the Middle East who enjoy such prestige are in the radical camp. But there have been cases of "repentant" radicals (in Egypt) who have retracted (albeit in jail and after due "convincing") their declarations of *takfir* against the regime. In Indonesia, the moderate Nahdlatul Ulama led by former President Abdurahman Wahid represents a genuine version of moderate Islam.

Shmuel Bar is a senior research fellow at the Institute for Policy and Strategy at the Interdisciplinary Center Herzliya in Israel and a veteran of the Israeli intelligence community.

Between Two Ages

GET USED TO IT

Address by WILLIAM VAN DUSEN WISHARD, *President, World Trends Research*
Delivered to the Coudert Institute, Palm Beach, Florida, December 1, 2001

Your topic of study "Living in an age of transition" couldn't be more appropriate to what we have been, are, and will continue to be living through probably for the rest of our lives.

In 2000, I published a new book, Between Two Ages. On the front cover appears this sentence: "The next three decades may be the most decisive 30 year period in the history of mankind." Then there's another sentence describing how the book examines that suggestion.

Nothing so dramatizes living between two ages as does the image of the fireball engulfing the World Trade Center, an image burned into the world's psyche September 11th. I'm not going to dwell on that event, except to say this. The image of the imploding World Trade Center must be seen as part of a panorama of images for its full significance to best be understood. The image, for instance, of death camps and crematoriums in Central Europe. The image of a mushroom cloud rising over the Pacific. Of Neil Armstrong stepping onto the Moon. Of Louise Brown, the first human to be conceived outside of the human body. Of a man standing near the summit of Mt. Everest talking on his cell phone to his wife in Australia. Of the first human embryo to be cloned. Of a computer performing billions of calculations in a second, calculations that could not have been performed by all the mathematicians who ever lived, even in their combined lifetimes. These are some of the images, representing both human greatness and depravity, that mark the end of one age and the approach of a new time in human experience.

It was in 1957 that Peter Drucker, who, more than any other person, defined management as a discipline, wrote: "No one born after the turn of the 20th century has ever known anything but a world uprooting its foundations, overturning its values and toppling its idols." So today I'm going to pursue Drucker's thought and suggest why I believe we're living at probably the most critical turning point of human history.

Between two ages. How are we to visualize the difference between those two ages? I offer some contrasts. From the dom-inance of print communication, to the emergence of electronic communication. From American immigration coming primarily from Europe, to immigration coming mainly from Asia and Latin America. From a time of relatively slow change, to change at an exponential rate. From economic development as a national endeavor, to economic development as part of a global system. From ultimate destructive power being confined to the state, to such power available to the individual. We could continue, but I think you see what I mean. We're in what the ancient Greeks called Kairos—the "right moment" for a fundamental change in principles and symbols.

Exactly what kind of era is opening up is far from clear. The only obvious fact is that it's going to be global, whatever else it is.

In the next few minutes I want to comment on three trends that are part of this shift between two ages. Let me start by stating my bias: I am bullish on the future. We've got unprecedented challenges ahead, clearly the most difficult humanity has ever faced. But I believe in the capacity of the human spirit to surmount any challenge if given the vision, the will and the leadership.

With this in mind, let's look at some trends that are moving us from one age to the next.

First trend: For the first time in human history, the world is forging an awareness of our existence as a single entity. Nations are incorporating the planetary dimensions of life into the fabric of our economics, politics, culture and international relations. The shorthand for this is "globalization."

We all have some idea of what globalization means. In my view, globalization represents the world's best chance to enrich the lives of the greatest number of people. The specter of terrorism, however, raises the question as to globalization's future. Will the 1990's "go-go" version be one of the casualties of terrorism? Yes and no. The economic pace of globalization may slow down, and certainly reaction to America's "soft power"— what other nations see as the "Americanization" of world culture—will continue to grow. But other aspects may actually accelerate. For example, we're already seeing the increased globalization of intelligence, security and humanitarian concerns.

Aside from that, globalization is far more than just economics and politics: more than non-western nations adopting free markets and democratic political systems. At its core, globalization means that western ideas are gradually seeping into the social and political fabric of the world. And even deeper, globalization is about culture, tradition and historic relationships; it's about existing institutions and why and how they evolved. In short, globalization goes to the very psychological foundations of a people.

Look at what's happening. Nations are adopting such ideas as the sanctity of the individual, due process of law, universal education, the equality of women, human rights, private property, legal safeguards governing business and finance, science as the engine of social growth, concepts of civil society, and perhaps most importantly, the ability of people to take charge of their destiny and not simply accept the hand dealt them in life. For millions of people these concepts are new modes of thought, which open undreamt of possibilities.

Is this good? From our perspective it is. But what do other nations feel as America's idea of creative destruction and entrepreneurship press deeper into the social fabric of countries such as China and India; as American cultural products uproot historic traditions?

In the Middle East, American culture as exemplified by a TV program such as Baywatch generates a unique resentment. Such a program presents Islamic civilization with a different nuance of feminine beauty and the dignity of women. Baywatch, and American culture in general, lure Muslims into an awkward position. On the one hand, their basic human appetites respond at a primal level. So it becomes part of them. Yet on another level, they fear the invasion of this new culture is undermining something sacred and irreplaceable in their very social fabric. Yes, it's their own fault; they don't have to import such entertainment. Yet it all seems to be part of so-called "modernization."

All of which illustrates how hard it is for us Americans to appreciate the underlying differences between western ideas and the foundations of other nations. Take some of the basic contrasts between Asia and the west. The west prizes individuality, while the east emphasizes relationships and community. The west sees humans dominating nature, while the east sees humans as part of nature. In the west there is a division between mind and heart, while in the east mind and heart are unified.

I mention this to illustrate the deep psychological trauma nations are experiencing as they confront the effects of globalization. We Americans, raised on the instinct of change, say, "Great. Let tradition go. Embrace the new." But much of the world says, "Wait a minute. Traditions are our connection to the past; they're part of our psychic roots. If we jettison them, we'll endanger our social coherence and stability."

Remember, it took centuries for our political, social and economic concepts to evolve in the West. They are the product of a unique western psychology and experience. Thus we cannot expect non-western nations to graft alien social attitudes onto an indigenous societal structure overnight.

Part of the upheaval created by globalization is the largest migration the world has ever seen, which is now under way. In China alone, 100 million people are on the move from the countryside to the city. In Europe, the OECD tells us that no country is reproducing its population; that the EU will need 180 million immigrants in the next three decades simply to keep its population at 1995 levels, as well as to keep the current ratio of retirees to workers.

As European population growth declines, and as immigration increases, the historic legends that are the basis of national identities tend to wane. As one British historian put it, "A white majority that invented the national mythologies underpinning modern European culture lives in an almost perpetual state of fear that it and its way of life are about to disappear." You realize what he means when you hear that the Church of England expects England to have more practicing Muslims than practicing Anglicans by next year. In Italy, the Archbishop of Bologna recently warned Italy is in danger of "losing its identity" due to the immigration from North Africa and Central Europe. This fear is the subtext for everything else we see happening in Europe today.

The question of identity is at the core of the world problem as globalization accelerates. It came sharply into focus in the 1960's when, for the first time in human history, we saw Earth from space, from the moon. An idea that had only existed in the minds of poets and philosophers suddenly became geopolitical reality—the human family is a single entity. We began to see national, cultural and ethnic distinctions for what they are—projections in our minds. We lost the clarity of identity—Herder's "collective soul"—that had given birth and meaning to nations and civilizations for centuries.

In my view, it's this continuing loss of identity—or the threat of it—that helps fuel terrorism. Granted, there's an individual psychotic aspect to any terrorist. But the context in which they live is a loss of a personal sense of identity, as well as a subsequent psychological identification with the God-image.

One aspect of globalization we sometimes find irritating is America's global role and the resulting world perception of America. This perception is shaped by many factors, some of which we control, many of which we don't. For example, nations have historically felt a natural antipathy toward the world's strongest empire, whoever it happened to be at the time. And make no mistake, we are perceived, at a minimum, as an empire of influence. That said, in my view no great nation has used its power as generously and with as little intention of territorial gain as has America. Nonetheless, if we don't understand what other nations feel about America, globalization will not succeed, and neither will the war on terrorism.

Consider a comment by the Norwegian newspaper, Aftenposten: "in Norway, Nepal, and New Zealand, all of us live in a world that is increasingly shaped by the United States." Now let's play with that thought for a moment and consider a hypothetical situation.

Imagine how we would feel if the world were increasingly shaped by, say, China. Suppose China had produced the information technology that is the engine of globalization, technology that we had to buy and incorporate into our social structure. Picture Chinese currency as the medium of world trade. Further envision Chinese as the international language of commerce. What if Chinese films and TV programs were flooding global entertainment markets, undermining bedrock American beliefs and values. Suppose China were the dominant military and economic world power. Imagine the Chinese having troops stationed for security and peacekeeping in over thirty countries around the world. What if the IMF and World Bank were primarily influenced by Chinese power and pressure. Suppose China had developed the economic and management theories that we had to adopt in order to compete in the global marketplace.

If this were the case, how would Americans feel? I'm not suggesting there's anything inherently wrong with U.S. world influence, I'm trying to illustrate the all pervasiveness of America's reach in the world in order to suggest why even our allies manifest uneasy concerns about America. Understanding this, and adjusting where warranted, is essential to the success of globalization, to say nothing of the future of America.

Consider another example. Think what it looks like to the rest of the world when we judge other nations on the basis of human rights and democracy, while at the same time systematically feeding our children a cultural diet considered by all religions and civilizations throughout history to be destructive of personal character and social cohesion. Two of America's foremost diplomats have commented on this anomaly. Zbigniew Brzezinski, former National Security Advisor to the president, writes, "I don't think Western secularism in its present shape is the best standard for human rights." He mentions consumption, self-gratification and hedonism as three characteristics of America's definition of the "good life," and then says, "The defense of the political individual doesn't mean a whole lot in such a spiritual and moral vacuum."

George F. Kennan, one of the giant U.S. diplomatic figures of the past half century, says simply, "This whole tendency to see ourselves as the center of political enlightenment and as teachers to a great part of the rest of the world strikes me as unthought-through, vainglorious and undesirable." I might add these comments were made before September 11th.

Such comments perhaps seem almost unpatriotic. But America's ability to provide world leadership may depend on whether we have the capacity to consider such reactions, and see what truth there may be in them. It's what the Scottish poet Robert Burns wrote: "Oh would some power the gift to give us, to see ourselves as others see us!"

I emphasize these points because if we're going to build a global age, it's got to be built on more than free markets and the Internet. Even more, it's got to be built on some view of life far broader than "my nation," "my race" or "my religion" is the greatest. Such views gave dynamism and meaning to the empires of the past. But the task now is to bring into being a global consciousness. It must have as its foundation some shared psychological and, ultimately, spiritual experience and expression. At the end of the day, globalization must have a legitimacy that validates itself in terms of a true democratic and moral order.

The second trend moving us between two ages is a new stage of technology development. This new phase is without precedent in the history of science and technology.

At least since Francis Bacon in the 1600's we have viewed the purpose of science and technology as being to improve the human condition. As Bacon put it, the "true and lawful end of the sciences is that human life be enriched by new discoveries and powers."

And indeed it has. Take America. During the last century, the real GDP, in constant dollars, increased by $48 trillion, much of this wealth built on the marvels of technology.

But along with technological wonders, uncertainties arise. Let me interject here that in 1997 I had a quadruple heart bypass operation using the most sophisticated medical technology in the world. So I'm a believer. Nonetheless, the question today is whether we're creating certain technologies not to improve the human condition, but for purposes that seem to be to replace human meaning and significance altogether.

The experts tell us is that by the year 2035, artificial robotic intelligence will surpass human intelligence. (Let's leave aside for a moment the question of what constitutes "intelligence.") And a decade after that, we shall have a robot with all the emotional and spiritual sensitivities of a human being.

Not long after that, computers—will go at such a speed that the totality of human existence will change so dramatically that it's beyond our capability to envision what life will be like. But never fear, we're told. The eventual marriage of human and machine will mean that humans will continue as a species, albeit not in a form we would recognize today.

Thus arrives what some would-be scientific intellectuals call the "Post-human Age." I emphasize, this is not science fiction. It is the projection of some of our foremost scientists.

Let's move from the general to the specific. Consider a remark by the co-founder of MIT's artificial intelligence lab and one of the world's leading authorities on artificial intelligence: "Suppose that the robot had all of the virtues of people and was smarter and understood things better. Then why would we want to prefer those grubby, old people? I don't see anything wrong with human life being devalued if we have something better." Now just absorb that thought for a moment. One of the world's leading scientists ready to "devalue human life" if we can create something he thinks is better. Setting aside the question of who decides what "better" is, to me, devaluing human life is a form of self-destruction.

The editor of Wired magazine says we're in the process of the "wiring of human and artificial minds into one planetary soul." Thus, he believes, we,ll be the first species "to create our own successors." He sees artificial intelligence "creating its own civilization."

These are not "mad scientists." They're America's best and brightest, and they believe they're ushering in the next stage of evolution.

In sum, we're creating technology that forces us to ask what are humans for once we've created super intelligent robots that can do anything humans can do, only do it a thousand times faster? Why do we need robots with emotional and spiritual capability, and what does that have to do with the seventy percent of humanity that simply seeks the basic necessities of life? What will it mean to be able to change the genetic structure not just of an individual child, but also of all future generations? Do we really want to be able to make genetic changes so subtle that it may be generations before we know what we've done to ourselves?

What we're talking about is a potential alteration of the human being at the level of the soul. This is a work proceeding absent any political debate, certainly without the assent of elected leaders. Yet it will change the definition of what it means to be a human being. It's the silent loss of freedom masquerading as technological progress.

Many other questions come to mind, but two in particular. Will it happen, and what is driving this self-destructive technological imperative?

On the first question—will it happen—my guess is probably not. In my judgment, there is a major issue the technological visionaries disregard. That is the question of how much manipulation and accelerated change the human being can take before he/she disintegrates psychologically and physiologically.

What we're experiencing is not simply the acceleration of the pace of change, but the acceleration of acceleration itself. In other words, change growing at an exponential rate. The experts tell us that the rate of change doubles every decade; that at today's rate of change, we'll experience 100 calendar years of change in the next twenty-five years; and that due to the nature of exponential growth, the 21st century as a whole will experience almost one thousand times greater technological change than did the 20th century.

I hasten to add that these are not my projections. They are the views of some of America's most accomplished and respected experts in computer science and artificial intelligence.

Onrushing change is already producing mounting dysfunction. The suicide rate among women has increased 200% in the past two decades. Thirty years ago, major corporations didn't have to think much about mental health programs for employees. Now, mental health is the fastest growing component of corporate health insurance programs. Think of the corporations that now provide special rooms for relaxation, naps, music or prayer and meditation. The issue now for corporations is not so much how to deal with stress; it's how to maintain the psychological integrity of the individual employee.

Other indicators of dysfunction tell us that teen suicide jumped 300% between 1960-90. Books are now written for eight and nine year old children advising them how to recognize the symptoms of stress, and to deal with it in their own lives. Anti-depressants and other character-controlling drugs are taken like aspirin. Rage has assumed a culture-like place in the national fabric, whether rage on the road, in stores, in schools and even in a popular video game called "Primal Rage," and, most tragically, in families.

Now, project forward the predicted increased speed of computers and the resulting ratcheting up of the pace of life over the next decades, and you end up asking, "How much more of this can the human metabolism take?" It's not the case that sooner or later something will give way. The multiplying social pathologies indicate that individual and collective psychological integrity is already giving way.

The second question is, what's driving this self-destructive activity? Certainly we as consumers are a major part of it. We're addicted to the latest electronic gizmo; whether it's the ubiquitous cell phone to keep us in touch with everyone everywhere, or one of those Sharper Image CD players you hang on the shower head so you can listen to Beethoven while taking a shower.

But let me offer three views that suggest a deeper story. Consider the comment of a former Carnegie-Mellon University computer scientist hired by Microsoft as a researcher. In an interview with the Washington Post, the good professor said, "This corporation is my power tool. It is the tool I wield to allow my ideas to shape the world."

My power tool. What clearer expression of ego-inflation could there be?

A second comment comes from the editor of Wired magazine, who famously wrote, "We are as gods, and we might as well be good at it." The Greeks had a word for identifying ourselves with the gods—hubris, pride reaching beyond proper human limits.

Perspective on all this comes from within the scientific community itself.

Freeman Dyson is one of the world's preeminent theoretical physicists. He talks about the "technical arrogance" that overcomes people "when they see what they can do with their minds."

My power tool; we are as gods; technical arrogance. The Greeks had another word that was even stronger than hubris. Pleonexia. An overweening resolve to reach beyond the limits, an insatiable greed for the unattainable. It is what one writer terms the "Masculine Sublime," which he describes as the "gendered characteristics out of which the myths of science are molded-myths of masculine power, control, rationality, objectivity."

From the earliest times, everything in human myth and religion warns us about overreaching. From the myths of Prometheus in ancient Greece, to the Hebrew story of Adam and Eve; from the Faust legend to Milton's Paradise Lost; from Mary Shelly's Frankenstein to Stevenson's Dr. Jekyll and Mr. Hyde; from Emily Dickinson to Robert Oppenheimer's lament that "in some sort of crude sense, the physicists have known sin"; through all these stories and experiences that come from the deepest level of the human soul, there has been a warning that limits exist on both human knowledge and endeavor; that to go beyond those limits is self-destructive.

No one knows exactly where such limits might be. But if they don't include the effort to create some technical/ human life form supposedly superior to human beings, if they don't include the capacity to genetically reconfigure human nature, if they don't include the attempt to introduce a "post-human" civilization, then it's hard to imagine where such limits would be drawn.

Keep in mind that myths are more than fanciful stories left over from the childhood of man. They emanate from the unconscious level of the psyche; that level which connects us to whatever transpersonal wisdom may exist. It's a level at which, as quantum physics suggests, there may exist some relationship between the human psyche and external matter. There may be some fundamental pattern of life common to both that is operating outside the understanding of contemporary science. In other words, we may be fooling around with phenomena that are, in fact, beyond human awareness; possibly even beyond the ability of humans to grasp. For at the heart of life is a great mystery which does not yield to rational interpretation. This eternal mystery induces a sense of wonder out of which all that humanity has of religion, art and science is born. The mystery is the giver of these gifts, and we only lose the gifts when we grasp at the mystery itself. In my view, Nature will not permit arrogant man to defy that mystery, that transcendent wisdom. In the end, Nature's going to win out.

Some people are already searching for the wisest way to approach such potential challenges as the new technologies present. Bill Joy, co-founder and former chief scientist of Sun Microsystems, suggests we've reached the point where we must "limit development of technologies that are too dangerous, by limiting our pursuit of certain kinds of knowledge." His concerns are based on the unknown potential of genetics, nanotechnology and robotics, driven by computers capable of infinite speeds, and the possible uncontrollable self-replication of these technologies this might pose. Joy acknowledges the pursuit of knowledge as one of the primary human goals since earliest times. But, he says, "If open access to, and unlimited development of, knowledge henceforth puts us all in clear danger of extinction, then common sense demands that we re-examine even these basic, long-held beliefs."

The third trend moving us between two ages is a longterm spiritual and psychological reorientation that's increasingly generating uncertainty and instability. This affects all of us, for we're all part of America's collective psychology, whether we realize it or not.

The best measure of America's psychological and spiritual life is not public opinion polls telling us what percentage of the population believes in God. Rather, it's the content and quality of our culture. For culture is to a nation what dreams are to an individual—an indication of what's going on in the inner life.

In my judgment, what's really going on is that the world is experiencing a long-term spiritual and psychological reorientation similar to what happened when the Greco-Roman era gave way to the start of the Feudal Age. That was a time of great disorientation and searching. The cry "Great Pan is dead," was heard throughout the ancient world as the traditional gods lost their hold on the collective psyche. The Greco-Roman world became awash in countless new religions and sects vying for supremacy.

Not too different from our times, beginning with Nietzsche's cry, "God is dead." When we look at what's happening today we see 1500 religions in America, including such anomalies as "Catholic-Buddhists." Beyond that, we see a smorgasbord of spiritual/psychological fare as seen in the popularity of books such as The Celestine Prophecy or the Chicken Soup series, in the rise of worldwide fundamentalism, in numerous cults such as "Heaven's Gate," in the New Age phenomenon, in interest in Nostradamus, in crop circles, in the supposed "Bible Code," in conspiracy theories, in fascination with the "other" as seen in movies such as "Planet of the Apes" or "Tomb Raiders," in the search for some extraterrestrial intelligence to save us from ourselves, and last but certainly not least, in terrorism, which, at its core, is a demonic hatred expressed in spiritual terms.

What happened in the Rome—early Feudal Age shift was played out over centuries. What's happening today has, yes, been evolving over the past few centuries. We see it first manifested in the emergence of the Faust legend; then in the Enlightenment's enthronement of the Goddess of Reason in Notre Dame and the ensuing acceptance of rationalism as life's highest authority; and in our own time in the ethos of "meaninglessness" that has virtually defined 20th century Western culture. But what's happening today—due to the 20th century electronic information technologies—is probably unfolding at a more rapid pace than the shift in the fourth-fifth-sixth centuries. For information technologies transmit not only information, but psychological dynamics as well.

While there are millions of devout Christians and Jews in America and Europe, the Judeo-Christian impulse is no longer the formative dynamic of Western culture, especially among the so-called "creative minority." Even so calm a journal as the Economist opines, "The West is secular." One need only look at the changing relationship between the roles of the priest and the psychologist to see what has been happening. Earlier in the 20th century, if someone had personal problems, he or she went to the priest for advice. Gradually that changed, and people started going to their psychologist. Recently, the leader of the Roman Catholic Church in England and Wales said that as a background for people's lives, Christianity "has almost been vanquished." His language mirrored a statement by the Archbishop of Canterbury who declared Britain to be a country where "tacit atheism prevails." Newsweek recently described Europe as a "post-Christian civilization." Throughout the continent, Newsweek reported, "churches stand empty."

Part of the psychological reorientation taking place is the breakup of our collective inner images of wholeness. For example, we used to talk about "heaven," which denoted the transcendent realm, eternity, the dwelling place of the gods. Now we just speak of "space," which has no spiritual connotation. We used to talk of "mother earth," which had a vital emotional association. From time immemorial, nature was filled with spirit. Now we just speak of "matter," a lifeless nature bereft of gods.

Thus transcendent meaning—which is the source of psychological wholeness is diminished. The function of symbolic language-words like "heaven" and "mother earth"— is to link our consciousness to the roots of our being, to link our consciousness to its base in the unconscious. When that link is devalued or discarded, there is little to sustain the inner life of the individual. So, few people are inwardly fed by any primal source of wholeness. In effect, our symbolic life and language have been displaced by a vocabulary of technology, a vocabulary that's increasingly devoid of transcendent meaning. The effect is a weakening of the structures that organize and, regulate our life-religion, self-government, education, culture and the family.

As a result, the soul of America—indeed, of the world—is in a giant search for some deeper and greater expression of life. Despite the benefits of modernization, technological society offers no underlying meaning to life. Thus the search taking place is both healthy and normal—given the seminal shift to an entirely new epoch that is occurring as we speak.

What we're discussing is at the core of the crisis of meaning that afflicts not only America and Europe, but Asia as well. For example, the Washington Post reports from Beijing, "Across China people are struggling to redefine notions of success and failure, right and wrong. The quest for something to believe in is one of the unifying characteristics of China today." A report from the East/West Center in Hawaii notes the decline in family and authority in Asia, and concludes by saying, "Eastern religion no longer is the binding force in Asian society." So it's a global crisis of meaning we're talking about.

Let me briefly summarize what we've been discussing. (1) Globalization possibly the most ambitious collective human experiment in history; (2) a new stage of technology the objective of which is to supplant human meaning and significance; and (3) a long-term psychological and spiritual reorientation. These are only three of the basic changes determining the future. And it's because of the magnitude and significance of such trends that I suggest the next three decades may be the most decisive thirty-year period in human history.

How do we respond to such a situation? We're already responding in the most sweeping redefinition of life America has ever known. We're redefining and restructuring all our institutions. Corporations are redefining their mission, structure and modus operandi. In education, we're trying countless new experiments, from vouchers to charter schools to home schooling. Alternative dispute resolution is helping lift the burden off the back of our legal system. Civic and charitable organizations are assuming functions formerly undertaken by local governments. More people are involved in efforts to help the elderly and those in poverty. In fact, it's estimated that well over fifty percent of all adult Americans donate a portion of their time to non-profit social efforts. Most importantly, there are countless efforts underway to redress the severe environmental imbalance we've created.

Against the background of the three trends I mentioned, perhaps this is a modest start, but at least it's a start. Clearly, there's another level of effort to move to, As Bill Joy suggests, such efforts must include a decision whether or not to continue research and development of technologies that could, in Joy's words, "bring the world to the edge of extinction." Obviously, such an examination must be done in a global context if it's to be valid.

But another question is, how are you and I to live in a world that's changing faster than individuals and institutions can assimilate? How do we maintain anchorage and balance when we're in between two ages?

I believe the starting place is understanding; simply to understand the fundamental changes taking place. That takes time and work.

As the most basic change taking place is in us as individuals, we must understand ourselves at a wholly new level. For the individual is the carrier of civilization. In the West, we tend to think in abstract categories of generality, such as civilizations, nations, historic trends, economic imperatives, social theories and philosophical concepts. These, we say, are the factors that make history. In my view, they're not. People make history, and all our concepts, theories and imperatives are projections of one kind or another that emanate from deep within the human psyche. It's what we are as individuals that shapes the future. So the issue boils down to how well do we know ourselves, both as individuals and as a nation?

We all know Socrates advice, "Know thyself." And most of us, if we pay any attention to that suggestion, think of knowing ourselves as knowing our conscious self. We think in terms of ego-consciousness. We think in terms of our persona, the mask we present to the world. The persona, however, is not the true, individual "me." The persona is usually a social identity—being a teacher, lawyer, banker or businessperson. As such, the persona derives from the collective psyche, not from any individual uniqueness.

But who we really are does not derive from our social role, from the work we do or our position on the social scale. Most of what we truly are resides in the unconscious, in the shadow side of our lives. My persona is who I like to think I am. My shadow is who I really am. My persona is the conscious "me." The shadow is the unconscious me. So getting to know the shadow is a prerequisite to knowing ourselves and who we truly are.

By and large, the shadow is a collection of repressed desires and "uncivilized" impulses. It's that part of our character we're not especially proud of and we'd rather not admit to. The British psychiatrist Anthony Stevens suggests that if you want to know what your shadow looks like, just write down a description of the sort of person you simply cannot stand. That description is your shadow. Everyone has a shadow. The problem is we easily see the other person's shadow, but not our own.

So what do we do with our shadow? Because we don't want to confront it, we usually project it on to others. We see our own devils in other people. This projection has been going on for millennia. It caused Christ to say, "And why do you see the mote that is in your brother's eye, but fail to see the beam that is in your own eye?" It's a form of denial, and there can be national denial as well as individual denial.

This failure to see our shadow is responsible for any amount of acrimony in relationships in a family, between friends or in an organization. On a collective level, it gives rise to political polarization, racial tension and international conflict. Hitler's projected shadow was a prime cause of the Holocaust. Every international conflict is, to some extent, a shadow projection. One reason we fail to resolve such international crises is because we don't recognize the critical dimension that is at the center of every crisis—the human psyche and its archetypal shadow. So how can you and I deal with our shadow, something that is unconscious?

The best way I've discovered is to study my reactions to other people. Reactions have two parts: First, an objective assessment of another person's character or actions; and second, the emotional intensity with which I react. No matter how accurate my assessment may be, that emotional intensity represents my shadow. So the instructive question to ask is not, "Why did the other person do what he or she did?" It's "Why am I reacting the way I am? What can my reaction tell me about my shadow?"

Let me make it personal. I have constant reactions to my wife. We've been married forty-four years, and I love her dearly. But that doesn't alter the fact that we react to each other. It's human nature. So when I react to her, no matter what the issue, I've learned to ask myself, "Where's the emotional steam coming from? Why am I reacting so strongly?" And I usually get an answer. And more often than not, the answer has to do with my loss of control of some particular situation. Something has happened that has taken away my control of my plan.

There's another feature of our shadow: the shadow includes aspects of ourselves that contain our unlived life-talents and abilities that, for various reasons, have been buried or never been made conscious. So the more we understand our shadow, the more likely these positive attributes are to develop.

As we confront our shadow, over time our negative qualities can be integrated with our positive qualities to make us more complete personalities. Becoming complete personalities is the whole object of life. That's what healing is all about; it's what growth is all about. It's a process of making conscious what has been unconscious. It's what one author wrote: "The full and joyful acceptance of the worst in oneself may be the only way of transforming it."

My task as a human being is to discover who I really am, and that means getting behind the persona and confronting the shadow. We can live on our persona only so long before life becomes stale and inauthentic, at which point we turn to trivia for distraction and entertainment. The same is true for nations. And while we Americans see our persona, the rest of the world sees our shadow. Indeed, Hollywood has made our shadow America's primary cultural export to the world.

Between two ages. There's a new epoch of human meaning struggling to take shape. Through the chaos and the killing, through the heartache and inner emptiness, the birth of a heightened consciousness is fighting its way out of the womb into the light.

The womb that nurtures this New Time is nothing less than the human unconscious, especially the deepest strata that is common to all humankind, the collective unconscious. The key to unlocking this deeper realm is to know ourselves in a new and deeper way; to become aware of life's opposites—the persona and the shadow, the good and evil, the loves and hatreds — that dwell within each of us, all of which constitute the totality of who we really are. The task is to strengthen the dialogue between consciousness and the limitless creative powers of the collective unconscious, wherein resides life's highest meaning.

A new time in history requires a fresh affirmation of the meaning and coherence of the human journey. That will not come from a speechwriter's pen or Madison Avenue. It must be born in the depths of the psyche of each one of us as we individually seek our own deeper meaning and relevance at a time of opportunity and danger unequaled in history. As we do this, we affirm that the sacred continuity of life continues. But it does not continue in a way we think of as normal. A new epoch will not emerge from conventional attitudes and habits. Living between two ages requires us to redefine what constitutes normalcy. A new normalcy can only come if we face our shadow so it can—over time—be integrated into a greater wholeness of personality. That's the price that must be paid in order that a new spiritual dispensation, a fresh expression of life's highest meaning, can come into being, and can shape the era that is to be.

Some eternal, infinite power is at work in each of us, as well as in the universe. This power is the source of renewal of all man's most vital and creative energies. With all our problems and possibilities, the future depends on how we—each in his or her own unique way-tap into that eternal renewing dynamic that dwells in the deepest reaches of the human soul.

In my view, this is some of what it means to live in an age of transition. Thank you.

Across the Great Divide

Our world: Capitalism and democracy are the two great forces of the age. They unleash creativity and human potential. But they can be destructive too; they challenge the old order. Are we ready for the wild ride of tomorrow?

By Fareed Zakaria

December 6, 1999 It has been only 10 years since the fall of the Berlin wall, but we are in a new age. In 1986 people would have seen their world of Reagan and Thatcher and Gorbachev as closely linked to the world of 1976 or, for that matter, of 1966 or 1956 or 1946. But today events, just 10 years old, are dim and quaint memories—remember the Nicaraguan contras? Having crossed a great historical divide, events on the other side of that chasm are like ancient history.

For almost a half century, the West has struggled mightily to spread capitalism and democracy around the world. Now it has gotten what it wanted—unbridled market and people power—and they will prove harder to handle than anyone imagined. Capitalism and democracy are the two dominant forces of modern history; they unleash human creativity and energy like nothing else. But they are also forces of destruction. They destroy old orders, hierarchy, tradition, communities, careers, stability and peace of mind itself. Unsentimental about the world as it exists, they surge forward, changing everything they encounter. The challenge of the West in the next century will be to find ways to channel the sweeping power of these two—the last surviving big ideas—as they reorganize all human activity. Otherwise for much of the world, it may be too fast a ride.

Things seem so different now because they are so different. For three genera-

tions, the world was defined by great political struggles: the Depression, World War II, the cold war, decolonization. Politics and diplomacy held center stage. Today the air is filled with a new sort of energy. "To get rich is glorious," goes a famous, recent tag line. It is the perfect sound bite for our age—because it was said by the leader of China's Communist Party. The heroes of the past may have been soldiers and statesmen, artists and writers: today they are entrepreneurs. Even countries like China, India and Brazil that once scoffed at the crass commercialism of the West now search desperately for ways to create export zones and high-tech corridors. Napoleon once derided England for being "a nation of shopkeepers." We are now a world of shopkeepers.

Intellectuals like to remind us that globalization is actually not that new. At the turn of the 20th century, free trade, free markets and democratic politics flourished. Today one does not need a visa to travel through much of Europe; then you did not even need a passport.

The point of this comparison is, of course, how it ended—badly. In the early 20th century prominent liberal thinkers believed that prosperity and interdependence had made war unthinkable. And yet it happened. World War I brought an end to the first great age of globalization.

But there are crucial differences between this turn of a century and the last one. Globalization today describes a far

more pervasive and deep phenomenon than has ever existed before. Thousands of goods, services and even ideas are manufactured globally, creating complex interconnections between states. A book, for example, can be written in New York, copy-edited in India, typeset in the Caribbean, printed in Singapore and then shipped worldwide. The Internet has made global manufacturing, distribution and communication simple and cheap.

There is another crucial difference between the last round of globalization and this one: the nature of the superpower. An open world economy rests upon the broad edifice of peace, which usually requires a great global hegemony—Britain in 1900, America in 2000. But in 1900 Britain was a declining power; World War I simply accelerated that trend. The picture today could not be more different. Not only is the United States securely the leading power in the world, its advantage is widening. For the past decade, American journalists, politicians and scholars have been searching for a new way to describe the post-cold-war world. It has been staring us in the face: we are living in the American Age.

The American economy has become the envy of the world, spearheading a series of technological breakthroughs that have defined a new post–Industrial Revolution. America's military outpaces any other by leaps and bounds. The Pentagon spends more on defense than the next five great powers combined. It spends more on defense research than *the rest of the world* put together. And Washington has no grand illusions that war is obsolete or that globalization does not require political stability. Whatever Bill Clinton's polemical rhetoric might suggest, there is no groundswell for isolationism in America.

America's edge is as visible in other sectors of society. The gap between American universities and foreign ones is fast widening. Harvard University recently announced that it had completed its $2 billion fund-raising drive months ahead of schedule. Oh, and by the way, it missed its target, overshooting by $0.3 billion. That's $300 million of spare change, which is more than the endowment of many of the best foreign universities. The World Bank recently calculated that the three richest men in America had a combined net worth that exceeds the total GDP of the 48 poorest countries in the world.

Of course, today's tranquil times could be upset by war. A stock-market crash could unnerve the booming economy. Bad foreign policy could bungle many of these extraordinary advantages. But none of these crises is likely to throw up a new superpower. In fact, when a crisis hits, America only becomes more indispensable—think of the East Asian economic collapse, or the Balkan wars. Even in lands where the backlash against America has deep roots, Americanization is pervasive. Listen to a 21-year-old woman, forced to attend an anti-American rally in Tehran: "It's a joke," she told *The New York Times*, pointing at the women clad in black chadors with bright blue colors flashing underneath. "How can you shout, 'Death to America!' when you're wearing blue jeans?" Or consider China. In November, Beijing compromised its gradual approach to economic reform when it agreed to join the World Trade Organization, largely under U.S. terms.

What can we expect in this new era? The short answer is, more of the same. More of global capitalism but also more of that other distinctive American export, democracy and popular power. Over the last 30 years, a great wave of democratization has swept the world. From Portugal and Greece in the 1970s to Latin America in the 1980s and Central Europe in the 1990s, elections have become a global phenomenon. The pressure will only get more intense. These two forces—capitalism and democracy—will hurl societies into modernity with all its glories and seductions. The companies of tomorrow will be efficient, but will also face brutal competition. Citizens will be able to enjoy culture from all over the world—from opera to Jerry Springer. Teenagers, at the click of a mouse, already have access to great encyclopedias—and racist propaganda.

It is a heady mix and it will only keep getting headier. The forces of creative destruction are beginning to operate at warp speed, creating new companies, careers and communities—but wrecking old ones at an equally dizzying pace. America has gotten used to this high-speed ride. Americans accept the chaos that comes from an ever-changing economy and a chaotic political system. They believe that in the end, it all works out for the best. But will the rest of the world be so understanding? Some countries will close themselves off from this world and stagnate. The wisest will find a balance between their own values and the requirements of modernity.

Most countries recognize the need to tame the fires of capitalism—in fact, they probably do so too much. It will be harder for them to determine how best to handle democratic populism. Some countries have already begun to see its dangers. They recognize that democracy without the rule of law, minority protections, property rights—what I have called illiberal democracy—can be a hollow shell. It was elections that fueled the fires of nationalism that still rage in the Balkans. It has been elections that have legitimized all manner of thugs from Venezuela to Belarus to Pakistan. In Russia, a well-functioning democracy has been combined with the wholesale corruption of economic reform, law, liberty and political institutions. The result: most Russians now dislike capitalism. They may soon come to dislike democracy.

The United States, the world's greatest democracy, has always kept its own popular pressures on a leash. Its court system is free from public oversight, its Bill of Rights designed to thwart majority rule and its regulatory apparatus keeps tabs on rogue traders and large corporations. Indeed, one could argue that the American way is so successful because both capitalism and democracy are tightly regulated by the rule of law. If the world wishes to learn a lesson about America, this should be the one it takes to heart.

Most difficult of all, societies must make these adjustments as the forces of change swirl around with gathering fury. Whatever the balance countries arrive at, they will still be riding farther, faster than they have ever done. The only advice one can give as we enter a brave new world is this: fasten your seat belts. It's going to be a bumpy ride.

Zakaria is managing editor of Foreign Affairs and author of a forthcoming book on the past, present and future of democracy.

Index

Index

Test Your Knowledge Form

We encourage you to photocopy and use this page as a tool to assess how the articles in *Annual Editions* expand on the information in your textbook. By reflecting on the articles you will gain enhanced text information. You can also access this useful form on a product's book support Web site at *http://www.dushkin.com/online/*.

NAME: _____

DATE: _____

TITLE AND NUMBER OF ARTICLE: _____

BRIEFLY STATE THE MAIN IDEA OF THIS ARTICLE:

_____

LIST THREE IMPORTANT FACTS THAT THE AUTHOR USES TO SUPPORT THE MAIN IDEA:

_____

WHAT INFORMATION OR IDEAS DISCUSSED IN THIS ARTICLE ARE ALSO DISCUSSED IN YOUR TEXTBOOK OR OTHER READINGS THAT YOU HAVE DONE? LIST THE TEXTBOOK CHAPTERS AND PAGE NUMBERS:

_____

LIST ANY EXAMPLES OF BIAS OR FAULTY REASONING THAT YOU FOUND IN THE ARTICLE:

_____

LIST ANY NEW TERMS/CONCEPTS THAT WERE DISCUSSED IN THE ARTICLE, AND WRITE A SHORT DEFINITION:

We Want Your Advice

ANNUAL EDITIONS revisions depend on two major opinion sources: one is our Advisory Board, listed in the front of this volume, which works with us in scanning the thousands of articles published in the public press each year; the other is you—the person actually using the book. Please help us and the users of the next edition by completing the prepaid article rating form on this page and returning it to us. Thank you for your help!

ANNUAL EDITIONS: Sociology 05/06

ARTICLE RATING FORM

Here is an opportunity for you to have direct input into the next revision of this volume.
We would like you to rate each of the articles listed below, using the following scale:

1. **Excellent: should definitely be retained**
2. **Above average: should probably be retained**
3. **Below average: should probably be deleted**
4. **Poor: should definitely be deleted**

Your ratings will play a vital part in the next revision.
Please mail this prepaid form to us as soon as possible.
Thanks for your help!

RATING	ARTICLE	RATING	ARTICLE
	1. The Kindness of Strangers		38. The Pentagon and Climate Change
	2. The Mountain People		39. The Secret Nuclear War
	3. The Atrophy of Social Life		40. Food and Agriculture in the 21st Century: Rethinking Our Paradigms
	4. Self-Reliance: Those Rugged Individuals		41. The New Terrorism: Securing the Nation against a Messianic Foe
	5. What's So Great About America?		
	6. What Makes You Who You Are		42. The Religious Sources of Islamic Terrorism
	7. The New Sex Scorecard		43. Between Two Ages
	8. The Criminal Menace: Shifting Global Trends		44. Across the Great Divide
	9. Parents or Prisons		
	10. The Aggregate Burden of Crime		
	11. The American Family		
	12. Living Better: Get Wed		
	13. Great Expectations		
	14. The Battle Over Gay Marriage		
	15. The Case for Staying Home		
	16. An Inner-City Renaissance		
	17. Community Building: Steps Toward a Good Society		
	18. For Richer: How the Permissive Capitalism of the Boom Destroyed American Equality		
	19. Working and Poor in the USA		
	20. Corporate Welfare		
	21. Requiem for Welfare		
	22. What's At Stake		
	23. Why We Hate		
	24. The Melting Pot, Part I: Are We There Yet?		
	25. Reversing the "Gender Gap"		
	26. Human Rights, Sex Trafficking, and Prostitution		
	27. The New Gender Gap		
	28. Who Rules America?		
	29. Where the Public Good Prevailed		
	30. Off the Books		
	31. Surveying the Global Marketplace		
	32. Where the Good Jobs Are Going		
	33. How I Joined Teach for America—and Got Sued for $20 Million		
	34. Whose Hospital Is It?		
	35. Are We a Nation "Under God?"		
	36. Coping with Methuselah		
	37. Rescuing a Planet Under Stress		

(Continued on next page)

ABOUT YOU

Name   Date
_____

Are you a teacher? ❏   A student? ❏
Your school's name
_____

Department
_____

Address   City   State   Zip
_____

School telephone #
_____

YOUR COMMENTS ARE IMPORTANT TO US!

Please fill in the following information:
For which course did you use this book?
_____

Did you use a text with this ANNUAL EDITION? ❏ yes ❏ no
What was the title of the text?
_____

What are your general reactions to the *Annual Editions* concept?
_____

Have you read any pertinent articles recently that you think should be included in the next edition? Explain.
_____

Are there any articles that you feel should be replaced in the next edition? Why?
_____

Are there any World Wide Web sites that you feel should be included in the next edition? Please annotate.
_____

May we contact you for editorial input? ❏ yes ❏ no
May we quote your comments? ❏ yes ❏ no